M A S T E R I N G
SPANISH

HEAR IT · SPEAK IT · WRITE IT · READ IT

Developed for the
FOREIGN SERVICE INSTITUTE,
DEPARTMENT OF STATE
by Robert P. Stockwell
J. Donald Bowen
Ismael Silva-Fuenzalida

BARRON'S

Cover design by Milton Glaser, Inc.

This course was developed for the Foreign Service Institute, Department of State.

The title of the original course is Spanish Basic Course

This edition published in 1985 by Barron's Educational Series, Inc.

All inquiries should be addressed to:
Barron's Educational Series, Inc.
250 Wireless Boulevard
Hauppauge, New York 11788

Paper Edition

International Standard Book No. 0-8120-2229-7

A large part of the text of this book is recorded on the accompanying tapes,
as follows:

Unit 1	Tape 1A		Unit 9	Tapes 6A and 6B
Unit 2	Tape 1B		Unit 10	Tapes 7A and 7B
Unit 3	Tape 2A		Unit 11	Tapes 8A and 8B
Unit 4	Tape 2B		Unit 12	Tapes 9A and 9B
Unit 5	Tape 3A		Unit 13	Tapes 10A and 10B
Unit 6	Tape 3B and Tape 4A (part)		Unit 14	Tapes 11A and 11B
Unit 7	Tape 4A (part) and Tape 4B		Unit 15	Tapes 12A and 12B
Unit 8	Tapes 5A and 5B			

On the tapes, selected statements about life
and customs in Spanish-speaking countries
adapted from

Spanish at a Glance by Heywood Wald

Learn Spanish the Fast and Fun Way by Gene Hammitt

PRINTED IN THE UNITED STATES OF AMERICA

5 6 7 8 9 800 28 27 26 25 24 23

INTRODUCTION

The materials in this book have been developed to present Spanish as a spoken language, and the skills of understanding and speaking are accordingly emphasized. The method of presentation will likely be new to students acquainted with more traditional methods of language teaching. In order to understand the materials, one must first understand the method upon which they are built.

Method of Teaching

The method is known as GUIDED IMITATION. There are two very important aspects of this method. First, learning a relatively small body of material so well that it requires very little effort to produce it. This is OVERLEARNING. The second aspect is learning to manipulate the sounds, sequences, and patterns of the language authentically. The important implication here is the reality of both the model and the imitation. The model (teacher, recording, etc.) must provide Spanish as people really speak it in actual conversations, and the student must be helped to an accurate imitation.

Pronunciation

The first two units are focused primarily on pronunciation problems. Drills on other aspects of the language are deliberately postponed because of the importance of developing good pronunciation habits from the very beginning of the course. Pronunciation is extremely important. It is the basis of all real fluency.

Aids to Listening

If speakers of English were not so highly literate, it might be possible to teach effectively without reference to any written symbolization, but most students are much more comfortable if some kind of representation of what they are imitating is also available for visual reference. There is, of course, a traditional writing system for Spanish which is used in all parts of the Spanish speaking world. It is a very adequate system for its purpose, which might be stated as providing visual cues for persons who already speak the language. For pedagogical purposes, a respelling, or phonetic representation of Spanish is also provided as a means of reminding the student of important features of the pronunciation which the traditional spelling system does not provide, such as significant sound distinctions, word groupings, intonation patterns, etc. The phonetic symbolization may at first look unfamiliar and somewhat foreboding, but this very unfamiliarity is a healthy reminder that none of the English sounds (which are so easily associated with the familiar letters of the alphabet) are exact duplications of the Spanish sounds to be mastered. This is also, of course, true in the respelling when familiar symbols are used: the appearance of the letter t does not mean the familiar English t-sound is indicated.

The intonations are marked in the respelling by a system of dots and accents placed at relative heights over the vowels. The patterns recorded in this way are not necessarily the only possibilities in spoken Spanish, but they are all normal patterns which have been thoroughly and widely tested.

The symbolization in the respelling will allow for a consistent interpretation of the pronunciation of any dialect area of the Spanish speaking world. For example, the /ş/ symbol is to be interpreted as a sound similar to the 's' of 'sink' in Spanish America, but as the 'th' of 'think' in Central Spain. Other regional pronunciation features are similarly marked.

The acquisition of a good pronunciation is first of all the result of careful listening and imitation plus whatever help can be obtained from initial pronunciation drills and description, and from the cues provided for continuing reference by the aids to listening.

Every unit (after the first two) is organized in the same way: part one is the basic dialog with a few pertinent notes; part two is grammar drills and discussion; part three is a set of recombination narratives and dialogs.

Basic Dialogs

The basic dialogs are the core of each unit. These dialogs are recreations of the real situations a student is most likely to encounter, and the vocabulary and sentences are those he or she is most likely to need. The dialogs are set in a mythical country called Surlandia, which is described as a typical Latin American republic, insofar as it is possible to extract common features from so diverse an area.

In the first part of the book new vocabularly is introduced mainly in the basic dialogs. Occasionally, in the illustrations of grammar points, new words are introduced in order to fill out patterns needed to do the exercises. New words are always clearly indicated by placing them on a line themselves, indented between the lines that are complete sentences. Since each new word is introduced in this fashion only once, the student should take pains to be sure he or she learns each word as it is presented. Careful pains have been taken to see that each word introduced will reappear many times later in the course to help the student assimilate each word in a variety of contexts.

The student should very carefully learn both the literal meanings of each individual word or phrase that is given on an indented line and the meaning that appears in the full sentences. It should not be cause for concern if the meaning in context is strikingly different from the literal meaning. In the construction of each dialog, the Spanish was written first, and the corresponding English is its closest equivalent and not a literal translation. It is therefore not at all surprising if the Spanish does not seem to 'follow' the English.

Drills and Grammar

Each unit can in some ways be likened to a musical theme with variations. The basic dialogs are the theme, and the drills provide the variations. Patterns of the structure of the language which have been learned in the basic sentences are expanded and manipulated in the drills.

There are four kinds of drills in each unit (three before Unit 6). Of these, two are designed to vary selected basic sentences within the structure and vocabulary the student has already learned. And two are oriented toward the structure of the language to provide a systematic coverage of all important patterns.

All of these drills are planned to be easily and rapidly answered. If a drill is found to be hard, the difficulty probably reflects inadequacy in the mastery of the dialogs and earlier drills.

Pattern drills are presented in a format which provides both practice and explanation. First appears a presentation of the pattern to be drilled, then various kinds of drills, and finally a more detailed discussion of the pattern.

The presentation consists of a listing of basic sentences (and a few new sentences when necessary) which illustrate the grammar point to be drilled. Then there is an extrapolation which shows the relationships involved in the pattern in a two-dimensional chart, which is further explained by a short note or two. This presentation should provide sufficient clues to enable the student to understand and use the pattern correctly in the drills that follow. These drills are mainly exercises making substitutions, responses, and translations, highlighting the grammar points covered. They are devised for oral answers to oral stimuli.

After the drills there is a more detailed discussion of the pattern drilled. While an effort was made to keep these discussions clear and readable, it has to be recognized that a description of a language is a technical subject.

The student may notice slight differences in the respelling used in the aids to listening and in the grammar charts and discussions. The respelling useful as a guide to pronunciation for an English speaking student records more details than a respelling to be used in grammar discussions where comparisons are made between Spanish forms, not between English and Spanish pronunciation.

Conversation

The conversation section of each unit is designed to help bridge the gap between the more or less mechanical stimulus-response activity of the drills and the skill of free conversation which is the ultimate aim of the course. These recombination monologues and dialogs extend the abilities of the student into ever more natural situations.

Preface

Mastering Spanish is part of a series of language courses being presented by Barron's Educational Series, Inc. This course is intended for the serious language student who wishes to speak Spanish fluently. The course book and accompanying tapes present Spanish as a spoken language, emphasizing pronunciation and verbal comprehension.

This course was developed by the Foreign Service Institute of the Department of State to train government officers who needed to speak Spanish fluently. In addition to being an excellent choice for those who wish to teach themselves Spanish, this course can be of great help to the student of Spanish who can read the language or is currently studying it in school but would like to achieve greater fluency.

SPOKEN SPANISH

Table of Contents

Tape 1A

225 million
14 million USA

1.1 BASIC SENTENCES. Useful phrases.

ENGLISH SPELLING	AID TO LISTENING	SPANISH SPELLING
Good morning.	bwénozđíàs↓	Buenos días.
Good morning, sir.	bwénozđíàs│séɲyór↓	Buenos días, señor.
Good afternoon, ma'am.	bwénastarđès│séɲyórà↓	Buenas tardes, señora.
Good evening, miss.	bwénaznochès│séɲyòrítà↓	Buenas noches, señorita.
how	kómò↓	cómo
are (to be)	està↓ estár↓	está (estar)
you	ùstéđ↓	usted
How are you?	kómǫestaụstéđ↓	¿Cómo está usted?
(I) am (to be)	estóy↓ estár↓	estoy (estar)
well	byén↓	bien
thanks	graşyàs↓	gracias
and	í↓	y
I'm fine, thanks. How are you?	estóybyéɲ│gráşyàs│ḁustéđ↑	Estoy bien, gracias, ¿y usted?

very	múy↓	muy
Very well, thanks.	múybyén∣grás̬yás↓	Muy bien, gracias
hello, hi	ólá↓	hola
what such	ké—tál↓	qué tal
Hi! How goes it? (1)	ólá↓ ketál↓	¡Hola! ¿Qué tal?
(it) goes (to go)	bá↓ ír↓	va (ir)
to you (it) goes	lé—bá↓	le va
How are you getting along?	kómolebá↓	¿Cómo le va?
Fine, thanks.	byén∣grás̬yás↓	Bien, gracias.
with	kóh↓	con
the permission	èl—pérmisô↓	el permiso
Excuse me. (2)	kómpèrmisô↓	Con permiso.
no, not	nó↓	no
Certainly.	kómonó↓	Cómo no.
excuse (to excuse)	dispénsè↓ dispènsár↓	dispense (dispensar)
Excuse me. (3)	dispénsèmè↓	Dispénseme

it (I) regret (to regret, to feel)	ló—syentó↓ séntír↓	lo siento (sentir)
much, lots, too much	múchó ↓	mucho
I'm very sorry.	lósyentomúchó ↓	Lo siento mucho.
That's okay.	éstabyén↓	Está bien.
many (f.pl.) (4)	múchás↓	muchas
Thanks a lot.	muchazgráşyàs↓	Muchas gracias.
of, from	dé˙↓	de
nothing	naďá↓	nada
You're welcome.	dénaďá↓	De nada.
there is, there are (there to be)	áy↓ abér↓	hay (haber)
Don't give it a thought. (5)	nọayďeké ↓	No hay de qué.
(I) want (to want)	kyeró↓ kèrér↓	quiero (querer)
to present	présèntár↓	presentar
to present to you	présèntarlé↓	presentarle

3

to	á↓	a
the (m. sg.)	él↓	el
to the	ál↓	al
I'd like to present Mr. Molina to you.	kyéro |préséntárlę|álséŋyórmólíná↓	Quiero presentarle al señor Molina.
the (f.sg.)	lá↓	la
I'd like to present Mrs. Molina to you.	kyéro |préséntárlę|áláséŋyóráđémólíná↓	Quiero presentarle a la señora de Molina.
the pleasure	él‑gustó↓	el gusto
Glad to meet you.	múchógustó↓	Mucho gusto.
equally (equal)	igwálméntě↓ igwál↓	igualmente (igual)
Same here, thanks.	igwálméntě |grásyás↓	Igualmente, gracias.
enchanted (to enchant)	ęŋkàntáđó↓ eŋkàntár↓	encantado (encantar)
to meet, get acquainted, to know	kónóşer↓	conocer
to meet you (f.)	kónóşerlá↓	conocerla

Delighted to meet you. (6)	èŋkàntác̣o	ɖèkȯnȯ̧ɛ̧erlà↓	Encantado de conocerla.
to meet you (m.)	kȯnȯ̧ɛ̧erlȯ↓	conocerlo
Glad to meet you. (6)	mứchȯgusto	ɖèkȯnȯ̧ɛ̧erlȯ↓	Mucho gusto de conocerlo.
Goodbye.	àɖyo͎s↓	Adiós.
until	ástà↓	hasta
tomorrow	màṇyanà↓	mañana
See you tomorrow.	àstàmàṇyanà↓	Hasta mañana.
then, later	lwegȯ↓	luego
So long.	àstàlwegȯ↓	Hasta luego.

1.10   Notes on the basic sentences

(1) /óla ↓ kétál ↓ / ¡*Hola! ¿Qué tal?* is a greeting generally used with a person whom you already know more than casually, and who occupies a status approximately equivalent to yours.

(2) /kompermíso ↓ / *Con permiso* is used to excuse yourself when, for example, you are on an elevator and need to squeeze between other people who are in front of you in order to get out; or, when you want to excuse yourself from a group you are talking with. It is not ordinarily interchangeable with /dɪspénseme ↓ / *dispénseme.*

5

(3) /dıspénseme ↓/ *dispénseme* is used as apology for a minor breach of etiquette, to interrupt a conversation to ask about something, etc.

(4) Note that /múchas↓/ *muchas* 'many' is simply the feminine plural of a word /múcho↓/ *mucho* 'much' that you also met in the phrase /múchogústo↓/ *mucho gusto*. The /—s/ is the plural part, while the /—a/ before the /—s/ is the feminine marker.

(5) /nǫáydeké↓/ *No hay de qué* is used when the other person thanks you for some small favor you have done for him; it is about the same as /denáda↓/ *De nada*.

(6) /enkantádo|dekonoşérla↓/ *Encantado de conocerla* is regularly used only when you are introduced to a woman (if you are a man). If you are a woman, a different form is used and you should not learn this sentence to use yourself. /múchogústo| dekonoşérlo↓/ *Mucho gusto de conocerlo* is what you say (if you are a man) to another man, or else just the short form /muchogústo↓/ *Mucho gusto*. In Spain, instead of /—lo/ you say /—le/.

1.2   DRILLS ON PRONUNCIATION

1.21   Vowel contrasts in weak-stressed syllables

In learning the basic sentences in the first section of this unit, you should have been repeatedly corrected for your pronunciation of the underlined vowels in such phrases as these:

1. bwenǫzdıás↓	—ǒ—	—à—
2. sęŋyór↓	—ę̀—	
3. bwenastaṙd̄ę̀s↓	—à—	—è—
4. sęŋyorà↓	—ę̀—	—à

5.	bwenáznochês↓	—á—		—è—
6.	grasyás↓	—á—		
7.	dispensémè↓	—í—	—é—	—è—
8.	múcházgrasyás↓	—á—		—á—
9.	présèntarlè ↓	—è—	—è—	—è—
1o.	mólinà ↓	—ò—		—à—
11.	ástàmànyanà ↓	—à—	—à—	—à—
12.	ástàlwegò ↓	—à—		—ò—

It is perfectly normal for you to have trouble with these vowels, because, as the dots over them indicate, *they are all under weak stress* in positions where such vowels *do not occur under weak stress in English.*

While it is normal to make these mistakes at first, they constitute a *very serious error* which must be corrected early in your efforts to form Spanish habits of pronunciation. The following lists are for the purpose of helping you to master these *vowels under weak stress.* They are arranged in *pairs of words* such that the *only* difference between the members of each pair is in the pronunciation of one weak-stressed vowel: such a pair of words is called a *minimally contrasting pair.*

Practice repeating these after your instructor until you can make the contrast *easily*, just as he does, and insist that he continue practicing them with you until they *do* come easily.

1.21.1 Exercises on minimal vowel contrasts under weak stress

/a/ and /e/ in contrast under weak stress

sedá↓	sedé↓	palón↓	pelón↓
sapá↓	sapé↓	fatál↓	fetál↓
lotá↓	loté↓	tañyir↓	teñyir↓
mesás↓	mesés↓	papitó↓	pepitó↓
bochá↓	boché↓	daditó↓	deditó↓
tintá↓	tinté↓	eskupá↓	eskupé↓
chinchá↓	chinché↓	şoketá↓	şoketé↓
kortá↓	korté↓	alumbrá↓	alumbré↓
sobrás↓	sobrés↓	franşesás↓	franşesés↓
basar↓	besar↓	kantorás↓	kantorés↓
manar↓	menar↓	birretá↓	birreté↓
machón↓	mechón↓	señyorás↓	señyorés↓
tachar↓	techar↓	pastorás↓	pastorés↓
tachón↓	techón↓	markadó↓	merkadó↓
panál↓	penál↓	apagár↓	apegár↓
tahón↓	tehón↓	portúgesás↓	portúgesés↓

/a/ and /i/ in contrast under weak stress

lában↓	líbán↓	pánya'l↓	pinya'l↓
pátón↓	pitón↓	másitá↓	misitá↓
nádár↓	nidár↓	látéra↓	lítéra↓
mátád↓	mitád↓	sáleró↓	siléró↓
chárlár↓	chirlár↓	pákétě↓	pikétě↓
pánşóń↓	pinşóń↓	fáharón↓	fiharón↓
pásandó↓	písandó↓	má(l)yádór↓	má(l)yidór↓

/a/ and /o/ in contrast under weak stress

árá↓	áró↓	kubá↓	kubó↓
tiá↓	tió↓	koká↓	kokó↓
şerá↓	şeró↓	kará↓	karó↓
pesá↓	pesó↓	pará↓	paró↓
pasá↓	pasó↓	chiná↓	chinó↓
malá↓	maló↓	kantá↓	kantó↓
mesá↓	mesó↓	mantá↓	mantó↓
mayá↓	mayó↓	şorrá↓	şorró↓
bolá↓	boló↓		

9

sántá̱ ↓	santó̱ ↓	dèréchá̱ ↓	dèréchó̱ ↓
swegrá̱ ↓	swegró̱ ↓	şigarrá̱ ↓	şigarró̱ ↓
negrá̱ ↓	negró̱ ↓	màriá ↓	móriá ↓
palmá̱ ↓	palmó̱ ↓	şápatá̱ ↓	şápató̱ ↓
pastá̱ ↓	pastó̱ ↓	èrmaná̱ ↓	èrmanó̱ ↓
trompá̱ ↓	trompó̱ ↓	mimosá̱ ↓	mimosó̱ ↓
rremá̱ ↓	rremó̱ ↓	pàrehá̱ ↓	pàrehó̱ ↓
kobrá̱ ↓	kobró̱ ↓	màreá̱ ↓	màreó̱ ↓
nyetá̱ ↓	nyetó̱ ↓	tèrnerá̱ ↓	tèrneró̱ ↓
índyá̱ ↓	índyó̱ ↓	şéresá̱ ↓	şéresó̱ ↓
kálór ↓	kólór ↓	(l)yámadá̱ ↓	(l)yámadó̱ ↓
èsposá̱ ↓	ésposó̱ ↓	làkoniká̱ ↓	làkonikó̱ ↓

/a/ and /u/ ın contrast under weak stress

pá̱hár ↓	pú̱hár ↓	lá̱neró ↓	lú̱neró ↓
tá̱rón ↓	tú̱rón ↓	kárakás ↓	kú̱rakás ↓
sá̱bidó ↓	sú̱bido ↓	bá̱rritá ↓	bú̱rritá ↓
pá̱pitá ↓	pù̱pitá ↓	pá̱rgitá ↓	pú̱rgitá ↓

málaṣó ↓	múlaṣó ↓	kányadó ↓	kúnyadó ↓
kánıtá ↓	kúnıtá ↓	márṣyanó ↓	múrṣyanó ↓
lánıtá ↓	lúnıtá ↓	pálıdéṣ ↓	púlıdéṣ ↓
málıtá ↓	múlıtá ↓	mátádor ↓	mútádor ↓

/e/ and /ı/ ın contrast under weak stress

pénár ↓	pınár ↓	péṣadó ↓	pıṣadó ↓
pétón ↓	pıtón ↓	pérıtá ↓	pırıtá ↓
pélón ↓	pılón ↓	péṣadá ↓	pıṣadá ↓
télón ↓	tılón ↓	péṣarón ↓	pıṣarón ↓
rrémár ↓	rrımár ↓	mé(l)yár ↓	mı(l)yár ↓
méṣerá ↓	mıṣerá ↓	pényıtá ↓	pınyıtá ↓

/e/ and /o/ ın contrast under weak stress

pasé ↓	pasó ↓	pepé ↓	pepó ↓
tomé ↓	tomó ↓	tıré ↓	tıró ↓
fumé ↓	fumó ↓	kabé ↓	kabó ↓
bıné ↓	bınó ↓	bıbé ↓	bıbó ↓

léchę ↓	léchǫ ↓	lę́syóh ↓	lǫ́syóh ↓
trahę́ ↓	trahǫ́ ↓	mę́sitá ↓	mǫ́sitá ↓
dehę́ ↓	dehǫ́ ↓	bę́litá ↓	bǫ́litá ↓
tehę́ ↓	tehǫ́ ↓	bę́taḍǒ ↓	bǫ́taḍǒ ↓
kyerę́ ↓	kyerǫ́ ↓	pę́saḍá ↓	pǫ́saḍá ↓
peynę́ ↓	peynǫ́ ↓	ę́rmitá ↓	ǫ́rmitá ↓
kobrę́ ↓	kobrǫ́ ↓	gę́rritá ↓	gǫ́rritá ↓
kantę́ ↓	kantǫ́ ↓	kǒntestę́ ↓	kǒntestǫ́ ↓
(l)yebę́ ↓	(l)yebǫ́ ↓	tę́neró ↓	tǫ́neró ↓
mandę́ ↓	mandǫ́ ↓	sę́rritǒ ↓	sǫ́rritǒ ↓
kambyę́ ↓	kambyǫ́ ↓	kǒmformę̌ ↓	kǒmformǫ́ ↓
komprę́ ↓	komprǫ́ ↓	ę́klipsę́ ↓	ę́klipsǫ́ ↓
pę́lar↓	pǫ́lar↓	trǎbahę̌ ↓	trǎbahǫ̌ ↓
mę́ntóh ↓	mǫ́ntóh ↓	prę́pósiṣyóh ↓	prǫ́pósiṣyóh ↓

/e/ and /u/ ın contrast under weak stress

tę́mór ↓	túmór ↓	sę́rrár ↓	sų́rrár ↓
lę́gár ↓	lúgár ↓	lę́chóh ↓	lúchóh ↓
lę́chár ↓	lúchár ↓	fę́stíh ↓	fų́stíh ↓

sḙ́kȿyòh ↓	sṳ̀kȿyòh ↓	pḙ́nsaďȯ ↓	pṳ́nȿaďȯ ↓
pḙ́nsyòh ↓	pṳ̀nȿyòh ↓	tḙ́nderȯ ↓	tṳ́nderȯ ↓
mḙsitá ↓	mṳsitá ↓	pḙ́cherȯ ↓	pṳ́cherȯ ↓
lḙ́litȯ ↓	lṳlitȯ ↓	pḙ̀ritá ↓	pṳ̀ritá ↓
ȿḙ̀rkaďȯ ↓	sṳ̀rkaďȯ ↓	rrḙ̀tiná ↓	rrṳ̀tiná ↓
tḙ́rkitȯ ↓	tṳ́rkitȯ ↓	ánḙ̀lar ↓	ánṳ̀lar ↓

/ɪ/   and   /o/   in contrast under weak stress

tḭmȯ́ ↓	tǫ̀mȯ́ ↓	miraďá ↓	móraďá ↓
figòh ↓	fǫ̀gòh ↓	pḭkitȯ ↓	pǫ̀kitȯ ↓
lisár ↓	lǫ̀sár ↓	pḭsaďá ↓	pǫ̀saďá ↓
miŕar ↓	mǫ̀rar ↓	tḭritȯ ↓	tǫ̀ritȯ ↓
misyòh ↓	mǫ̀ȿyòh ↓	ihitȯ ↓	ǫ̀hitȯ ↓
triŋkár ↓	trǫ̀ŋkár ↓	imitȯ ↓	ǫ̀mitȯ ↓
mḭ(l)yar ↓	mǫ̀(l)yar ↓	tḭntisimȯ ↓	tǫ́ntisimȯ ↓

/ɪ/   and   /u/   in contrast under weak stress

ligár ↓	lṳgár ↓	miŕar ↓	mṳ́rar ↓
miròh ↓	mṳ́ròh ↓	piɲyòh ↓	pṳ̀ɲyòh ↓

bi̱(l)ya'r ↓	bu̱(l)ya'r ↓	mi̱nítá ↓	mu̱nítá ↓
pi̱nṣo'n ↓	pu̱nṣo'n ↓	chi̱nche'ro̱ ↓	chu̱nche'ro̱ ↓
pi̱nta'r ↓	pu̱nta'r ↓	ni̱ɗoso̱' ↓	nu̱ɗoso̱' ↓
fi̱syo'n ↓	fu̱syo'n ↓	pi̱ɗyendo̱' ↓	pu̱ɗyendo̱' ↓
fi̱ŋhi'r ↓	fu̱ŋhi'r ↓	rri̱mítá ↓	rru̱mítá ↓
mi̱sítá ↓	mu̱sítá ↓	mi̱rahe̱s ↓	mu̱rahe̱s ↓
i̱míto̱ ↓	u̱míto̱ ↓	pi̱ntaɗá ↓	pu̱ntaɗá ↓
mi̱lítá ↓	mu̱lítá ↓	rri̱kítá ↓	rru̱kítá ↓
li̱noso̱' ↓	lu̱noso̱' ↓	bi̱rlaɗo'r ↓	bu̱rlaɗo'r ↓
ti̱nero̱' ↓	tu̱nero̱' ↓	pi̱ritá ↓	pu̱ritá ↓
fi̱lerá ↓	fu̱lerá ↓	li̱nare̱s ↓	lu̱nare̱s ↓
ṣi̱rkíto̱ ↓	su̱rkíto̱ ↓		

/o/ and /u/ in contrast under weak stress

to̱pe' ↓	tu̱pe' ↓	o̱míto̱ ↓	u̱míto̱ ↓
bo̱ka'l ↓	bu̱ka'l ↓	mo̱nítá ↓	mu̱nítá ↓
o̱late̱ ↓	u̱late̱ ↓	plo̱mero̱' ↓	plu̱mero̱' ↓
tro̱ŋka'r ↓	tru̱ŋka'r ↓	mo̱ṣítá ↓	mu̱ṣítá ↓
lo̱nítá ↓	lu̱nítá ↓	rro̱kítá ↓	rru̱kítá ↓

sótanà↓   sûtanà↓   mótilár↓   mútilár↓

póritò↓   púritò↓   ákòsár↓   ákùsár↓

1.21.2 Discussion of minimal vowel contrasts under weak stress

English speakers of course also distinguish words in this same minimal way - *pit, pet, pat, pot, putt, put,* for example--but only rarely *under weak stress.* That is, English has similar differences only in syllables that are noticeably *louder* than any of the Spanish syllables you have been practicing. The underlined vowels in the following English words are all the *same* vowel sound in actual speech, no matter how they are spelled.

president   precedent   bottom   plot'em   warden   pardon

They would *not* be the same in Spanish.

By careful repetition of these Spanish words after a native speaker, and by observing closely the point of difference between each pair, you can begin to *hear* and, having *heard,* to *imitate* differences of a type and frequency that are quite strange to an English speaker's way of talking.

In learning the basic sentences you were probably also corrected for placing too much stress on some syllables, too little stress on others. There are only *two levels of stress* in Spanish (English has four, as we will discover). These two levels are indicated in the 'Aids to Listening' by an acute accent / ′ / over the vowels that have louder stress and a dot / · / over the vowels that have softer stress. We will call these STRONG STRESS and WEAK STRESS.

1.22 The stress system in Spanish

There are two things that are important about stress. One is to get the two stresses placed on the right syllables. The other is to make each of them the right strength. Let us examine these two aspects one at a time.

The following pairs of words differ only in the placement of stress, and, as you can see, the difference in meaning that results is considerable.

1.22.1 Exercises on minimal stress contrasts

1.	ésta↓	'this'	èstá↓	'is'
2.	iŋglès↓	'groins'	iŋglés↓	'English'
3.	pesó↓	'monetary unit'	pèsó↓	'he weighed'
4.	pernó↓	'bolt'	pèrnó↓	'a kind of wine'
5.	pikó↓	'peak'	pikó↓	'he stung'
6.	baldè↓	'bucket'	bàldé↓	'I crippled'
7.	libró↓	'book'	libró↓	'he freed'
8.	ará↓	'altar'	àrá↓	'he will do'
9.	àbrá↓	'open'	àbrá↓	'there will be'

1.22.2 Discussion of minimal stress contrasts

In short, you can be rather drastically misunderstood if you fail to place the stresses correctly when you speak. This, of course, is also true in English, but not so obviously true in view of the greater complexity of the English stress system. We have in English also a fair number of items which can have the stresses arranged in more than one way:

áddrèss↓ or àddréss↓   Càribbéán↓ or Càríbbéàn↓

Chiléán↓ or Chileán↓   Nèw Órlèáns↓ or Nèw Órléáns↓

Since we do not have as many nice neat minimal pairs in English as there are in Spanish (like /ésta — /está/), we may at first be deceived into thinking that Spanish uses stress in a way that English does not, but this is not true.

The other important thing to learn in drilling on stress is to stress syllables with the right amount of force or strength. It is at this point that the four stresses of English interfere with the *two* stresses of Spanish. Let us first learn what the four stresses of English are. Listen to yourself say this phrase:

elevator — operator.

Which syllable is loudest? el— in elevator.   Let us indicate this by writing an acute accent over the e;

élevator — operator.

Which syllable is next loudest? op— in operator. We'll write it with a circumflex accent:

élevator — ôperator.

Then we can hear that —vat — and —rat— are about equally loud, but softer than op—, so we will write a grave accent:

élevàtor — ôperàtor

The syllables that are left over are the weakest, so we write:

$$\acute{e}l\breve{e}v\grave{a}t\breve{o}r \;-\; \hat{o}p\breve{e}r\grave{a}t\breve{o}r$$

In doing this we have marked four levels of stress, which we can label:

primary   —   <u>el</u>—   secondary   —   <u>ôp</u>—

tertiary   —   <u>vàt</u>— <u>ràt</u>—   weak   —   <u>ĕ</u> <u>ŏr</u> <u>ĕ</u> <u>ŏr</u>

This represents a great many different levels of stress, but every English speaker (native) uses all four quite regularly and unconsciously every time he makes an utterance.

Now, how do these four English stresses affect your Spanish? If we remember that Spanish only has TWO stresses, then it seems likely that you will get your FOUR mixed up with these two, with the result that you will put too much stress on some syllables, not enough on others. The correspondence between the English stresses and those of Spanish is roughly this:

<u>English</u>   <u>Spanish</u>

Primary   /ʹ/ ⎤
                      ⎬   Strong /ʹ/
Secondary   /ˆ/ ⎦

Tertiary   /ˋ/ ⎤
                      ⎬   Weak   /˘/
Weak   /˘/ ⎦

Let us look back now at the basic sentences and see if any of the difficulties you had with them can be traced to this difference between the two languages.

RIGHT	YOUR PROBABLE ERROR
1. kômpêrmisô↓	kômpêrmisô↓
2. dispensêmê↓	dispensêmê↓
3. prêsêntarlê↓	prêsêntarlê↓
4. làsêŋyorademolinà↓	làsêŋyôràdemolinà↓
5. igwalméntê↓	igwalmentê↓
6. êŋkàntadô↓	êŋkàntadô↓
7. àstàmàŋyanà↓	âstàmàŋyanà↓

Now because we consider this a very important point indeed, and because it is a point which is rarely drilled elsewhere, we have put together the following long list, arranged according to the number of syllables and placement of stress. Until you can say these using only the two stresses that are marked instead of the four of English you cannot expect to go on and learn complex utterances successfully. Time spent practicing these, therefore, will be very well spent.

1.22.3   Exercises on contrasting stress patterns

´ ⌐↓		⌐ ´↓	
rrohà↓	komô↓	êstà↓	kôlór↓
muchô↓	gustô↓	kàlór↓	ústéd↓
tantô↓	bwenô↓	êstóy↓	àdyós↓
astà↓	lwegô↓	sêŋyór↓	kôrtés↓
dondê↓	frasês↓	rràsón↓	fûmár↓

fúmŏ ↓	áɓrȧ ↓	pȧsár ↓	fȧbór ↓
bȧŋyŏ ↓	bɪsȧ́ ↓	ȧbrɪ́r ↓	pḙrɗóʼn ↓
téŋgȧ ↓	táksɪ ↓	dḙ́şɪ̀r ↓	bɪstéʼ ↓
áŋyŏ ↓	yɛ́lŏ ↓	şyúɗa̋ɗ ↓	tȧmbyéʼn ↓
tárɗė ↓	şérkȧ ↓	sḙrbɪ́r ↓	şḙrrár ↓

́ ⁼ ⁼ ↓	⁼ ́ ⁼ ↓	⁼ ⁼ ́ ↓
rrápiɗŏ ↓	trȧɓahȧ̋ ↓	trȧɓȧhár ↓
lástimȧ ↓	sȧlúɗŏs ↓	ȯrȧ́şyóʼn ↓
fósfŏrŏ ↓	mȧŋyanȧ̋ ↓	ḙntḙndéʼr ↓
syéntḙsḙ ↓	sḙŋyorȧ̋ ↓	ḙspȧŋyóʼl ↓
dehḙ́mḙ ↓	difɪşil ↓	ȧwtŏbúʼs ↓
únikŏ ↓	mŏlestȧ̋ ↓	ḙstȧ́şyóʼn ↓
bȧrbȧ̋rŏ ↓	ḙskuchḙ̋ ↓	kȯrȧ́şóʼn ↓
méɗikŏ ↓	bḙntanȧ̋ ↓	sȧlúɗȧ́r ↓
ᵐyerkŏ̋lḙs ↓	mɪnútŏs ↓	rrḙgúlȧ́r ↓
sȧbȧ̋ɗŏ ↓	tɪkétḙs ↓	kȯnŏşéʼr ↓
şéntimŏ ↓	şḙ́ntaɓŏs ↓	pȧrȧ́gwáʼy ↓

saŋwichê ↓   bôletôs ↓   úrúgwaý ↓
últimô ↓   sâbemôs ↓   sâlbâdôr ↓
proksimô ↓   ɑyêgadâ↓   kôntêstár ↓

⌐ ⌐ ⌐ ⌐ ↓   ⌐ ⌐ ⌐ ⌐ ↓   ⌐ ⌐ ⌐ ⌐ ↓   ⌐ ⌐ ⌐ ⌐ ↓

dígâmêlô ↓   têlefônô ↓   têlêgramâ ↓   trâbâhâré ↓
prestêsêlô ↓   simpatikô ↓   inmêdyatâ ↓   kâswâlidâd ↓
tomêsêlô ↓   dêşidâsê ↓   dêspêdidâs ↓   libêrâşyón ↓
traygâmêlô ↓   mâgnifikô ↓   âbsôlutô ↓   âbilidâd ↓
beâsêlô ↓   múchisimô ↓   súfişyentê ↓   kômúnikár↓
kwentêmêlô ↓   própositô ↓   prêsêntarlê ↓   fêrrôkârríl↓
dandômêlô ↓   fânatikô ↓   sêŋyôritâ ↓   mêntâlidâd ↓
byendôsêlô ↓   pêrdonêmê ↓   kônôşyendô ↓   âgrikúltor ↓
kambyêmêlô ↓   âltimêtrô ↓   âdêlantê ↓   êntônâşyón ↓
sakésêlô ↓   figurêsê ↓   dêmâsyadô ↓   êŋkôntrârá ↓
mwebâsêlô ↓   âmerikâ ↓   pânôramâ ↓   kâminâré ↓
subâmêlâs ↓   milésimô↓   mônôgramâ ↓   âmârişâr ↓
komâsêlô ↓   tântisimô ↓   êntêndidô ↓   âmânêşér ↓
buskâmêlô ↓   bwênisimô ↓   kômfúndidô ↓   fâşilitár ↓

21

˘ ˘ ´ ˘ ˘ ↓   ˘ ˘ ˘ ´ ˘ ↓   ˘ ˘ ˘ ˘ ´ ˘ ↓

kȯnȯşyendȯsė↓   prėsėntȧşyonės↓   ȧntėryȯrid̶ȧd̶↓

ȧşėrkandȯsė↓   ȧmėrikanȯ↓   pȯstėryȯrid̶ȧd̶↓

prėşyȯsısımȯ↓   lȧbȯrȧtoryȯ↓   kristȧlişȧşyȯn↓

prėsėntandȯlė↓   kȯmbėrsȧşyonės↓   kȯmȕnikȧşyȯn↓

primėrısımȯ↓   kȯnsėrbȧtoryȯ↓   nȧşyȯnȧlid̶ȧd̶↓

ėŋkȯntrandȯlȧ↓   kȧmisėrıȧ↓   ȧrgȕmėntȧşyȯn↓

˘ ˘ ˘ ˘ ˘ ´ ˘ ↓   ˘ ˘ ˘ ˘ ˘ ˘ ´ ˘ ↓

hėnėrȧlişȧşyȯn↓   ėspėşyȧlişȧşyȯn↓   institȕşyȯnȧlid̶ȧd̶↓   dėznȧtȕrȧlişȧşyȯn↓

id̶ėntifikȧşyȯn↓   dėkȯntȧminȧşyȯn↓   imprėsyȯnȧbilid̶ȧd̶↓   impėrsȯnȧlişȧşyȯn↓

nȧtȕrȧlişȧşyȯn↓   rrėspȯnsȧbilid̶ȧd̶↓   kȯnstitȕşyȯnȧlid̶ȧd̶↓   ȧgrikȕltȕrişȧşyȯn↓

rrėkȧpitȕlȧşyȯn↓   rrėspėtȧbilid̶ȧd̶↓   sȕpėrnȧtȕrȧlid̶ȧd̶↓   ȧmėrikȧnişȧşyȯn↓

kȧpitȧlişȧşyȯn↓   irrėgȕlȧrid̶ȧd̶↓   dėskȧpitȧlişȧşyȯn↓   sȕpėrȧlimėntȧşyȯn↓

˘ ˘ ´ ˘ ↓   ˘ ˘ ˘ ´ ˘ ↓

igwalmėntė↓   ȧktwalmėntė↓   hėnėralmėntė↓   mȧtėryalmėntė↓

ȕswalmėntė↓   kȯrd̶yalmėntė↓   litėralmėntė↓   ėlsėŋyorkartėr↓

séɲyorkártèr↓   séɲyorkástró↓   álsèɲyorkástró↓   èspèşyálmèntè↓

dóktorkampós↓   ásiⓐşè↓   inmóralmèntè↓   èlkólornégró↓

kólorbèrdè↓   áⓂyabyenè↓   imfórmalmèntè↓   èlsèɲyorbargás↓

1.22.4 Discussion of contrasting stress patterns

You probably noticed, in listening to and imitating these items, that they seem to be pronounced *faster* than English words of similar length. Actually they are not, but there is a big difference in *rhythm* which makes it *seem* that they are. This difference in rhythm can be indicated something like this, using longer lines to indicate longer syllables and shorter lines to indicate shorter syllables:

English Speaker

Where do you think it'll be found?

Spanish Speaker

Where do you think it will be found?

Thus the Spanish way is to make every syllable almost equally long, giving a machine-gun effect, whereas the English way is to make the louder syllables longer. The two languages divide up their time differently.

1.23 The intonation system of Spanish

Up to this point we have discussed two errors you were corrected for in learning the basic sentences: UNSTRESSED VOWELS and SYLLABLE STRESS. The third problem which occurs from the very beginning and will be with you to mar your Spanish for a very long time is INTONATION: the rise and fall of the pitch of the voice. We have indicated this by placing our accent marks at *three different heights* over the vowel:

Low pitch: directly over the vowel   /à ó/

Middle pitch: one space above the vowel   /à ò/

High pitch: two spaces above the vowel   /a o/

All three in sequence look like this: /à à a/   /á à a/

These are analogous to steps in a musical scale: 

In addition to these various levels of pitch, there may be a slight rise / ↑ / or a slight fall / ↓ / after the last pitch, or it may remain level / | / .

Now let us return to the basic sentences and see what you were corrected on.

<table>
<tr><td>RIGHT</td><td>YOUR PROBABLE ERROR</td></tr>
</table>

	RIGHT	YOUR PROBABLE ERROR
1.	bwènozdías |sèŋyór ↓	bwènozdías |seŋyor ↑
2.	bwènastardès |sèŋyórà ↓	bwènastardès |seŋyorà ↑
3.	bwènaznochès |sèŋyòrítà ↓	bwènaznochès |seŋyorita ↑
4.	komǫestaųstéd ↓	komǫestaųstéd ↓
5.	mùybyeŋ |grásyàs ↓	mùybyeŋ |grásyàs ↑
6.	kómolebá↓	kómoleba ↓
7.	kómonó ↓	kómono ↓

8. múchazgráşyàs ↓   múchazgraşyàs ↓

9. dènadà ↓   denádà ↑

10. nọaydeké ↓   nọaydeké ↑

11. igwálmentè|gráşyàs ↓   igwálmentè|gráşyàs ↑

12. àdyós ↓   adyos ↑

13. àstámàŋyanà ↓   astamaŋyana ↑

14. àstálwegó ↓   astalwego ↑

It will be evident to you that all of the mistaken patterns of the right-hand column above are attributable to some very common pattern that such utterances have in English. A few of the common non-Spanish interference patterns that English sets up are these:

1. Good morning|Bill ↑   5. Good bye ↑

2. Fine | thanks ↑   6. Good bye ↑

3. How are you ↓   7. Many thanks ↓

4. How are you ↓

The only way to get these (and other) English patterns out of your way in talking Spanish is by the correct repetition of Spanish patterns so often that they automatically replace the English ones when they are supposed to. The following exercise is directed toward that end.

1.23.1 Exercises on contrasting intonation patterns

1. beṇgaká ↓

2. klarokesí↓

3. sonlastrés ↓

4. ⓪yeggenabyón ↓

5. nolokré∂ ↓

6. nómeimpórtá ↓

7. byenemaŋyáná ↓

8. ⓪yègomaríà ↓

9. àkisèbáylà ↓

10. komọestá ↓

11. dondestá↓

12. komolebá ↓

13. kyene(s)són ↓

14. kelepásà ↓

15. kwando⓪yégà ↓

Group 1
All of a 'falling' pattern

16. kwántokwéstá ↓

17. kékomémós ↓

18. déꝺondesón ↓

19. páráꝺondebán ↓

20. pórkesefwé ↓

21. pórkwántotyémpó ↓

22. ákwantoestámós ↓

1. yáseba ↑

2. kyérekafé ↑

3. bínokonustéꝺ↑

4. kómyéronya ↑

5. tyenꬱunlápis ↑

6. sébakonmigo ↑

7. légústomaría ↑

8. léyoꬱldyaryo ↑

9. tyenenótro ↑

10. lépásólaléche ↑

Group 2
All of a 'rising' pattern

11.   tráhosukárro ↑

12.   légustasutrabáho ↑

1.   grásyàs |sèŋyór ↓

2.   mùybyeŋ |grásyàs ↓

3.   sı |sèŋyórà ↓

4.   no |sèŋyòrítà ↓

5.   nọay |ómbrè ↓

6.   beŋgà |màríà ↓

7.   nó |múchàzgrásyàs ↓

8.   nòbyenẹ |èntónşès ↓

9.   sı |pàpá ↓

1o.   no |màmá ↓

11.   àđyos |sèŋyórès ↓

12.   àstàmàŋyanà |sèŋyórès ↓

Group 3
All ending in a low level pattern

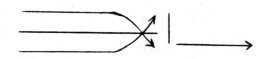

End of Tape 1A

28

Tape 1B

2.1   BASIC SENTENCES. Useful phrases.

ENGLISH SPELLING	AID TO LISTENING	SPANISH SPELLING
ahead, forward	ådèlantè↓	adelante
Come on in.	ådèlantè↓	¡Adelante!
seat (to seat)	syentè↓ sèntár↓	siente (sentar)
seat yourself (to seat oneself)	syentèsè↓ sèntarsè↓	siéntese (sentarse)
Sit down.	syentèsè↓	Siéntese.
(you) have (to have)	tyenè↓ tènér↓	tiene (tener)
a, an (one)	ún↓ únò↓	un (uno)
the pencil	èl—lápiş↓	el lápiz
Do you have a pencil?	tyenęunlápiş↓	¿Tiene un lápiz?
(I) have (to have)	teŋgò↓ tènér↓	tengo (tener)
No, I don't.	nó↓notéŋgò↓	No, no tengo.
yes	si↓	sí

Yes, I do.	síↆsitéŋgòↆ	Sí, sí tengo.
repeat (to repeat)	rrépításↆ rrépétírↆ	repita (repetir)
Say it again.	rrépitáↆ	Repita.
translate (to translate)	tráduşkáↆ tráduşírↆ	traduzca (traducir)
Translate.	tráduşkáↆ	Traduzca.
another	ótráↆ	otra
the time	lá‑béşↆ	la vez
again	ótrá‑béşↆ	otra vez
for	pórↆ	por
the favor	él‑fábórↆ	el favor
please	pór‑fábórↆ	por favor
Again, please.	ótrabéş │pórfábórↆ	Otra vez, por favor.
the pardon	él‑pérdónↆ	el perdón
(you) say (to say)	dişéↆ déşírↆ	dice (decir)
Excuse me, what did you say? [1]	pérdónↆ kómodişęusteɑ↑	Perdón. ¿Cómo dice usted?
give (to give)	déↆ dárↆ	dé (dar)
to me	meↆ	me

the pen	là‑p lúmà↓	la pluma
Give me the pen.	démelaplúmà↓	Déme la pluma.
pass (to pass, to hand)	pásé↓ pàsár↓	pase (pasar)
pass me	pásémé↓	páseme
the book	èl—líbrò↓	el libro
Pass me the book.	páseme(l)líbrò↓	Páseme el libro.
is (to be)	é's↓ sér↓	es (ser)
that	ésò↓	eso
What's that?	kes̩ésò↓	¿Qué es eso?
this	éstò↓	esto
the ashtray	èl—s̩énis̩erò↓	el cenicero
This is an ashtray.	ésto̩|ésùns̩énis̩erò↓	Esto es un cenicero.
wants (to want)	kyéré↓ kèrér↓	quiere (querer)
to say	dès̩ír↓	decir
(it) means	kyéré—dès̩ír↓	quiere decir

What does *cenicero* mean?   kékyéreɖeşír |şeníşéró↓   ¿Qué quiere decir *cenicero*?

It means *ashtray*.   kyéreɖeşír |æshtréy↓   Quiere decir *ashtray*.

    says itself, is said (to say)   sě—ɖíşé↓ děşír↓   se dice (decir)

    in   én↓   en

    the Spanish   él—éspàŋyól↓   el español

How do you say *table* in Spanish?   kómoseɖíşe |teybɨl |éŋéspàŋyól↓   ¿Cómo se dice *table* en español?

    the table   là—mesá↓   la mesa

You say *mesa*. (2)   sěɖíşe |mesá↓   Se dice *mesa*.

    the English   él—iŋglés↓   el inglés

    the chair   là—síɰyá↓   la silla

How do you say *silla* in English?   kómoseɖíşe |síɰyȧ |éniŋglés↓   ¿Cómo se dice *silla* en inglés?

You say *chair*.   sěɖíşe |chéhr↓   Se dice *chair*.

    where   dóndě↓   dónde

    the embassy   lạ—ěmbàhaɖá↓   la embajada

    American   àměrikáná↓   americana

Where's the American Embassy?	dóndestá|laḁémbảhaḁamerɪkánảↆ	¿Dónde está la Embajada Americana?
the bathroom	él—baɲyỏↆ	el baño
Where's the bathroom?	dóndestá|ẹlbaɲyỏↆ	¿Dónde está el baño?
there	áɪↆ	ahí
at, to	áↆ	a
the left	lạ—ɪşkyérɗảↆ	la izquierda
There to the left.	áɪ|álạɪşkyérɗảↆ	Ahí a la izquierda.
the right	lả—ɗérechảↆ	la derecha
There to the right.	áɪ|álảɗérechảↆ	Ahí a la derecha.
There straight ahead.	áɪ|áɗélantềↆ	Ahí adelante.
take, carry (to take)	Ꞙyébềↆ Ꞙyébảrↆ	lleve (llevar)
take us	Ꞙyébềnỏsↆ	llévenos
the center (of town)	él—şentrỏↆ	el centro
Take us downtown.	Ꞙyébenòs|alşéntrỏↆ	Llévenos al centro.
are (to be)	éstánↆ éstárↆ	están (estar)

the (m. pl.)	lós↓	los
Where're the books?	dóndestán|lozlíbròs↓	¿Dónde están los libros?
take me	Ɑyebémȩ́↓	lléveme
the hotel	ȩ̀l—òtél↓	el hotel
Take me to the hotel.	Ⱡyebemȩ|alotél↓	Lléveme al hotel.
(it) goes down (to go down)	subȩ̀↓ súbìr↓	sube (subir)
or	ó↓	o
(it) goes down (to go down)	bahȧ↓ bȧhȧr↓	baja (bajar)
Going up or down? (3)	subȩobáhȧ↓	¿Sube o baja?
how much	kwantó↓	cuánto
How much is it?	kwantȩȩs↓	¿Cuánto es?

one	unó↓	uno	six	séys↓	seis
two	dós↓	dos	seven	syetȩ̀↓	siete
three	trés↓	tres	eight	ochó↓	ocho
four	kwatró↓	cuatro	nine	nwebȩ̀↓	nueve
five	ṣiŋkó↓	cinco	ten	dyé ṣ↓	diez

34

eleven	ónșê↓	once		fifteen	kínșê↓	quince
twelve	dóșê↓	doce		sixteen	dyéșiseys↓	dieciséis
thirteen	treșê↓	trece		twenty	beyntê↓	veinte
fourteen	kåtorșê↓	catorce		twenty-one	beyntiunó↓	veintiuno

2.10   Notes on the basic sentences

(1) Instead of using the entire phrase 'What did you say?', The Spanish speaker frequently uses only the first word, i.e. /kómo↑/, just as we may say only 'What?'

(2) Note that here, and in the other phrases above and below which also have the form /se-díșe↓/ in them, that the idea of 'someone' actually *saying* the word is not given: rather, the word *says itself*, which makes this construction *impersonal*, and which is translated into English as 'is said' or 'you say'. The Spanish construction used is the *reflexive* construction, which will be examined in detail in Unit 24.

(3) More literally, 'Does it (the elevator) go up or does it go down?'

2.2   DRILLS ON PRONUNCIATION

In the first unit we examined the vowels under weak stress, the stress system, the intonation system, and the resulting rhythmic effect.

Before going on to an examination of consonants, and vowels under strong stress, notice in the lists below how in words which sound familiar, you are liable to make some rather serious mistakes because of the very familiarity of the words.

2.21   Typical errors from English vowel influence in similar-sounding words.

CORRECT	YOUR PROBABLE ERROR	FAMILIAR ENGLISH PRONUNCIATION	ENGLISH SPELLING
ófiṣinà↓	àfiṣinà↓	áfis↓ — ófis↓	office
dóktór↓	dáktór↓	dáktə̀r↓	doctor
ópórtúnidàd↓	àpə̀rtúnidàd↓	àpə́rtuwnìtiy↓	opportunity
kóŋgresó↓	káŋgresó↓	kàŋgris↓	congress
kómférenṣyà↓	kámférenṣyà↓	kánfə̀rins↓	conference
trópikál↓	trápikál↓	trapìkə̀l↓	tropical
átomikà↓	àtamikà↓	ə́tamik↓	atomic
óndurás↓	àndurás↓	hə̀ndurìs↓	Honduras
kómbérsàṣyón↓	kámbérsàṣyón↓	kànvə̀rseyšìn↓	conversation
óspitál↓	àspitál↓	haspitìl↓	hospital
kóntrató↓	kántrató↓	kantrǽkt↓	contract
pósiblé↓	pásiblé↓	pasìbìl↓	possible

bómbárdeð↓	bâmbárdeð↓	bàmbardmɛnt↓	bombardment
prontó↓	prantó↓	prantòw↓	pronto
proksimá↓	praksimá↓	ə́praksimɛ̀t↓	approximate
fosfóró↓	fasfóró↓	fasfɔ̀rəs↓	phosphorous
kostó↓	kastó↓	ka'st↓ - ko'st↓	cost

blaŋká↓	blæŋká↓	blæŋk↓	blank
kansás↓	kænsás↓	kænzɨz↓	Kansas
pasé↓	pæsé↓	pæ's↓	pass
klasé↓	klæsé↓	klæ's↓	class
grasyás↓	græsyás↓	græ's↓	grass
lastimá↓	læstimá↓	læst↓	last
ɛspáŋyol↓	ɛspǽŋyol↓	spæniš↓	Spanish
àbsólutó↓	æbsólutó↓	æbsə̀lùwt↓	absolute

From these examples it is no doubt clear that many words which *look* easy, because they seem very much like English words, are in fact the most misleading because of their similarity. If you are alert to the possibility of this error, however, it is a relatively easy one to correct.

2.22   Voiced stop consonants

2.22.1   /d/ in Spanish

The problem that arises from /d/ is that it has two varieties of pronunciation which are, from the point of view of English speakers, actually different sounds; but from the point of view of Spanish speakers, they are one and the same sound.

How can there be such a difference in point of view? A sound is, one would think, either the same as another or it isn't. But this is an instance where the 'common sense' viewpoint does not hold. From infancy speakers of Spanish are taught to ignore the difference between [d] and [đ]. English speakers are taught to respect that difference but ignore others (such as the puff of air that comes after the /p/ of *pill* but does not come after the /p/ of *spill*).

The symbol [d] represents the initial sound of English *den, do, die, dare,* etc., but the tip of the tongue actually touches the back side of the upper teeth when this sound is produced in Spanish, whereas in English it touches somewhat further back.

The symbol [đ] represents the initial sound of English *then, thee, the, those, that, there,* etc., or the middle sound of *either, mother, other, father,* etc., or the final sound of *lathe, bathe.* However, it must be distinguished carefully from the *other* sound which English writes with *th,* the initial sound of *thin, thick, thistle,* or the middle sound of *ether, Ethel,* or the final sound of *bath.* This other sound is written [ş] in this book, and it has no connection with /d/.

Examples of the two /d/ sounds are below.

dáđó↓	áđondé↓
déđó↓	ándađó↓
dúđár↓	sóldađó↓
dúđosó↓	tildađó↓
gwárdađó↓	dézđéɲyađó↓
kárdađó↓	dézđíchađó↓

You will of course notice that both kinds of / d / appear here, and wonder how you can tell which variety to expect. The rule is reasonably clear and consistent, though in some dialect areas, slight variations may occur:

	pause	/n/	/l/	/↓/	/↑/	vowels	/y/	/w/	other consonants
[d] appears after	x	x	x	x	x				
[đ] appears after						x	x	x	x

The real importance of producing the right variety of / d / at the right time becomes evident upon examination of the contrasts below, where the use of [d] instead of [đ] in the left-hand column will cause the word to be misinterpreted as being the one in the right-hand column.

2.22.11   Exercise on / d / and / r / between vowels

óđá↓	orá↓	píđá↓	pírá↓
tóđó↓	toró↓	lóđó↓	loró↓
káđá↓	kará↓	kóđó↓	koró↓
seđá↓	será↓	muđó↓	muró↓
móđó↓	moró↓	ađá↓	ará↓
míđá↓	mírá↓		

2.22.2   /b/   in Spanish

The problem of /b/ is similar to that of /d/.   There are two varieties which are the *same* from the Spanish point of view but noticeably different from the English point of vew.

The symbol [b] represents the initial sound of English words like *bee, bill, buy, borrow,* the middle sound in *baby, tabby, tubby,* the final sound in *tub, hub, rub, flub.*

The symbol [ɓ] represents a sound which does not exist in English. It is produced by bringing the lips close to each other, but not allowing them to touch, so that the air passes through them with a slight friction noise. The result sounds like a cross between a *b, v,* and *w.* The easiest way to learn to produce it is to start out as though to make a [b] in a word like *about,* but not allow the lips to touch so that the resulting sound is *v*-like in character (but remember that it is *not* a *v*).

Examples of [b] and [ɓ] follow:

bėbér↓   silbabá↓

bibír↓   sálbabá↓

bábór↓   ėnérbabá↓

bábosá↓   érbabá↓

şúmbabá↓   ėzbóşabá↓

kámbyabá↓   ėzbobó↓

	pause	/m/	/i/	/↓/	/↑/	vowels	y	w	other consonants
[b] appears after	x	x	x	x	x				
[b] appears after						x	x	x	x

To make a mistake in the production of /b/ is not as serious as with the /d/, but errors can lead to misunderstanding. More important, there is no *v* sound in Spanish, even though it is in the writing system. The Spanish sound which Americans may hear as *v* in a word like *Havana* is actually the [b] sound.

2.22.3 /g/ in Spanish

The problem of /g/ is similar to that of /d/ and /b/. There are two varieties which are the same from the Spanish point of view but noticeably different from the English point of view.

The symbol [g] represents the initial sound of English words like *go, get, got, guess*, the middle sound in *ago, again*, the final sound in *tug, tag, tog*.

The symbol [ǥ] represents a sound which is heard only rarely in English, in a word like *sugar*. It is produced by raising the back part of the tongue up towards the roof of the mouth as though to make a [g] but without allowing the tongue to touch, so that the air is free to pass through with a slight friction noise.

Examples of [g] and [g] follow:

galgó↓   éstégalgó↓

gagá↓   élgagó↓

grégoryò↓   làgárgantá↓

gágerà↓   làgorgá↓

àgriŋgadò↓   ézgrégoryò↓

àgàŋgrénarsé↓   ézgágerá↓

As with /d/ and /b/, the distribution of the two varieties of /g/ is fairly clear and consistent:

	pause	[ŋ]	/l/	/↓/	/↑/	vowels	y	w	other consonants
[g] appears after	x	x	x	x	x				
[g] appears after						x	x	x	x

To make a mistake in the production of /g/ is not serious, but unless you learn to produce the [g] variety you will find that it is difficult to identify when you are listening to a Spanish speaker. So for the purpose of comprehension it is worth the trouble to master it.

2.23   Vibrants / r / and / rr / in Spanish

Even though we write these sounds with the letter *r*, the student should take special note of the very important fact that these /r/–sounds do not even vaguely resemble the / r /–sounds that occur in most varieties of English. Any attempt to transfer one's English / r / over into Spanish will result in utter failure to produce a satisfactory imitation of the Spanish sound.

You have already (2.22.11) gone through a session of drill-work on the difference between / r / and the variety of / d / that appears between vowel-contrasts like [tóđó↓] - [tóró↓].   Now it is necessary to distinguish this *single* / r / (the one which is so much like English *tt* or *d* or *dd* in words like *Betty, cottage, lettuce, better, wader, waiter, shutter, shudder*) from the *double* / rr /. The / rr / is a rapid trill of the tongue-tip, and it can usually be learned only by careful imitation. The following drill is to help you hear and learn to reproduce the difference between the two kinds of / r /.

2.23.1   Exercise on / r / and /rr/ between vowels

peró↓	perró↓
karó↓	karró↓
pará↓	parrá↓
bará↓	barrá↓
koró↓	korró↓
şeró↓	şerró↓
yeró↓	yerró↓
foró↓	forró↓
fyeró↓	fyerró↓
ámará↓	ámarrá↓

Not only is the Spanish /r/ quite different from the English *r* when it occurs between vowels, as in the preceding drill; it is also quite different in association with consonants. Take the Spanish word [tárdė↓] for example. Your first attempt will probably sound something like the English words *tar day*. If you will try to make it sound more like *totter-they* (spoken rapidly), you will come pretty close to the Spanish pronunciation.

The following drill will allow you to practice /r/ in all combinations with other consonants.

2.23.2   Excercise on /r/ before and after consonants

prontó↓	kwerpó↓	grandé↓	amargó↓
primó↓	torpé↓	frió↓	marfíl↓
tres↓	kartá↓	frasé↓	perfíl↓
trató↓	pwertá↓		farsá↓
krudó↓	şerká↓		irsé↓
kreó↓	parké↓		arhentiná↓
brasíl↓	arból↓		surhyó↓
bromá↓	kurbá↓		dormí↓
dramá↓	tardé↓		armá↓
drogá↓	gwardá↓		byernés↓
graşyás↓	gárgantá↓		ornó↓

Whenever /r/ occurs at the very end of an utterance (*not* the end of a word, but the end just before pause), and especially when that final syllable is a *stressed* syllable, it has a different pronunciation from what is heard elsewhere. It is more like /rr/, but the vocal cords do not vibrate during it. The effect is almost like combining /r/ with /s/ except that the tongue-tip remains *up* at the end. This sound can be practiced by imitation of the following words.

2.23.3   Exercise on Spanish /r/ at the end of an utterance

sė́ŋyo'r↓	ȧ̧ukȧ́r↓
ȧbla'r↓	nakȧ́r↓
mė́tė'r↓	etė́r↓
kȧnsa'r↓	kanṣė́r↓
rrė́bólbė'r↓	rrė́bólbė́r↓
pȧrti'r↓	mártir↓
fȧbó'r↓	bȯ́líbȧ́r↓

In the preceding pages the *gross* differences in the pronunciation of sounds that are similar in Spanish and English have been illustrated and discussed. These are the differences which if unmastered will cause great difficulty and misunderstanding in an attempt to communicate in Spanish, and their mastery is therefore of the utmost importance to a student. However, there are other pronunciation features that should be understood and learned, to reduce the 'gringo accent' that will inevitably distract the listener's attention and thus impair the communication efficiency. The following lists of similar sounding words pronounced by a Spanish speaker and an English speaker respectively will illustrate important differences in the pronunciation of what might be considered the same vowels. Note especially that the English vowels seem to be more prolonged, more drawn out, and especially note that they do *not* seem to maintain the same quality from the beginning to the end of the vowel, whereas the Spanish vowel *does*.

2.24   Vowel nuclei in Spanish

2.24.1   English /ey/ and Spanish /e/

day	dé↓
Kay	ké↓
say	sé↓
bay	bé↓
Fay	fé↓
May	mé↓
lay	lé↓

2.24.2   English /ow/ and Spanish /o/

no	nó↓
low	ló↓
yoe	yó↓
so	só↓

2.24.3   English /ɪy/ and Spanish /ɪ/

me	mí↓
tea	tí↓
see	sí↓
bee	bí↓
Dee	dí↓
knee	ní↓

2.24:4   English /uw/ and Spanish /u/

too	tú↓
sue	sú↓
pooh	pú↓
coo	kú↓
boo	bú↓
moo	mú↓

Generally if you are imitating a native or near-native pronunciation at full normal colloquial speed, errors of the type illustrated above are not likely to be obtrusive. Probably the most important detail to remember is to say words which contain these vowels without allowing the quality to change in the course of producing them. For /u/ and /o/, this means rounding the lips during the production of the preceding consonant so that the lips are properly rounded in anticipation of the rounding required for the vowel.

2.25   Lateral —/l/ in Spanish

/l/ in English is a sound that is produced by raising the tip of the tongue up to touch the roof of the mouth in such a way that the air column is forced to pass around either side of it: this way of producing a sound is called *lateral* (i.e. 'side') *articulation*.

In Spanish, the /l/ is actually a *laterally-released* [d], and it has a *very* different sound from the English /l/. If you will try to follow by manipulating your own tongue, a technical description will be helpful: produce a [d] as in the word *did*. Notice that to make the [d], you release the whole tip of the tongue so that the air can flow suddenly out across the top of it. Now instead of releasing the entire tongue downward, keep the tip locked in its [d] position at the end of the word *did* but release the air through one side as though you were going to say the word *diddle*, but without lowering the back part of the tongue as you would in *diddle*. If you have followed these instructions, you are producing a Spanish /l/.

Compare the following pairs which are approximately alike except for the /l/-sounds and try to imitate the difference.

2.25.1   Exercise on Spanish /l/

feel	fíl↓	dell	dél↓	coal	kól↓
hotel	ótél↓	tall	tál↓	tool	túl↓
el	él↓				

2.26   Voiceless stops

2.26.1   /p/ in Spanish

It was mentioned earlier that in English there are at least two conspicuously different kinds of p-sounds: the p of *pin*, *pill*, which has the puff of air called *aspiration*, and the p of *spin*, *spill*, which has no aspiration.

The Spanish /p/ is always produced *without* aspiration. One way for an American to get at the mastery of it is by thinking of an *s* before Spanish words that begin with /p/ in order to transfer the English pattern of producing unaspirated p after *s*.

The following list will give you a basis for comparing the p-sound in the two languages and learning to reproduce the difference.

2.26.11   Exercise on Spanish /p/

pace	péş↓
Peru	pèrú↓
pawn	páǹ↓
par	pár↓
pore	pór↓
pone	póǹ↓
pooh	pú↓
plan	pláǹ↓

2.26.2   /t/ in Spanish

The /t/ problem is like the /p/ problem: in English it is aspirated, in Spanish it is not. In addition, the tongue touches a point that is more forward in the mouth to produce a Spanish /t/: it literally touches the back side of the upper teeth, which it does not do in English.

2.26.21   Exercise on Spanish /t/

tea	tí↓
ten	tén↓
toss	tás↓
taboo	tåbú↓

2.26.3   /k/ in Spanish

If you have mastered /p/ and /t/, /k/ will be a breeze since it involves again the aspiration problem.

2.26.31   Exercise on Spanish /k/

kilo	kiló↓
Kay	ké↓
call	kál↓
can	kán↓
cafe	kåfé↓

2.27   **Voiceless spirants**

2.27.1   /s/ in Spanish

Spanish has an [s] and a [z] , but unlike English they are considered as variants of a single sound, /s/ . That is to say, two Spanish words are never distinguished solely by the difference [s–z] as are the English words 'seal and 'zeal'. Note the following pairs of words in Spanish which have partly similar sequences of sounds.

2.27.11   Exercise on the distribution of the variants of /s/

ézbóşó↓	ésposó↓
rrázga'r↓	rráska'r↓
ézḃeltá↓	éspeltá↓
áznó↓	askó↓
mɪzmó↓	mɪstó↓
húẓga'r↓	búska'r↓
dézɖéŋya'r↓	déstéŋyi'r↓
dɪzgústó↓	dɪskursó↓
dézɖé↓	desté↓ (dę esté)
ézɖé↓ (ez dé)	esté↓

2.27.12   Discussion of the distribution of the variants of /s/

You will notice that the [z] occurs in Spanish only in a syllable-final position before a *voiced consonant*, namely [b, d, g, m, n, l, r]. Anywhere else, [s] occurs, except before semi-vowels /y/ and /w/ where both [s] and [z] occur, depending on whether the syllable begins with the /s/ or with the semivowel. Since there is no choice on the part of the speaker-only one or the other occurs in any given situation, but not both-they are *not in contrast* and belong to only one basic sound unit, /s/.

But in some dialects and styles of speaking Spanish, another variety of [s] occurs. Note these pronunciations of some Caribbean and South American dialects.

$$\text{bwéna}^h\text{noché}^h\downarrow \qquad\qquad \text{múcha}^h\text{grásyá}^h\downarrow$$

$$\text{kómọe}^h\text{táụ}^h\text{té}\downarrow \qquad\qquad \text{á}^h\text{támáŋyáná}\downarrow$$

$$\text{kẹórạé}^h\downarrow \qquad\qquad\qquad \text{ésọé}^h\downarrow$$

The /s/ is *not* dropped entirely in these dialects. Actually there are some rather complex differences in distribution from one dialect to another, so that Argentineans may say that Chileans 'eat their *s*'s', and Colombians will say the Argentineans eat *their s's*, and so on, without any of these stereotypes reflecting the facts. Thus, for example, since the Chileans use the [h] variety of /s/ in all syllable-final occurrences, they are accused of eating their *s*'s by Argentineans who use the [h] variety only in those syllable - final ocurrences that are followed by a syllable which begins with a consonant. Such details are not pertinent to the development of your pronunciation, since in *any* case you should imitate your instructor's pronunciation. But you may hear other varieties some day, and it is well to understand the patterns they follow. Remember that in *no* dialect does the syllable-initial /s/ appear as [h] .

There are certain groups of words in which the / s / will bother you more than elsewhere, because the words sound familiar and lead you back into English / z / —channels. Such are the words listed below.

2.27.13 Typical errors frcm English / z /—influence on Spanish / s /

CORRECT	YOUR PROBABLE ERROR	FAMILIAR ENGLISH PRONUNCIATION	ENGLISH SPELLING
kansás↓	kanzás↓	kǽnzɨs↓	Kansas
ímflwenşá↓	ímflwenzá↓	ìnflúwenzə↓	influenza
bènèşwelá↓	bènèzwelá↓	vènɨzúwelə↓	Venezuela
èksámènès↓	ègzámènès↓	ègzǽmz↓	exams
rráşón↓	rrázón↓	ríyzɨn↓	reason
dibísyón↓	dibízyón↓	dɨvížɨn↓	division
própósitó↓	própózitó↓	prápəzíšɨn↓	proposition
présiɗentè↓	prèzíɗentè↓	prezɨdɨnt↓	president
présèntè↓	prèzèntè↓	priyzéht↓	present
présèntár↓	prèzèntár↓	prezɨnt↓	present
présèntáşyonès↓	prèzèntáşyonès↓	prèzinteyšɨn↓	presentation
bisitár↓	bizitár↓	vízit↓	visit
sántàrrosá↓	sántàrrozá↓	sǽntə rowzə↓	Santa Rosa
rrósálíndá↓	rrózálíndá↓	ròwzəlíndə↓	Rosalinda

2.27.14   American Spanish / s / and Castilian /ş/

In Castilian Spanish, a dialect used in some areas of Spain, but having a prestige status that far outweighs its geographical distribution, the sounds   / s /   and   / ş /   are different. The / s / is pronounced with the tongue tip raised toward the top of the mouth, so that an effect like a very slight lisp is noticeable. The / ş / is pronounced something like the *th* of the English word *thin*. Thus words like the following, which are alike in other dialects, are distinguished in Castilian Spanish.

kásá↓	kaşá↓	lásó↓	láşó↓
ás↓	áş↓	masá↓	maşá↓
pesès↓	peşès↓	lósá↓	lóşá↓
kóse'r↓	kóşe'r↓	pásó↓	páşó↓
pósó↓	póşó↓	asá↓	aşá↓

This distinction can be ignored by anyone who expects to use Spanish among speakers of American Spanish dialects.

2.27.2   /h/ in Spanish

Another consonant that marks an American accent is the   /h/ . The following lists of similar sounding words pronounced by an English speaker and a Spanish speaker will illustrate the difference between English *h* and Spanish /h/ .

2.27.21   Exercise on Spanish /h/

heater	hırá↓
hurrah	húra'r↓
holly	halé↓
hotter	hará↓
hoosegow	húʒgadó↓

Hilda	hílda↓
junta	húntá↓
aha	áha·↓
Mohican	mòhıká↓

2.27.22 Discussion of Spanish /h/

When you produce *h* in English your tongue is relaxed and low in your mouth, so that you merely breathe easily across it before beginning the vowel that follows. For a Spanish /h/, the tongue must be tenser and higher in the mouth, near the roof but not touching it, so that more friction noise is created when air is forced past. It is especially difficult for an English speaker to produce Spanish /h/ between vowels and after a stressed syllable as in /méhıko↓ déheme/, etc. Though always stronger than English *h* Spanish /h/ carries more or less friction noise depending on the area of the Spanish speaking world. Listen carefully and imitate what you hear to the best of your ability.

2.28 Nasals and palatals

2.28.1 /n/ in Spanish

Spanish /n/ differs from English *n* in that it is usually produced against the back of the upper teeth, instead of on the gum ridge above the teeth. In this respect it is similar to Spanish /t/ and /d/. The correct articulation of /n/ is not too difficult for English speakers, but there are a couple of combinations of /n/ plus another consonant that create problems.

2.28.11 The cluster /nt/ in Spanish

quantity	kántıdád↓
Tonto	tantó↓
lentil	lenté↓

canto	kántô↓
antidote	ántɪdôtô↓
Tantalus	tántâlô↓
pinto	pɪntô↓
junta	huntâ↓
Santa Mónica	sántâ—monɪkâ↓

The close yoking of n͟t in English in words like the ones above, especially when not pronounced slowly and in expressions like 'I wanta', does not happen in the pronunciation of Spanish /nt/ , where the /n/ is clearly resonated through the nose before the /t/ begins.

2.28.2   /ŋy/ and /ny/ in Spanish

Speakers from practically all dialect areas can, when they try, make a difference between forms with /ŋy/ and those with /ny/ . It seems, however, that this difference is unimportant from the point of view of its limited usefulness, since the distinction is frequently obscured at normal utterance speed. It is somewhat like the difference between medial *tt* and *dd* after stress in words like *shutter* and *shudder:* the difference is there, and we can make it if we try to, but we usually do not. In the hierarchy of importance of the various details of learning Spanish pronunciation, this is one of the last.

2.28.21   English /nɪy/ , /ny/ and Spanish /ŋy/ , /ny/

<u>1</u>	<u>2</u>	<u>3</u>	<u>4</u>
uranium		úraŋyô↓	úranyô↓
lineal		álɪŋyâ↓	álɪnyâ↓
matrimonial		moŋyô↓	mâtrimonyô↓

Antonio		ótoṇyó↓	ántonyó↓
linear	vineyard	lá‑bıṇyá↓	lábınyá↓
	minion	mıṇyó↓	mınyó↓
	onion	dě‑moṇyó↓	děmonyó↓
	Hispania	ěspaṇyá↓	ispaṇyá↓
	Hispaniola	ěspåṇyolá↓	ispåṇyolá↓
	canyon	ěskaṇyó↓	åskanyó↓
	annual	aṇyó↓	hěranyó↓
	pinion, piñon	pıṇyoń↓	opınyoń↓

The English and Spanish pronunciations of /n/ and /y/ together (columns 2 and 4) do not sound alike largely because in English, the syllable division is *after* the /n/, but in Spanish it is *before* the /n/. Column 3 really hardly needs to be given except that purists would be uncomfortable if we failed to indicate that the contrast can be, and sometimes is, made.

2.28.3   /ly/, /(l)y/,, and /y/ in Spanish

2.28.31   English /lı̌y/, /ly/ and Spanish /ly/, /(l)y/, and /y/

Balearic	dahlia	bályá↓	ba(l)y̌á↓	báyá↓
polio	pavillion	pólyó↓	po(l)yó↓	poyó↓
alias	stallion	ályás↓	a(l)yás↓	ayás↓

malleable	Amelia	ámalyá↓	ámaⒻyá↓	ámayá↓
oleo	collier	ólyô↓	óⒻyô↓	oyô↓
oleography	goliard	ólyár↓	óⒻyár↓	ôyár↓
Ilion	million	ilyón↓	miⒻyón↓	mi‑yó↓
alien	billion	élyô↓	éⒻyô↓	
Quintilian	quintillion	fílyô↓	fíⒻyô↓	

The preceding lists are not so much for drill as for illustration of an important and widespread dialect difference. To distinguish the important dialect difference, the [l] of the forms in column four is placed in parenthesis, /(l)y/ , since it drops in all dialects except in some parts of Castile in Spain, in upland Colombia, Ecuador, Bolivia, Paraguay, and a few other areas. In most of these dialects the minimal difference between /ly/ and /(l)y/ (the similar forms in columns 3 and 4) can be made, but has the same limited usefulness as the /ny/ –/ɲy/ distinction. For all the other dialect areas, the similar forms of columns 4 and 5 are not distinguished; both have the [y] variant of /y/ , described below.

2.28.4   /y/ in Spanish

/y/ has two variants which are obvious to the English ear because they are like two entirely separate sounds in English. We write these variants with [y] for the one that is the y's of *yea, yes, bay, buy, yacht*, etc., and with [y] for the one that varies all the way from [y] to (ɔ) as in *judge*. In the English words below, either of the two words on each line begins with a sound that is equally likely to occur in the Spanish items of the right-hand column.

2.28.41   English *y* and *j* and Spanish [y]

| | yes | Jess | yesô↓ |
| | yellow | jello | yelô↓ |

yah	jaw	yá↓
yoe	Joe	yó↓
uke	juke	yugó↓
yearn	germ	yérnó↓
yabber	jabber	yabá↓
yea	jay	yé↓

In Spanish these are variants of the same sound. It often puzzles an English speaker to hear both variants because he does not know which one to imitate. Actually both Spanish variants may be used by a single speaker. The significant difference in English is no longer significant, and you must learn to ignore it.

Not all /y/ 's in Spanish can be pronounced both ways: only those which are syllable initial, and especially those which are utterance initial. Another way of saying this is that Spanish [y] will appear at the end of a word or before or after consonants within a word, pretty much like the English y. In other positions the Spanish /y/ varies from a [y], to sounds English speakers would interpret as the z in azure or the j of judge. As you have probably noticed, we have transcribed this latter variant as [y], to distinguish it from the [y] which cannot be pronounced like English j.

2.29   Conclusion

There are, be it admitted, other difficulties in the pronunciation of Spanish than those which have been pointed out here. One is the handling of juncture - that is, the way words run together in a sequence. We call attention to this by the way in which we transcribe utterances in the text (without spaces separating words). Another is the problem of pronouncing various unfamiliar consonant sequences like /bw/, /trw/, /yw/ etc. These we are inclined to leave to the correction of the pronunciation of complete phrases as they happen to turn up - not on the assumption that they are less important, but because there are no drills which will help the student learn them except repetition of the utterances themselves. If the student has learned to make all the contrasts described in the foregoing material, and to avoid the most serious pitfalls that have also been described, he is well on his way toward accurate pronunciation of Spanish and should find that mastery of the utterances comes much easier than it otherwise would.

2.3   DRILLS AND GRAMMAR

2.31   Pattern drills

2.31.1   Some demonstratives

A.   Presentation of pattern [1]

ILLUSTRATIONS

———————	1 keşésò↓	¿Qué es *eso?*
———————	2 estǫ̀|èsůnşènişerò↓	*Esto* es un cenicero. *ashtray*
What's this?	3 keşéstò↓	¿Qué es *esto?*
a, an (f.)	unà↓	una
That's a chair.	4 esǫ̀|èsůnàsi(l)yà↓	*Eso* es una silla.

---

(1) The 'presentation of pattern' is a device that will be used here and in subsequent pattern drills to briefly explain the grammar principles and chart the illustrative forms that make up the pattern. It will usually consist of three parts: illustrations, extrapolation, and notes.

The illustrations are a group of sentences, some of which have previously appeared as basic sentences and some of which have not. New sentences can be identified by the appearance of an English translation in the left hand column. These 'structural filler' sentences contain forms needed to fill out the pattern of the point being drilled and should be memorized just as basic sentences. In these sentences the forms to be drilled are underlined or italicized.

The extrapolation is an arrangement of the forms to be drilled that shows the relationships between these forms. These relationships are analytically 'extrapolated' and shown in a chart for the benefit of those who can grasp the relationships more easily when they are presented visually in a spacial configuration.

The notes, when they occur, are designed to very briefly explain the extrapolation.

A fuller discussion of the pattern is presented after the drills in section B, entitled 'discussion of pattern'. Further explanation and correlation with other grammar points can be found in the appendix.

That's good.	5 ésǫezbwénȯ↓	*Eso* es bueno.
Translate this.	6 tráduşkạéstȯ↓	Traduzca *esto*.
Repeat that.	7 rrépitạésȯ↓	Repita *eso*.

EXTRAPOLATION

ésto	thıs
éso	that

NOTES

a. English 'this' and 'that' can sometimes be translated
/ésto/ and /éso/ in Spanish.

2.31.11 Response drill [1]

(1) This and subsequent response drills are made up of four groups of questions which are designed to elicit answers that require the use of the grammar point previously illustrated, but at the same time to insure answers that are completely natural in their most probable contexts. The four groups are: (1) choice questions, which normally require full sentence replies. (2) Information questions, the answers to which are listed and can be given *sotto voce* just before the questions. These will also normally require full sentence replies. (3) Yes-no questions to be answered 'no'. The correct answer is listed and can be given *sotto voce* just before the questions. These too will normally require full sentence replies. (4) Yes-no questions to be answered 'yes'. These will normally require just /sí↓/ or a partial sentence reply.

The student's cue for the kind of answer he should give is the presence or absence of a *sotto voce* prompting before the question and whether the question has an intonation ending with a /↓/ or /↑/ . The first and second groups end with /↓/ and require answers which are chosen by the student in group one and suggested *sotto voce* by the instructor in group two. The third and fourth groups end with /↑/ and require /nó↓/ with a correction which is given *sotto voce* by the instructor in group three and /sí↓/ with or without additional elaboration, usually in the form of a partial sentence, in group four.

The student should not need to look at the materials to do this drill orally.

Model Problem:

      1 eséstǫespáŋyóltǫiŋglést

[élşéntró↓] 2 keséśó↓

 [ùnsyétè↓] 3 eséstǫunwébet

      4 esésǫuntrést

Model Answer:

      1 esot ésèspàŋyólt

      2 esot ésèlşéntró↓

      3 éstot nó↓ésùnsyétè↓

      4 éstot sí↓ésùntrést↓

———————————————————————————————————

Model Problem:

          1 ¿Es esto español o inglés?
(el centro) 2 ¿Qué es eso?
 (un siete) 3 ¿Es esto un nueve?
          4 ¿Es eso un tres?

Model Answer:

          1 ¿Eso? Es español.
          2 ¿Eso? Es el centro.
          3 ¿Esto? No, es un siete.
          4 ¿Esto? Sí, es un tres.

1 és̞ést̞o̞unlápis̞t̞o̞unaplúma̱↓   éso↑ és̱únᶏplúma̱↓

2 és̞ést̞o̞unasí(l)ɣa↑t̞o̞unamésa̱↓   ésto↑ és̱únᶏmésa̱↓

[únlíbro̱↓] 3 kés̞éstó↓   éso↑ és̱únlíbro↓

[únş̌énis̞ero̱↓] 4 kés̞ésó↓   ésto↑ és̱únş̌énis̞ero↓

[únlápis̞↓] 5 és̞és̞o̞unaplúma↑   ésto↑ nó↓és̱únlápis̞↓

[únᶏplúma̱↓] 6 és̞ést̞o̞unlápis̞↑   éso↑ nó↓és̱únᶏplúma̱↓

7 és̞és̞o̞unóte̱l↑   éso↑ si↓és̱únǒté'l↓

8 és̞ést̞o̞unş̌énis̞ero↑   éso↑ si↓és̱únş̌énis̞ero↓

9 és̞és̞o̞unasí(l)ɣa↑   ésto↑ si↓és̱únásí(l)ɣa̱↓

---

1 ¿Es esto un lápiz o una pluma?   ¿Eso? Es una pluma.
2 ¿Es esto una silla o una mesa?   ¿Esto? Es una mesa.

(un libro) 3 ¿Qué es esto?   ¿Eso? Es un libro.
(un cenicero) 4 ¿Qué es eso?   ¿Esto? Es un cenicero.

(un lápiz) 5 ¿Es eso una pluma?   ¿Esto? No, es un lápiz.
(una pluma) 6 ¿Es esto un lápiz?   ¿Eso? No, es una pluma.

7 ¿Es eso un hotel?   ¿Eso? Sí, es un hotel.
8 ¿Es esto un cenicero?   ¿Eso? Sí, es un cenicero.
9 ¿Es eso una silla?   ¿Esto? Sí, es una silla.

2.31.12   Translation drill (1)

1 That's good.	éso︎ |ezbwénó↓	Eso es bueno.
2 This isn't Spanish.	ésto |no︎es︎español↓	Esto no es español·
3 How's that going?	ketál |baésó↓	¿Qué tal va eso?
4 What's that?	kesésó↓	¿Qué es eso?
5 What's this?	keséstó↓	¿Qué es esto?
6 That's too much.	éso︎ezmúchó↓	Eso es mucho.
7 I don't want that until tomorrow.	nokyero︎eso︎ |ástámáṇyaná↓	No quiero eso hasta mañana.
8 I want that later.	kyero︎eso |lwégó↓	Quiero eso luego.
9 I regret this very much.	syentomucho︎ |éstó↓	Siento mucho esto.
10 This is going very well.	éstoba |muybyén↓	Esto va muy bien.
11 The young lady wants this.	láseṇyórita |kyeréstó↓	La señorita quiere esto.

End of Tape 1B

_____

(1) Translate the English sentences to Spanish. The student should cover the Spanish answers while doing this drill orally.

B. Discussion of pattern [1]

Basically, /éso/ is used to refer to an object which is relatively nearer the person being addressed than it is to the person speaking, whereas /ésto/ refers to an object relatively nearer to the person speaking. Roughly, then, they correspond to the English words *that* and *this*, but in Spanish the ending /—o/ on these two words indicates that the speaker does not know what the Spanish word for the object is (as when asking the question 'What is this?'), or that the speaker is answering a question in which /ésto/ or /éso/ is used, or that the speaker is referring to a situation or set of circumstances instead of to an object (as in /ésǫesbwéno↓/. Otherwise the speaker would choose these forms with other endings, which will be presented in Unit 7.

---

(1) This and subsequent discussions of pattern are not designed for use in the classroom. They are explanations of the structural patterns of the drills for the orientation of students who feel that such explanations are helpful to their efforts to master the language. Classroom time should be reserved for drilling the language itself, leaving grammar explanations largely for home study or special grammar sessions of the class.

Tape 2A

3.1   BASIC SENTENCES.   White's arrival in Surlandia.

John White, an American arriving for the first time in Surlandia, a country south of the United States, has been met at the airport and seen through customs to his hotel by American friends. They leave him at the hotel, were he checks in at the desk and then is accompanied to his room by the porter carrying his bags. He arrives in the room.

ENGLISH SPELLING	AID TO LISTENING	SPANISH SPELLING
to you	lé↓	le
(it) pleases, is pleasing (to please)	gustá↓ gústar↓	gusta (gustar)
to you is pleasing	lè͟gustá↓	le gusta
the room	èl‑kwartó↓	el cuarto
Porter Do you like the room? (1)	lègustaelkwartó↑	*Mozo* ¿Le gusta el cuarto?
to me is pleasing	mè͟gustá↓	me gusta
White Yes, I do.	sí·|mègustá↓	*White* Sí, me gusta.
(you) want (to want)	kyérè↓ kérér↓	quiere (querer)
the water	èl‑agwá↓	el agua (f.)
mineral	minèrál↓	mineral
soda water	agwa‑minerál↓	agua mineral

Porter
Do you want soda water? [2]

kyéręustéđ|agwaminéral↑

Mozo
¿Quiere usted agua mineral?

rise, bring up (to go up)

subá↓ subír↓

suba (subir)

it

lá↓

la (f.)

bring it up to me [3]

subámēlá↓

súbamela

later

dēspwé·s↓

después

White
Yes. Bring it up to me later.

si↓ subámēlá|dēspwés↓

White
Sí. Súbamela después.

(you) need (to need)

nęśęsitá↓ nęśęsitár↓

necesita (necesitar)

anything, something

algó↓

algo

else

ma·s↓

más

anything else

algo—más↓

algo más

Porter
Do you need anything else?

nęśęsitalcomas↑

Mozo
¿Necesita algo más?

near [4]

şerká↓

cerca

near to

şerká—đé↓

cerca de

here

àki↓

aquí

White
Yes, Is the American Embassy

near here?

    far

    the avenue

    Columbus

Porter
No. It's quite a distance.

On Columbus avenue.

    that

    there is that, it's necessary [5]

    to take

    the taxi

It's necessary to take a taxi.

White
Thanks. Here you are.

Porter
Thank you very much, sir.

    the elevator

---

sí↓ éstalaẹmbahaḍamerikana|

ṣerkaḍẹakí↑

léhòs↓

lạ—ábénìḍà↓

kòlòn↓

nó↓ éstalehòs↓

énlàbénìḍa|ḍekolón↓

ké↓

ay—kè↓

tòmár↓

èl—taksi↓

ayketomaruntáksi↓

graṣyàs↓ àkityénè↓

muchazgráṣyàs |sènyór↓

èl—às(ṣ)ènsór↓

White
Sí. ¿Está la Embajada Ameri-

cana cerca de aquí?

    lejos

    la avenida

    Colón

Mozo
No. Está lejos.

En la avenida de Colón.

    que

    hay que

    tomar

    el taxi

Hay que tomar un taxi.

White
Gracias. Aquí tiene.

Mozo
Muchas gracias, señor.

    el ascensor

Are you going down in the elevator?	báha̦en̦elas(ş)ensór↑	¿Baja en el ascensor?
now	áorá↓	ahora
same	mízmó↓	mismo
right now	áora‒mízmó↓	ahora mismo

White
Yes. Right now.　　　　　　　sí↓ áoramízmó↓　　　　　　　**White**
Sí, ahora mismo.

the box, the cashier's desk	lá‒kahá↓	la caja
Where's the cashier's desk?	dóndestalakáhá↓	¿Dónde está la caja?
first	primér↓ primeró↓	primer (primero)
the floor	él‒pisó↓	el piso
the entrance	la̦‒éntraḋá↓	la entrada

Porter
On the first floor to the right
of the entrance.　　　　　énélprimérpísǫ|álaḋérecha|deląentráḋá↓　　　**Mozo**
En el primer piso, a la derecha
de la entrada.

(Mr. White goes down on the elevator and up to the cashier's window.)

(you) can (to be able)	pweḋé↓ póḋér↓	puede (poder)
to change, exchange	kámbyár↓	cambiar
to change for me	kámbyarmé↓	cambiarme

some, a few	únòs↓	unos
the dollar	èl—dólár↓	el dólar
some dollars	únòz—dólárès↓	unos dólares

White
Can you change a few dollars for me?

pwéḍe |kàmbyármẹ |ùnòzḍólarest

White
¿Puede cambiarme unos dólares?

Cashier
Yes. How many?

si↓ kwántòs↓

Cajero
Sí. ¿Cuántos?

how, at what	à—kómò↓	a cómo
the change, exchange	èl—kámbyò↓	el cambio

White
Ten. What's the rate of exchange?

dyé̦ş↓ àkómoẹsta |ẹlkámbyò↓

White
Diez. ¿A cómo está el cambio?

the bill	èl—biꞥyétè↓	el billete
the bills	lòz—biꞥyétès↓	los billetes
the check	èl—chékè↓	el cheque

Cashier
In bills or in a check?

èmbiꞥyétes |ọenchékè↓

Cajero
¿En billetes o en cheque?

this	éstè↓	este
traveler	byàhérò↓	viajero

White
This traveler's check.

éstechékè |byàhérò↓

White
Este cheque viajero.

70

then	èntónşès↓	entonces
Cashier Five to one, then.	àşiŋkoporúnǫ‖èntónşès↓	**Cajero** A cinco por uno, entonces.
it	ló↓	lo (m.)
How do you want it?	kómolokyérè↓	¿Cómo lo quiere?
the coin, the change	là—mónedà↓	la moneda
White Eight in bills and two in change.	ochǫembillyétes↑idósęnmonédà↓	**White** Ocho en billetes y dos en moneda.
(it) costs (to cost)	kwestà↓ kòstár↓	cuesta (costar)
How much does a taxi to the American Embassy cost?	kwantokwestǫuntaksı‖àlǫèmbàhadamerikánà↓	¿Cuánto cuesta un taxi a la Embajada Americana?
the peso	èl—pésò↓	el peso
the pesos	lòs—pésòs↓	los pesos
less	menòs↓	menos

Cashier
Two pesos more or less.

dóspésŏz |mäsŏménŏs↓

Cajero
Dos pesos más o menos.

    for, in exchange for

    pór↓

    por

    the information

    lä—imfórmäşyón↓

    la información

White
Thanks for the information.

gräşyas |pórlaimfórmäşyón↓

White
Gracias por la información.

3.10   Notes on the basic sentences

(1) As can be seen by comparing the literal translation in the build-up with the free translation given in this sentence, there is simply not any literal way to equate the English idea of 'liking' something with a word in Spanish which takes an object as the English word *like* does. Rather, one has to say that the object which he likes is 'pleasing' to him. Thus 'I like it' becomes 'It's pleasing to me'.

(2) *Agua mineral*, which literally means 'mineral water', may be carbonated 'soda water' or it may simply be purified drinking water. The terms used for purified drinking water differ from one area to another. Sometimes such water is called by the trade name of the company that distributes it, such as 'Agua Güitig' in Ecuador, or 'Agua Chuqüitanta' in Peru. At other times it is called *agua cristal*. At any rate, one should be certain that he finds out *what* to ask for, since the public water supply is safe in only a very few places in the Spanish-speaking world.

(3) The forms /me/ and /la/ in the utterance /súbamela/ are called *clitic pronouns*, or, for short, just *clitics*. They will be discussed in detail beginning with Unit 10.

(4) Note that the word /şérka/ 'near' modifies a verb, but does not function as a phrase relator. The *English* word *near*, however, functions in both capacities. That is, in English we can say 'He didn't even get *near*' or 'He didn't even get near the house.' The Spanish equivalent of *near* is /şérka/, in the first example, but /şérka/ *plus* /de/ , 'near of, near to', in the second.

(5) This idiom is especially useful to bear in mind. It is the equivalent of several English expressions. The closest is 'It is necessary to...', but the most frequent is 'You've got to...' or 'You have to...' or 'Ya gotta...', in all three of which the *you* does not refer to you personally, but really means something like 'One should...' or 'One ought to...'.

3.2   DRILLS AND GRAMMAR

3.21   Pattern drills

3.21.1   Gender of singular nouns and adjectives

Presentation of pattern

ILLUSTRATIONS

_____	1.	pásemęęⓁlíbrȯ↓	Páseme *el libro.*
_____	2.	deme laplúmȧ↓	Déme *la pluma.*
_____	3.	tyenęunlapiṣ↑	¿Tiene *un lápiz?*
Do you have a pen?	4.	tyenęunaplumá↑	¿Tiene *una pluma?*
_____	5.	muchoǫústȯ↓	*Mucho gusto.*
(it) has (to have)		tyénȩ↓ ténȩr↓	tiene (tener)
_____	6.	tyenemuchaǥwá↑	¿Tiene *mucha agua?*
_____	7.	estechekebyahérȯ↓	Este *cheque viajero.*
_____	8.	dondesta│lȧȩmbȧhadamerikánȧ↓	¿Dónde está *la Embajada Americana?*

EXTRAPOLATION

	Masculine		Feminine		
	article	noun	article	noun	
Definite	el	líbro	la	mésa	'the'
Indefinite	un	líbro	una	mésa	'a(n)'

Gender forms of adjectives

Masculine	Feminine
········ o	········ a

········ e
········ C

NOTES

a. All Spanish nouns can be divided into two groups, or subclasses, called 'masculine' and 'feminine'.

b. Spanish articles, like many other Spanish adjectives, have distinct masculine and feminine forms.

c. The masculine form of adjectives appears only with masculine nouns, the feminine form with feminine nouns.

d. Many Spanish adjectives have gender marking endings (distinct masculine and feminine forms /múcho — múcha/); others, primarily those ending in /—e/ or in a consonant /minerál, trés, syéte/, etc.), do not have different endings when used with masculine or feminine nouns.

3.21.11 Substitution drill [1] — item substitution

Model Problem:

AID TO LISTENING   SPANISH SPELLING

éstọeṣ̣unlápiṣ̣↓   Esto es un lápiz.

_____ṣeniṣérȯ↓   _____ cenicero.

Model Answer:

éstọeṣ̣unṣeniṣérȯ↓   Esto es un cenicero.

(1)   This and subsequent substitution drills are designed to elicit from the student slight variations on given sentences. These variations concern the structural relationships within the grammar point being drilled, such as the agreement between articles and nouns in the present drill. The model problem and answer are given only this once. All subsequent substitution drills are to be carried out in the same way.

The student should not need to look at the materials to do this drill orally. Both the *Aids to Listening* and the *Spanish Spelling* are given for all drills (on top half and bottom half of page, respectively); they are for the instructor to use in class and for the student to use in home study: not in class.

1   ésǫesụnaplúmȧ↓   ésǫesụnotél↓
    _____otél↓   ésǫesụmbįǫyétė↓
    _____bįǫyétė↓   ésǫesụnamésȧ↓
    _____mésȧ↓   ésǫesụnlíbrȯ↓
    _____líbrȯ↓

2   ésˏestǫunabenįɖa↑   ésˏestǫunamonéɖa↑
    _____monéɖa↑   ésˏestǫuŋkwarto↑
    _____kwarto↑   ésˏestǫunasįǫya↑
    _____sįǫya↑   ésˏestǫumpeso↑
    _____peso↑

---

1 Eso es una pluma.   Eso es un hotel.
  _____hotel.   Eso es un billete.
  _____billete.   Eso es una mesa.
  _____mesa.   Eso es un libro.
  _____libro.

2 ¿Es esto una avenida?   ¿Es esto una moneda?
  ¿_____moneda?   ¿Es esto un cuarto?
  ¿_____cuarto?   ¿Es esto una silla?
  ¿_____silla?   ¿Es esto un peso?
  ¿_____peso?

75

3 dóndestá|lakáhà↓

_____sęñyór↓   dóndestá|ęlsęñyór↓

_____sęñyorítà↓   dóndestá|lasęñyorítà↓

_____embaháđà↓   dóndestá|lạembaháđà↓

_____as(ş)ensór↓   dóndestá|ęlas(ş)ensór↓

4 gráşyas|porlaplúmà↓

_____şenişérò↓   gráşyas|porelşenişérò↓

_____ımformaşyón↓   gráşyas|porlạımformaşyón↓

_____lápiş↓   gráşyas|porel()lápiş↓

_____chékè↓   gráşyas|porelchékè↓

---

3 ¿Dónde está la caja?
   ¿ _____ señor?   ¿Dónde está el señor?
   ¿ _____ señorita?   ¿Dónde está la señorita?
   ¿ _____ Embajada?   ¿Dónde está la Embajada?
   ¿ _____ ascensor?   ¿Dónde está el ascensor?

4 Gracias por la pluma.
   _____ cenicero.   Gracias por el cenicero.
   _____ información.   Gracias por la información.
   _____ lápiz.   Gracias por el lápiz.
   _____ cheque   Gracias por el cheque.

5 àiestaelágwà↓
        _____señórà↓   àiestalaseñórà↓
        _____mésà↓   àiestalamésà↓
        _____entrádà↓   àiestalaentrádà↓
        _____táksi↓   àiestaeltáksi↓

6 dondesta|làséñyoramerikánà↓
        _____señor_____↓   dondesta|elseñyoramerikáno↓
        _____señórita_____↓   dondesta|làseñyóritamerikánà↓
        _____ótel_____↓   dondesta|elótelamerikáno↓
        _____moneda_____↓   dondesta|làmónedamerikánà↓

---

5 Ahí está el agua.
    _____ señora.   Ahí está la señora.
    _____ mesa.   Ahí está la mesa.
    _____ entrada.   Ahí está la entrada.
    _____ taxi.   Ahí está el taxi.

6 Dónde está la señora americana?
    ¿_____ señor _____?   ¿Dónde está el señor americano?
    ¿_____ señorita _____? ¿Dónde está la señorita americana?
    ¿_____ hotel _____?   ¿Dónde está el hotel americano?
    ¿_____ moneda _____? ¿Dónde está la moneda americana?

77

7 ái̯ęsta|lȧmízmasíǫ̀ya᷄ḷ

_____ șenișérȯ̀ḷ   ái̯ęsta|ęlmízmoșenișérȯ̀ḷ

_____plúma᷄ḷ   ái̯ęsta|lȧmízmaplúma᷄ḷ

_____seņyór̀ḷ   ái̯ęsta|ęlmízmoseņyór̀ḷ

_____seņyóra᷄ḷ   ái̯ęsta|lȧmízmaseņyóra᷄ḷ

8 ái̯ęsta|ęló̀trochékè̀ḷ

_____ entrádȧḷ   ái̯ęsta|la̤otra̤entrádȧḷ

_____táksi᷄ḷ   ái̯ęsta|ęló̀trotáksi᷄ḷ

_____mésȧḷ   ái̯ęsta|la̤otramésȧḷ

_____líbrȯ̀ḷ   ái̯ęsta|ęló̀trolíbrȯ̀ḷ

---

7 Ahí está la misma silla.

_____ cenicero.   Ahí está el mismo cenicero.

_____pluma.   Ahí está la misma pluma.

_____ señor.   Ahí está el mismo señor.

_____ señora.   Ahí está la misma señora.

8 Ahí está el otro cheque.

_____ entrada.   Ahí está la otra entrada.

_____ taxi.   Ahí está el otro taxi.

_____ mesa.   Ahí está la otra mesa.

_____ libro.   Ahí está el otro libro.

9   tyéne̦ |únáplumabwéná↓

_____ lápis _____↓   tyéne̦ |únlápiȥbwéno↓

_____ síꞖya _____↓   tyéne̦ |únásiꞖya̱bwéná↓

_____ líbro _____↓   tyéne̦ |únlíbrobwéno↓

_____ mésa _____↓   tyéne̦ |únámesabwéná↓

10   téŋgo |trézdíazmás↓

_____ tárdez ↓   téŋgo |tréstárdezmás↓

_____ biꞖyetez ↓   téŋgo |trézbiꞖyetezmás↓

_____ nóchez ___↓   téŋgo |tréznochezmás↓

_____ dólarez __↓   téŋgo |trézdólarezmás↓

---

9 Tiene una pluma buena.

_____ lápiz _____.   Tiene un lápiz bueno.

_____ silla _____.   Tiene un libro bueno.

_____ mesa _____.   Tiene una mesa buena.

10 Tengo tres días más.

_____ tardes __.   Tengo tres tardes más.

_____ billetes_.   Tengo tres billetes más.

_____ noches __.   Tengo tres noches más.

_____ dólares __.   Tengo tres dólares más.

11   tyéne |ṣiŋkonóchezmás↓

_____díaz_____↓   tyéne |ṣiŋkodíazmás↓

_____tardez_____↓   tyéne |ṣiŋkotardezmás↓

_____biḷḷyetez___↓   tyéne |ṣiŋkobiḷḷyetezmás↓

_____dólarez_____↓   tyéne |ṣiŋkodólarezmás↓

3.21.12 Response drill

1   estáláentrada | aláderecha↑oalaiṣkyérda↓   estáláderechá↓

2   kyérounlápiṣ↑ounaplúmà↓   kyérounáplúmà↓

3   kyérounlíbro↑ounchéké↓   kyérounchéké↓

---

11 Tiene cinco noches más.

_____días_____.   Tiene cinco días más.

_____tardes_____.   Tiene cinco tardes más.

_____billetes___.   Tiene cinco billetes más.

_____dólares___.   Tiene cinco dólares más.

1 ¿Está la entrada a la derecha o a la izquierda?   Está a la derecha.

2 ¿Quiere un lápiz o una pluma?   Quiero una pluma.

3 ¿Quiere un libro o un cheque?   Quiero un cheque.

```
                 4   tyeneumbi()yetet ǫunamonéďá↓              téŋgǫúnámǒneďá↓

                 5   áiayunseŋyort ǫunaseŋyórá↓               áyúnásèŋyorá↓

[ènélkwártǒ]     6   dóndestalasí()yá↓                        èstaęnęlkwártǒ↓

[ènélsentrǒ]     7   dóndęayunǫtél↓                           ayunǫtél|ènélsèntrǒ↓

[láplumà]        8   lègustaę()lápiṣt                         nǒ↓ mègústálàplúmà↓

[ènęlsęntrǒ]     9   èstalaseŋyorà|ďèmòlínakít               nǒ↓ èsta|ęnélsèntrǒ↓

[únlapiṣ]       10   tyenęunaplúmat                          nǒ↓ téŋgǫúnlapiṣ↓

                11   lègustaęlsęntrot                        sí↓ mègústàmuchǒ↓

                12   èstalaseŋyorakít                        sí↓ sięstákí↓

                13   áyunamésaít                             sí↓ sìáy↓
```

---

	4 ¿Tiene un billete o una moneda?	Tengo una moneda.
	5 ¿Ahí hay un señor o una señora?	Hay una señora.
(en el cuarto)	6 ¿Dónde está la silla?	Está en el cuarto.
(en el centro)	7 ¿Dónde hay un hotel?	Hay un hotel en el centro.
(la pluma)	8 ¿Le gusta el lápiz?	No, me gusta la pluma.
(en el centro)	9 ¿Está la señora de Molina aquí?	No, está en el centro.
(un lápiz)	10 ¿Tiene una pluma?	No, tengo un lápiz.
	11 ¿Le gusta el centro?	Sí, me gusta mucho.
	12 ¿Está la señora aquí?	Sí, sí está aquí.
	13 ¿Hay una mesa ahí?	Sí, sí hay.

3.21.13   Translation drill

1. That's a coin.	esǫesunamonédà↓	Eso es una moneda.
2. No, this is not a bill.	no↓ éstònǫes ǀùmbiꞔyéte↓	No, esto no es un billete.
3. The young lady is at the Embassy.	làsènyòritą ǀèstąęnląembahádà↓	La señorita está en la embajada.
4. Do you want a chair?	kyeręunasiꞔyá↑	¿Quiere una silla?
5. Do you have the check or not?	tyenelchekętonó↓	¿Tiene el cheque o no?
6. The teller's window is to the left.	làkahą ǀestaląįşkyérdà↓	La caja está a la izquierda.
7. The Embassy is not far from here.	ląėmbàhadą ǀnoęstálehòz ǀdęąkí↓	La embajada no está lejos de aquí.
8. I want you to meet a young lady.	kyeropresentarlę ǀąunàsènyòritá↓	Quiero presentarle a una señorita.
9. Do you like Columbus Avenue?	lęꞔusta ǀlàbénidakolon↑	¿Le gusta la Avenida Colón?
10. The bathroom is to the right.	èlbaŋyǫ ǀèstaladęréchà↓	El baño está a la derecha.
11. I have a room in the hotel.	tengǫuŋkwartǫ ǀenelotél↓	Tengo un cuarto en el hotel.
12. Do you want a pencil?	kyeręunlápiş↑	¿Quiere un lápiz?
13. Do you need a pen?	nęşėsitąunapluma↑	¿Necesita una pluma?
14. Where's there a chair?	dondęay ǀunasiꞔyà↓	¿Dónde hay una silla?
15. Is the hotel downtown?	èstaęlotel ǀenelşentro↑	¿Está el hotel en el centro?

B   Discussion of pattern

In Spanish there is a large class of words to which the label *noun* can be applied. A noun can be identified by the fact that it can have endings added to it to change its reference from one to more than one (as explained in Unit 4) and by the fact that it belongs to one of two subclasses, called *masculine* and *feminine*. While a noun can change for number, it has only one gender or the other, which is inherent and does not change. The terms masculine and feminine are convenient but more or less arbitrary tags to represent grammatical categories and have nothing to do with gender or sex in the real world. Nouns that have appeared so far include /el—gústo, el—lápıṣ, la—béṣ, el—líbro, el—ṣenıṣéro, el—espaɲyól, la—síⱱya, la—embaháda, el—báɲyo, el—ṣéntro, el—otél, el—kwárto, el—ágwa, la—abenída, el—táksı, el—as(ṣ)ensór, la—káha, el—píso, la—entráda, el—chéke, el—dólar, el—kámbyo, el—bıⱱyéte, la—monéda, la—ımformaṣyón/.

You will notice that the word /el/ or the word /la/ precedes each noun. These are the singular forms of the definite article: /el/ is masculine, and /la/ is feminine. When memorizing each noun it is well to memorize its gender at the same time. Usually this can be done by memorizing the appropriate form of the definite article with the noun. (/el—ágwa/ is an exception, since it is actually feminine.) The words /el/ and /la/, called *definite articles*, are usually the equivalent of English 'the'. The words /un/ and /una/, called *indefinite articles*, are usually the equivalent of English 'a' or 'an'.

The articles, and other adjectives which change for gender, *must appear in the same gender category as the noun* with which they are associated. This is called *gender agreement*, and the associated adjective is said to *agree with* the noun. Thus adjectives differ from nouns in having two gender forms in order to agree with nouns from either subclass.

There are two subclasses of adjectives - those which show a gender change, and those for which distinct gender forms are only potential. In certain circumstances the latter subclass *can* show a change (see Unit 39 for a discussion of diminutives) but usually they have the same endings for masculine or feminine agreement. Usually the forms which change have a final /—o/ for masculine and /—a/ for feminine forms, though sometimes the masculine form may end in a consonant, as /espaɲyól — espaɲyóla, ınglés — ınglésa/ when these are used as adjectives.

Other adjectives, like /minerál, séys, syéte/, which end in /—e/ or in a consonant do not change. Thus:

múch**o**—gústo	múch**a**—ımformaṣyón
mén**os**—gústo	mén**os**—ımformaṣyón

Note that in Spanish adjectives usually *follow* the noun modified: /embaháda—amerikána, chéke—byahéro/ etc. Some adjectives, like the articles /el, la/, etc. always precede : /la—abenída, dós—pésos/, etc. These are usually 'number' or 'limiting' adjectives. Some adjectives, however, may follow or precede the noun: /plúma—bwéna, bwéna—plúma/.

3.22   Replacement drills [1]

        Model Problem:

tyéne̯únlápiş↑

_____plúma↑

kyére̯_____↑

    Model Answer:

tyéne̯únáplúma↑

kyére̯únáplúma↑

        Model Problem:

¿Tiene un lápiz?
¿ _____ pluma?
¿Quiere _____ ?

        Model Answer:

¿Tiene una pluma?
¿Quiere una pluma?

---

    (1) This and subsequent replacement drills are designed as a fast moving substitution-type drill on selected basic sentences, with the substitutions occurring in different parts of the sentence, each being a single change -plus any obligatory associated change(s)- of the sentence immediately preceding.

    The student should not need to look at the materials to do this drill orally.

A   kómo̧e̦stau̦stéd↓

1 _____laseɲórà↓   kómoe̦stá|laseɲóra↓

2 _____ seɲór↓   kómoe̦stá|e̦lseɲór↓

3 dónde_____ ↓   dóndestá|e̦lseɲór↓

4 _____seɲorítà↓   dóndestá|laseɲorítà↓

5 kómo_____ ↓   kómoe̦stá|laseɲorítà↓

6 _____e̦lse̦ɲyorhwáyt↓   kómoe̦stá|e̦lse̦ɲyorhwáyt↓

7 dónde _____ ↓   dóndestá|e̦lse̦ɲyorhwáyt↓

A   ¿Cómo está usted?

1 ¿ _____ la señora?   ¿Cómo está la señora?

2 ¿ _____ señor?   ¿Cómo está el señor?

3 ¿Dónde _____ ?   ¿Dónde está el señor?

4 ¿ _____ señorita?   ¿Dónde está la señorita?

5 ¿Cómo _____ ?   ¿Cómo está la señorita?

6 ¿ _____ el Sr. White?   ¿Cómo está el Sr. White?

7 ¿Dónde _____ ?   ¿Dónde está el Sr. White?

B   kyérẹustéd|ágwaminerál↑

1 _____álgomás↑   kyérẹustéd|álgomás↑

2 ____elsenyorhwáyt|____↑   kyérelsenyorhwáyt|álgomás↑

3 nẹ̀sẹ́sitạ_____↑   nẹ̀sẹ́sitạelsenyorhwáyt|álgomás↑

4 ____ustéd_____↑   nẹ̀sẹ́sitạustéd|álgomás↑

5 _____álgo↑   nẹ̀sẹ́sitạustéd|álgo↑

6 dísẹ_____↑   dísẹustéd|álgo↑

7 _____bwénòzdías↑   dísẹustéd|bwénòzdías↑

B   ¿Quiere usted agua mineral?

1 ¿ _____ algo más?   ¿Quiere usted algo más?

2 ¿ ____ el Sr. White ____?   ¿Quiere el Sr. White algo más?

3 ¿Necesita _____?   ¿Necesita el Sr. White algo más?

4 ¿ ____ usted _____?   ¿Necesita usted algo más?

5 ¿ _____ algo?   ¿Necesita usted algo?

6 ¿Dice _____?   ¿Dice usted algo?

7 ¿ _____ 'buenos días'?   ¿Dice usted 'buenos días'?

C   néşésıta̧ |algomás↑

1 _____uno____↑   néşésıta̧ |unomás↑

2 tyeņe_____↑   tyeņe |unomás↑

3 _____ɗoz____↑   tyene |ɗozmás↑

4 kyere_____↑   kyere |ɗozmás↑

5 _____menos↑   kyere |ɗozmenos↑

6 ay_____↑   ayɗozmenos↑

7 _____trez___↑   ay |trezmenos↑

C   ¿Necesita algo más?

1 ¿_____uno ____?   ¿Necesita uno más?

2 ¿Tiene _____?   ¿Tiene uno más?

3 ¿ _____dos ____?   ¿Tiene dos más?

4 ¿Quiere_____?   ¿Quiere dos más?

5 ¿_____ menos?   ¿Quiere dos menos?

6 ¿Hay_____?   ¿Hay dos menos?

7 ¿_____ tres_____?   ¿Hay tres menos?

D   èstá|la̯embahaḋamerikána|s̟ěrkáḋe̯ákí↑

1 _____e̯lotél_____↑   èstá|e̯lotelamerikáno|s̟ěrkáḋe̯ákí↑

2 _____iŋglés_____↑   èstá|e̯loteliŋglés|s̟ěrkáḋe̯ákí↑

3 _____léhôz_____↑   èstá|e̯loteliŋglés|léhôzḋe̯ákí↑

4 _____ḋe̯áí↑   èstá|e̯loteliŋglés|léhôzḋe̯áí↑

5 ____la̯embaháḋa_____↑   èstá|la̯embaháḋa̯iŋglésa|léhôzḋe̯áí↑

6 _____espaɲyóla_____↑   èstá|la̯embaháḋe̯espaɲyóla|léhôzḋe̯áí↑

7 ____ otél_____↑   èstá|e̯lotelespaɲyól|léhôzḋe̯áí↑

D   ¿Está la Embajada Americana cerca de aquí?

1 ¿____el Hotel_____?   ¿Está el Hotel Americano cerca de aquí?

2 ¿_____ inglés _____?   ¿Está el Hotel Inglés cerca de aquí?

3 ¿_____ lejos_____?   ¿Está el Hotel Inglés lejos de aquí?

4 ¿_____ de ahí?   ¿Está el Hotel Inglés lejos de ahí?

5 ¿____la Embajada _____?   ¿Está la Embajada Inglesa lejos de ahí?

6 ¿_____ Española _____?   ¿Está la Embajada Española lejos de ahí?

7 ¿____el Hotel_____?   ¿Está el Hotel Español lejos de ahí?

E dóndestálakáhà↓

1 _____ otél↓   dóndestaęlotél↓

2 _____ seŋyórà↓   dóndestalaseŋyórà↓

3 kómo _____ ↓   kómoęstalaseŋyórà↓

4 _____ ustéđ↓   kómoęstaųstéđ↓

5 _____ hwán↓   kómoęstahwán↓

6 dónde _____ ↓   dóndestahwán↓

7 _____ lęentráđà↓   dóndestalęentráđà↓

E ¿Dónde está la caja?

1 ¿_____ hotel?   ¿Dónde está el hotel?

2 ¿_____ señora?   ¿Dónde está la señora?

3 ¿Cómo _____ ?   ¿Cómo está la señora?

4 ¿_____ usted?   ¿Cómo está usted?

5 ¿_____ Juan?   ¿Cómo está Juan?

6 ¿Dónde _____ ?   ¿Dónde está Juan?

7 ¿_____ la entrada?   ¿Dónde está la entrada?

F   kómolokyérè↓

1 _____dísè↓   kómolodísè↓

2 _____nesesítà↓   kómolonesesítà↓

3 dónde_____↓   dóndelonesesítà↓

4 kóŋke_____↓   kóŋkelonesesítà↓

5 _____kyérè↓   kóŋkelokyérè↓

6 dónde_____↓   dóndelokyérè↓

7 _____tyénè↓   dóndelotyénè↓

F   ¿Cómo lo quiere?

1 ¿-_____dice?   ¿Cómo lo dice?

2 ¿_____necesita?   ¿Cómo lo necesita?

3 ¿Dónde_____?   ¿Dónde lo necesita?

4 ¿Con qué_____?   ¿Con qué lo necesita?

5 ¿_____quiere?   ¿Con qué lo quiere?

6 ¿Dónde_____?   ¿Dónde lo quiere?

7 ¿_____tiene?   ¿Dónde lo tiene?

3.23   Variation drills [1]

A   démelaplúmá↓   Déme la pluma.

   1   Give me the book.   deme(l)líbró↓   Déme el libro.

   2   Pass me the pen.   pasemelaplúmá↓   Páseme la pluma.

   3   Give us the book.   denos.e(l)líbró↓   Dénos el libro.

   4   Give us that.   denos.ésó↓   Dénos eso.

   5   Take us downtown.   (l)yebenos.alşéntró↓   Llévenos al centro.

   6   Take me downtown.   (l)yebemẹalşéntró↓   Lléveme al centro.

   7   Take me to the hotel.   (l)yebemẹalotél↓   Lléveme al hotel.

(1) This and subsequent variation drills consist of translations of sentences similar to and within the basic structural frame of selected basic sentences.

The student should cover the Spanish answers while doing this drill orally.

B lègustaͅelkwártot   ¿Le gusta el cuarto?

1 Do you like the book?   lègustaͅeͅḽḽibrot   ¿Le gusta el libro?

2 Do you like the hotel?   lègustaͅelotélt   ¿Le gusta el hotel?

3 Do you like the Embassy?   lègustalaͅembahaḏat   ¿Le gusta la embajada?

4 Do you like the avenue?   lègustalabeniḏat   ¿Le gusta la avenida?

5 Do you like (the) Spanish?   lègustaͅelespaɲólt   ¿Le gusta el español?

6 Do you like (the) English?   lègustaͅeliŋglést   ¿Le gusta el inglés?

7 Do you like (the) Miss Molina? lègustalaseɲyoritamolínat   ¿Le gusta la señorita Molina?

C nót èstaléhòs↓   No, está lejos.

1 No, it's near.   nót èstaͅśérkà↓   No, está cerca.

2 No, it's to the right.   nót èstalaḏeréchà↓   No, está a la derecha.

3 No, it's to the left.   nót èstalaͅiͅskyérḏà↓   No, está a la izquierda.

4 No, it's up ahead.   nót èstaḏelánté↓   No, está adelante.

5 Yes, it's at the entrance.   sí↓ èstálǎentrádà↓   Sí, está a la entrada.

6 Yes, it's here.   sí↓ éstàkí↓   Sí, está aquí.

7 Yes, it's there.   sí↓ éstàí↓   Sí, está ahí.

D   áyketomár|untáksi↑   ¿Hay que tomar un taxi?

1 Is it necessary to take a room?   áyketomár|uŋkwárto↑   ¿Hay que tomar un cuarto?

2 Is it necessary to take the   áyketomár|elas(ṣ)ensór↑   ¿Hay que tomar el ascensor?
  elevator?

3 Is it necessary to take anything   áyketomár|algomás↑   ¿Hay que tomar algo más?
  else?

4 Is it necessary to say that?   áykedeṣír|eso↑   ¿Hay que decir eso?

5 Is it necessary to translate that?   áyketraduṣír|eso↑   ¿Hay que traducir eso?

6 Is it necessary to cash a check?   áykekambyár|unchéke↑   ¿Hay que cambiar un cheque?

7 Is it necessary to have   áyketenér|chékezbyahéros↑   ¿Hay que tener cheques viajeros?
  traveler's checks?

E   pwéde |kambyárme |estechéket   ¿Puede cambiarme este cheque?

1 Can you break this bill for me?   pwéde |kambyárme |estebilyétet   ¿Puede cambiarme este billete?

2 Can you change one dollar for me?   pwéde |kambyárme |undólart   ¿Puede cambiarme un dólar?

3 Can you change the pen for me?   pwéde |kambyárme |laplúmat   ¿Puede cambiarme la pluma?

4 Can you take me to the hotel?   pwéde |λyebárme |alotélt   ¿Puede llevarme al hotel?

5 Can you introduce Mr. Molina to me?   pwéde |presentárme |alsenyormolinat   ¿Puede presentarme al señor Molina?

6 Can you tell me that?   pwéde |deşírme |esot   ¿Puede decirme eso?

7 Can you repeat that for me?   pwéde |rrepetírme |esot   ¿Puede repetirme eso?

F   kwantokwéstauntaksị |alaémbàhadamerikáná↓   ¿Cuánto cuesta un taxi a la Embajada Americana?

1 How much does a taxi to the Embassy cost?   kwantokwéstauntaksị |alaémbàhadà↓   ¿Cuánto cuesta un taxi a la Embajada?

2 How much does a taxi to the hotel cost?   kwantokwéstauntaksị |alótél↓   ¿Cuánto cuesta un taxi al hotel?

3 How much does a taxi to
   Columbus Avenue cost?

kwantokwestaṷuntaksɨ|àlàbénidakolón↓

¿Cuánto cuesta un taxi a la
   Avenida Colón?

4 How much does a taxi
   downtown cost?

kwantokwestaṷuntaksɨ|àlşentró↓

¿Cuánto cuesta un taxi al centro?

5 How much does the book
   cost?

kwantokwestaⓔllíbrò↓

¿Cuánto cuesta el libro?

6 How much does the room cost?

kwantokwestaelkwártò↓

¿Cuánto cuesta el cuarto?

7 How much does it cost?

kwantokwestà↓

¿Cuánto cuesta?

3.3   CONVERSATION STIMULUS (1)

NARRATIVE I

1 Mr. White is at the Columbus Hotel.	élséṇyorhwáyt |éstá |ẹṇélótélkolónↆ	El Sr. White está en el Hotel Colón.
2 He has a room there.	tyenẹuŋkwárto |áíↆ	Tiene un cuarto ahí.
3 He likes his room.	légustạ |elkwártóↆ	Le gusta el cuarto.

---

(1) This and subsequent conversation stimuli are designed to help bridge the gap between pattern-drill sentence practice and actual conversation. They are divided into one, two, or more combinations of narratives and dialogs. The narrative part is a translation drill of sentences in a sequence context, which sets the stage for the dialog following. The dialog is elicited from the participants by the teacher, acting as a prompter for players who have not learned their lines very well. He tells each what he should say (until such time as the lines are memorized), making sure that the participants address each other, talk naturally and meaningfully, and fully understand what they are saying.

The student should cover the Spanish answers while doing the narratives orally. He should not need to look at the materials to do the dialogs orally.

The following expressions are necessary for the prompting or direction of the dialogs.

Tell him (that)...	dígale |kẻ...	Dígale que...
Answer him (that)...	kǒntéstele |kẻ...	Contéstele que...
Ask him if...	préguntele |si...	Pregúntele si....
Tell him again (that)...	rrẻpítale |kẻ...	Repítale que...

4 He needs something.	nèṣèsítálgò↓	Necesita algo.
5 He needs to change a twenty dollar bill.	nèṣèsitakambyár | ùmbi(l)yete | dèbeyntedólàrès↓	Necesita cambiar un billete de veinte dólares.
6 The cashier's desk is to the right.	làkáhạestáladerécha↓	La caja está a la derecha.

DIALOG 1

Juan, dígale 'buenos días' a la señorita.	bwenozdías |sèɲyóríta↓	Juan: Buenos días, señorita.
Srta., contéstele 'buenos días' al Sr. White y pregúntele si le gusta el cuarto.	bwenozdías |sèɲyórhwáyt↓ lègustạelkwartó↑	Srta.: Buenos días, Sr. White. ¿Le gusta el cuarto?
Juan, contéstele que sí, que le gusta mucho, y que gracias.	sí↓ mègustamúchò |gráṣyàs↓	Juan: Sí, me gusta mucho, gracias.
Srta., pregúntele si necesita algo.	nèṣèsítálgo↑	Srta.: ¿Necesita algo?
Juan, dígale que sí, que Ud. quiere cambiar un billete de veinte dólares. Pregúntele que dónde está la caja.	sí↓ kyerokambyár |ùmbi(l)yéte | dèbeyntedólàrès↓ dondestalakáhà↓	Juan: Sí, quiero cambiar un billete de veinte dólares. ¿Dónde está la caja?

Srta., dígale que está ahí, a la derecha.

èstaí|àlàdèrechà↓

Juan, dígale que muchas gracias.

muchazgráşyàs↓

Juan: Muchas gracias.

NARRATIVE 2

1 He goes there.

baí↓

Va ahí.

2 The rate of exchange is three to one.

èlkambyoestá|atresporúnò↓

El cambio está a tres por uno.

3 He wants to change twenty dollars.

kyerekambyar|beynteꝺólàrès↓

Quiere cambiar veinte dólares.

4 And how does he want it?

ikomolokyere↑

Y ¿cómo lo quiere?

5 He wants two twenties and two tens.

kyere|ꝺozꝺebeyntę|iꝺozꝺeꝺyéş↓

Quiere dos de veinte y dos de diez.

DIALOG 2

Juan, dígale al cajero que dispense y pregúntele que a cómo está el cambio.	dispensé↓ akómo|ęstaęlkámbyô↓	Juan: Dispense, ¿a cómo está el cambio?
Cajero, contéstele que está a tres por uno.	ęstátrésporúnô↓	Caj: Está a tres por uno.
Juan, pregúntele si puede cambiarle este billete.	pweḍekambyarmestebiⓁyeté↑	Juan: ¿Puede cambiarme este billete?
Cajero, pregúntele que de cuánto es.	dękwantǫés↓	Caj: ¿De cuánto es?
Juan, contéstele que es de veinte dólares.	ézḍebeynteḍólàrés↓	Juan: Es de veinte dólares.
Cajero, dígale que con mucho gusto, y pregúntele que cómo lo quiere.	kónmuchoçústô↓ **komolokyérè↓**	Caj: Con mucho gusto. ¿Cómo lo quiere?
Juan, dígale que dos de veinte y dos de diez, por favor.	dozḍebeynte↑iḍozḍedyéş|pôrfàbór↓	Juan: Dos de veinte y dos de diez, por favor.
Cajero, contéstele que cómo no, que aquí tiene.	kómonó↓ àkítyénè↓	Caj: Cómo no, aquí tiene.

NARRATIVE 3

1 He goes to the American
  Embassy in a taxi.

bálaémbàhádàmèrikàna | entáksi↓

Va a la Embajada Americana en
  taxi.

2 The Embassy isn't far.

laémbàhadanoestaléhòs↓

La Embajada no está lejos.

3 It's on Columbus Avenue.

èsta | enlàbènidakolón↓

Está en la Avenida Colón.

4 The taxi costs two and a
  quarter.

èltaksi | kwésta | dozbeyntişínkò↓

El taxi cuesta dos veinticinco.

DIALOG 3

Juan, dígale al chofer que lo
  lleve a la Embajada Americana.

Qyebeme | àlaémbàhadamerikáná↓

Juan: Lléveme a la Embajada
  Americana.

Chofer, dígale que perdón, que
  cómo dice.

pérdón↓ komodişe↑

Chof: Perdón, ¿cómo dice?

Juan, repítale que a la Embajada
  Americana, y pregúntele si está
  muy lejos de aquí.

àlaémbàhadamèrikáná↓
èstamuylehoz | deaki↑

Juan: A la Embajada Americana.

¿Está muy lejos de aquí?

Chofer, contéstele que no mucho,
  que está en la Avenida Colón.

nomúchò↓ èstaenlàbènidakolón↓

Chof: No mucho, está en la
  Avenida Colón.

Juan, pregúntele que cuánto es.   kwantoés↓   Juan: ¿Cuánto es?

Chofer, dígale que dos veinticinco.   dózbeyntiʂíŋkò↓   Chof: Dos veinticinco.

Juan, dígale que aquí tiene, que   àkityéné↓ graʂyàs↓   Juan: Aquí tiene, gracias.
gracias.

Chofer, dígale que gracias a él.   graʂyasạustéd |sèŋyór↓   Chof: Gracias a usted, señor.

                                                                              End of Tape 2A

Tape 2B

4.1   BASIC SENTENCES.   White meets Molina at the Embassy.

Mr. White arrives at the Embassy by taxi and pays the driver.

ENGLISH SPELLING	AID TO LISTENING	SPANISH SPELLING
(I) owe (to owe)	debó↓ debér↓	debo (deber)
to you (I) owe	le-debó↓	le debo

White
How much do I owe you?

kwantoledébó↓

White
¿Cuánto le debo?

| (they) are (to be) | son↓ sér↓ | son (ser) |
| the chauffeur | el-chofér↓ | el chofer |

Taxi Driver
It's four pesos.

soŋkwatropésós↓

Chofer de taxi
Son cuatro pesos.

(they) told, said (to tell, to say) (1)	diherón↓ deşír↓	dijeron (decir)
to me (they) told	me-diherón↓	me dijeron
they would be (to be)	serián↓ sér↓	serían (ser)

White
At the hotel they told me it'd be two. (2)

enelótél |mediheron |ke
seriandós↓

White
En el hotel me dijeron que
serían dos.

(I) give (to give)	dóy↓ dár↓	doy (dar)
to you (I) give [3]	lè—doy↓	le doy
the tip	là—propinà↓	la propina
I'll give you three. One for a tip.	lèdoytrés↓ unodepropínà↓	Le doy tres. Uno de propina.
good , OK	bwenô↓	bueno
Taxi driver		*Chofer de taxi*
O.K. Thank you, sir.	bwenô↓ gra§yàs│sèŋyór↓	Bueno, gracias, señor.

(Mr. White enters the Embassy and goes to the Administrative Office. He is taken to the consular section where he is going to work and introduced to one of the young local employees with whom he is going to be associated.)

Administrative officer		*Oficial administrativo*
Mr. Molina, this is Mr. White. [4]	sèŋyormolinà↑ estes.elsèŋyorhwáyt↓	Señor Molina, éste es el señor White.
(he) goes (to go)	bá↓ ír↓	va (ir)
to work	tràbàhár↓	trabajar
we, us	nòsotrôs↓	nosotros
He is going to work with us.	bàtràbàhar│kò(n)nòsótròs↓	Va a trabajar con nosotros.
so much	tantô↓	tanto
to know him [5]	kònó§erlô↓	conocerlo

Molina
I'm very glad to know you, Mr. White.

tántogústo|dekonoşérlð|señyórhwáyt↓

Molina
Tanto gusto de conocerlo, señor White.

mine

mióↄ

mío

White
The pleasure's mine.

èlgústọezmíðↄ

White
El gusto es mío.

since

dézdèↄ

desde

when

kwandóↄ

cuando

Molina
How long have you been here?

dézdèkwandọ|estakíↄ

Molina
¿Desde cuándo está aquí?

yesterday

àyérↄ

ayer

White
Since yesterday.

dézdọàyérↄ

White
Desde ayer.

such

tálↄ

tal

how, how goes it

ke—tálↄ

qué tal

the trip

èl—byahèↄ

el viaje

Molina
How was the trip?

kétalelbyáhèↄ

Molina
¿Qué tal el viaje?

excellent	èks(ş)élentè↓	excelente

White
Excellent.

èks(ş)élentè↓

White
Excelente.

the movement	èl—mòbimyéntò↓	el movimiento
the section	là—sèkşyón↓	la sección
consular	kònsùláŕ↓	consular

Is there much activity in the consular section here?	ay |múchomòbimyéntọ |ènlàsèkşyóŋ |kònsúláraki↑	¿Hay mucho movimiento en la sección consular aquí?

almost	kásì↓	casi
always	syémprè↓	siempre
(we) are (to be)	èstámòs↓ èstáŕ↓	estamos (estar)
busy (to occupy)	òkùpaďòs↓ òkùpáŕ↓	ocupados (ocupar)

Molina
Yes. We're almost always very busy.

sí↓ kásisyemprestámoz \|múyokupáďòs↓

Molina
Sí. Casi siempre estamos muy ocupados.

(you) speak (to speak)	ablà↓ àbláŕ↓	habla (hablar)

White
Do you speak English, Mr. Molina?

àblạustèďiŋgles \|sèŋyórmòlínà↓

White
¿Habla usted inglés, señor Molina?

(I) speak (to speak)   ȧblő↓ ȧblár↓   hablo (hablar)

little   pőkő↓   poco

a little   ùm‑pőkő↓   un poco

Molina
Yes. I speak a little.   sí↓ ȧblọump őkő↓   *Molina*
Sí, hablo un poco.

but   peró↓   pero

(you) must, ought (must, ought)   dėbė↓ dėbér↓   debe (deber)

to practice   prȧktikár↓   practicar

But you ought to practice your Spanish.   pėrọústėḋ|ḋebepraktikár|elespaŋyol↓   Pero usted debe practicar el español.

the purpose   ėl‑prőpősitő↓   el propósito

by the way   ȧ‑prőpősitő↓   a propósito

(you) pronounce (to pronounce)   prőnúnşyȧ↓ prőnúnşyár↓   pronuncia (pronunciar)

(you) learned (to learn) (6)   ȧprėndyő↓ ȧprėndér↓   aprendió (aprender)

By the way.   ȧprőpősitő↓   A propósito.

You speak it and pronounce it very well.   lọȧblạ|ilőprőnúnşyȧ|múybyén↓   Lo habla y lo pronuncia muy bien.

Where did you learn it?   dőndelọȧprėndyő↓   ¿Dónde lo aprendió?

the school	la̧—éskwélá↓	la escuela
the language, tongue	lá—léŋgwá↓	la lengua
school of languages	éskwela—de—léŋgwàs↓	escuela de lenguas
the state	él—éstadò↓	el estado
united (to unite)	únidò↓ únìr↓	unido (unir)
the United States	lós—éstádòs—únídòs↓	los Estados Unidos

White
At a language school in the States.

énúṇa̧éskwéládélẹŋgwas |énlós̟éstádos̟unídòs↓

White
En una escuela de lenguas en los Estados Unidos.

the thing	lá—kósá↓	la cosa
say (to say) [7]	dígá↓ dèṣír↓	diga (decir)
not to me say	no—me—dígá↓	no me diga

Molina
Another thing. Don't call me Mr. Molina.

ótrakósá↓ nómedíga |seŋyórmolíná↓

Molina
Otra cosa. No me diga señor Molina.

| my (mine) | mí↓ mìó↓ | mi (mío) |
| the name | èl—nómbrè↓ | el nombre |

My name is Joe.

mínómbreshosé↓

Mi nombre es José.

| oh | á↓ | ah |
| the mine | èl—mìó↓ | el mío |

White
Oh. All right. Mine is John.

á↓ múybyén↓ èlmiọeshwán↓

White
Ah, muy bien. El mío es Juan.

107

4.10   Notes on the basic sentences

(1) /dɪhéron/ *dijeron* is a Past I tense form of a fairly irregular type which will not be drilled in detail until Unit 23.

(2) Notice that in the English translation the word /ke/ 'that' is left untranslated, even though we can also say 'They told me that it'd be two.' This omission in English is *very* common, but *it never happens in Spanish.* While there will be drills on this matter later in this text, it would be well for the student to fix in his mind here and now the fact that the verb /deşír/ 'to say, to tell' always requires /ke/ 'that' after it if there is another verb being introduced by it.

(3) Notice that the word /le/ *le* is '(to) you' in the context of the complete utterance. Formal usage in contexts that mean 'you' is actually the same as in those that mean 'him, her'. The sentence /ledóytrés↓/ *le dcy tres* can be translated either 'I'll give you three', 'I'll give him three', or 'I'll give her three', and only the context will distinguish which translation is appropriate.

(4) One of the *very* common uses of the definite article in Spanish where it is *never* used in English is in *talking about* a person whose name is cited with /seɲyór/ or /seɲyoríta/ or /seɲyóra/: 'The Mister White', 'The Mrs. Smith', etc.

(5) The form /lo/ *lo* which appears here in the literal meaning 'him', but referring to the person being addressed (that is, 'you' — see note (3) above), often has the form /le/ *le* in Spain. For this reason a person who plans to go to Spain should practice saying /konoşérle/ *conocerle* as well as /konoşérlo/ *conocerlo*. We will not bother to point out this difference throughout this book, since the teacher can readily point out which form he himself uses (/le/ or /lo/), and that is the one the student should imitate. It may be noted here that the difference between Spain and Latin America on this point is easily stated by rule: the form /le/ is used in Latin America *only* as an indirect clitic form but in Spain it occurs also as the direct clitic form if the reference is to a male human being where /lo/ would be used in Latin America.

(6) /aprendyó/ *aprendió* is a regular Past I tense form which will be drilled in Unit 17.

(7) The form /díga/ *diga* is a command form which will be drilled, along with others of the type, in Unit 27. As in the present sentence, it can be used with the meaning 'call'.

4.2   DRILLS AND GRAMMAR

4.21   Pattern drills

4.21.1   Number in nouns and adjectives

   A.   Presentation of pattern

ILLUSTRATIONS

Hand me the books.	1 pásemelozlíbrȯs↓	Páseme *los libros.*
Give me the pens.	2 demelasplúmȧs↓	Déme *las plumas.*
_____	3 pwéɖe |kȧmbyȧrmȩ |únȯzɖólarest↑	¿Puede cambiarme *unos dólares?*
Give me some pens.	4 demȩunasplúmȧs↓	Déme *unas plumas.*
_____	5 bwenozɖɪȧs |sȩ̇ɲyór↓	° *Buenos días,* señor.
_____	6 bwenaznochės |sȩ̇ɲyȯrítȧ↓	*Buenas noches,* señorita.
_____	7 muchazgráşyȧs |sȩ̇ɲyór↓	*Muchas gracias,* señor.

EXTRAPOLATION

Nouns and adjectives

singular	plural
..........vowel	..........vowel —s
.....consonant	.....consonant —es

Partially irregular patterns of articles

Indefinite articles

	sg	pl
m	un	un<u>o</u>s
f	una	unas

Definite articles

	sg	pl
m	<u>e</u>l	l<u>o</u>s
f	la	las

NOTES

a. Spanish nouns, like English nouns, have different forms in the plural.

b. Spanish adjectives, *unlike* most English adjectives, also have different forms in the plural.

4.21.11   Substitution drill - number substitution [1]

Model Problem:

àkí |áyúnótélbwénò↓

Model Answer:

àkí |áyúnósótélezbwénòs↓

1   téŋgọúnáplumạeks(ṣ)eléntè↓   téŋgọúnásplumạeks(ṣ)eléntès↓

2   tyénèlmízmolíbrò↓   tyénélòzmízmozlíbròs↓

3   kyérọelótrodólàr↓   kyérolosọotrozdólàrès↓

_____

Model Problem:

`Aquí hay un hotel bueno.

Model Answer:

Aquí hay unos hoteles buenos.

1 Tengo una pluma excelente.   Tengo unas plumas excelentes.

2 Tiene el mismo libro.   Tiene los mismos libros.

3 Quiero el otro dólar.   Quiero los otros dólares.

_____

(1)   Number substitution involves a change between singular and plural forms. In the present drill these forms are nouns; change the singular nouns (and any associated adjectives) to plural and plural nouns (with any associated adjectives) to singular.

4 téngǫúncheke̞byahéró↓   téngǫúnóschekezbyahérǫs↓

5 áblo|kǒnlás̞e̞ņyǒríta̞espaņyólá↓   áblo|kǒnlá(s)s̞e̞ņyǒrítas,espaņyólás↓

6 ne̞s̞és̞ita̞unamesabwéná↓   ne̞s̞és̞ita̞unazmesazbwénás↓

7 ábla|kǒne̞lmízmǫamerikánó↓   ábla|kǒnlǒzmízmos,amerikánǒs↓

---

4 Tengo un cheque viajero.   Tengo unos cheques viajeros.

5 Hablo con la señorita española.   Hablo con las señoritas españolas.

6 Necesita una mesa buena.   Necesita unas mesas buenas.

7 Habla con el mismo americano.   Habla con los mismos americanos.

4.21.12   Response drill

1   kyérèpókágwa̧tomúchà↓   kyéròpókà↓

2   áblạustéd|kònèlmízmosèṇyortokonótró↓   áblo|kònèlmízmò↓

3   tyéṇȩ|ótraplúma̧tolamízmà↓   téŋgotrà↓

4   áblạùstéd|muchǫespaŋyóltopókò↓   áblópokò↓

5   tyéṇȩ|ótrozlíbrostolozmízmòs↓   teŋgo|lòzmízmòs↓

[èṇèlṣéntrò↓]   6   dóndestá|làsèṇyòritạespaŋyólà↓   làsèṇyòritạespaŋyola̧|éstáȩn èlṣéntrò↓

[ènlàmésà↓]   7   dóndestá|làmònédamerikánà↓   làmònédàmèrikána̧|estáȩnlamésà↓

---

1 ¿Quiere poca agua o mucha?   Quiero poca.
2 ¿Habla Ud. con el mismo señor o con otro?   Hablo con el mismo.
3 ¿Tiene otra pluma o la misma?   Tengo otra.
4 ¿Habla usted mucho español o poco?   Hablo poco.
5 ¿Tiene otros libros o los mismos?   Tengo los mismos.

(en el centro) 6 ¿Dónde está la señorita española?   La señorita española está en el centro.
(en la mesa)   7 ¿Dónde está la moneda americana?   La moneda americana está en la mesa.

[åkí↓]   8 dóndestá |e(l)líbróbwénó↓   é(l)líbróbwéno̧ |eståkí↓

[kȯnlá(s)sȇŋyȯràs↓] 9 ablȧustéd |kȯnló(s)sȇŋyȯresiŋglésés↑   nó↓ ablo |kȯnlà(s)sȇŋyȯrasiŋglésȧs↓

[èlmízmȯ↓]   10 tyénȩustéd |otrolíbro↑   nó↓ téŋgȯȩlmízmȯ↓

[pókȯ↓]   11 ablȧustéd |muchȯespaŋyól↑   nó↓ áblópókȯ↓

                      12 ay |muchoșótélezbwénos |akí↑   sí↓ áymúchȯs↓

                      13 tyéne(l)ȧ |muchazmonédas |åmȇrikánas↑ sí↓ tyénèmúchȧs↓

                      14 ay |muchomobɩmyéntȯ |ênlȧsékȿyóŋ   sí↓ áymúchȯ↓
                          kȯnsúlar↑

                      15 nȇȿésitȧ |únȯschékèzbyȧheros↑   sí↓ nȇȿésitȯúnȯs↓

(aquí)   8 ¿Dónde está el libro bueno?   El libro bueno está aquí.

(con las señoras) 9 ¿Habla usted con los señores ingleses?   No, hablo con las señoras inglesas.

(el mismo)   10 ¿Tiene usted otro libro?   No, tengo el mismo.

(poco)   11 ¿Habla usted mucho español?   No, hablo poco.

                  12 ¿Hay muchos hoteles buenos aquí?   Sí, hay muchos.

                  13 ¿Tiene ella muchas monedas americanas?   Sí, tiene muchas.

                  14 ¿Hay mucho movimiento en la sección consular? Sí, hay mucho.

                  15 ¿Necesita unos cheques viajeros?   Sí, necesito unos.

4.21.13   Translation drill

1 There're many good
   schools here.

ákíáy |múchaseskwelazbwénàs↓

Aquí hay muchas escuelas
buenas.

2 There's an excellent
   school there.

áìay |únaèskwelaeks(ṣ)eléntè↓

Ahí hay una escuela
excelente.

3 I always speak with
   the same ladies.

syempreabló |kònlázmɪzma(s)seɲóràs↓

Siempre hablo con las mismas
señoras.

4 Can you change some
   American coins for me?

pwedekambyarmȩ |únázmónedas,amerikanas↑

¿Puede cambiarme unas
monedas americanas?

5 I haven't got the other
   dollars now.

nóteŋgo |lòṣotrozdólàrès |àórá↓

No tengo los otros dólares
ahora.

6 I have very few bills.

téŋgò |múypókozbiʎyétès↓

Tengo muy pocos billetes.

7 Hand me another pencil.

pásemȩ |ótrolápiṣ↓

Páseme otro lápiz.

8 Give me the other checks.

déme |lòṣotroschékès↓

Déme los otros cheques.

9 I always leave good tips.

syempredoy |própinazbwénàs↓

Siempre doy propinas buenas.

B. Discussion of pattern [1]

      Both English and Spanish use the concept of *number*, which distinguishes *one* (singular) from *more than one* (plural). English nouns regularly add an ending for plural forms, e.g., the endings of the words 'cat<u>s</u>, dog<u>s</u>, horse<u>s</u>', the particular ending that appears depending on what sound the singular form ends with. In Spanish the plural ending also depends on the last sound of the singular form, though with a different formula: words ending with a vowel add /—s/, with a consonant, /—es/, as /mésa — mésa<u>s</u> otél — otél<u>es</u>/.

      Adjectives in English do not usually change in form when modifying plural nouns: '*the* boy - *the* boys, *good* book - *good* books'. However, the indefinite article <u>a</u> (a special kind of adjective) can appear only with singular nouns: '*a* boy' but '*some* boys'; and the demonstratives (another special kind of adjective, often used when pointing) genuinely change when modifying plural nouns: '*this* boy - *these* boys, *that* book - *those* books'.

      Almost *all* Spanish adjectives change forms for singular and plural in the same way nouns do; that is, add /—s/ if the word ends in a vowel, /—es/ if in a consonant.

      The patterns of pluralization of the articles (the special adjectives, equivalent to 'a, an, some, the' in English, used before nouns to limit their application, definitely or indefinitely) are slightly irregular. The irregularities are charted in the presentation of pattern that began this section, with irregular elements underlined.

(1) There are irregular forms. See appendix for presentation of them.

4.21.2   The irregular verb /estár/

A.   Presentation of pattern

ILLUSTRATIONS

_____

I

I'm in the bathroom.

you (fam.)

(you) are (to be)

How are you?

_____

he

How is he?

she

How is she?

_____

(you) are (pl.) (to be)

1   éstoybyén |grášyàs↓   *Estoy* bien, gracias.

yó↓   yo

2   yo̜ęstóy |en̥elbáŋyò↓   Yo *estoy* en el baño.

tú↓   tú

éstàs↓ éstár↓   estás (estar)

3   kómo̜estastú↓   ¿Cómo *estás* tú?

4   kómo̜estaus̜téd↓   ¿Cómo *está* usted?

él↓   él

5   kómo̜estaél↓   ¿Cómo *está* él?

é()yà↓   ella

6   kómo̜estaé()yà↓   ¿Cómo *está* ella?

7   kásisyémprestámoz |múyokupádòs↓   Casi siempre *estamos* muy
                                                   ocupados.

éstán↓ éstár↓   están (estar) you (pl.)   ústedés↓   ustedes

How are you all?   8 kómǫestánųstédés↓   ¿Cómo *están* ustedes?

they (m.)   éⱡⱡɥòs↓   ellos

How are they?   9 kómǫestánéⱡⱡɥòs↓   ¿Cómo *están* ellos?

EXTRAPOLATION

	sg	pl
1st person	estóy	estámos
2nd person familiar	estás	
2nd person formal / 3rd person	está	están

NOTES

a. Spanish verbs change to agree with their subject for singular and plural, for first person (I), second person (you), and third person (he or anything else).

b. Second person is further distinguished for familiar or formal.

c. Second person formal and third person take the same verb form in the singular; all second and third person take the same form in the plural.

4.21.21   Substitution drills - number substitution

Model Problem:

éstámos.en.elotél↓

Model Answer:

éstóyen.elotél↓

1 éstanái↓   éstaí↓
2 éstamozbyén↓   éstoybyén↓

Model Problem:

Estamos en el hotel.

Model Answer:

Estoy en el hotel

1 Están ahí.   Está ahí.
2 Estamos bien.   Estoy bien.

3 èstámbyén│àkí↓   èstábyén│àkí↓

4 èstá│ęnląeskwélà↓   èstán│ęnląeskwélà↓

5 èstóy│ęnląembahádà↓   èstámos│ęnląembahádà↓

6 nòęstabyén│àí↓   nòęstambyén│àí↓

7 èstámos│enelşéntrò↓   èstóyenelşéntrò↓

---

3 Están bien aquí.   Está bien aquí.

4 Está en la escuela.   Están en la escuela.

5 Estoy en la Embajada.   Estamos en la Embajada.

6 No está bien ahí.   No están bien ahí.

7 Estamos en el centro.   Estoy en el centro.

Person - number substitution

Model Problem:

> àntónyo̧ | estàȩn̦el ş̦éntró↓
>
> ùsteḑes_____↓

Model Answer:

> èstàȩn̦el ş̦éntró↓

1 y̧ó̧ȩstóy | mùyby̧én̦àkí↓

àlíş̦y̧ḁ_____↓   èstá | mùyby̧én̦àkí↓

nòsótròs_____↓   èstámò̧z | mùyby̧én̦àkí↓

àlíş̦y̧àḁàn̦tón̦yo̧____↓   èstán | mùyby̧én̦àkí↓

ùstéḑ_____↓   èstá | mùyby̧én̦àkí↓

___

Model Problem:

> *Antonio* está en el centro.
> Ustedes_____

Model Answer:

> Están en el centro.

1 *Yo* estoy muy bien aquí.
   Alicia _____   Está muy bien aquí.
   Nosotros _____   Estamos muy bien aquí.
   Alicia y Antonio_____   Están muy bien aquí.
   Usted_____   Está muy bien aquí.

2   páblo|estaęnlaembaháđà↓

   yo_____↓   èstoyenlaembaháđà↓

   àntonyo_____↓   èstaęnlaembaháđà↓

   lòsèŋyores_____↓   èstanenlaembaháđà↓

   làsèŋyòritą_____↓   èstaęnlaembaháđà↓

3   àlişyaįyo|ęstamos.en.elotél↓

   yo_____↓   èstoyen.elotél↓

   ùsteđes_____↓   èstan.en.elotél↓

   elįantonyo_____↓   èstan.en.elotél↓

   e01yą_____↓   èstaęn.elotél↓

---

2   *Pablo* está en la Embajada.

   Yo_____   Estoy en la Embajada.
   Antonio_____   Está en la Embajada.
   Los señores_____   Están en la Embajada.
   La señorita_____   Está en la Embajada.

3   *Alicia* y yo estamos en el hotel.

   Yo_____.   Estoy en el hotel.
   Ustedes_____   Están en el hotel.
   El y Antonio_____   Están en el hotel.
   Ella_____   Está en el hotel.

4.21.22   Response drill

1   èstálaseņyorą|ènèlòtél↑
    ǫenląembahádà↓   èstáęnląèmbàhàďà↓

2   èstanlozbiꝇyetes|àki↑ǫaí↓   èstánàki↓

3   èstànusteđes|ènląèskwelà↑
    ǫenelotél↓   èstámòs.ènląèskwelà↓

4   èstánlo(s)seņyóres|àki↑
    ǫenelşéntrò↓   èstán, ènèlşentró↓

[byén↓]   5   komǫestáųstéđ↓   èstóybyeŋ|gráşyàs↓

[ènèlşentrò↓] 6   dóndestaęlotél↓   èstáęnèlşentrò↓

[byén↓]   7   komǫestánustéđès↓   èstámózbyeŋ|gráşyàs↓

---

1 ¿Está la señora en el hotel o en la Embajada?   Está en la Embajada.

2 ¿Están los billetes aquí o ahí?   Están aquí.

3 ¿Están Uds. en la escuela o en el hotel?   Estamos en la escuela.

4 ¿Están los señores aquí o en el centro?   Están en el centro.

(bien)   5 ¿Cómo está usted?   Estoy bien. Gracias.

(en el centro) 6 ¿Dónde está el hotel?   Está en el centro.

(bien)   7 ¿Cómo están ustedes?   Estamos bien. Gracias.

[şérkà↓]   8   èstalaémbàhàda|léhozdelşéntro↑   nó↓ èstáşérkà↓

[ènèlşéntró↓]   9   èstánlo(s)señyóres|àkí↑   nó↓ èstánènèlşéntró↓

[ènlaémbàhàda↓] 10   èstaustéd|ènèlótel↑   nó↓ èstóyènlaémbàhàdà↓

                   11 èstáneⱡⱡaz|byénàkí↑   sí↓ èstánmuybyén↓

                   12 èstanustédes|ókùpádos↑   sí↓ èstámozmuy|ókùpádos↓

                   13 èstaustéd|ókùpádo↑   sí↓ èstóymuy|ókùpádo↓

       (cerca)   8 ¿Está la Embajada lejos del centro?   No, está cerca.
   (en el centro)   9 ¿Están los señores aquí?   No, están en el centro.
(en la Embajada)   10 ¿Está usted en el hotel?   No, estoy en la Embajada.

                   11 ¿Están ellas bien aquí?   Sí, están muy bien.
                   12 ¿Están ustedes ocupados?   Sí, estamos muy ocupados.
                   13 ¿Está usted ocupado?   Sí, estoy muy ocupado.

4.21.23   Translation drill

1 The books are on the table.

lózlíbros | estánenlamésà↓

Los libros están en la mesa.

2 We're in a hotel a long way
    from here.

éstamos | énùnótel | léhozdęakí↓

Estamos en un hotel lejos de aquí.

3 How are you?

komǫestaųstéđ↓

¿Cómo está usted?

4 Are you busy?

éstaųsteđ | ókùpađo↑

¿Está usted ocupado?

5 The elevator is to the left.

élàs(ş)énsór | estálaįşkyérđà↓

El ascensor está a la izquierda.

6 Where's the cashier?

dóndestá | lakáhà↓

¿Dónde está la caja?

7 Columbus Avenue is very near
    here.

làbèníđàkólon | èstámuyşerkà | dęàkí↓

La Avenida Colón está muy cerca
de aquí.

8 They're very busy.

ę̇(l)yos | èstánmúyokùpáđós↓

Ellos están muy ocupados.

9 Good evening. How are you?

bwenaznochès↓ komǫestaųstéđ↓

Buenas noches. ¿Cómo está usted?

B. Discussion of pattern

The following discussion needs the prior clarification of two concepts:

verb — a word identified in English by the endings it can occur with, as: 'work, works, worked, working', or some internal modification, as: 'sing, sings, sang, sung, singing.' Spanish verbs are similarly identified by comparable (though more numerous and complex) endings and changes. Verbs in English and Spanish commonly express action, occurrence, etc.

pronoun — one of a relatively small group of words which contain the categories of person, number, and case. The following chart lists the English pronouns which can occur as subjects of verbs:

	sg	pl
1st person	I	we (you and I) (Bill and I)
2nd person	you	you (you and he) (you and Bill)
3rd person	he she it (the book)	they (he and she) (Bill and he) (the books)

The concept of *person* exists in English pronouns, but has a very limited application to English verbs. Most verbs in English occur with an ending in what might be called the 3rd person singular forms: 'I hit - he hits, I dig - he digs, I miss - he misses'. In Spanish there are usually five (1) widely used forms, which accompany and agree with different pronoun subjects, showing person and number distinctions. The following chart gives examples of these forms, with the verb /estár/.

yó estóy	nosótros estámos
tú estás	
ustéd él está éⱀya	ustédes éⱀyos están éⱀyas

Second and third person verb forms are identical, except that the concept of *familiarity* makes a distinction between second person singular *familiar* and second person singular *formal* forms. In Spanish, two persons addressing each other will select one of two subject pronouns, i.e./ustéd/ or/tú/. Automatically, the accompanying verb will take specific endings depending on which pronoun has been selected. Thus, the sentence 'How are you?' can be translated either as /kómo‿está‿ustéd↓/ or /kómo‿estás‿tú↓/

This selection involves a pattern of personal relationships which is by no means simple or even the same throughout the Spanish speaking world. Furthermore, it implies that the speaker *must* select one set of forms or the other when addressing another individual depending on their personal relationship. For the sake of brevity, the distinctions involved have been termed *formal* /ustéd/ and *familiar*/tú/, and in general way correspond to the usage of 'Sir' or 'Mister' and first names in English. However, the Spanish and English usages do not correlate one hundred per cent, and in Spanish there is a finer gradation from formality to familiarity in which *both* the selection of/ustéd/or /tú/ and the use of titles, first names, and last names play an important part. Thus, in greeting Mr. Juan Molina, there are the following possibilities:

¿Cómo está usted, señor Molina?   ¿Cómo está usted, Juan?
¿Cómo está usted, Molina?   ¿Cómo estás tú, Juan?

---

(1)   Two other forms exist: /bosótros/ , a 2nd person familiar plural form, is still used in parts of Spain, though considered archaic in other dialect areas; and /bós/, a 2nd person familiar singular form, used in some areas in place of or alongside /tú/, the more common form. Both /bosótros/ and /bós/ require separate and distinct equivalent verb forms. See Appendix.

It does *not* follow that in his answer to a greeting, Mr. Molina is automatically going to use the *same* set of forms selected by the first speaker. For the status of personal relationships between two individuals depends on such factors as their difference in age, period of mutual acquaintance, sex, rank, and family relationship.

There are no rules of thumb which can guide the student in his selection of *usted* or *tú* forms. Rather, it is a question of feeling for differences which he will develop as he adjusts to the cultural patterns of the individuals in any specific Spanish speaking area.

Spanish verbs, unlike English (except in the case of commands), can appear with no accompanying pronoun or noun subject with no loss of meaning content, i.e., they contain their pronominal reference. Indeed they most frequently *do* appear alone, unless the pronouns are present for special emphasis or contrast or unless (as is possible with 3rd person forms) the context does not make the reference clear. Thus the following translation correlations are usually correct.

/estóy/	I am	/yó estóy/	*I* am
/estás/	you are	/tú estás/	*you* are
/está/	he(she)is(you are)	/él está/	*he* is
/estámos/	we are	/nosótros estámos/	*we* are
/están/	they(you)are	/él᷉yos están/	*they* are

The verb /estár/ has certain irregularities in its pattern, namely the addition of /—y/ to the first person singular form and the occurrence of stress on the endings of all singular and second - third person plural forms. These irregularities will become more obvious by contrast with the regular pattern which will be presented in Unit 6.

4.22   Replacement drills

A   sóŋkwatropésòs↓

1 _____señyorítàs↓   sóŋkwatrosenyorítàs↓

2 ___una_____↓   ès̗unasenyorítà↓

3 _____señyór↓   ès̗unsenyór↓

4 ___ocho_____↓   sónochosenyórès↓

5 _____ðólàrès↓   sónochoðólàrès↓

6 débò_____↓   débochoðólàrès↓

7 téŋgó_____↓   téŋgochoðólàrès↓

A   Son cuatro pesos.

1 _____ señoritas.   Son cuatro señoritas.

2 ___una _____.   Es una señorita.

3 _____ señor.   Es un señor.

4 ___ocho _____.   Son ocho señores.

5 _____ dólares.   Son ocho dólares.

6 Debo _____.   Debo ocho dólares.

7 Tengo_____.   Tengo ocho dólares.

B dézđékwandǫ|estakíↆ

1 ástá_____ↆ   ástákwandǫ|estakíↆ

2 _____estamos____ↆ   ástákwandǫ|estamos̩akíↆ

3 _____okupáđòsↆ   ástákwandǫ|estamos̩okupáđòsↆ

4 dézđé_____ↆ   dézđékwandǫ|estamos̩okupáđòsↆ

5 _____ènlòs̩ės̩tađos̩uníđòsↆ   dézđékwandǫ|estamos|ènlòs̩ės̩tađos̩uníđòsↆ

6 _____estoy_____ↆ   dézđékwandǫ|estoy|ènlòs̩ės̩tađos̩uníđòsↆ

7 _____esta_____ↆ   dézđékwandǫ|esta|ǫnlòs̩ės̩tađos̩uníđòsↆ

B ¿Desde cuándo está aquí?

1 ¿Hasta _____?   ¿Hasta cuándo está aquí?

2 ¿_____estamos____?   ¿Hasta cuándo estamos aquí?

3 ¿_____ ocupados?   ¿Hasta cuándo estamos ocupados?

4 ¿Desde_____?   ¿Desde cuándo estamos ocupados?

5 ¿_____ en los Estados Unidos?   ¿Desde cuándo estamos en los Estados Unidos?

6 ¿_____estoy _____?   ¿Desde cuándo estoy en los Estados Unidos?

7 ¿_____está_____?   ¿Desde cuándo está en los Estados Unidos?

C   áymúcho |mobimyéntọ |énlásékşyọŋkonsulár↑

1 _____akí↑   áymúcho |mobimyéntọ |akí↑

2 _____kósas _____↑   áymúchas |kósas |akí↑

3 _____aora↑   áymúchas |kósas |aora↑

4 __pókas _____↑   aypókas |kósas |aora↑

5 _____aí↑   aypókas |kósas |aí↑

6 _____libros_____↑   aypókoz |libros |aí↑

7 _____mesas_____↑   aypókaz |mesas |aí↑

C   ¿Hay mucho movimiento en la Sección Consular?

1 ¿_____aquí?   ¿Hay mucho movimiento aquí?

2 ¿_____ cosas _____?   ¿Hay muchas cosas aquí?

3 ¿_____ahora?   ¿Hay muchas cosas ahora?

4 ¿_____ pocas _____?   ¿Hay pocas cosas ahora?

5 ¿_____ahí?   ¿Hay pocas cosas ahí?

6 ¿_____libros_____?   ¿Hay pocos libros ahí?

7 ¿_____mesas_____?   ¿Hay pocas mesas ahí?

D   siↂ kásisyemprȩ|ėstámȯs,ȯkȗpáɗosↂ

1 _____ȧkíↂ   siↂ kásisyemprȩ|ėstámȯs,ȧkíↂ

2 _____ėstóy_____ↂ   siↂ kásisyemprȩ|ėstóyȧkíↂ

3 ___únȧzbȩȿes_____ↂ   siↂ únȧzbȩȿes|ėstóyȧkíↂ

4 _____ȯkȗpáɗoↂ   siↂ únȧzbȩȿes|ėstóyȯkȗpáɗoↂ

5 ___ótrȧzbȩȿes_____ↂ   siↂ ótrȧzbȩȿes|ėstóyȯkȗpáɗoↂ

6 _____estamos____ↂ   siↂ ótrȧzbȩȿes|ėstámȯs,ȯkȗpáɗosↂ

7 ___kásisyemprȩ_____ↂ   siↂ kásisyemprȩ|ėstámȯs,ȯkȗpáɗosↂ

D   Sí, casi siempre estamos ocupados.

1 _____aquí.   Sí, casi siempre estamos aquí.

2 _____estoy_____.   Sí, casi siempre estoy aquí.

3 ___unas veces_____.   Sí, unas veces estoy aquí.

4 _____ocupado.   Sí, unas veces estoy ocupado.

5 ___otras veces_____.   Sí, otras veces estoy ocupado.

6 _____estamos_____.   Sí, otras veces estamos ocupados.

7 ___casi siempre_____.   Sí, casi siempre estamos ocupados.

E ábláustédiŋglés |señyormolina↑

1 és_____↑   ésústédiŋglés |señyormolina↑

2 _____ámèrikano |_____↑   ésústédámèrikano |señyormolina↑

3 _____ |señyorita_____↑   ésústédámèrikana |señyoritamolina↑

4 _____éspáñyola |_____↑   ésústédèspáñyola |señyoritamolina↑

5 ábla_____↑   ábláustedespañyol |señyoritamolina↑

6 _____yo_____↑   ábloyoespáñyol |señyoritamolina↑

7 _____byén |_____↑   ábloyobyen |señyoritamolina↑

E ¿Habla usted inglés, señor Molina?

1 ¿Es_____?   ¿Es usted inglés, Sr. Molina?

2 ¿_____ americano_____?   ¿Es usted americano, Sr. Molina?

3 ¿_____ señorita____?   ¿Es usted americana, Srta. Molina?

4 ¿_____española _____?   ¿Es usted española, Srta. Molina?

5 ¿Habla_____ ?   ¿Habla usted español, Srta. Molina?

6 ¿____ yo_____?   ¿Hablo yo español, Srta. Molina?

7 ¿_____ bien_____?   ¿Hablo yo bien, Srta. Molina?

F minómbreshosé↓

1 _____ıŋglés↓   minómbresıŋglés↓

2 _____ésté↓   mínombresésté↓

3 __lıbro___↓   mílıbroesésté↓

4 _____eks(ş)elénté↓   mílıbroes eks(ş)elénté↓

5 __lıbros_____↓   mızlıbro(s)sonek(ş)eléntés↓

6 _____bwénos↓   mızlıbro(s)sombwénos↓

7 __plumas_____↓   míspluma(s)sombwénàs↓

F   Mi nombre es José.

1 _____inglés.   Mi nombre es inglés.

2 _____éste.   Mi nombre es éste.

3 __libro_____.   Mi libro es éste.

4 _____excelente.   Mi libro es excelente.

5 __libros_____.   Mis libros son excelentes.

6 _____ buenos.   Mis libros son buenos.

7 plumas_____.   Mis plumas son buenas.

4.23   Variation drills

A   kwántoleɗébò↓   ¿Cuánto le debo?

1 What do I owe you?   keleɗébò↓   ¿Qué le debo?

2 What are you telling him?   keleɗíṣé↓   ¿Qué le dice?

3 What did they tell him?   keleɗihérón↓   ¿Qué le dijeron?

4 When did they tell him?   kwandoleɗihérón↓   ¿Cuándo le dijeron?

5 Where did they tell him?   dondeleɗihérón↓   ¿Dónde le dijeron?

6 How did they tell him?   kómoleɗihérón↓   ¿Cómo le dijeron?

7 How is he getting along?   kómolebá↓   ¿Cómo le va?

B   leɗóytrés↓ únoɗepropíná↓   Le doy tres, uno de propina.

1 Here are four, two for a tip.   leɗóykwatró↓ dozɗepropíná↓   Le doy cuatro, dos de propina.

2 Here are twenty, ten for a tip. leɗóybeyntè↓ dyezɗepropíná↓   Le doy veinte, diez de propina.

3 Here are ten, five for a tip.   leɗóydyéṣ↓ ṣɪŋkoɗepropíná↓   Le doy diez, cinco de propina.

4 Here are eleven, one for a tip.   lèdóyonşè↓ únodepropínà↓   Le doy once, uno de propina.

5 Here's a dollar and no tip.   lèdóyundólàr↓ nádadepropínà↓   Le doy un dólar, nada de propina.

6 Here's this, that's for a tip.   lèdóyestò↓ ésodepropínà↓   Le doy esto, eso de propina.

7 I'll give you this, not that.   lèdóyestò↓ ésonó↓   Le doy esto, eso no.

C   bátràbàhar|kò(n)nòsótròs↓   Va a trabajar con nosotros.

1 He's going to work with you all.   bátràbàhar|kònùstédès↓   Va a trabajar con ustedes.

2 She's going to work here.   bátràbàhar|àkí↓   Va a trabajar aquí.

3 She's going to speak Spanish.   báblár|èspàŋyól↓   Va a hablar español.

4 He's going to learn English.   báprèndér|iŋglés↓   Va a aprender inglés.

5 He's going to say something.   bádèşirálgó↓   Va a decir algo.

6 She's going to translate the name.   bátràdùşír|èlnombrè↓   Va a traducir el nombre.

7 You're going to be very busy.   báęstár|muyokupádó↓   Va a estar muy ocupado.

D   sí↓ yọabloͅumpókò↓   Sí, yo hablo un poco.

1 Yes, I speak a lot.   sí↓ yọablomúchò↓   Sí, yo hablo mucho.

2 Yes, you speak more.   sí↓ ústeḍablamás↓   Sí, usted habla más.

3 Yes, he speaks less.   sí↓ elablaménòs↓   Sí, él habla menos.

4 Yes, I have five dollars. sí↓ yótéŋgóşiŋkoḍólàrès↓   Sí, yo tengo cinco dólares.

5 Yes, you have fifteen.   sí↓ ústeḍtyénekínşè↓   Sí, usted tiene quince.

6 No, I don't have much.   no↓ yonoteŋgomúchò↓   No, yo no tengo mucho.

7 No, I don't owe much.   no↓ yonoḍebomúchò↓   No, yo no debo mucho.

E   pérọúste|ḍébèpràktikár|èlèspàŋyól↓   Pero usted debe practicar el español.

1 But you ought to practice English.   pérọústé|ḍébèpràktikár|èliŋglés↓   Pero usted debe practicar el inglés.

2 But you ought to say something.   pérọústé|ḍébèḍèşirálgò↓   Pero usted debe decir algo.

3 But you ought to take a taxi.   pérọústé|ḍébètòmár|ùntáksi↓   Pero usted debe tomar un taxi.

4 But you ought to speak less. pérọusté|ɖébẹầblarménós↓ Pero usted debe hablar menos.

5 But you ought to speak more. pérọusté|ɖébẹầblarmás↓ Pero usted debe hablar más.

6 But you ought to go to the Embassy. pérọusté|ɖébẹír|àlạėmbàhàɖà↓ Pero usted debe ir a la Embajada.

7 But you ought to go up in the elevator. pérọusté|ɖébèsúbír|ėnẹlàs(ṣ)ènsór↓ Pero usted debe subir en el ascensor.

F ótrakósà↓ nómeɖiga|sèṇyórmólìnà↓ Otra cosa, no me diga Sr. Molina.

1 Another thing, don't tell me that. ótrakósà↓ nómeɖigạ ésó↓ Otra cosa, no me diga eso.

2 Another thing, don't repeat that to me. ótrakósà↓ nómerrepitạésó↓ Otra cosa, no me repita eso.

3 Another thing, don't translate that for me. ótrakósà↓ nómetraɖuṣkạésó↓ Otra cosa, no me traduzca eso.

4 Another thing, don't give me a tip. ótrakósà↓ nómeɖepropínà↓ Otra cosa, no me dé propina.

5 Another thing, don't pass me the book. ótrakósà↓ nòṃepaseⓁlíbrò↓ Otra cosa, no me pase el libro.

6 Another thing, don't **take**
  me to the hotel.

ótrakósà↓ nóme(l)yèbąạlotél↓

Otra cosa, no me lleve al hotel.

7 Another thing, don't take
  me to the Embassy.

ótrakósà↓ nóme(l)yèbạalạembàhádà↓

Otra cosa, no me lleve a la
Embajada.

4.3   CONVERSATION STIMULUS

NARRATIVE 1

1 Mr. Smith and Mr. White are
  at the Embassy.

èlsèŋyórsmiş|ఫèlsèŋyórhwàyt|
èstánènlạèmbàhàdà↓

El Sr. Smith y el Sr. White están

en la Embajada.

2 Mr. Smith wants him to meet
  Mr. Molina.

èlsèŋyórsmiş|kyérèprèsèntarlę|ál
sèŋyormolínà↓

El Sr. Smith quiere presentarle al

Sr. Molina.

3 Mr. White speaks Spanish
  very well.

èlsèŋyórhwàyt|áblàmúybyén|
espaŋyól↓

El Sr. White habla muy bien

español.

4 He learned it in school.

lọàpréndyó|ęnlạèskwélà↓

Lo aprendió en la escuela.

5 Mr. Molina speaks English a
  little, not much.

èlsèŋyórmólinạ|áblạiŋglés|
úmpókò↓nomúchó↓

El Sr. Molina habla inglés un

poco, no mucho.

DIALOG 1

Sr. Smith, dígale a Juan que Ud. quiere presentarle al Sr. Molina.	hwán↓ kyérópreséntarle̡ │ álse̡ŋyórmòlínà↓	Smith: Juan, quiero presentarle al Sr. Molina.
José, déle su nombre -José Molina- y dígale que mucho gusto.	hòsémolíná↓ múchogústò↓	José: José Molina, mucho gusto.
Juan, dígale que igualmente y déle su nombre -John White. Pregúntele que cómo se dice John en español, que si Juan.	igwalménte̡↓ ɉáŋhwáyt↓ kómose dìṣe │ɉán │ éné̡spà̡ŋyól↓ hwán↑	Juan: Igualmente, John White. ¿Cómo se dice 'John' en español?, ¿Juan?
José, dígale que sí, que Juan y dígale que él habla muy bien el español.	sí↓hwán↓ ústedàbla │múybyén │ él̡éspà̡ŋyól↓	José: Sí, Juan. Usted habla muy bien el español.
Juan, dígale que muchas gracias.	múchazgráṣyàs↓	Juan: Muchas gracias.
José, pregúntele que dónde lo aprendió.	dòndelo̡aprendyó↓	José: Dónde lo aprendió?
Juan, dígale que en la escuela. Pregúntele si él habla inglés.	énla̡èskwélà↓ ɹ̥ustéd̡↓ àbla̡iŋglés↑	Juan: En la escuela. Y usted ¿habla inglés?
José, contéstele que Ud. habla un poco, no más.	áblo̡ùmpokò │nòmás↓	José: Hablo un poco, no más.

NARRATIVE 2

1 John's been here since yesterday.	hwanestakí |dezdęayér↓	Juan está aquí desde ayer.
2 He's going to work in the Consular Section.	batrabahár |ènlàsèkşyoŋkonsulár↓	Va a trabajar en la Sección Consular.
3 The Consular Section is on the main floor.	làsèkşyóŋkònsúlar | èstáęnèlprimerpísó↓	La Sección Consular está en el primer piso.
4 It's to the right of the entrance.	èstáláděrecha |deląentráďà↓	Está a la derecha de la entrada.
5 Most of the time they're very busy in the Consular Section.	kásisyemprę |èstánmuyokupáďòs | ènlàsèkşyóŋkònsúlár↓	Casi siempre están muy ocupados en la Sección Consular.
6 But right now there isn't much doing there.	pérǫàóràmizmo |nǫaymucho mobimyéntǫ |àí↓	Pero ahora mismo no hay mucho movimiento ahí.

DIALOG 2

Spanish prompt	Phonetic	Spanish
José, pregúntele al Sr. White que desde cuando está aquí?	dézdèkwandǫ |estakí |sèŋyórhwáyt↓	José: Desde cuándo está aquí, Sr. White?
Juan, dígale que no le diga 'Sr. White', que le diga 'John' o 'Juan'.	nómeďıga |seŋyorhwáyt↓ dígàmèjàh |óhwàn↓	Juan: No me diga 'Sr. White'. Dígame 'John' o 'Juan'.

José, dígale que está bien, y
  otra vez pregúntele que desde
  cuándo está aquí?

èstàbyén |hwán↓ dézdèkwándǫ |estàkí↓

José: Está bien, Juan. ¿Desde
  cuándo está aquí?

Juan, dígale que desde ayer.

dézdęàyér↓

Juan: Desde ayer.

José, dígale que a Ud. le dijeron que él va a trabajar
  con ustedes.

médihèrǫn |kèbátràbàhár |kò(n)nósótròs↓

José: Me dijeron que va a trabajar
  con nosotros.

Juan, dígale que sí, y pregúntele que dónde está la Sección Consular.

sí↓ dondestá |làsèkęyóŋkònsúlár↓

Juan: Sí. ¿Dónde está la Sección
  Consular?

José, dígale que en el primer piso,
  a la derecha de la entrada.

énęlprimèrpísó↓ àládèrecha

dęlęentrádà↓

José: En el primer piso, a la

  derecha de la entrada.

Juan, pregúntele si hay mucho
  movimiento ahí ahora.

ay |múchomobɪmyéntǫ |aiąórat

Juan: ¿Hay mucho movimiento
  ahí ahora?

José, contéstele que casi siempre
  ustedes están muy ocupados, pero
  que ahora mismo no hay mucho
  movimiento.

kásɪsyémprę |èstámòz |múyokupáđòs↓

pérǫáoramɪzmot nǫaymuchomobɪmyéntó↓

José: Casi siempre estamos muy
  ocupados, pero ahora mismo
  no hay mucho movimiento.

End of Tape 2B

Tape 3A

5.1   BASIC SENTENCES.   White's first day at work.

In their office, John White and José Molina begin to get better acquainted.

ENGLISH SPELLING	AID TO LISTENING	SPANISH SPELLING
to be	sér↓	ser
your (yours)	sú↓ súyȯ↓	su (suyo)
the desk	él—éskritóryȯ↓	el escritorio

Molina
John, this is going to be your desk.

hwán↓ éstebasér |syéskritóryȯ↓

Molina
Juan, éste va a ser su escritorio.

whatever	kwálkyér↓ kwálkyérȧ↓	cualquier (cualquiera)
that (you) may need (to need) [1]	ké—néṣésité↓ néṣésitár↓	que necesite (necesitar)
notify (to notify)	ȧbisé↓ ȧbisár↓	avise (avisar)
notify me	ȧbisémé↓	aviseme

Whatever you need, let me know.

kwálkyérkósa |keneṣesité↑ȧbisémé↓

Cualquier cosa que necesite, avíseme.

| very much (much) | múchisimȯs↓ muchȯ↓ | muchísimos (mucho) |

White
O. K. Thanks a lot.

múybyén↓ múchisimazgráṣyás↓

White
Muy bien. Muchísimas gracias.

the part	lå—pártê↓	la parte

Molina
What part of the States are you from?

dèképarte |dèlòsȩstaɗosˌuníɗòs |ésˌùstéɗ↓

Molina
¿De qué parte de los Estados Unidos es usted?

(I) am (to be)

sóy↓ sér↓

soy (ser)

White
I'm from San Francisco, California.

sóy |ɗèsåmfrànʂiskò |kålîfórnyå↓

White
Soy de San Francisco, California.

Where are you from?

ˌ̩ustéɗeɗóndés↓

Y usted, ¿de dónde es?

Molina
I'm from here.

sóyɗȩakí↓

Molina
Soy de aquí.

(you) came (to come)

binò↓ bènî́r↓

vino (venir)

the family

lå—fåmilyå↓

la familia

Did you come with your family?

binȯustéɗ |kònsûfåmilyaↃ

¿Vino usted con su familia?

bachelor

sôlterò↓

soltero

White
No, I'm a bachelor.

noↃ sóy |sôlterò↓

White
No, soy soltero.

married (to marry)

kåsaɗò↓ kåsár↓

casado (casar)

What about you? Are you married?	¿ùstéȧ↓ éskàsȧȧoↂ	Y usted, ¿es casado?
also, too	tàmbyén↓	también
Molina No, I'm a bachelor, too.	nó↓ sóysòlteró⎮tàmbyén↓	**Molina** No, soy soltero también.
the hour	la̧—orȧ↓	la hora
White What time is it?	kȩoȩrȧés↓	**White** ¿Qué hora es?
the quarter	èl—kwȧrtȯ↓	el cuarto
Molina It's a quarter to twelve.	sónlȧzȧoȩe⎮menoskwártó↓	**Molina** Son las doce menos cuarto.
it is that	és—kè↓	es que
already	yȧ↓	ya
the hunger	èl—ambré↓	el hambre (f)
to be hungry	téner—ambré↓	tener hambre
Are you hungry already?	és⎮kȩyátyenȩambreↂ	¿Es que ya tiene hambre?
enough, quite (a bit)	bástánté↓	bastante
good	bwén↓ bwenȯ↓	buen (bueno)
the restaurant	èl—rrèstóran↓	el restorán

145

White
Yes, quite hungry. Is there a good

restaurant near here?

  the turn

  around the corner

  cheap, inexpensive

Molina
Yes, there's one around the corner

that's good and inexpensive.

  (we) can (to be able)

  to lunch

  together

  (it) seems (to seem)

  to you (it) seems

We can have lunch together.

O. K with you?

  let's go, we go (to go)

White
Sure. Let's go.

146

sí↓ bàstántê↓ áyumbwén

rrestorán|șerkaɖęakí↑

lá—bwéltà↓

à—lá—bwéltà↓

bàratô↓

sí↓ áyúnǫ|àlàbwélta|

kézbwenǫibàrátô↓

pôɖemôs↓ pôɖe'r↓

àlmôrșàr↓

huntôs↓

pàreșê↓ pàreșe'r↓

lê—pàreșê↓

pôɖemos.almorșar|húntôs↓

lêpàreșebyén↑

bámôs↓ ír↓

komonó↓ bamôs↓

White
Sí, bastante. ¿Hay un buen

restorán cerca de aquí?

  la vuelta

  a la vuelta

  barato

Molina
Sí, hay uno a la vuelta

que es bueno y barato.

  podemos (poder)

  almorzar

  juntos

  parece (parecer)

  le parece

Podemos almorzar juntos.

¿Le parece bien?

  vamos (ir)

White
Cómo no. Vamos.

5.10   Notes on the basic sentences

(1) /neꞅesíte/ *necesite* is an example of a verb form which has no exact equivalent in English. Forms of this type are called 'subjunctive.' The particular use of a subjunctive construction illustrated in the present sentence will be drilled in Unit 40. Subjunctive forms will be designated in English by the translation device 'that (you) may...'

5.2   DRILLS AND GRAMMAR

5.21.1   Pattern drills

5.21.1   The irregular verb /sér/

A.   Presentation of pattern

ILLUSTRATIONS

_____	1 nó↓ sóysólteró↓	No, *soy* soltero.
(you) are (to be)	érés↓ sér↓	eres (ser)
And you, are you married?	2 itú↓ éréskàsàdo↑	Y tú, ¿*eres* casado?
- - - - - - - - - -	3 ꞌùstéd↓ éskàsàdo↑	Y usted, ¿*es* casado?
_____	4 minómbreꞌeshosé↓	Mi nombre *es* José.
(we) are (to be)	sómòs↓ sér↓	somos (ser)
No, we're single.	5 nó↓ sómò(s)sólteròs↓	No, *somos* solteros.
(you) (pl.) are (to be)	són↓ sér↓	son (ser)

And are you all married?   6   ¡ústedés↓ sóŋkásaɗos↑   Y ustedes, ¿son casados?

_____   7   són|làzɗoșeménoskwártò↓   Son las doce menos cuarto.

EXTRAPOLATION

		sg	pl
1		sóy	sómos
2	fam	éres	
2-3	for	és	són

NOTES

a. Spanish has two verbs which translate English 'to be':
/estár/, presented in Unit 4, and /sér/, presented
in this unit.

148

5.21.11   Substitution drills

Number substitution

1 sóyàmèrikanò↓   sómòs̩àmérikanòs↓

2 sóŋkàsaɗós↓   éskàsaɗò↓

3 sómò(s)sòlteròs↓   sóysòlteró↓

4 sóndęàkı̇́↓   ézɗę̀àkı̇́↓

5 ézɗèkàlifornyà↓   sóndèkàlifornyà↓

6 sóyɗę̀àkı̇́↓   sómòzɗę̀àkı̇́↓

7 és̩àmèrikanò↓   sónàmèrikanòs↓

---

1 Soy americano.   Somos americanos.

2 Son casados.   Es casado.

3 Somos solteros.   Soy soltero.

4 Son de aquí.   Es de aquí.

5 Es de California.   Son de California.

6 Soy de aquí.   Somos de aquí.

7 Es americano.   Son americanos.

Person - number substitution

1 ántonyoezdechíle↓

   yo＿＿＿＿＿＿＿↓　　　　　　　　　　　　　　　　　　soydechíle↓

   pablo＿＿＿＿＿↓　　　　　　　　　　　　　　　　　　ezdechíle↓

   ántonyo|álisya＿＿＿＿↓　　　　　　　　　　　　　sondechíle↓

   ùsted＿＿＿＿＿↓　　　　　　　　　　　　　　　　　　ezdechíle↓

2 nòsotro(s)somos|àmérikános↓

   álisya＿＿＿＿＿＿＿↓　　　　　　　　　　　　　　esamerikáná↓

   ùstedes＿＿＿＿＿＿↓　　　　　　　　　　　　　　sonamerikános↓

---

1 *Antonio* es de Chile.

   Yo＿＿＿＿＿＿.　　　　　　　　　　　　　　　　Soy de Chile.

   Pablo＿＿＿＿＿.　　　　　　　　　　　　　　　Es de Chile.

   Antonio y Alicia＿＿.　　　　　　　　　　　Son de Chile.

   Usted＿＿＿＿＿.　　　　　　　　　　　　　　Es de Chile.

2 *Nosotros* somos americanos.

   Alicia＿＿＿＿＿＿＿.　　　　　　　　　　　Es americana.

   Ustedes＿＿＿＿＿＿＿.　　　　　　　　　　Son americanos.

```
yó_____↓                    sóyamerikánò↓
éλyos_____↓                    son̬amerikánòs↓


3  ȧlịsyae(s)soltéra↓              sómo(s)soltérós↓
   pabloịyo_____↓               sonsoltérós↓
   elịantónyo_____↓               é(s)soltéra↓
   éλya_____↓                sóysoltéró↓
   yó_____↓
```

Yo _____ .	Soy americano.
Ellos_____ .	Son americanos.
3 *Alicia* es soltera.	
Pablo y yo _____ .	Somos solteros.
El y Antonio _____ .	Son solteros.
Ella _____ .	Es soltera.
Yo_____ .	Soy soltero.

5.21.12   Response drill

1 álısyąe(s) soltérątokasádá↓   é(s)sóltérá↓

2 esustédámerikanotoespanyól↓   sóyámerikanó↓

3 són,ɛ(l)yózdechiletodelos,estados.   són |delós,estádósúnidós↓
    unídós↓

[lós,estádósúnidós]   4 dédondesonustédés↓   somoz |delós,estádósúnidós↓

[sámfránşiskó]   5 dédondesustéd↓   sóydesámfránşiskó↓

[láuná]   6 keorąés↓   ezláuná↓

[kálifórnyá]   7 dékepartes,ɛ(l)yá↓   ézdekálifórnyá↓

---

1 ¿Alicia es soltera o casada?   Es soltera.

2 ¿Es usted americano o español?   Soy americano.

3 ¿Son ellos de Chile o de los   Son de los Estados Unidos.
    Estados Unidos?

(los Estados Unidos)   4 ¿De dónde son ustedes?   Somos de los Estados Unidos.

(San Francisco)   5 ¿De dónde es usted?   Soy de San Francisco.

(la una)   6 ¿Qué hora es?   Es la una.

(California)   7 ¿De que parte es ella?   Es de California.

[lòs,èstádòs,únidòs]   8 ésèldechílet   no↓ ézdèlòs,èstádòs,únidòs↓

[làzdòşè]   9 sónlàzdòşe|ménoskwártot   no↓ sónlàzdòşè↓

[kàsadó]   10 és,ùstedsolterot   no↓ sóykàsadó↓

[àmèrikanòs]   11 són,ùstedes|espaŋyólest no↓ sómòs,àmèrikanós↓

                         12 és,ùstedkasadot   sí↓ sóykàsadó↓

                         13 sóne()yos,amèrikànost   sí↓ sónàmèrikanòs↓

(los Estados Unidos)   8 ¿Es él de Chile?   No, es de los Estados Unidos.

        (las 12)   9 ¿Son las doce menos cuarto?   No, son las doce.

        (casado)   10 ¿Es usted soltero?   No, soy casado.

    (americanos)   11 ¿Son ustedes españoles?   No, somos americanos.

                      12 ¿Es usted casado?   Sí, soy casado.

                      13 ¿Son ellos americanos ?   Sí, son americanos.

5.21.13   Translation drill

1 We're from San Francisco.	sómoz │dèsámfrànṣiskò↓	Somos de San Francisco.
2 She's married, too.	ê()yaéskàsadà │tàmbyén↓	Ella es casada también.
3 The hotels are excellent.	lòṣótéles │soneks(ṣ)eléntès↓	Los hoteles son excelentes.
4 Where's the lady from?	dèképarté │ezlaseņyórà↓	¿De qué parte es la señora?
5 Where're you from?	dèdondesustéd↓	¿De dónde es usted?
6 My name is Pancho.	minombrespánchò↓	Mi nombre es Pancho.
7 I'm (an) American.	sóyamerikánò↓	Soy americano.
8 How much is the tip?	kwantoezlapropínà↓	¿Cuánto es la propina?
9 They're from the Consular Section.	ê()yos │sóndèlàsèkṣyoŋkonsulár↓	Ellos son de la sección consular.
10 When is the trip?	kwandoeṣelbyáhè↓	¿Cuándo es el viaje?
11 The pleasure is mine.	èlgustoezmíó↓	El gusto es mío.
12 We're married, too.	sómòskàsadòs │tàmbyén↓	Somos casados también.
13 The restaurants are not expensive.	lózrrèstóranes │sombarátòs↓	Los restoranes son baratos.

B. Discussion of pattern

The verb /sér/ is highly irregular in the present tense, as will be seen by comparing it to regular verb patterns presented in Unit 7.

Both /estár/ and /sér/ translate the English verb 'be'. They are not, however, equivalent. Rather they divide an area of meaning which is included in the content of a single English concept, named by the verb 'be'. Therefore a confusion between the two cannot be thought of as a relatively minor mistake simply because they express aspects of what is considered 'the same thing' in English; in Spanish /sér/ and /estár/ are as genuinely different as any other two verbs, and the use of one when the other is expected is painfully obvious.

The difference between /sér/ and /estár/ can perhaps best be generalized by other English concepts: /sér/ is the link of *identity*, (the essential, inherent or permanent), /estár/ the link of *association*, (the casual, accidental or temporary). This generalization is more useful descriptively in some cases than in others. Thus when a noun follows the linking verb to express complete identity, /sér/ is always selected·

/hwán |ésmɪermáno↓/   John is my brother.

When an adjective follows the linking verb, one has to decide whether the link of identity or the link of association is appropriate. The choice may often seem quite arbitrary to Americans, but when identity is involved (/sér/), there seems to be a more inherent connection between the noun and the quality; when association is involved (/estár/), the connection is more or less incidental.

Thus even though /sér/ and /estár/ appear in utterances which show no other difference, the two utterances will never have the same 'meaning'. If a person describes a house with an adjective like pretty, saying 'The house is pretty', he cannot, in Spanish, express only this much of the idea. He must also say either that the house is intrinsically pretty,

/lakásą |esboníta↓/

or that it presents an unusually attractive appearance on a specific occasion (looks pretty),

/lakásą |estáboníta↓/

There is no way to make the incomplete statement (from the Spanish point of view) that the house 'is' pretty; additional refinements in meaning are obligatory in the choice of /sér/ or /estár/ . Through this choice the Spanish speaker indicates the circumstances he considers *identity* and distinguishes them from those he considers *association*.

The distinction is, to be sure, forced by the structure of the language (the divided linking verb), but it is no less real to the speaker of Spanish, who never hesitates to select the correct form. It is only the American, whose background lacks the experience of making a meaning distinction, nonsignificant in English but highly significant in Spanish, who experiences a confusion between the two forms. In a very real sense, using /sér/ and /estár/ correctly involves an entire way of life, and an American seeking proficiency in spoken Spanish needs to acquire a 'feel' for the distinction by making a large number of sentences his own through memorization in meaningful contexts.

When a verb modifier appears with the linking verb, association is generally selected (/estár/), though not exclusively. Notice the following contrasts, most of which are illustrated in basic sentences:

/estár/	association	/sér/	identity
/kómọestámaría↓/	How's Mary?	/kómọésmaría↓/	What's Mary like?
/dóndestásyespós6↓/	Where's your husband?	/dedóndé(s)syespóso↓/	Where's your husband from?
/dóndestálafyésta↓/	Where's the party?	/dóndéslafyésta↓/	Where's the party being held?

Other classifications and examples can be found in the appendix.

5.22   Replacement drills

A   dèképárte|dèlòs,èstádòs,únidòs|ès,ùstéd↓

1 _____ éⁿyòs↓   dèképárte|dèlòs,èstádòs,únidòs|sónéⁿyòs↓

2 _____ès ____↓   dèképárte|dèlòs,èstádòs,únidòs|ès,él↓

3 _____kálifornya_____↓   dèképárte|dèkàlifornya|ès,él↓

4 _____là(s)sèŋyóràs↓   dèképárte|dèkàlifornyà|sónlà(s)sèŋyóràs↓

5 _dónde_____↓   dèdondesón|là(s)sèŋyóràs↓

6 _____ùstéd↓   dèdondè|ès,ùstéd↓

7 _____sómòz____↓   dèdondè|sómòznòsótròs↓

A   ¿De qué parte de los Estados Unidos es usted?

1 ¿ _____ ellos?   ¿De qué parte de los Estados Unidos son ellos?

2 ¿ _____es ____?   ¿De qué parte de los Estados Unidos es él?

3 ¿ _____California _____?   ¿De qué parte de California es él?

4 ¿ _____las señoras?   ¿De qué parte de California son las señoras?

5 ¿ _dónde_____?   ¿De dónde son las señoras?

6 ¿ _____usted?   ¿De dónde es usted?

7 ¿ _____somos ____?   ¿De dónde somos nosotros?

B bíno|kónsufamílya↑   bíno|kónmifamílya↑

1 _____mi_____↑   baha|konmifamílya↑

2 baha_____↑   baha|konlafamílya↑

3 _____la_____↑   baha|konlasfamílyas↑

4 _____famílyas↑   baha|konelsenyor↑

5 _____senyor↑   baha|konelsenyor↑

6 trábaha_____↑   trábaha|konelsenyor↑

7 _____los____↑   trábaha|konlo(s)senyores↑

B   ¿Vino con su familia?

1 ¿ _____ mi_____?   ¿Vino con mi familia?

2 ¿Baja_____?   ¿Baja con mi familia?

3 ¿ _____ la_____?   ¿Baja con la familia?

4 ¿ _____ familias?   ¿Baja con las familias?

5 ¿ _____ señor__?   ¿Baja con el señor?

6 ¿Trabaja_____?   ¿Trabaja con el señor?

7 ¿ _____ los_____?   ¿Trabaja con los señores?

C noↆ sóysòlteròↆ

1 ____sómòs____↓   noↆ sómò(s)sòlteròsↆ

2 _____ṣiŋkòↆ   noↆ sómòs(ṣ)iŋkòↆ

3 ____són____↓   nòↆ sónṣiŋkòↆ

4 _____bwenàsↆ   noↆ sómbwenàsↆ

5 _____màsↆ   noↆ sónmàsↆ

6 ____áy____↓   noↆ áymàsↆ

7 ____kyérò__↓   noↆ kyéròmàsↆ

C No, soy soltero.

1 ___ somos ____.   No, somos solteros.

2 _____ cinco.   No, somos cinco.

3 ___ son _____.   No, son cinco.

4 _____ buenas.   No, son buenas.

5 _____ más.   No, son más.

6 ___ hay _____.   No, hay más.

7 ___ quiero_____   No, quiero más.

D   ¿ùstéd↓ éskàsàďo↑

1 _____sóŋ_____↑   ¿ùstéďès↓sóŋkàsàďos↑

2 _____sòltéros↑   ¿ùstéďès↓sónsóltéros↑

3 _éꝇyạ_____↑   ¿éꝇyạ↓é(s)sòltèrạ↑

4 _____sóy_____↑   iyó↓ sóysòltéro↑

5 _____sòltéras↑   ¿éꝇyás↓sónsóltéras↑

6 _nósótròs_____↑   inósótròs↓sómò(s)sòltéros↑

7 _____àmérikànos↑   inósótròs↓sómòs àmérikànos↑

D   Y usted, ¿es casado?

1 _____ ¿son____?   Y ustedes, ¿son casados?

2 _____ ¿__solteros?   Y ustedes, ¿son solteros?

3 _ella, ¿_____?   Y ella, ¿es soltera?

4 _____ ¿soy_____?   Y yo, ¿soy soltero?

5 _____ ¿__solteras?   Y ellas, ¿son solteras?

6 _nosotros¿_____?   Y nosotros, ¿somos solteros?

7 _____ ¿__americanos?   Y nosotros, ¿somos americanos?

E   ay |únrrestòrán |şerkaḑęakí↑

1   ____òtél_____↑   ay |únọótel |şerkaḑęakí↑

2   __múchos_____↑   ay |múchosọóteles |(ş)érkaḑęakí↑

3   _____abeníḑas_____↑   ay |múchas,abeníḑas |(ş)érkaḑęakí↑

4   _____aí↑   ay |múchas,abeníḑas |(ş)érkaḑęaí↑

5   ___bástantes_____↑   ay |bástantes,abeníḑas |(ş)érkaḑęaí↑

6   _____taksıs____↑   ay |bástantestaksıs |(ş)érkaḑęaí↑

7   _____lạembahaḑa↑   ay |bástantestaksıs |(ş)érkaḑelạembahaḑa↑

E   ¿Hay un restorán cerca de aquí?

1 ¿ ____hotel_____ ?   ¿Hay un hotel cerca de aquí?

2 ¿ __ muchos_____ ?   ¿Hay muchos hoteles cerca de aquí?

3 ¿ _____ avenidas_____ ?   ¿Hay muchas avenidas cerca de aquí?

4 ¿ _____ahí?   ¿Hay muchas avenidas cerca de ahí?

5 ¿ ___bastantes _____ ?   ¿Hay bastantes avenidas cerca de ahí?

6 ¿ _____ taxis_____ ?   ¿Hay bastantes taxis cerca de ahí?

7 ¿ _____ la Embajada?   ¿Hay bastantes taxis cerca de la Embajada?

F póḍemos|ȧlmȯrȿȧr|húntȯs↓

1 _____ȯtrȧbéȿ↓   póḍemos|ȧlmȯrȿȧr|ȯtrȧbéȿ↓

2 kyérǫ_____↓   kyérǫ|ȧlmȯrȿȧr|ȯtrȧbéȿ↓

3 _____ir_____↓   kyérǫir|ȯtrȧbéȿ↓

4 _____ȧí↓   kyérǫirȧí↓

5 pweḍę_____↓   pweḍęirȧí↓

6 _____tambyén↓   pweḍęir|tambyén↓

7 nęȿęsitǫ_____↓   nęȿęsitǫir|tambyén↓

F Podemos almorzar juntos.

1 _____ otra vez.   Podemos almorzar otra vez.

2 Quiero_____.   Quiero almorzar otra vez.

3 _____ir_____.   Quiero ir otra vez.

4 _____ahí.   Quiero ir ahí.

5 Puede_____.   Puede ir ahí.

6 _____ también.   Puede ir también.

7 Necesita_____.   Necesita ir también.

5.23   Variation drills

A   ¿ùstéd↓ dèdòndés↓   Y usted, ¿de dónde es?

    1 And where's the gentleman   ¿èlsèɳyór↓ dèdòndés↓   Y el señor, ¿de dónde es?
       from?

    2 And where's Mrs. Molina   ìlàsèɳyoramolínà↓ dèdòndés↓   Y la señora Molina, ¿ de dónde es?
       from?

    3 And where's the taxi   ¿èlchóférdètaksi↓ dèdòndés↓   Y el chofer de taxi, ¿de dónde es?
       driver from?

    4 And where's the waiter from?   ¿èlmoşó↓ dèdòndés↓   Y el mozo, ¿de dónde es?

    5 And where's the cashier from?   ¿èlkàheró↓ dèdòndés↓   Y el cajero, ¿de dónde es?

    6 And where're John and Joseph   ìhwànìhosé↓ dèdòndesón↓   Y Juan y José, ¿de dónde son?
       from?

    7 And where're the Molinas from?   ìlózmòlínà↓ dèdòndesón↓   Y los Molina, ¿de dónde son?

B sóyđèsàmfránṣiskò|kàlifórnyàↆ

Soy de San Francisco, California.

1 I'm from the United States.   sóy|đèlòsèstáđòsùnıđòsↆ

Soy de los Estados Unidos.

2 I'm from Florida.   sóyđèflórıđàↆ

Soy de Florida.

3 I'm from here.   sóyđẹàkıↆ

Soy de aquí.

4 I'm a bachelor.   sóysóltéróↆ

Soy soltero.

5 I'm a taxi driver.   sóychòférđétaksiↆ

Soy chofer de taxi.

6 We're married.   sómòskàsađòsↆ

Somos casados.

7 We're single.   sómò(s)sòlteròsↆ

Somos solteros.

C kẹórạẹ́sↆ

¿Qué hora es?

1 What day is it?   kéđıạẹ́sↆ

¿Qué día es?

2 What language is it?   kéleŋgwạẹ́sↆ

¿Qué lengua es?

3 What hotel is it?   kẹotélés↓   ¿Qué hotel es ?

4 What school is it?   kẹskwelạés↓   ¿Qué escuela es?

5 What tables are they?   kemésa(s)són↓   ¿Qué mesas son ?

6 What books are they?   kélibro(s)són↓   ¿Qué libros son?

7 What (kind of a) thing is it?   kekosạés↓   ¿Qué cosa es ?

D   són│lázdoṣemenoskwárto↓   Son las doce menos cuarto.

1 It's fifteen to twelve.   són│làzdoṣemenoskínṣè↓   Son las doce menos quince.

2 It's ten to eleven.   són│làṣonṣemenozdyéṣ↓   Son las once menos diez.

3 It's twenty to seven.   ·són│là(s)syetemenozbéynté↓   Son las siete menos veinte.

4 It's five to nine.   són│làznwebemeno(s)ṣíŋkò↓   Son las nueve menos cinco.

5 It's a quarter to eight.   són│làṣochomenoskwárto↓   Son las ocho menos cuarto.

165

6 It's six.   són│là(s) séys↓   Son las seis.

7 It's one.   éz│launà↓   Es la una.

E   yatyeneambre↑   ¿Ya tiene hambre?

1 Have you got the dollars already?   yatyene│lozdolares↑   ¿Ya tiene los dólares?

2 Have you got the check already?   yatyene│elcheke↑   ¿Ya tiene el cheque?

3 Has she got a room already?   yatyene│unkwarto↑   ¿Ya tiene un cuarto?

4 Has she got a table already?   yatyene│unamesa↑   ¿Ya tiene una mesa?

5 Has he got twenty dollars already?   yatyene│beyntedolares↑   ¿Ya tiene veinte dólares?

6 Does he have a hotel?   tyeneunotel↑   ¿Tiene un hotel?

7 Does he have a taxi?   tyeneuntaksi↑   ¿Tiene un taxi?

F   síↆ áyunǫ│àlàƀwéltą│kὲzƀwénǫibarátôↆ   Sí, hay uno a la vuelta que es bueno
                                                            y barato.

1 Yes, there's one here that's   síↆ áyunǫ│àkì│kὲzmúybwénôↆ   Sí, hay uno aquí que es muy bueno.
  very good.

2 Yes, there's one here that's   síↆ áyunǫ│àkì│kὲsὲks(ş)èlénteↆ   Sí, hay uno aquí que es excelente.
  excellent.

3 Yes, there's one there, but it   síↆ áyunǫ│aì│pérókwestamuchôↆ   Sí, hay uno ahí, pero cuesta mucho.
  costs a lot.

4 Yes, there's one at the Embassy   síↆ áyunǫ│ènląὲmbàhàđa│pérǫ   Sí, hay uno en la Embajada pero
  but it's busy.   èstaǫkupáđôↆ   está ocupado.

5 Yes, there's one on the first   síↆ áyunǫ│ènèlprimérpiso│   Sí, hay uno en el primer piso
  floor who is an American.   kὲsàmὲrikanôↆ   que es americano.

6 No, there's not another one to   nóↆ nǫayótrǫ│àląişkyérđàↆ   No, no hay otro a la izquierda.
  the left.

7 No, there's not another school   nóↆ nǫayótrą│èskwélàđèléŋgwàsↆ   No, no hay otra escuela de lenguas.
  of languages.

5.3   CONVERSATION STIMULUS

NARRATIVE 1

1 It's almost twelve o'clock.	sóŋkasilazdóşė↓	Son casi las doce.
2 Jose is going to have lunch with John.	hóse|bálmorşar|koŋhwán↓	José va a almorzar con Juan.
3 John isn't very hungry.	hwán|nótyéne|muchámbrė↓	Juan no tiene mucha hambre.
4 There's a good restaurant around the corner.	áyúmbwénrrestorán|alabwélta̧↓	Hay un buen restorán a la vuelta.
5 The restaurant is quite inexpensive.	ėlrrėstorán|ėzbàstántebarátò↓	El restorán es bastante barato.

DIALOG 1

| José, pregúntele a Juan si no va a almorzar. | nóbalmorşar\|hwán↑ | José: ¿No va a almorzar, Juan? |
| Juan, contéstele que Ud. no tiene mucha hambre y pregúntele que qué hora es. | nótéŋgomuchámbrė↓ kę̇orą̇és↓ | Juan: No tengo mucha hambre. ¿Qué hora es? |

José, dígale que son casi las doce, y pregúntele si pueden almorzar juntos.	sóŋkásilazdóşè↓ pódemos almorşar |huntos↑	José: Son casi las doce. ¿Podemos almorzar juntos?
Juan, contéstele que muy bien, que vayan, y pregúntele que adónde pueden ir.	múybyém↓bamòs↓ ádónde podemosír↓	Juan: Muy bien, vamos. ¿A dónde podemos ir?
José, dígale que a la vuelta, que hay un buen restorán ahí.	àlàbweltà↓ áy |ùm bwenrrestorán|àí↓	José: A la vuelta. Hay un buen restorán ahí.
Juan, preguntele si es barato.	ezbárató↑	Juan: ¿Es barato?
José, dígale que sí, que es bastante barato.	sí↓ ézbàstántebaráto↓	José: Sí, es bastante barato.

NARRATIVE 2

1 Carmen del Valle is in the restaurant.	kármendelbaȰyẹ |éstaẹnẹlrrestorán↓	Carmen del Valle está en el restorán.
2 John wants to meet her.	hwaŋkyérekonoşérlà↓	Juan quiere conocerla.
3 She is at a table on the left.	eȰyạestá |ẹnùnàmesalạişkyérdà↓	Ella está en una mesa a la izquierda.
4 Carmen speaks English very well.	kármen |áblạiŋglez |múybyén↓	Carmen habla inglés muy bien.

5 She learned it in school, in   lọáprẻndyó|ẹnlạẻskweláↆ   Lo aprendió en la escuela,
   the States.
                                        ẻnlỏs̩ẻstạd̦os̩uníd̦osↆ   en los Estados Unidos.

                                        DIALOG 2

José, dígale a Juan que ahí está   áiẹsta|kármendelbáↄyẻↆ   José: Ahí está Carmen del Valle.
Carmen del Valle. Pregúntele
si quiere conocerla.   kyerekonos̩erlaↇ   ¿Quiere conocerla?

Juan, contéstele que sí, que cómo   síↆ kómỏnóↆ dondestáↆ   Juan: Sí, cómo no. ¿Dónde está?
no. Pregúntele que dónde está.

José, dígale que está ahí a la   ẻstáiↆ̩álạiṣkyerdáↆ   José: Está ahí, a la izquierda.
izquierda.

Juan, pregúntele a José si Carmen   ảblạiŋgléskármenↇ   Juan: ¿Habla inglés Carmen?
habla inglés.

José, contéstele que sí, que lo habla   síↆ lọáblảmuybyénↆ lọáprẻndyó| José: Sí, lo habla muy bien. Lo
muy bien, que lo aprendió en los
Estados Unidos en la escuela.   ẹnlỏs̩ẻstạd̦os̩uníd̦os|ẹnlạẻskweláↆ   aprendió en los Estados
                                                                              Unidos en la escuela.

NARRATIVE 3

1 John is delighted to meet Carmen.	hwan │ ėstáęŋkàntaďo │ďėkŏnóşéra kármęn↓	Juan está encantado de conocer a Carmen.
2 He talks with her in English and then in Spanish.	ábla │konéỹ̧ąeniŋglés↑ilwégǫ enępspaŋyól↓	Habla con ella en inglés y luego en español.
3 He says that he is from California.	éldişe │kézďėkàlifórnyà↓	El dice que es de California.
4 No, he isn't from San Francisco, he's from San Diego.	no↓ élnǫezďesamfranşískò↓ ézďėsándyeǫò↓	No, él no es de San Francisco, es de San Diego.
5 He arrived yesterday.	binǫayér↓	Vino ayer.
6 He didn't come with his family.	nóbinokónlafamílyà↓	No vino con la familia.
7 He's single.	é(s)sólterò↓	Es soltero.

DIALOG 3

José, dígale hola a Carmen y   olà |kármèn↓ ketál↓   José: Hola, Carmen, ¿qué tal?
pregúntele que qué tal.

Carmen, dígale hola también y   olà |hósé↓ ketál↓ komolebá↓   Carmen: Hola, José ¿qué tal?
pregúntele que qué tal, que   ¿Cómo le va?
cómo le va.

José, contéstele que bastante bien,   bàstantebyéŋ |grásyàs↓   José: Bastante bien, gracias
que gracias, y dígale que quiere   karmèn↓ kyeropresentarlè| Carmen, quiero presentarle
presentarle al Sr. White, Juan White. alseŋyorhwáyt↓ hwaŋhwáyt↓   al Sr. White, Juan White.

Carmen, dígale a Juan que mucho   muchoqustŏ |seŋyór↓   Carmen: Mucho gusto, señor.
gusto.

Juan, dígale a la señorita que   èŋkàntadodekonoşerlà |sèŋyòrítá↓ Juan: Encantado de conocerla,
encantado de conocerla.   señorita.

José, pregúntele a Carmen si   pòdemos |àlmòrşar |kònústed |kármen↑ José: ¿Podemos almorzar con
pueden almorzar con ella.   usted, Carmen?

Carmen, contéstele que sí, cómo no,   si↓ kómóno↓ èŋkàntadá↓ syéntènsé↓ Carmen: Sí, cómo no, encantada.
que encantada. Dígales a los dos   Siéntense.
que se sienten.

Jose, dígale a Carmen que Juan es   hwanezdekalifórnyà |kármèn↓   José: Juan es de California,
de California.   Carmen.

Carmen, dígale que dispense, que cómo dice.

dispensé↓ kómoɑiṣe↑

Carmen: Dispense, ¿cómo dice?

José, repítale que Juan es de California.

kèhwanezɑekalifórnyà↓

José: Que Juan es de California.

Carmen, diga ¿ah, sí? y pregúntele a Juan que de qué parte, si de San Francisco.

á|sí↑ dèképártè↓ dèsàmfrànṣisko↑

Carmen: ¿Ah, sí? ¿De qué parte? ¿De San Francisco?

Juan, contéstele que no, que Ud. es de San Diego.

nó↓ sóyɑèsàndyègò↓

Juan: No, soy de San Diego.

Carmen, pregúntele que cuándo vino.

kwándobínò↓

Carmen: ¿Cuándo vino?

Juan, contéstele que ayer.

àyér↓

Juan: Ayer.

Carmen, pregúntele si vino con la familia.

bíno|konlafamílya↑

Carmen: ¿Vino con la familia?

Juan, contéstele que no, que Ud. no tiene familia, que es soltero.

nó↓ yonotengofamílyà↓ sóysòlterò↓

Juan: No, yo no tengo familia, soy soltero.

End of Tape 3A

6.1   BASIC SENTENCES.   White and Molina have lunch together.

John White and Jose Molina enter the restaurant.

ENGLISH SPELLING	AID TO LISTENING	SPANISH SPELLING
there (in that place)	àⱴyi↓	allí
empty (to vacate, empty)	dèsòkúpàd̶ò↓ dèsòkúpár↓	desocupado (desocupar)
Jose Molina		*José Molina*
There's an empty table over there.	àⱴyiay |únàmésà |dèsòkúpád̶à↓	Allí hay una mesa desocupada.
to seat	sèntár↓	sentar
ourselves	nòs↓	nos
to seat ourselves (to seat oneself, to sit down)	sèntárnòs↓ sèntársè↓	sentarnos (sentarse)
John White		*John White*
Let's sit down.	bamos.asentárnòs↓	Vamos a sentarnos.
let's see (to see)	béamòs↓ bér↓	veamos (ver)
the menu	èl—ménú↓	el menú
Jose Molina		*José Molina*
Let's see the menu.	béamos.elmenú↓	Veamos el menú.
(you) wish (to wish)	dèseán↓ dèseár↓	desean (desear)

Waiter
What will you have, gentlemen?

kedesean̯ustédės |sèn̟yórės↓

the sandwich

èl—san̟wich↓

the ham

èl—hámon̟↓

John White
I want a ham sandwich.

ỵokyerọunsan̟wich |dehamón↓

the salad

lạ—énsáladạ↓

the lettuce

lá—léchuɡạ↓

the tomato

èl—tòmaté↓

Also a lettuce and tomato salad.

tàmbyén |énsáladạ |dèléchuɡạitomáté↓

the beer

lá—ṣérbeṣạ↓

And a beer.

ịunaṣerbéṣạ↓

to me

à—mí↓

bring (to bring)

tráyɡạ↓ trạér↓

bring me

tráyɡàmė↓

Mesero
¿Qué desean ustedes, señores?

el sandwich

el jamón

John White
Yo quiero un sandwich de jamón.

la ensalada

la lechuga

el tomate

También ensalada de lechuga y tomate.

la cerveza

Y una cerveza.

a mí

traiga (traer)

tráigame

the soup	là—sopà↓	la sopa
the vegetable	là—léǥumbrè↓	la legumbre
the chop	là—chùletà↓	la chuleta
the pork, pig	èl—ṣerǿò↓	el cerdo
the wine	èl—bìnò↓	el vino

Jose Molina
Bring *me* vegetable soup, pork chops and wine. (1)

àmɪ|trayǥamesópa|ɗeleǥúmbrès↑
chùlétàzɗèṣerɗọibínò↓

José Molina
A mí tráigame sopa de legumbres, chuletas de cerdo y vino.

the dessert	èl—postrè↓	el postre
of (for) dessert	dè—postrè↓	de postre
(you) want (to want)	kyerén↓ kéré⁀r↓	quieren (querer)

Waiter
What'll you have for dessert?

dèpostre|kekyérèn↓

Mesero
De postre, ¿qué quieren?

the pie	èl—pàstél↓	el pastel
the apple	là—mànṣanà↓	la manzana

There's some apple pie, that's very good.

áy|úmpàstéldémánṣana|kézmuybwénò↓

Hay un pastel de manzana que es muy bueno.

(we) try (to try, to taste)	pròbamòs↓ pròbá⁀r↓	probamos (probar)

John White
Shall we try it?

lòpròbamòs↑

John White
¿Lo probamos?

176

(I) have (to have)	é↓ ḁ̇ḙ́r↓	he (haber)
eaten (to eat)	kȯ̇mi̇d̊ó↓ kȯ̇me̊r↓	comido (comer)
(I) have eaten [2]	ė̇—kȯ̇mi̇d̊ó↓	he comido

Jose Molina
I've already had it. It's excellent.

yo̊yålo̊ekȯ̇mi̇d̊ó↓ e̊zbwé̊nó↓

José Molina
Yo ya lo he comido. Es bueno.

for	pårá↓	para
Bring us both some.	tråygåpårålozd̊ós↓	Traiga para los dos.
if	si̊↓	si
to treat	tråtår↓	tratar
ourselves (we) treat of you (to address as)	nós—tråtåmoz—d̊e—tú↓ tråtårse̊—d̊é↓	nos tratamos de tú (tratarse de)

What do you say if we just use 'tú'? [3]

ke̊le̊påre̊şe̊ |si̊no̊stråtåmoz |d̊e̊tú↓

¿Qué le parece si nos tratamos de tú?

(you) have (to have)	tye̊né̊s↓ te̊né̊r↓	tienes (tener)
the reason	lå—rråşó̊n↓	la razón

John White
You're right. Good idea.

tye̊ne̊zrråşón↓ mu̇ybyé̊n↓

John White
Tienes razón. Muy bien.

(you) go (to go)	bås↓ i̊r↓	vas (ir)

177

to live	bìbír↓	vivir
Jose Molina		**José Molina**
Are you going to live at the hotel?	basabíbir∣enelotél↑	¿Vas a vivir en el hotel?
(I) think (to think)	pyensó↓ pènsár↓	pienso (pensar)
to look for (4)	búskár↓	buscar
the apartment	èl—ápártámentó↓	el apartamento
John White		**John White**
No, I plan to look for an apartment.	nó↓ pyensó∣búskárúnápártámentó↓	No, pienso buscar un apartamento.
easy	fași̇l↓	fácil
to find	éŋkòntrár↓	encontrar
Is it easy to find one here?	esfași̇l∣déŋkòntrárákí↑	¿Es fácil de encontrar aquí?
(I) believe (to believe)	kreó↓ kr̥ée̥r↓	creo (creer)
Jose Molina		**José Molina**
I think so.	yokréo∣késí↓	Yo creo que sí.
(you fam.) want (to want)	kyerès↓ kèré̥r↓	quieres (querer)
you, to you (fam)	té↓	te
(I) can (to be able)	pwedó↓ pòdé̥r↓	puedo (poder)
to help	àyúdár↓	ayudar
If you want, I can help you.	sikyeres↑yo∣tèpwédòȧyúdár↓	Si quieres, yo te puedo ayudar.
the check, the bill	là—kwentá↓	la cuenta
Waiter! the check.	moșó↓ làkwentá↓	¡Mozo! La cuenta.

178

6.10   Notes on the basic sentences

(1) The Spanish equivalent of 'bring *me*' in this sentence is [amí|tráyɡame] *a mí tráigame* 'to me bring me'. The reason why *a mí* is present is to indicate contrast with what the other person is having. This is shown in English by extra stress on the word *me*, but in Spanish one cannot make the contrast by placing stress on the *me* of [tráyɡame].

(2) Note that there are two verbs meaning 'have' in Spanish. You have already had *tener*, which means 'have' in the sense of 'possess'. This new verb, *haber*, means 'have' the auxiliary verb form in verb constructions like 'have gone, have been,' etc. Constructions with *haber* will be drilled and explained in detail in Unit 9.

(3) This is the first occurrence in the dialogs of the use of the verb and pronoun forms that are ordinarily called the *familiar forms*. They are in contrast with the *formal forms* that go with the pronouns *usted* and *ustedes*. As explained in Unit 4, the problem of when to use *tú* and when to use *usted* is a very complex one indeed, and you should observe throughout all the remainder of the text which people use the *tú* forms with each other and which ones use *usted*.

(4) Notice that the single word [buskár] *buscar* means 'to look for', not just 'to look' — that is, no preposition is needed to translate the 'for' part of 'look for'.

6.2   DRILLS AND GRAMMAR

6.21   Pattern drills

6.21.1 Present tense forms of regular /—ár/ verbs

A.   Presentation of pattern

ILLUSTRATIONS

————————————	1 sí↓ ábloumpókó↓	Sí, *hablo* un poco.
I ('ll) help you.	2 yoteayúdó↓	Yo te *ayudo*.
Do you speak English?	3 ablas.inglés↑	¿*Hablas* inglés?
Are you looking for an apartment?	4 buskas |un.apartamento↑	¿*Buscas* un apartamento?

179

─────────	5	ábląustéđinglést	¿Habla usted inglés?
─────────	6	nèşésítálgomást	¿Necesita algo más?
John works with us.	7	hwantrabáha|kò(n̥)nòsotròs↓	Juan trabaja con nosotros.
─────────	8	nóstrátámozđetut↑	¿Nos tratamos de 'tú'?
Yes, we speak a little.	9	sí↓ ábląmos͜umpókò↓	Sí, hablamos un poco.
─────────	10	keđéséanustedés|sènyórès↓	¿Qué desean ustedes, señores?
The gentlemen take a taxi.	11	lò(s)sènyores|tómanuntáksi↓	Los señores toman un taxi.
The ladies practice a lot.	12	là(s)sènyoras|pràktíkanmúchò↓	Las señoras practican mucho.

EXTRAPOLATION

	sg	pl
1	─o	─ámos
2 fam	─as	
2_3	─a	─an

NOTES

a. Spanish regular verbs can be grouped into *theme classes*. Which set of endings a verb takes depends on which theme class the verb belongs to.

b. Regular /─ár/ verbs have the theme /a/ recurring in the endings of all present tense forms except 1 sg.

180

6.21.11   Substitution drills — number substitution

1   trábaho |nwebęórás↓

2   áblanespaŋyól↓

3   nónęsę́sita(n)náďá↓

4   trábáhamozmúchó↓

5   áblaniŋglés↓

6   notrabáhanaí↓

7   nęsę́sitotrolíbró↓

trábáhamoz |nwebęórás↓

áblaespaŋyól↓

nónęsę́sitanáďá↓

trábahomúchó↓

áblaiŋglés↓

notrabahaí↓

nęsę́sitamosotrolíbró↓

---

1   Trabajo nueve horas.

2   Hablan español.

3   No necesitan nada.

4   Trabajamos mucho.

5   Hablan inglés.

6   No trabajan ahí.

7   Necesito otro libro.

Trabajamos nueve horas.

Habla español.

No necesita nada.

Trabajo mucho.

Habla inglés.

No trabaja ahí.

Necesitamos otro libro.

Person — number substitution

1 nòsotrostrabàhámos,akíↆ

   yǫ_____ↆ   tràbahǫakíↆ

   àliṣyaḷantónyo_____ↆ   tràbahanakíↆ

   el_____ↆ   tràbahakíↆ

   ústeₑes_____ↆ   tràbahanakíↆ

2 yǫáblòpokǫespaŋyólↆ

   éꞈyạ_____ↆ   áblàpokǫespaŋyólↆ

   àntonyǫipablǫ____ↆ   áblàmpokǫespaŋyólↆ

---

1 *Nosotros* trabajamos aquí.

   Yo_____.   Trabajo aquí.

   Alicia y Antonio_____.   Trabajan aquí.

   El_____.   Trabaja aquí.

   Ustedes_____.   Trabajan aquí.

2 *Yo* hablo poco español.

   Ella_____.   Habla poco español.

   Antonio y Pablo_.   Hablan poco español.

álisyaįyo_____↓　　　　　　　　　ȧblámòspokǫespaŋyól↓

ústeđ_____↓　　　　　　　　　　　ȧblȧpokǫespaŋyól↓

3　álisya |nónèȿèsitapermísò↓

yo_____↓　　　　　　　　　　　nónèȿèsitopermísò↓

nósotroz_____↓　　　　　　　　nónèȿèsitamospermísò↓

e͡ŋaz_____↓　　　　　　　　　　nónèȿèsitampermísò↓

ústeđez_____↓　　　　　　　　　nónèȿèsitampermísò↓

Alicia y yo_____.　　　　　　　　Hablamos poco español.

Usted_____.　　　　　　　　　　Habla poco español.

3　*Alicia* no necesita permiso.

Yo_____.　　　　　　　　　　　No necesito permiso.

Nosotros_____.　　　　　　　　No necesitamos permiso.

Ellas_____.　　　　　　　　　　No necesitan permiso.

Ustedes_____.,　　　　　　　　No necesitan permiso.

6.21.12   Response drill

	1	trábahąusteɖakí↑ǫeŋkalifórnyá↓	trábáhǫàkí↓
	2	áblanųsteɖezbyén |elespaŋyól↑ǫeliŋglés↓	áblámózbyen |èliŋglés↓
	3	trábahąel |enląembahaɖa↑ǫakí↓	trábáhàkí↓
	4	nèşésitąusteɖ |unlápiş↑ǫunaplúmá↓	nèşésítǫùnàplumá↓
[èspáŋyól↓]	5	kęablàn |ᶜⁿyósàkí↓	áblánęspàŋyól↓
[àkí↓]	6	dondetrabáhą |ùstéɖ↓	trábáhǫàkí↓
[èspáŋyól↓]	7	kę̨ablą |ùstéɖàkí↓	áblǫéspàŋyól↓

	1	¿Trabaja usted aquí o en California?	Trabajo aquí.
	2	¿Hablan ustedes bien el español o el inglés?	Hablamos bien el inglés.
	3	¿Trabaja él en la Embajada o aquí?	Trabaja aquí.
	4	¿Necesita usted un lápiz o una pluma?	Necesito una pluma.
(español)	5	¿Qué hablan ellos aquí?	Hablan español.
(aquí)	6	¿Dónde trabaja usṭed?	Trabajo aquí.
(español)	7	¿Qué habla usted aquí?	Hablo español.

[séys↓]   8 kwántasórás |trábáhámóznósótrós↓   trábáhámòs |seysórás↓

[si0yàs↓] 9 néşésitanustédez |mazmésast   nó↓ néşésitámòzmá(s)si0yás↓

[àki↓]   10 trábáhaeleŋkalifórnyat   nó↓ trábáhàki↓

[iŋgles↓] 11 ábláusteđbyen |elespaŋyolt   nó↓ áblobyénéliŋgles↓

       12 áblamoseliyo |espaŋyolt   si↓ ústedes |áblánéspáŋyól↓

       13 trábáhaustedbastantet   si↓ trábáhòbástanté↓

(seis)   8 ¿Cuántas horas trabajamos nosotros?   Trabajamos seis horas.

(sillas) 9 ¿Necesitan ustedes más mesas?   No, necesitamos más sillas.

(aquí)   10 ¿Trabaja él en California?   No, trabaja aquí.

(inglés) 11 ¿Habla usted bien el español?   No, hablo bien el inglés.

       12 ¿Hablamos él y yo español?   Sí, ustedes hablan español.

       13 ¿Trabaja usted bastante?   Sí, trabajo bastante.

6.21.13   Translation drill

1 I don't pronounce very well.   nópronúnşyó |múybyén↓   No pronuncio muy bien.

2 We don't speak much Spanish.   nọablamoz |muchọespaŋyól↓   No hablamos mucho español.

3 When do you all need the desk?   kwándonẹşesítanustẹḍes |éléskritóryọ↓   ¿Cuándo necesitan ustedes el escritorio?

4 She doesn't need anything now.   éⁿ ya |nónẹşesíta |naḍaórá↓   Ella no necesita nada ahora.

5 I always take a taxi.   syémpre |tómọuntáksi↓   Siempre tomo un taxi.

6 Where do you work?   dondetrabaha |ústéḍ↓   ¿Dónde trabaja usted?

7 Do you all speak Spanish?   ablanustéḍes |éspáŋyol↑   ¿Hablan ustedes español?

8 I haven't worked since yesterday.   notrabaho |ḍézḍẹ̀ayér↓   No trabajo desde ayer.

9 Do I pronounce well?   prónunşyoyó |byén↑   ¿Pronuncio yo bien?

10 We'll cash the checks later.   déspwes |kámbyamoz loschékès↓   Después cambiamos los cheques.

11 They almost always speak in Spanish. éⁿyos |kásisyémprẹ |ablanénespaŋyól↓   Ellos casi siempre hablan en español.

12 We work in a language school.   tràbáhamos|énúnạẻskwelaḍeléŋgwàs↓   Trabajamos en una escuela de lenguas.

13 Do you speak Spanish?   ablạústeḍ|éspàṇyòl↑   ¿Habla usted español?

B. Discussion of pattern

Determining which verbs are *regular* and which are *irregular* in a language like Spanish is a matter of statistics. When one examines all the verbs in the lexicon, the largest group which has similar changes within a patterned frame is considered regular; other verb patterns are most economically described in terms of their deviation from this established norm.

An examination of Spanish verbs shows that the *infinitive* forms (traditionally the 'center' or 'point of beginning' in the verb pattern) can be divided into three groups, according to what vowel precedes the final $/-r/$. The three groups can be referred to as $/-ár/$, $/-ér/$, and $/-ír/$ verbs. The identifying vowel is called the *theme vowel*, since it recurs in many of the conjugated forms of the verb. That part of the infinitive which remains when the $/-Vr/$ (*vowels* plus $/r/$) is removed is known as the *stem*.

From among these three subclasses of verbs, the present discussion describes those of the $/-ár/$ theme class which are regular in the present tense.

One of the characteristics of regular verbs in Spanish is that person, number, and tense categories are signalled by changes in the *endings*. In regular verbs (and in some irregular verbs) there are no changes in the stem other than the occurrence or non-occurrence of strong stress, which is shifted to the ending for 1 pl forms in the present tense:

	sg	pl
1	´ o	—ámos
2 fam	´ as	
2 - 3	´ a	´ an

The importance of the correct placement of strong stress cannot be over-emphasized. As other tense forms are presented where the only difference from some of the forms above is a different placement of the strong stress, it will be seen that this feature carries the entire burden of distinguishing the otherwise identical forms. A mistake in stress placement will more likely lead to misunderstanding than a malpronunciation of several sounds. The results will be every bit as striking as 'Abbot' $\sim$ 'a bat'

187

are in English when stress (and a structurally obligatory, corresponding vowel substitution characteristic of the English phonological pattern) is shifted from the first to the second syllable.

In the Spanish pattern the /—o/ ending of the 1 sg form is distinct. In the other endings the theme vowel /a/ appears, followed by /—s, —mos, —n/. These are the regular signals of 2 sg fam, 1pl, and 2 - 3 pl respectively; these endings recur in other theme class and tense form patterns.

6.21.2   The semantic differences between /está(n)/ and /áy/

A.   Presentation of pattern

ILLUSTRATIONS

----

1   dondestaelbáņyò↓   ¿Dónde *está* el baño?

Where is (there) a bathroom?   2   dondeayumbáņyò↓   ¿Dónde *hay* un baño?

EXTRAPOLATION

Definite	está el...
Indefinite	áy un...

NOTES

a. /está/ translates 'is'.

b. /áy/ translates 'there is' or 'is there?'

6.21.21   Substitution drill

1   dondeayunotél↓
    _____ ęl____↓   dóndestaęlotél↓

2   ákięstaełlíbrò↓
    _____un____↓   ákɪayunlíbrò↓

3   áɪayunasęnyorítá↓
    _____la____↓   áięstalasęnyorítá↓

4   dondeayuna(s)síꞶyàs↓
    _____las____↓   dondestánla(s)síꞶyàs↓

5   ákięstánlozlápişès↓
    _____unoz____↓   ákɪayunozlápişès↓

---

1 ¿Dónde hay un hotel?
   ¿_____ el____ ?   ¿Dónde está el hotel?

2 Aquí está el libro.
   _____ un____ .   Aquí hay un libro.

3 Ahí hay una señorita.
   _____ la_____.   Ahí está la señorita.

4 ¿Dónde hay unas sillas?
   ¿_____ las_____?   ¿Dónde están las sillas?

5 Aquí están los lápices.
   _____unos_____.   Aquí hay unos lápices.

6.21.22   Translation drill

1 Where is there a cheap restaurant?

   Where's the cheap restaurant?

   dondẹay |ùnrrėstòrámbarátò↓

   dondesta |ẹlrrėstòrámbarátò↓

   ¿Dónde hay un restorán barato?

   ¿Dónde está el restorán barato?

2 There's a room for you all.

   There's the room for you all.

   àıay |ùŋkwártò |pàrạústéᴅès↓

   àıẹsta |ẹlkwártò |pàrạústéᴅès↓

   Ahí hay un cuarto para ustedes.

   Ahí está el cuarto para ustedes.

3 There're the empty tables.

   There're some empty tables.

   àıẹstan |làzmesazᴅesokupáᴅàs↓

   àıay |ùnàzmesazᴅesokupáᴅàs↓

   Ahí están las mesas desocupadas.

   Ahí hay unas mesas desocupadas.

4 There isn't a chauffeur here.

   The chauffeur's not here.

   nọayunchofer |àkí↓

   nọẹstaẹlchofer |àkí↓

   No hay un chofer aquí.

   No está el chofer aquí.

5 Is the pie good?

   Is there a good pie?

   èstaẹlpastelbwenó↑

   ayumpastelbwenó↑

   ¿Está el pastel bueno?

   ¿Hay un pastel bueno?

6 Is the hotel around the corner?

   Is there a hotel around the corner?

   èstaẹlotel |alabwelta↑

   ayunọtel |alabwelta↑

   ¿Está el hotel a la vuelta?

   ¿Hay un hotel a la vuelta?

7 The waiters are here already.

   There're some waiters here already.

   yaẹstan |lozmóṣòs,àkí↓

   yay |unozmóṣòs,àkí↓

   Ya están los mozos aquí.

   Ya hay unos mozos aquí.

8 Where's the apartment with two rooms?

dóndestá |ęlápártámento |kòndoskwártós↓

¿Dónde está el apartamento con dos cuartos?

Where is there an apartment with two rooms?

dóndęay |únápártámento |kòndoskwártós↓

¿Dónde hay un apartamento con dos cuartos?

9 There's a restaurant up ahead.

áiądelantę |áyunrrestorán↓

Ahí adelante hay un restorán.

The restaurant's up ahead.

áiądelantę |estaęlrrestorán↓

Ahí adelante está el restorán.

B. Discussion of pattern

When a reference to the location of something is definite, /está/ is used, with the definiteness marked by the occurrence of a definite article. When the reference is not definite, the uniquely irregular form /áy/ (from the verb /abér/) is used, usually but not necessarily accompanied by an indefinite article.

When the definite reference occurs, the normal agreement for number between subject and verb prevails:

/dondestálasíⁿyá↓/

Where's the chair?

/dondestánla(s)síⁿyás↓/

Where're the chairs?

but when indefinite reference occurs, there is no corresponding change in the verb form; /áy/ can appear with either singular or plural forms:

/àyunlibrǫenlamésá↓/

There's a book on the table.

/àyunóslibros.enlamésá↓/

There're some books on the table.

One may be definite in number, but still indefinite in reference. Thus:

/àydosplumàs |àkí↓/

There're two pens here.

compared to: /làsdosplumàs |éstánàkí↓/

The two pens are here.

191

6.22   Replacement drills

A   áꟙyıay |únámesaꬵesokupáꬵà↓

1 _____ kwarto _____ ↓   áꟙyıay |úŋkwartoꬵesokupáꬵò↓

2 ákı _____ ↓   ákıay |úŋkwartoꬵesokupáꬵò↓

3 _____ ꬵesokupáꬵòs↓   ákıay |únòskwartozꬵesokupáꬵòs↓

4 _____ sıꟙyaz _____ ↓   ákıay |únà(s)sıꟙyazꬵesokupáꬵàs↓

5 _____ lá _____ ↓   ákıꬾsta |lásıꟙyaꬵesokupáꬵà↓

6 _____ bwénà↓   ákıꬾsta |làsıꟙyabwénà↓

7 _____ únàs _____ ↓   ákıay |únà(s)sıꟙyazbwénàs↓

A   Allí hay una mesa desocupada.

1 _____ cuarto _____ .   Allí hay un cuarto desocupado.

2 Aquí _____ .   Aquí hay un cuarto desocupado.

3 _____ desocupados.   Aquí hay unos cuartos desocupados.

4 _____ sillas _____ .   Aquí hay unas sillas desocupadas.

5 _____ la _____ .   Aquí está la silla desocupada.

6 _____ buena.   Aquí está la silla buena.

7 _____ unas _____ .   Aquí hay unas sillas buenas.

192

B   béamos.elmenú↓   béamozlakwéntá↓

1 _____ kwéntá↓   béamozlakwéntá↓

2 kyero _____ ↓   kyerolakwéntá↓

3 _____ manşánás↓   kyerolazmanşánás↓

4 ___dyez _____ ↓   kyéródyezmanşánás↓

5 _____ biŋyétés↓   kyéródyezbiŋyétés↓

6 ___menoz _____ ↓   kyérómenozbiŋyétés↓

7 téŋgó _____ ↓   téŋgómenozbiŋyétés↓

B   Veamos el menú.

1 _____ cuenta.   Veamos la cuenta.

2 Quiero _____ .   Quiero la cuenta.

3 _____ manzanas.   Quiero las manzanas.

4 _____ diez _____ .   Quiero diez manzanas.

5 _____ billetes.   Quiero diez billetes.

6 _____ menos _____ .   Quiero menos billetes.

7 Tengo _____ .   Tengo menos billetes.

C   kedeseán |ùstédès |sèŋyórès↓

1 _____ùstéd _____↓   kedeseą |ùstéd |sèŋyór↓

2 ___kyerę_____↓   kekyerę |ùstéd |sèŋyór↓

3 ___dįsę_____↓   kedįsę |ùstéd |sèŋyór↓

4 komo_____↓   komodįsę |ùstéd |sèŋyór↓

5 ___están_____↓   komǫestanųstédès |sèŋyórès↓

6 _____sèŋyórítà↓   komǫestaųstéd |sèŋyórítà↓

7 dèdonde_____↓   dèdondesųstéd |sèŋyórítà↓

C   ¿Qué desean ustedes, señores?

1 ¿ _____ usted, _____?   ¿Qué desea usted, señor?

2 ¿___quiere___ , ___?   ¿Qué quiere usted, señor?

3 ¿___dice___ , ___?   ¿Qué dice usted, señor?

4 ¿Cómo___ , ___?   ¿Cómo dice usted, señor?

5 ¿___están___ , ___?   ¿Cómo están ustedes, señores?

6 ¿_____ , señorita?   ¿Cómo está usted, señorita?

7 ¿De dónde___ , ___?   ¿De dónde es usted, señorita?

D   yókyerǫ |únsaŋẉichɗehamón↓   yókyerǫ |úmpokoɗehamón↓

1   _____ poko _____↓   yókyerǫ |úmpokoɗetomátė↓

2   _____ tomátė↓   yókyerǫ |únàsopaɗetomátė↓

3   _____ sopa _____↓   yókyero |làsopaɗetomátė↓

4   _____ lá _____↓   yoꞔyebo |làsopaɗetomátė↓

5   __ꞔyebo _____↓   nósotroz |ꞔyébamoz |làsopaɗetomátė↓

6   nósotroz _____↓   nósotroz |ꞔyébamoz |làsopaɗelegúmbrès↓

7   _____ legúmbrès↓

D   Yo quiero un sandwich de jamón.

1   _____ poco _____.   Yo quiero un poco de jamón.

2   _____ tomate.   Yo quiero un poco de tomate.

3   _____ sopa _____.   Yo quiero una sopa de tomate.

4   _____ la _____.   Yo quiero la sopa de tomate.

5   __ llevo _____.   Yo llevo la sopa de tomate.

6   Nosotros _____.   Nosotros llevamos la sopa de tomate.

7   _____ legumbres.   Nosotros llevamos la sopa de legumbres.

E   basaḃıḃır|eṇeloteĺ↑

1 _____eṣtaḋoṣuniḋoṣ↑   baṣaḃıḃır|enloṣeṣtaḋoṣuniḋoṣ↑

2 ____trabahar_____↑   baṣatrabahar|enloṣeṣtaḋoṣuniḋoṣ↑

3 ḋeṣean _____↑   ḋeṣeantrabahar|enloṣeṣtaḋoṣuniḋoṣ↑

4 _____embahaḋa↑   ḋeṣeantrabahar|enlaembahaḋa↑

5 kyere_____↑   kyeretrabahar|enlaembahaḋa↑

6 ____almorşar_____↑   kyerealmorşar|enlaembahaḋa↑

7 póḋemos_____↑   póḋemoṣalmorşar|enlaembahaḋa↑

E   ¿Vas a vivir en el hotel?

1 ¿ _____ Estados Unidos?   ¿Vas a vivir en los Estados Unidos?

2 ¿ ____ trabajar_____ ?   ¿Vas a trabajar en los Estados Unidos?

3 ¿Desean_____ ?   ¿Desean trabajar en los Estados Unidos?

4 ¿_____ Embajada?   ¿Desean trabajar en la Embajada?

5 ¿Quiere_____?   ¿Quiere trabajar en la Embajada?

6 ¿____almorzar_____?   ¿Quiere almorzar en la Embajada?

7 ¿Podemos_____?   ¿Podemos almorzar en la Embajada?

F   nó↓ pyénsobuskár |unₐapartaméntó↓

1   ____ kyéro_____↓   nó↓ kyérobuskár |unₐapartaméntó↓

2   _____otél↓   nó↓ kyérobuskárunₒotél↓

3   _____el____↓   nó↓ kyérobuskárelotél↓

4   ____ pódemoz_____↓   nó↓ pódemozbuskárelotél↓

5   sí↓_____↓   sí↓ pódemozbuskárelotél↓

6   _____enkontrar____↓   sí↓ pódemos,enkontrárelotél↓

7   _____apartaméntòs↓   sí↓ pódemos,enkontrár |los

                                              apartaméntòs↓

F   No, pienso buscar un apartamento.

1   __, quiero_____.   No, quiero buscar un apartamento.

2   __, _____hotel.   No, quiero buscar un hotel.

3   __, _____el____.   No, quiero buscar el hotel.

4   __, podemos_____.   No, podemos buscar el hotel.

5   Sí, _____.   Sí, podemos buscar el hotel.

6   __, _____encontrar_____.   Sí, podemos encontrar el hotel.

7   __, _____apartamentos.   Sí, podemos encontrar los apartamentos.

End of Tape 3B

Tape 4A

6.23   **Variation drills**

A   ȧmí |tráygame |sópaᵈelegúmbrés↓   A mí tráigame sopa de legumbres.

    1 Bring *me* a sandwich.   ȧmí |tráygamȩunsáṇwich↓   A mí tráigame un sandwich.

    2 Bring *me* an apple pie.   ȧmí |tráygamȩ |úmpásteldemanşáná↓   A mí tráigame un pastel de manzana.

    3 Bring *me* a tomato salad.   ȧmí |tráygamȩ |úna̧énsáladᵃᵈetomáté↓   A mí tráigame una ensalada de tomate.

    4 Bring *me* a beer.   ȧmí |tráygamȩuna̧şerbéşȧ↓   A mí tráigame una cerveza.

    5 Give *me* (some) more soup.   ȧmí |ᵈemema(s)sópȧ↓   A mí déme más sopa.

    6 Give *me* (some) more chops.   ȧmí |ᵈememaschulétȧs↓   A mí déme más chuletas.

    7 Hand *me* an apple.   ȧmí |pasemȩunamanşánȧ↓   A mí páseme una manzana.

B   ayumpastél |demanşáná↑kézmúybwénó↓   Hay un pastel de manzana que es muy
                                                                             bueno.

    1 There's an American wine that's   ayumbíno̧ |amerikáno↑kézmúybwénȯ↓   Hay un vino americano que es muy bueno.
      very good.

    2 There's a school of languages   ayuna̧eskwéla |ᵈeléṇgwas↑kézmúybwénȧ↓   Hay una escuela de lenguas que es muy
      that's very good.   buena.

3 There's a restaurant that's not very good.

ayunrrestoraŋ↑kènoęzmuybwénò↓

Hay un restorán que no es muy bueno.

4 There are some Americans in the hotel who are from Kansas.

ayunos.amerikanos |en.elotel↑kèsondekánsàs↓

Hay unos americanos en el hotel que son de Kansas.

5 There's a gentleman here who doesn't speak Spanish.

ayunseŋyoraki↑kèngàblạespaŋyól↓

Hay un señor aquí que no habla español.

6 There're some apartments, but they're not very good.

ayúnós.àpàrtàmentòs↓pérónoson |muybwénòs↓

Hay unos apartamentos, pero no son muy buenos.

7 There're some pens on the desk, but they're not very good.

ayunasplumas |ènèlèskritoryò↓
pérónoson |muybwénàs↓

Hay unas plumas en el escritorio, pero no son muy buenas.

C trayga |paralozdós↓

Traiga para los dos.

1 Bring (enough) for the three (of us).

trayga |paralostrés↓

Traiga para los tres.

2 Bring vegetable soup.

trayga |sopadelegúmbrès↓

Traiga sopa de legumbres.

3 Bring more ham.

trayga |mashamón↓

Traiga más jamón.

4 Hand me the water.

pasemelágwà↓

Páseme el agua.

5 Give me more wine.

deme |mazbínò↓

Déme más vino.

6 Give me the bill.   démelåkwéntà↓   Déme la cuenta.

7 Let me know this afternoon.   ábisemestatárdé↓   Avíseme esta tarde.

D   keleparéşe|sinóstràtámozdetú↓   ¿Qué le parece si nos tratamos de 'tú'?

   1 What do you say (if) we speak   keleparéşe|siàblamos,espaɲól↓   ¿Qué le parece si hablamos español?
     Spanish?

   2 What do you say (if) we practice Spanish?   keleparéşe|sipràktikamos,espaɲól↓   ¿Qué le parece si practicamos español?

   3 What do you say (if) we drink wine?   keleparéşe|sitómamozbínò↓   ¿Qué le parece si tomamos vino?

   4 What do you say (if) we take the   keleparéşe|sitómamos,elas(ş)ensór↓   ¿Qué le parece si tomamos el ascensor?
     elevator?

   5 What do you say (if) we come in?   keleparéşe|sipàsamos,adelánté↓   ¿Qué le parece si pasamos adelante?

   6 What do you say (if) we go   keleparéşe|sibàmozmaɲánà↓   ¿Qué le parece si vamos mañana?
     tomorrow?

   7 What do you say (if) we eat lunch now?   keleparéşe|siàlmórşamos,aórà↓   ¿Qué le parece si almorzamos ahora?

E   tyenezrraşón↓   Tienes razón.

   1 You're right, Joseph.   tyenezrraşoɲ|hósé↓   Tienes razón, José.

2 You're not right, Joseph.   nótyénezrraşón |hòsé↓   No tienes razón, José.

3 He's right.   tyénerraşón↓   Tiene razón.

4 I'm right.   téŋgorraşón↓   Tengo razón.

5 I'm hungry.   téŋgoámbrè↓   Tengo hambre.

6 Charles and Mary are very hungry. kárlosimaria |tyénènmuchámbrè↓ Carlos y María tienen mucha hambre.

7 You're very hungry.   ústedes |tyénènmuchámbrè↓   Ustedes tienen mucha hambre.

F moşó↓ làkwentà↓   ¡Mozo! La cuenta.

1 Miss! The check.   sèŋyórità↓ làkwentà↓   ¡Señorita! La cuenta.

2 Sir! The book.   sèŋyó'r↓ è⓪librò↓   ¡Señor! El libro.

3 Joseph! The pencil.   hòsé↓ è⓪lapiş↓   ¡José! El lápiz.

4 Waiter! To the right.   moşó↓ àládèrechà↓   ¡Mozo! A la derecha.

5 Waiter! Mineral water.   moşó↓ àgwamineral↓   ¡Mozo! Agua mineral.

6 Madam! To the left.   sèŋyorà↓ àlaişkyerdà↓   ¡Señora! A la izquierda.

7 Gentlemen! Come in.   sèŋyorès↓ àdèlantè↓   ¡Señores! Adelante.

6.24   Review drill [(1)] — The use of the definite articles with titles

1 How are you, Mr. Molina?	komǫestaystéɗ |séŋyórmólínà↓	¿Cómo está usted, Sr. Molina?
How's Mr. Molina?	komǫesta |ǫlséŋyórmolínà↓	¿Cómo está el Sr. Molina?
2 How are you, Miss White?	komǫestaystéɗ |séŋyórítàhwáyt↓	¿Cómo está usted, señorita White?
How's Miss White?	komǫesta |làséŋyórítahwáyt↓	¿Cómo está la señorita White?
3 Mr. Molina, how's Miss White?	séŋyórmólínà↓ komǫesta |laseŋyoritahwáyt↓	Sr. Molina, ¿cómo está la señorita White?
4 Miss Molina, How's Miss White?	séŋyórítàmólínà↓ komǫesta |laseŋyoritahwáyt↓	Señorita Molina, ¿cómo está la señorita White?
5 Mrs. Molina, how's Mrs. White?	séŋyóràmólínà↓ komǫestalaseŋyorahwáyt↓	Sra. Molina, ¿cómo está la señora White?
6 Mrs. Molina, is Mrs. White here?	séŋyóràmólínà↓ ėstalaseŋyorahwayt |àki↑	Sra. Molina, ¿está la Sra. White aquí?
7 Miss Molina, is Miss White here?	séŋyórítàmólínà↓ ėstalaseŋyorítahwayt |àki↑	Señorita Molina, ¿está la señorita White aquí?
8 Mr. Molina, is Mr. White here?	séŋyórmólínà↓ ėstaǫlseŋyorhwayt |àki↑	Sr. Molina, ¿está el Sr. White aquí?
9 Mr. Molina, where's Mr. White from?	séŋyórmólínà↓ dėɗondes |ėlséŋyorhwáyt↓	Sr. Molina, ¿de dónde es el Sr. White?
10 Miss Molina, where's Miss White from?	séŋyórítàmólínà↓ dėɗondez |làséŋyórita hwáyt↓	Señorita Molina, ¿de dónde es la señorita White?

---

(1) Review drills will be a regular part of the format of unit six and subsequent units. They will review and correlate structure points previously presented or will enlarge on structural details which were not sufficiently developed. They will usually be translation drills, though substitution and response drills will occasionally be used.

11 Where're you from, Mrs. Molina?   dèḍondeșustéd̦ |séɲyórámólínà↓   ¿De dónde es usted, Sra. Molina?

    And Mrs. White?   ilaseɲyorahwayt↑   ¿Y la señora White?

12 Mr. Molina, is Mr. White (an) American?   séɲyórmólínà↓ eșelseɲyorhwayt |ámèrikano↑   Señor Molina, ¿es el señor White americano?

13 Miss Molina, is Miss White (an) American?   séɲyórítámólínà↓ ézlaseɲyorítahwayt | Señorita Molina, ¿es la señorita White americana?
                                              ámèrikana↑

6.3   CONVERSATION STIMULUS

NARRATIVE 1

1 It's eleven o'clock.   sónlàșonșé↓   Son las once.

2 Jose and John take a table.   hósęḻhwan |tomanụnamésà↓   José y Juan toman una mesa.

3 They want to see the menu.   kyerémberelmenú↓   Quieren ver el menú.

4 Jose wants to try the pork chops.   hósekyereprobár |làschùlétazḍeşérḍò↓   José quiere probar las chuletas de cerdo.

5 He's also going to have a green salad.   támbyembakomér |únạénsàlaḍaḍeleǵúmbrès↓   También va a comer una ensalada de legumbres.

6 He's very hungry.   tyénemuchámbrè↓   Tiene mucha hambre.

7 Juan's going to have a ham sandwich   hwám|bákomér|únsánwichdehamóŋ|kồn   Juan va a comer un sandwich de jamón
   with lettuce and tomato.   con lechuga y tomate.

                                              léchugaitomátè↓

8 Jose and John want a beer.   hóseịhwáŋ|kyérenụunaṣerbéṣà↓   José y Juan quieren una cerveza.

                                              DIALOG 1

Mozo, dígales 'buenos días' a los señores   bwénôzɔ́ɪás|séŋyórès↓ déseámberelmenú↑   Mozo: Buenos días, señores. ¿Desean
   y pregúnteles si desean ver el menú.   ver el menú?

José, contéstele que sí, que por favor, y   sí|pórfấṿ6r↓ komọestán|láschúletaz   José: Sí, por favor. ¿Cómo están las
   pregúntele que cómo están las chuletas   chuletas de cerdo?
   de cerdo.   σeṣérơò↓

Mozo, contéstele que están muy buenas.   éstánmuybwénàs↓   Mozo: Están muy buenas.

José, pregúntele a Juan que qué le parece   kéleparéṣé|hwán|siprồbamos.ésó↓   José: ¿Qué le parece, Juan, si probamos
   si prueban eso, que Ud. tiene mucha   eso? Yo tengo mucha hambre.
   hambre.   yo|téŋgònǔuchámbré↓

Juan, contéstele a José que no, que Ud.   nó↓ yokyerọunsánwich|dekwàlkyerkósá↓   Juan: No, yo quiero un sandwich de
   quiere un sandwich de cualquier cosa.   cualquier cosa.

Mozo, dígale al señor (Juan) que qué le   kéleparéṣé|únsánwichdehàmon| Mozo: ¿Qué le parece un sandwich de
   parece un sandwich de jamón con   jamón con lechuga y tomate?
   lechuga y tomate.   kồnléchugaitomáté↓

Juan, contéstele que está bien, y que una cerveza también por favor.

èstabyén↓ ɪ̀ùnáx̧èrḇèx̧atambyén |pòrfàḇór↓

Juan: Está bien. Y una cerveza también, por favor.

José, dígale al mozo que a Ud. otra, con las chuletas.

ámɪ |otrá↓ kónlàschúlétàs↓

José: A mí otra, con las chuletas.

NARRATIVE 2

1 John likes the sandwich very much.

àhwan |lég̈ústámuchǫelsá ŋ̱wich↓

A Juan le gusta mucho el sandwich.

2 It's very good.

èstámuyḻwénò↓

Está muy bueno.

3 The pork chops are good, too.

làschúlétàzd̊èx̧érd̊ǫ |èstámbwenastambyén↓

Las chuletas de cerdo están buenas también.

4 Jose wants another beer.

hósekyerǫ |ótrax̧erḇéx̧à↓

José quiere otra cerveza.

5 So does John.

ìhwantàmbyén↓

Y Juan también.

6 Jose wants to use the familiar 'tu' with John.

hóse |kyérètràtáràhwàn |detú↓

José quiere tratar a Juan de 'tú'.

7 John says it's okay.

hwàndix̧e |kèstabyén↓

Juan dice que está bien.

DIALOG 2

José, pregúntele a Juan que qué tal el sandwich.

kétálelsáŋwich |hwán↓

José: ¿Qué tal el sandwich, Juan?

Juan, contéstele que le gusta mucho, que está muy bueno. Pregúntele a José que qué tal las chuletas.

mégustamúcho↓ éstámuybwéno↓ iláschúletás↓ ketál↓

Juan: Me gusta mucho, está muy bueno. Y las chuletas, ¿qué tal?

José, contéstele que están muy buenas también. Pregúntele si quiere otra cerveza.

éstánmuybwénás |támbyén↓ kyére otraşerbéşa↑

José: Están muy buenas también. ¿Quiere otra cerveza?

Juan, dígale que Ud. cree que sí, y que si él también.

kreokesí↓ ๅustéๅtambyén↑

Juan: Creo que sí, ¿Y usted también?

José, dígale que sí, que Ud. también, pero pregúntele que qué le parece si se tratan de 'tú'.

si |yotambyén↓ pérokéleparéşe | sinóstrátamozdetú↓

José: Sí, yo también. Pero, ¿qué le parece si nos tratamos de 'tú'?

Juan, dígale que está bien, si él quiere.

éstabyén↓ sitúkyéres↓

Juan: Está bien...si tú quieres...

NARRATIVE 3

1 John needs an apartment.

hwán |néşésitaunapartaméntó↓

Juan necesita un apartamento.

2 He's going to look for one.

bábuskárúnó↓

Va a buscar uno.

3 Jose's going to help John find one.

hóse │báyúɾárahwan │ạẹŋkòntrarúnó↓

José va a ayudar a Juan a encontrar uno.

4 He's going to go with him tomorrow.

baír │kónẹl │màɲyanà↓

Va a ir con él mañana.

5 He's going to be busy in the morning, but not in the afternoon.

pòrlàmàɲyana │báẹstárókúpaɾo │pérò pòrlàtarɾe │nó↓

Por la mañana va a estar ocupado, pero por la tarde no.

6 John wants to go at three o'clock.

hwaŋkyerẹir │alastrés↓

Juan quiere ir a las tres.

7 John likes the hotel where he's staying.

àhwan │léǥustạ │ẹlótẹl │dondestá↓

A Juan le gusta el hotel donde está.

8 But it's cheaper to live in an apartment.

pérọẹzmazbaráto │ƀibirenụnapartaméntó↓

Pero es más barato vivir en un apartamento.

DIALOG 3

Juan, dígale a José que Ud. necesita buscar un apartamento; y pregúntele si quiere ayudarle.

hósé↓ nẹsẹsito │búskarunạapartaméntó↓ kyeres̬ạyuɾarme↑

Juan: José, necesito buscar un apartamento. ¿Quieres ayudarme?

José, dígale que cómo no, que Ud. le puede ayudar con mucho gusto.

komonó↓ yotepwéɾọayuɾar │kònmuchoǥústó↓

José: Cómo no, yo te puedo ayudar con mucho gusto.

Juan, pregúntele si él va a estar ocupado mañana.

tu │bas̬ạestár │ókúpaɾomaɲana↑

Juan: ¿Tú vas a estar ocupado mañana?

207

José, contéstele que por la mañana
sí, pero que pueden ir por la tarde.

pórlámáɲyanasí↓ pérópóɖemos│ir

porlatarɖè↓

José: Por la mañana sí, pero podemos ir
por la tarde.

Juan, pregúntele que a qué hora.

àkҽorà↓

Juan: ¿A qué hora?

José, dígale que a las dos o a las
tres, si le parece.

àlàɾɖos │ɡalastrés↓sitépáréşè↓

José: A las dos o a las tres, si te parece.

Juan, dígale que a las tres le parece bien.

àlàstréz │meparҽşebyén↓

Juan: A las tres me parece bien.

José, pregúntele si no le gusta el hotel
donde está.

nótéɡustҽelotél │dòndestàs↑

José: ¿No te gusta el hotel donde estás?

Juan, dígale que sí, pero que Ud. piensa
que es más barato vivir en un
apartamento.

sí↓ pérópyenso │kézmazbaratò │

bibírénúnąpártáméntó↓

Juan: Sí, pero pienso que es más barato
vivir en un apartamento.

7.1   BASIC SENTENCES.   White and Molina look for an apartment.

        John White and José Molina leave the restaurant; on the way out they pick up a newspaper to check on apartment leads. They are walking over to Molina's car.

ENGLISH SPELLING	AID TO LISTENING	SPANISH SPELLING
the car	èl—áwtò↓	el auto
Molina This is my car.	éstezmįáwtò↓	*Molina* Este es mi auto.
old	byéhò↓	viejo
It's old, but pretty decent.	ézbyého ǀpérobwénò↓	Es viejo pero bueno.
the newspaper	èl—pèryóđikò↓	el periódico
Let's see the paper.	bámos.abér ǀelpéryóđikò↓	Vamos a ver el periódico.
the amount, quantity	là—kàntiđáđ↓	la cantidad
what a (large) quantity	ké—kàntiđáđ↓	qué cantidad
the advertisement	èl—ánunşyò↓	el anuncio

White
What a bunch of ads!

ké |kàntiđađęanúnşyòs↓

White
¡Qué cantidad de anuncios!

too much

dėmàsyađô↓

demasiado

too many

dėmàsyađôs↓

demasiados

why

pór─ké↓

por qué

(we) see (to see)

bemós↓ bér↓

vemos (ver)

the friend

èl─àmıgô↓

el amigo

the agency

lą─àhenşyà↓

la agencia

Molina
Too many. Why don't we see
a friend of mine who has a
(rental) agency? (1)

dėmàsyađôs↓ pórkénobémos |
ąưŋàmıgomıo |kètyęnęunahénşyà↓

Molina
Demasiados. ¿Por qué no vemos
a un amigo mío que tiene una
agencia?

(They go to the rental agency as Molina suggested. After the introduction of White and other formalities, they inquire about apartments.)

to rent

àlkilár↓

alquilar

Molina
Mr. White wants to rent an
apartment.

èlsèŋyor |đęséálkilár |ûnàpàrtàméntô↓

Molina
El señor desea alquilar un
apartamento.

right now	pòr—áorà↓	por ahora
only	sólô↓	sólo
available,(unoccupied), (to vacate)	dèsòkúpàdò↓ dèsòkúpár↓	desocupado (desocupar)

Agent
Right now I have only two available.

pòràora|sólotéŋgoàóz|àèsòkúpádòs↓

Agente
Por ahora sólo tengo dos
desocupados.

| the building | èl—èdifìşyò↓ | el edificio |
| the field, the country | èl—kámpò↓ | el campo |

One downtown, in the Del Campo
building.

úngenelşéntrò↑ ènèlèdifìşyo|dèlkámpò↓

Uno en el centro, en el edificio
'Del Campo'.

without	sín↓	sin
the piece of furniture (2)	èl—mwéblè↓	el mueble
the furnitures	lòz—mwéblès↓	los muebles

sinmwéblès↑

White
Unfurnished?

àmwèbladò↓ àmwèblár↓

White
¿Sin muebles?

furnished (to furnish)

amueblado (amueblar)

Agent
No, furnished.

nó↓ àmwèbladò↓

Agente
No, amueblado.

the month

èl—més↓

el mes

per month	ȧl—mė́s↓	al mes

White
How much per month?

kwȧntọalmȇ́s↓

White
¿Cuánto al mes?

hundred	ṣyentó↓	ciento
two hundred	dȯs(ṣ)yentȯs↓	doscientos
to include	iŋklwír↓	incluir
the light	lȧ—lúṣ↓	la luz
nor	niì↓	ni
the gas	ėl—gȧ́s↓	el gas

Agent
Two hundred not including electricity, water, or gas.

dȯs(ṣ)yentos |siniŋklwír |lúṣ |
ȧgwa |nigás↓

Agente
Doscientos, sin incluir luz, agua ni gas.

White
And where's the other?

iḋondestȧ̧lótró↓

White
¿Y dónde está el otro?

that	ėsė́↓	ese
the outskirts	lȧs—ȧfwerȧ́s↓	las afueras
big, great	grȧndė̀↓	grande

Agent
That one's in the outskirts and it's bigger.

ȇsestá |ȩnlȧsȧfwerȧs↑ȩezmazgrȧ́ndė̀↓

Agente
Ese está en las afueras y es más grande.

(to) me (it) suits (to suit)	mê—kómbyéné↓ kómbènír↓	me conviene (convenir)

White
I think the first suits me better.

kréo |kêmêkómbyénémás |élprimeró↓

White
Creo que me conviene más el primero.

Can we see it?

pódemozbérlo↑

¿Podemos verlo?

the key

lâ—①yabé↓

la llave

clear, of course

kláró↓

claro

Agent
Yes, of course, Here's the key.

sí |kláró↓ ákityénela①yábé↓

Agente
Sí, claro; aquí tiene la llave.

7.10   Notes on the basic sentences

(1) The /a/ *a* which appears in /bémos̬aųṇamígo/ *bemos a un amigo* is not to be translated 'to' or in any of the several other possibilities for the translation of /a/ . It only indicates that the direct object of the verb is *personalized*, that is, either *is* a person or is *thought of* as a person. It will be taken up in detail in Unit 10.

(2) The Spanish word /mwébles/ *muebles* is an example of a count noun (a noun that names items customarily measured by number) which is correlated with an English word 'furniture', an example of a mass noun (one that names items customarily measured by amount). Thus /mwéble/ can be translated only in a roundabout way by saying 'a piece of furniture', since 'a furniture' is an impossible combination of 'a' directly preceding a mass noun. Further discussion and other examples will be presented in Unit 58.

213

7.2   DRILLS AND GRAMMAR

7.21   Pattern drills

7.21.1   Present tense forms of regular /-ér/ verbs

A.   Presentation of pattern

ILLUSTRATIONS

————————	1 yókréokesí↓	Yo *creo* que sí.
————————	2 kwántoledébó↓	¿Cuánto le *debo?*
Are learning Spanish?	3 áprendes.espaɲyol↑	¿*Aprendes* español?
Do you eat in the restaurant?	4 kómes │enelrrestoran↑	¿*Comes* en el restorán?
You eat very little.	5 ústedkome │múypókó↓	Usted *come* muy poco.
How much does he owe you?	6 kwántoledébé↓	¿Cuánto le *debe?*
We are learning a lot.	7 áprendemozmúchó↓	*Aprendemos* mucho.

How much do we owe you?

8   kwántoledebémòs↓

¿Cuánto le *debemos*?

They eat together.

9   eĺẏoskómeɲhúntòs↓

Ellos *comen* juntos.

Do they believe that?

10   kréeneĺẏoséso↑

¿*Creen* ellos eso?

EXTRAPOLATION

		sg	pl
1		—o	—émos
2	fam	—es	
2 - 3		—e	—en

NOTES

a. Where /—ár/ verb endings have the theme /a/ recurring,
    /—ér/ verb endings have the theme /e/ .

b. The endings are otherwise identical.

7.21.11   Substitution drills

Number substitution

1   àprendoespañól↓   àpréndemos,españól↓

2   kómemospastél↓   komopastél↓

3   débébeyntepésòs↓   débémbeyntepésòs↓

4   kómènmuchopóstrè↓   kómèmuchopóstrè↓

5   débemosumpókò↓   debọumpókò↓

6   àprendeiŋglés↓   àprendeniŋglés↓

7   kreọkesí↓   kręemoskesí↓

---

1 *Aprendo* español.   Aprendemos español.

2 *Comemos* pastel.   Como pastel.

3 *Debe* veinte pesos.   Deben veinte pesos.

4 *Comen* mucho postre.   Come mucho postre.

5 *Debemos* un poco.   Debo un poco.

6 *Aprende* inglés.   Aprenden inglés.

7 *Creo* que sí.   Creemos que sí.

Person - number substitution

1   yókomǫały íↆ   kómęały íↆ

    áli̧şya_____ↆ   komenały íↆ

    ę0yos_____ↆ   kómemosały íↆ

    àntonyçiyó_____ↆ   komęały íↆ

    ústeď_____ↆ

2   àpréndémòzmúchǫaíↆ   àpréndòmúchǫaíↆ

    yó_____ↆ

_____

1 *Yo* como allí.

    Alicia _____.   Come allí.

    Ellos _____.   Comen allí.

    Antonio y yo _____ .   Comemos allí.

    Usted _____.   Come allí.

2 Aprendemos mucho ahí.

    Yo _____ .   Aprendo mucho ahí.

```
     ústedes_____↓              ápréndénmúchọaí↓

     álịṣya_____↓               ápréndémúchọaí↓

     hwan_____↓                ápréndémúchọaí↓


  3  ántonyọdebenẹlotél↓

     nósotroz_____↓                 dèbemosẹnẹlotél↓

     pablo_____↓                  debenẹlotél↓

     álịṣyạıkármen____↓                debenenẹlotél↓

     yo_____↓                   debọenẹlotél↓
```

```
     Ustedes _____.           Aprenden mucho ahí.

     Alicia_____.            Aprende mucho ahí.

     Juan_____.             Aprende mucho ahí.


  3  Antonio debe en el hotel.

     Nosotros _____.            Debemos en el hotel.

     Pablo_____.             Debe en el hotel.

     Alicia y Carmen_____.           Deben en el hotel.

     Yo_____.              Debo en el hotel.
```

7.21.12 Response drills

1 kómeustéd|enelşéntrot̯enelapartaméntó↓   kómo̯enélşéntró↓

2 áprendenustédes|espaŋyólt̯o̯inglés↓   áprendémo̯se̯spaŋyól↓

3 debene(l)yozmúcho̯t̯opókó↓   débempokó↓

[enélşéntró↓]   4 dondekómenustédés↓   kómemosenelşéntró↓

[espáŋyól]   5 kea̯prénde̯|ústédakí↓   áprendo̯espaŋyól↓

[dyéşíseyspésós↓]   6 kwántodebél↓   debe|dyéşíseyspésós↓

---

1 ¿Come usted en el centro o en el apartamento?   Como en el centro.

2 ¿Aprenden ustedes español o inglés?   Aprendemos español.

3 ¿Deben ellos mucho o poco?   Deben poco.

(en el centro) 4 ¿Dónde comen ustedes?   Comemos en el centro.

(español)   5 ¿Qué aprende usted aquí?   Aprendo español.

(16 pesos)   6 ¿Cuánto debe él?   Debe 16 pesos.

[lègumbrès↓]   7 kome⑩ya |hamón↑   nó↓ kómèlègumbrès↓

[èlàpàrtàméntò↓]   8 komęustéđ |enęlrrestoràn↑   nó↓ kómǫènèlàpàrtàmentò↓

[muchò↓]   9 àprendenę⑩yos |pókǫakí↑   nó↓ àpréndènmuchò↓

                    10 kómenųstéđez |múchęensaláđa↑ sí↓ kòmémòzmuchęensaláđà↓

                    11 àprendelespąnyol↑   sí↓ àpréndèspąnyó↓

(legumbres)   7 ¿Come ella jamón?   No, come legumbres.

(el apartamento) 8 ¿Come usted en el restorán? No, como en el apartamento.

(mucho)   9 ¿Aprenden ellos poco aquí?   No, aprenden mucho.

          10 ¿Comen ustedes mucha ensalada?   Sí, comemos mucha ensalada.

          11 ¿Aprende él español?   Sí, aprende español.

                                                  End of Tape 4A

Tape 4B

7.21.13   Translation drill

1   *I* always eat dessert.   yósyémpre |kómópóstrè↓   Yo siempre como postre.

2   *He* eats lots of pork chops.   elkómè |múchas |chúlétazdeşérdó↓   El come muchas chuletas de
                                                                                          cerdo.

3   We learn a lot here.   àpréndémozmuchọ |àkí↓   Aprendemos mucho aquí.

4   *They* (f) owe 21 pesos.   eꞩyàz |débèm |bèyntɟumpésós↓   Ellas deben 21 pesos.

5   *I* owe the whole (all the)   yódébò |todalakwéntà↓   Yo debo toda la cuenta.
    bill.

6   Where does she eat?   dondekómeꞩyà↓   ¿Dónde come ella?

7   By the way, where do you eat?   àpróposító↓ dondekómẹustéd↓   A propósito, ¿dónde come Ud?

8   They·learn very well.   eꞩyos |àprénden |múybyén↓   Ellos aprenden muy bien.

9   We don't believe that.   nokrẹémòs |ésò↓   No creemos eso.

10 What do you believe?   kékrẹẹ |ustéd↓   ¿Qué cree Ud?

11 Does he eat lettuce?   kómel |léchuga↑   ¿Come·él lechuga?

B. Discussion of pattern

As the extrapolation above shows, the pattern for /—ér/ theme class regular verbs is very similar to that of /—ár/ verbs. The only difference is the appearance of theme /—e—/ immediately after the stem and preceding the person-number indicators, the same places where the theme /—a—/ appears in /—ár/ verb forms.

Stress patterns are identical for /—ér/ and /—ár/ verbs. Strong stress occurs on the stem in all forms except 1 pl, where the first syllable of the ending receives the strong stress.

7.21.2   The demonstratives /éste, ése, akél/

A.   Presentation of pattern

ILLUSTRATIONS

────────────	1 estechékeḃyahéró↓	*Este* cheque viajero.
This soup is (tastes) good.	2 estasópạ |ẹstáḃwenạ̀↓	*Esta* sopa está buena.
These are my cars.	3 esto(s) son |misáwtòs↓	*Estos* son mis autos.
I like these chairs.	4 mẹgustan |esta(s)sỉ0yạ̀s↓	Me gustan *estas* sillas.
────────────	5 ese|ẹstáẹnlạ̀sạ̀fwerạ̀s↓	*Ese* está en las afueras.
That lady is American.	6 esasẹnyorạ |ẹsạ̀mẹrikanạ̀↓	*Esa* señora es americana.
I don't want those (pieces of) furniture.	7 nokyerọ |esozmwéblẹ̀s↓	No quiero *esos* muebles.

| Those ladies are American. | 8 | ésa(s) señyóras \|sónåmèrikánås↓ | *Esas* señoras son americanas. |
| that over there (m) | | åkél↓ | aquél |

| That's my car over there. | 9 | åkélezmįáwtó↓ | *Aquél* es mi auto. |
| that over there (fem) | | åké()yá↓ | aquélla |

| That lady there is American. | 10 | åké()yasenyórą \|èsåmèrikánå↓ | *Aquella* señora es americana. |

| I like those cars over there. | 11 | mègustán \|åké()yòsáwtòs↓ | Me gustan *aquellos* autos. |

| Those tables over there are empty. | 12 | åké()yazmèsas \|èstándesokupádås↓ | *Aquellas* mesas están desocupadas. |

EXTRAPOLATION

	near me		near you		near him	(away from us)
	sg	pl	sg	pl	sg	pl
m	éste	éstos	ése	ésos	akél	aké()yos
f	ésta	éstas	ésa	ésas	aké()ya	aké()yas

NOTES

a. Demonstratives, which are special kinds of adjectives, have distinct forms for gender and number.

b. Spanish has one set of forms which corresponds to English 'this', two that correspond to 'that'.

7.21.21 Substitution drills

Form substitution

1 làmesa̧ |èstac̄esokupác̄a̧↓

   éstá_____↓   éstàmesa̧ |èstac̄esokupác̄a̧↓

   ésà_____↓   ésàmesa̧ |èstac̄esokupác̄a̧↓

   àké⑩ya̧_____↓   àké⑩ya̧mésa̧ |èstác̄esokupác̄a̧↓

2 èlkwártǫezbwénó↓

   éstè_____↓   éstèkwártǫ |ezbwénó↓

   ésè_____↓   ésèkwártǫ |ezbwénó↓

---

1 *La* mesa está desocupada.

   Esta_____.   Esta mesa está desocupada.

   Esa_____.   Esa mesa está desocupada.

   Aquella_____.   Aquella mesa está desocupada.

2 *El* cuarto es bueno.

   Este_____.   Este cuarto es bueno.

   Ese_____.   Ese cuarto es bueno.

àkél_____↓   àkélkwártọ|ezbwénỏ↓

3 lỏs̩ápàrtámentos|sómbarátòs↓   éstỏs̩ápàrtámentos|sómbarátòs↓

   éstỏs_____↓   ésòs̩ápàrtámentos|sómbarátòs↓

   ésòs_____↓   àké(l)yòs̩ápàrtámentos|sómbarátòs↓

   àké(l)yòs_____↓

Aquel_____.   Aquel cuarto es bueno.

3 Los apartamentos son baratos.

   Estos_____....   Estos apartamentos son baratos.

   Esos_____..   Esos apartamentos son baratos.

   Aquellos_____..   Aquellos apartamentos son baratos.

225

Number substitution

1 tráygamése |şenışéró↓

_____şenışérós↓   tráygamésos |şenışérós↓

2 dèseǫır |ǫesahénşyà↓

_____ahénşyàs↓   dèseǫır |ǫesas,ahénşyàs↓

3 àkeꞮyòs |èdıfışyos |soŋgrándés↓

_____edıfışyǫ_____↓   àkeledıfışyǫ |ezgrándè↓

---

1 Tráigame ese *cenicero*.

_____ *ceniceros*.   Tráigame esos ceniceros.

2 Deseo ir a esa *agencia*.

_____ *agencias*.   Deseo ir a esas agencias.

3 Aquellos *edificios* son grandes.

_____ *edificio* _____.   Aquel edificio es grande.

4 éstòs,èskritoryos |sombarátós↓   éstèskritoryọ |ezbarátó↓
   _____èskritoryọ_____↓

5 bamos,abér |esosperyóɗikós↓   bamos,abér |eseperyóɗikó↓
   _____peryóɗikò↓

6 éstámesa |nọezgrándè↓   éstázmesaz |nosọŋgrándès↓
   ____mesaz_____↓

7 àke(ll)ya,seɲyora |es,espaɲyólà↓   àke(ll)ya(s)seɲyoras |sọnespaɲyólàs↓
   _____seɲyoras_____↓

---

4 Estos *escritorios* son baratos.   Este escritorio es barato.

  _____*escritorio*_____.

5 Vamos a ver esos *periódicos*.   Vamos a ver ese periódico.
  _____*periódico*.

6 Esta *mesa* no es grande.   Estas mesas no son grandes.

  _____*mesas*_____.

7 Aquella *señora* es española.   Aquellas señoras son españolas.

  _____*señoras*_____.

Item substitution

1 kyérópresèntárlę |aèsasenyórà↓

_____senyór↓   kyérópresèntárlę |aèsesenyór↓

2 ésósapàrtámentos |sombwénôs↓

___èskwelas_____↓   ésàsèskwelas |sombwénàs↓

3 demęake()yozlíbròs↓

_____plúmàs↓   demęake()yasplúmàs↓

---

1 Quiero presentarle a esa *señora*.

_____ señor.   Quiero presentarle a ese señor.

2 Esos *apartamentos* son buenos.

___ *escuelas* _____   Esas escuelas son buenas.

3 Dème aquellos *libros*

_____ *plumas*   Déme aquellas plumas.

4 pásemeselápiṣ↓

 _____ plúmả↓

    pásemesaplúmả↓

5 ȧkelȧwtọ│ésta◌̇esokupá◌̇ȯ↓

 ____mesạ_____↓

    ȧke◌̇yamésạ│ésta◌̇esokupá◌̇ả↓

6 éstȧsék̦yon│ezgránde̊↓

 ____e◌̇ífɪ̧yọ_____↓

    ésté◌̇ífɪ̧yọ│ezgránde̊↓

7 ȧke◌̇yamésạ│ésta◌̇esokupá◌̇ả↓

 _____eskrɪtóryọ_____↓

    ȧkeleskrɪtóryọ│ésta◌̇esokupá◌̇ȯ↓

---

4 Páseme ese *lápiz.*

 _____ *pluma.*

    Páseme esa pluma.

5 Aquel *auto* está desocupado.

 ____*mesạ*_____ .

    Aquella mesa está desocupada.

6 Esta *sección* es grande.

 ____*edificio*_____ .

    Este edificio es grande.

7 Aquella *mesa* está desocupada.

 _____ *escritorio*_____ .

    Aquel escritorio está desocupado.

7.21.22 Response drill [1]

1 kyéréstelápiş↑ǫestaplúmá↓   ésélápiş↓

2 kyéréstozlapişes↑ǫestasplúmás↓   ésásplúmás↓

_____

1 ¿Quiere este lápiz o esta pluma?   Ese lápiz.

2 ¿Quiere estos lápices o estas plumas?   Esas plumas.

(1) The implicit spacial reference of the demonstratives can be most effectively presented by the use of gestures to indicate position. Both tutor and the student should independently use /éste/ for items near themselves and /ése/ for items near each other or away from both.

[éstôzlíbròs↓]   3   kékyérẹ|ùstéá↓   ésôzlíbròs↓

[éstásplúmàs↓]   4   kékyérél↓   ésásplúmàs↓

[esé↓]   5   lègústạ|éstelíbro↑   ésenó↓ éstê↓

[esòs↓]   6   kyérẹ|estôzlíbros↑   ésoznó↓ éstôs↓

[esàs↓]   7   kyérẹ|estasplúmas↑   ésaznó↓ éstàs↓

[esá↓]   8   lègústạ|éstaplúma↑   ésanó↓ éstá↓

(estos libros)   3   ¿Qué quiere Ud.?   Esos libros.
(estas plumas)   4   ¿Qué quiere él?   Esas plumas.

(ése)   5   ¿Le gusta este libro?   Ese no, éste.
(ésos)   6   ¿Quiere estos libros?   Esos no, éstos.
(ésas)   7   ¿Quiere estas plumas?   Esas no, éstas.
(ésa)   8   ¿Le gusta esta pluma?   Esa no, ésta.

231

9 èzbwéno|eselíbro↑   éstet sↄↄ èzmúybwénↄ↓

10 èzbwéno|estelíbro↑   éset sↄↄ èzmúybwénↄ↓

11 èzbwéna|estaplúma↑   ésat sↄↄ èzmúybwénà↓

12 èzbwéna|esaplúma↑   ésta↑ sↄↄ èzmúybwénà↓

13 sómbwénos|esozlíbros↑   éstos↑ sↄↄ sónmúybwénos↓

---

9 ¿Es bueno ese libro?   ¿Este? Sí, es muy bueno.

10 ¿Es bueno este libro?   ¿Ese? Sí, es muy bueno.

11 ¿Es buena esta pluma?   ¿Esa? Sí, es muy buena.

12 ¿Es buena esa pluma?   ¿Esta? Sí, es muy buena.

13 ¿Son buenos esos libros?   ¿Estos? Sí, son muy buenos.

7.21.23 Translation drill

1 This salad is very good.

éstą̀ènsàlácą |èstámúybwénà↓

Esta ensalada está muy buena.

2 Those (over there) gentlemen speak English.

àkeⓁyo(s) señóres |àblaniŋglés↓

Aquellos señores hablan inglés.

3 That room to the left.

ésèkwartọalạịşkyérdà↓

Ese cuarto a la izquierda.

4 That's my room over there.

àkelezmɪkwártò↓

Aquél es mi cuarto.

5 Can we see those pieces of furniture?

pòdemozbér |esozmwéblest↑

¿Podemos ver esos muebles?

6 Hand me those keys.

pásemésazⓁyábès↓

Páseme esas llaves.

7 That (over there) young lady is American.

àkeⓁyasenyoritą |es,amerikánà↓

Aquella señorita es americana.

8 This building is large.

éstèdifịşyọ |ezgrándè↓

Este edificio es grande.

9 In this section we are very busy.

èn,éstàsèkşyón |èstámòzmúyokupádòs↓

En esta sección estamos muy ocupados.

10 Do you need these books?

nèşèsítạ̀estozlíbrost↑

¿Necesita estos libros?

11 That's Mrs. Molina.

ésą |èzlàsènyoramolínà↓

Esa es la señora Molina.

B. Discussion of pattern

Demonstratives are words which designate or point out, usually in terms of spatial arrangement, but sometimes in terms of time relation. They are a special kind of 'limiting' adjectives which always precede the nouns they modify. Besides the forms listed in the presentation above, demonstratives include definite articles, which have been separately presented because of special functions that they have.

English as well as Spanish has words that can be classed as demonstratives. The English demonstratives provide a relatively rare example of modifier forms which change in English for number reference, as the following chart shows:

	near	far
sg	this	that
pl	these	those

This change in form is called 'inflection for number', and an agreement in form with an associated noun is obligatory; i.e., we cannot say 'these book' or 'that apples'. As has already been shown in unit 4, agreement in number between nouns and adjectives in Spanish is almost always shown by number inflection in the adjective, just as it is in this one case in English.

The spatial contrast in English demonstratives is a two-way pattern: near and not near. The Spanish demonstratives, however, have a three-way pattern: near me, near you (or a short way off), and near him (or a long way off). Thus /akél/ implies more distant in space or more remote in time. This extra distinction, coupled with three distinct gender forms, gives Spanish an inventory of 15 forms, compared to 4 in English, as follows

	sg	pl	sg	pl
	this	these	that	those
m	éste	éstos	ése, akél	ésos, akéⓁyos
f	ésta	éstas	ésa, akéⓁya	ésas, akéⓁyas
n	ésto		éso, (akéⓁyo)	

Note that the pattern of the Spanish forms deviates from the normal pattern of Spanish modifiers in one important respect. The regular pattern:

	sg	pl
m	— o	— os
f	— a	— as

is present except in the m sg forms, where the endings are /—e/ (/éste, ése/) or zero (/akél/). A form which has a final /—o/ appears in the pattern with unmarked, or neuter, gender. The forms /ésto/ and /éso/ were presented and explained in Unit 2; /akél)yo/, though appearing less frequently, occurs in similar patterns.

The demonstratives can occur as modifiers (adjectives modifying nouns) or as nominalized forms (taking the place of nouns). Both uses are illustrated in the following sentence:

/éstelíbro |esmásbaráto |keése↓/   'This book is cheaper than that one'

Note that in English the singular forms are not readily nominalized, so that 'one' replaces the noun.

The neuter forms almost always occur nominalized, since there are no neuter nouns they can modify.

Spelling conventions have established the practice of marking a written accent on the stressed vowel in masculine and feminine nominalized forms, except when the letter is printed with upper case type.

7.22   Replacement drills

A   éstezmɹáwtò↓

1 àkel_____↓   àkelezmɹáwtò↓

2 _____ ṣerbéṣà↓   àke(l)ɹạezmɹṣerbéṣà↓

3 ésạ_____↓   esạezmɹṣerbéṣà↓

4 _____lápiṣ↓   ésezmɹlápiṣ↓

5 _____mésà↓   esạezmɹmésà↓

6 ____la_____↓   esạezlamésà↓

7 ésas_____↓   ésa(s)sonlazmésàs↓

A   Este es mi auto.

1 Aquél_____.   Aquél es mi auto.

2 _____cerveza.   Aquélla es mi cerveza.

3 Esa_____.   Esa es mi cerveza.

4 _____lápiz.   Ese es mi lápiz.

5 _____mesa.   Esa es mi mesa.

6 _____la_____.   Esa es la mesa.

7 Esas_____.   Esas son las mesas.

B   èlsèŋyórhwáyt|dèséàlkilár|un̩apartaméntò↓

1 _____ búskar _____↓   èlsèŋyórhwáyt|dèséàbúskar|un̩apartaméntò↓

2 __sèŋyórà_____↓   làsèŋyóràhwayt|dèséàbúskar|un̩apartaméntò↓

3 _____mwéblès↓   làsèŋyóràhwayt|dèséàbúskar|un̩ozmwéblès↓

4 _____bér_____↓   làsèŋyóràhwayt|dèséàber|un̩ozmwéblès↓

5 _____máz_____↓   làsèŋyóràhwayt|dèséàber|mazmwéblès↓

6 _____kyérè_____↓   làsèŋyóràhwayt|kyéreber|mazmwéblès↓

7 lòs_____↓   lò(s)sèŋyórèshwayt|kyérèmbér|mazmwéblès↓

B   El señor White desea alquilar un apartamento.

1 _____ buscar _____.   El señor White desea buscar un apartamento.

2 __señora_____.   La señora White desea buscar un apartamento.

3 _____muebles.   La señora White desea buscar unos muebles.

4 _____ver_____.   La señora White desea ver unos muebles.

5 _____más_____.   La señora White desea ver más muebles.

6 _____quiere_____.   La señora White quiere ver más muebles.

7 Los_____.   Los señores White quieren ver más muebles.

C　idóndestaęlótról

1 ＿＿＿＿＿mésá↓　　　　　　　　　　　　idóndestalamésá↓

2 ＿＿＿＿＿ęsa＿↓　　　　　　　　　　　　idóndestaęsamésá↓

3 ＿＿＿＿＿sí()yá↓　　　　　　　　　　　idóndestaęsasí()yá↓

4 ＿＿＿＿la＿＿↓　　　　　　　　　　　idóndestalasí()yá↓

5 ＿＿＿＿＿sęņyórás↓　　　　　　　　　idóndestanla(s)sęņyórás↓

6 ＿kómǫ＿＿＿＿＿↓　　　　　　　　ikómǫestanla(s)sęņyórás↓

7 ＿＿＿＿ęl＿＿＿↓　　　　　　　　ikómǫestaęlsęņyór↓

C　¿Y dónde está el otro?

1 ¿＿＿＿＿＿mesa?　　　　　　　　　¿Y dónde está la mesa?

2 ¿＿＿＿＿ esa ＿＿?　　　　　　　　¿Y dónde está esa mesa?

3 ¿＿＿＿＿ silla?　　　　　　　　　¿Y dónde está esa silla?

4 ¿＿＿＿＿ la ＿＿?　　　　　　　　¿Y dónde está la silla?

5 ¿＿＿＿＿ señoras?　　　　　　　　¿Y dónde están las señoras?

6 ¿＿cómo＿＿＿＿?　　　　　　　　¿Y cómo están las señoras?

7 ¿＿＿＿＿ el＿＿?　　　　　　　　¿Y cómo está el señor?

D   kreó|kềmềkỏmbyénềmas|elpriméró↓

1 _____ótró↓   kreó|kềmềkỏmbyénềmas|elótró↓

2 _____muchọ_____↓   kreó|kềmềkỏmbyénềmuchọ|elótró↓

3 _____gústả_____↓   kreó|kềmềgústảmuchọ|elótró↓

4 ___lề_____↓   kreó|kềlềgústảmuchọ|elótró↓

5 _____pókọ_____↓   kreó|kềlềgústảpókọ|elótró↓

6 kreẹ_____↓   kreẹ|kềlềgústảpókọ|elótró↓

7 _____ótrả↓   kreẹ|kềlềgústảpoko|lạótrả↓

D   Creo que me conviene más el primero.

1 _____ otro.   Creo que me conviene más el otro.

2 _____mucho___ .   Creo que me conviene mucho el otro.

3 _____gusta_____ .   Creo que me gusta mucho el otro.

4 ___le_____ .   Creo que le gusta mucho el otro.

5 _____poco___ .   Creo que le gusta poco el otro.

6 Cree_____ ,   Cree que le gusta poco el otro.

7 _____ otra.   Cree que le gusta poco la otra.

E   pòdemozbérloↃ

1 _____buskárloↃ   pòdemozbuskárloↃ

2 kyére_____Ↄ   kyérebuskárloↃ

3 _____ótrabeşↃ   kyére|buskárlǫ|ótrabeşↃ

4 _____ir_____Ↄ   kyérǫir|ótrabeşↃ

5 _____ḓespwésↃ   kyérǫir|ḓespwésↃ

6 _____benir_____Ↄ   kyérebenir|ḓespwésↃ

7 kyérem_____Ↄ   kyérembenir|ḓespwésↃ

E   ¿Podemos verlo?

1 ¿_____buscarlo?   ¿Podemos buscarlo?

2 ¿Quiere _____?   ¿Quiere buscarlo?

3 ¿_____otra vez?   ¿Quiere buscarlo otra vez?

4 ¿_____ir_____?   ¿Quiere ir otra vez?

5 ¿_____después?   ¿Quiere ir después?

6 ¿_____venir_____?   ¿Quiere venir después?

7 ¿Quieren_____?   ¿Quieren venir después?

F   síↆ åkityéne |laɲyábèↆ

1 _____laz_____↓   síↆ åkityéne |lazɲyábèsↆ

2 _____biɲyétèsↆ   síↆ åkityéne |lozbiɲyétèsↆ

3 __åí_____↓   síↆ åítyéne |lozbiɲyétèsↆ

4 _____um_____↓   síↆ åítyenε |umbiɲyétèↆ

5 _____monéɗàↆ   síↆ åítyenε |unamonéɗàↆ

6 _____ésaz_____↓   síↆ åítyenε |ésazmonéɗàsↆ

7 _____chékéↆ   síↆ åítyenε |ésechékèↆ

F   Sí, aquí tiene la llave.

1 _____ las _____ .   Sí, aquí tiene las llaves.

2 _____billetes.   Sí, aquí tiene los billetes.

3 __ ahí _____ .   Sí, ahí tiene los billetes.

4 _____un_____ .   Sí, ahí tiene un billete.

5 _____ moneda.   Sí, ahí tiene una moneda.

6 _____esas_____.   Sí, ahí tiene esas monedas.

7 _____cheque.   Sí, ahí tiene ese cheque.

7.23   Variation drills

A   ézbyeho |péróbwenót   Es viejo, pero bueno.

1 It's old but inexpensive.   ézbyeho |péróbàratót   Es viejo, pero barato.

2 It's old but excellent.   ézbyeho |pérọéks(ṣ)élenté↓   Es viejo, pero excelente.

3 It's big but inexpensive.   ézgrande |péróbàratót   Es grande, pero barato.

4 They're old but inexpensive.   sómbyehos |péróbàratòs↓   Son viejos, pero baratos.

5 They're good and inexpensive.   sómbwenos₁barátòs↓   Son buenos y baratos

6 They're big and good.   sóŋgrandes₁bwénós↓   Son grandes y buenos.

7 They're inexpensive and good.   sómbàratos₁bwénós↓   Son baratos y buenos.

B   bamos₁abér|elperyódikò↓   Vamos a ver el periódico.

1 Let's go see the apartment   bamos₁abér |elapartaméntó↓   Vamos a ver el apartamento

2 Let's go see the building.   bamos₁abér |eledifíṣyò↓   Vamos a ver el edificio.

3 Let's go see the rooms.

bámos&abér | loskwártôs↓

Vamos a ver los cuartos.

4 Let's go get acquainted with the downtown section.

bámos&akonoşér | elşéntrô↓

Vamos a conocer el centro.

5 Let's go eat in the restaurant.

bámos&akomér | enelrrestorán↓

Vamos a comer en el restorán.

6 Let's go to work now.

bámos&atrabahár | aórà↓

Vamos a trabajar ahora.

7 Let's go look for an apartment.

bámos&abuskár | un&apartaméntô↓

Vamos a buscar un apartamento.

C pórkénobémos | ạun&amígomíô↓

¿Por qué no vemos a un amigo mío?

1 Why don't we see Joseph?

pórkénobémos | ahosé↓

¿Por qué no vemos a José?

2 Why don't we eat in the restaurant?

pórkénokomémos | enelrrestorán↓

¿Por qué no comemos en el restorán?

3 Why don't we eat later?

pórkénokomémoz | despwés↓

¿Por qué no comemos después?

4 Why don't we go down in the elevator?

pórkénobahámos | enelas(ş)ensór↓

¿Por qué no bajamos en el ascensor?

5 Why don't we speak Spanish?

pórkénọablamos | espaŋyól↓

¿Por qué no hablamos español?

6 Why don't we look for another apartment?

pórkenobuskámos |otrǫapartaméntǒↆ

¿Por qué no buscamos otro apartamento?

7 Why don't we rent another building?

pórkenǫalkilámos |otrǫedifíşyǒↆ

¿Por qué no alquilamos otro edificio?

D   sólotengo |dozdesokupádǒsↆ

Sólo tengo dos desocupados.

1 I only have five available.

sólotengo |şınkodesokupádǒsↆ

Sólo tengo cinco desocupados.

2 I only have one available.

sólotengǫ |unodesokupádǒↆ

Sólo tengo uno desocupado.

3 I only have one table available.

sólotengǫ |unamesa |desokupádàↆ

Sólo tengo una mesa desocupada.

4 I only have one apartment available.

sólotengǫ |unapartamento |desokupádǒↆ

Sólo tengo un apartamento desocupado.

5 I only have one desk available.

sólotengǫ |uneskritoryo |desokupádǒↆ

Sólo tengo un escritorio desocupado.

6 I only have five chairs available.

sólotengo |şınkosiꝏyaz |desokupádàsↆ

Sólo tengo cinco sillas desocupadas.

7 He only has two rooms available.

sólotyéne |doskwártoz |desokupádǒsↆ

Sólo tiene dos cuartos desocupados.

E   dôs(ṣ)yéntôs↓sininklwír|luṣ↑

   ágwanigás↓

                                                                Doscientos, sin incluir luz, agua
          ni gas.

1 Three hundred, not including electricity, water or gas.

trés(ṣ)yéntôs↓sininklwír|luṣ↑

ágwanigás↓

Trescientos, sin incluir luz, agua ni gas.

2 Four hundred, not including electricity, water or gas.

kwátrôṣyéntôs↓sininklwír|luṣ↑

ágwanigás↓

Cuatrocientos, sin incluir luz, agua ni gas.

3 Two hundred twenty, not including water or gas.

dôs(ṣ)yéntozbéyntê↓sininklwír|

ágwanigás↓

Doscientos veinte, sin incluir agua ni gas.

4 Seven pesos, not including beer or wine.

syetepésôs↓sininklwír|ṣêrbéṣa

nibínô↓

Siete pesos, sin incluir cerveza ni vino.

5 Fifteen dollars, not including the taxi or the tip.

kinṣedólárês↓sininklwír|êl

taksinilapropína↓

Quince dólares, sin incluir el taxi ni la propina.

6 Two hundred dollars without furniture.

dôs(ṣ)yéntozdólares|sinmwéblês↓

Doscientos dólares sin muebles.

7 Three hundred dollars furnished.

trés(ṣ)yéntozdólares|amwebládô↓

Trescientos dólares amueblado.

F ése|éstáẹnlàs̩àfwéras|ẓézmáz

    grándè↓

                                                                      Ese está en las afueras y es más grande.

1 That one is downtown and is larger.   ése|éstáẹnélṣéntro|ẓézmázgrándè↓   Ese está en el centro y es más grande.

2 That one is on Columbus Avenue and is less expensive.   ése|éstáẹnlàbèníⱡàkólon|ẓézmáz   Ese está en la Avenida Colón y es más barato.

                                                báráto̩↓

3 That one is near the American Embassy.   ésestaṣérka|ⱡèl̩ạèmbàhaⱡamerikánà↓   Ese está cerca de la Embajada Americana.

4 That one is to the right.   ésestaladerécha̩↓   Ese está a la derecha.

5 That one is to the left.   ésestalạiṣkyérⱡà↓   Ese está a la izquierda.

6 That one is very far.   ése|éstámuyléhòs↓   Ese está muy lejos.

7 That one is very good.   ése|éstámuybwéno̩↓   Ese está muy bueno.

7.24   Review drill - The distribution of /sér/ and /estár/

1 I'm not an American but   nosóyamerıkánò↓péroestóy|enlòs.   No soy americano, pero estoy
   I'm in the United States.   èstaɗos,uníɗòs↓   en los Estados Unidos.

2 We're not Americans, but   nosomos|amerıkánòs↓péroéstamos| No somos americanos, pero
   we're in the United States.   enlòs.èstaɗos,uníɗòs↓   estamos en los Estados Unidos.

3 He's not an American, but   elnoes,amerıkánò↓péroésta|enlòs.   El no es americano, pero está
   he's in the United States.   èstaɗos,uníɗòs↓   en los Estados Unidos.

4 They're from Chile, but   éꞎyò(s)sóndèchılè↓péroestánénkòlombyà↓ Ellos son de Chile, pero están en
   they're in Colombia.   Colombia.

5 Carmen's from Chile, but   karmen|èzɗèchılè↓péroestáénèlpérú↓   Carmen es de Chile, pero está
   she's in Peru.   en el Perú.

6 They (f) are married, and   éꞎyà(s)sóŋkásaɗas|ꞎestanéŋkalıfórnyà↓ Ellas son casadas y están en
   they're in California.   California.

7 She's married, and she's in   éꞎyaéskásaɗa|ꞎestaéŋkalıfórnyà↓   Ella es casada y está en
   California.   California.

8 He's single, and he's in Cuba.   élè(s)sóltero|ꞎestaéŋkúbà↓   El es soltero y está en Cuba.

9 The hotel is good, and it's   élótelezbweno|inoéstaléhòs↓   El hotel es bueno y no está lejos.
   not far.

10 The buildings are big and they're near.

lósėċifíṣyòs |sóŋgrándes |ẓèstánṣérkà↓

Los edificios son grandes y están cerca.

11 The restaurant isn't cheap and it's very far.

èlrrèstòrán|nọẹzbarátò↓ẓèstámuyléhòs↓

El restorán no es barato y está muy lejos.

7.3   CONVERSATION STIMULUS

NARRATIVE 1

1 Juan talks with the young lady that works in the cashier's office.

hwan |áblàkònlàsėŋyòrita |
kėtràbahạenlakáhà↓

Juan habla con la señorita que

trabaja en la caja.

2 He says he's planing to look for an apartment.

eldị̣ẹ |kėpyensa |búskaruṇapartaméntò↓

El dice que piensa buscar un apartamento.

3 He likes this hotel.

lėgustạẹstẹotél↓

Le gusta este hotel.

4 But it's cheaper living in an apartment.

pérọẹzmázbarátòîbıbír |ėnụ̀napártà
mentò↓

Pero es más barato vivır en un apartamento.

5 He wants it furnished.

lòkyérẹ |àmwèbladò↓

Lo quiere amueblado.

6 But if there isn't (one)
  furnished he'll take
  one unfurnished.

péròsinọay│ámwéblaḍot
tomạunosınmwéblès↓

Pero si no hay amueblado,

toma uno sin muebles.

7 A friend who works with him
  in the consular section is
  going to help him.

únạmıgo│kètràbahakonél│
ênlàsèkṣyóŋkònsúlart
bayuḍárlè↓

Un amigo que trabaja con él

en la sección consular, va a

ayudarle.

8 They're going to go this
  afternoon.

bánạir│estatárdè↓

Van a ir esta tarde.

9 Juan thinks it's easy to find
  an apartment.

hwaŋ│kréẹkésfaṣil│êŋkòntráràpàrtà
méntò↓

Juan cree que es fácil encontrar
apartamento.

DIALOG 1

Juan, dígale a la Srta. que Ud.
piensa buscar un apartamento.

pyénsobuskar│unạpartaméntò│sèŋyòrítà↓

Juan: Pienso buscar un apartamento, señorita.

Srta., pregúntele si no le gusta
este hotel.

nólègustạestẹotelt

Srta.: ¿No le gusta este hotel?

Juan, contéstele que sí, es excelente
pero que es más barato vivir en un
apartamento.

sı↓ẹsẹèks(ṣ)èlèntè↓ pérọèzmazbarátôt
bıbır│ênụnạpàrtàmentò↓

Juan: Sí, es excelente, peio es

más barato vivir en un
apartamento.

Srta., pregúntele si él cree que es fácil encontrar.

ústeɑ̀kreę̀ |késfaɡ̀ıleŋkontrár↑

Srta.: ¿Ud. cree que es fácil encontrar?

Juan, dígale que Ud. cree que sí.

kréo̱ |késí↓

Juan: Creo que sí.

Srta., pregúntele si lo quiere amueblado o sin muebles.

lòkyérę̀ |àmwèbladɑ̱o̱tosınmwéblés↓

Srta.: ¿Lo quiere amueblado o sin muebles?

Juan, contéstele que le conviene más amueblado, pero que si no hay, toma uno sin muebles.

mèkòmbyénemás |àmwèblaɑ̀ò↓
pérósıno |ay↑tomo̱unosınmwéblés↓

Juan: Me conviene más amueblado; pero si no hay, tomo uno sin muebles.

NARRATIVE 2

1 It's almost three o'clock.

soŋkasılastrés↓

Son casi las tres.

2 Jose and Juan go down in the elevator.

hòseı̱hwàm |bahaṇeṇelas(ş)ensór↓

José y Juan bajan en el ascensor.

3 Jose has yesterday's paper.

hòsétyenę̀ |èlpèryóɑ̀ıkoɑ̀ęa̱yér↓

José tiene el periódico de ayer.

4 They look at the ad section.

bén |làsékşyondęanúnşyòs↓

Ven la sección de anuncios.

5 There are many apartments.

áymuchos‚apartaméntòs↓

Hay muchos apartamentos.

6 One ad says: 'Three-room   úninánunşyodíşè↓ àpàrtàmento| Un anuncio dice: 'Apartamento
  apartment, furnished, two   dètreskwártòs↓ àmwèblàdô↓   de tres cuartos, amueblado,
  hundred a month.'   dôs(ş)yentos.almés↓   doscientos al mes.

7 It's too big for Juan.   ézdèmàsyadográndè |páràhwán↓   Es demasiado grande para Juan.

                                    DIALOG 2

Juan, dígale a José que son   soŋkasilastrés |hòsé↓   Juan: Son casi las tres, José.
  casi las tres.

José, dígale que tiene razón,   tyenezrraşóm↓bamòs↓   José: Tienes razón, vamos.
  que 'vamos', y que a esta   àestaora |nọaymuchomobimyéntò↓   A esta hora no hay mucho
  hora no hay mucho movi-   movimiento.
  miento.

Juan, pregúntele a José si lleva (l)yebas|elperyodikodeayer↑   Juan: ¿Llevas el periódico de
  el periódico de ayer.   ayer?

José, contéstele que sí, que aquí sí↓ àkiestá↓ béamoslos.anúnşyòs↓ José: Sí, aquí está. Veamos
  está, y que vean los anuncios.   los anuncios.

Juan, pregúntele si ve algo.   bes.algo↑   Juan: ¿Ves algo?

Jose, dígale que aquí hay uno: sí↓ ák̯ayúnò↓ ápàrtàmento│   José: Sí, aquí hay uno: 'Apartamento
  'Apartamento de tres cuartos,   dètreskwartos↑àmwéblàdo↑   de tres cuartos, amueblado,
  amueblado, agua, luz; dos-   agwa↑lus̩↑dòs(s̩)yentos̩almés↓   agua, luz; doscientos al mes.
  cientos al mes.

Juan, dígale que no le conviene,   nomekombyéné↓dèmàsyadográndè↓   Juan: No me conviene, demasiado
  que demasiado grande.   grande.

NARRATIVE 3

1 Another one says: 'Unfurnished   otrodís̩é↓ ápàrtàmento│sin   Otro dice: 'Apartamento sin muebles,
  apartment, cheap....'   mwebles↑ bàrato↑   barato....'

2 No, Juan wants it furnished.   no↓hwanlokyére̩│amwebládò↓   No, Juan lo quiere amueblado.

3 Here's a furnished one-room   àk̯ı│áyúnàpàrtàmento̩│àmwébládo̩↑   Aquí hay un apartamento amueblado
  apartment.   idẹuŋkwártò↓   y de un cuarto.

4 But it's a long ways from down-   pérọèsta│muylehoz│dèls̩éntrò↓   Pero está muy lejos del centro,
  town, almost in the outskirts.   kas̯ı│ènlàsàfweràs↓   casi en las afueras.

5 And Juan wants to live downtown.   ihwaŋkyérebıbır│ènèls̩éntrò↓   Y Juan quiere vivir en el centro.

6 There are others but they're
    either too big or they're
    too far away.

áyótròs↓ péròsónmúygrándès↑

qèstánmúyléhòs↓

Hay otros, pero o son muy grandes

o están muy lejos.

7 Jose has a friend who works
    for an agency.

hósétyenҫun̩amigo|kètrábahą

en̩unahénşyà↓

José tiene un amigo que trabaja

en una agencia.

8 They're going to see him.

bánàberlò↓

Van a verlo.

DIALOG 3

José, dígale que aquí hay otro:
'Apartamento sin muebles,
barato....'

àkɹ̩ayótró↓ àpàrtàméntosin

mwéblèz↑bàrato|

José: Aquí hay otro: 'Apartamento

sin muebles, barato....'

Juan, dígale que no, que Ud. quiere
uno amueblado.

nó↓ kyérọunọ|àmwèblado↓

Juan: No, quiero uno amueblado.

José, dígale que aquí hay uno
amueblado y de un cuarto.

àki|áyúnọàmwèblado↑idҫuŋkwártò↓

José: Aquí hay uno amueblado y

de un cuarto.

Juan, pregúntele si dice dónde
está.

dişe|dondesta↑

Juan: ¿Dice dónde está?

José, contéstele que sí, que en la Avenida Colón, 1621.

sí↓ ènlàbènídàkòlón↓

dyèșiseyzḃeyntyúnò↓

José: Sí, en la Avenida Colón, 1621.

Juan, pregúntele que dónde está eso.

dondestaésò↓

Juan: ¿Dónde está eso?

Jose, contéstele que un poco lejos, que casi en las afueras.

ùmpokolehòs↓ kási |ènlàsàfwerás↓

José: Un poco lejos, casi en las afueras.

Juan, dígale que no le conviene a Ud., que Ud. quiere vivir en el centro.

nomekombyénè↓ yokyérobibir |

ènèlșentrò↓

Juan: No me conviene; yo quiero

vivir en el centro.

José, dígale que muy bien, que Ud. tiene un amigo que trabaja en la Agencia del Valle; que pueden ir a hablar con el.

muyḃyén↓ yótéŋgoúnàmigo |

kètrábahą |ènlàhenșya

ďelbáļyè↓ póďemos.ir |àḃlàrkonél↓

José: Muy bien. Yo tengo un amigo que trabaja en la Agencia del Valle; podemos ir a hablar con él.

End of Tape 4B

8.1   BASIC SENTENCES. Molina tells White about his neighbors' apartment.

After having seen several apartments that were not suitable, Jose Molina and John White return to the hotel to talk it over.

ENGLISH SPELLING	AID TO LISTENING	SPANISH SPELLING
gosh	kárambá↓	caramba
(I) remember (to remember)	rrékwérdó↓ rrékórdár↓	recuerdo (recordar)
Molina Gosh, now I remember.	kárambá↓ áorakerrekwérdó↓	*Molina* ¡Caramba! Ahora que recuerdo.
the neighbor	él—béşinó↓	el vecino
(they) go (to go)	bán↓ ír↓	van (ir)
to remove	múdár↓	mudar
the house	lá—kasá↓	la casa
to move (one's residence)	múdarse—de—kásá↓	mudarse de casa
the week	lá—sémaná↓	la semana
My neighbors are going to move this week.	mizbéşinoz |banamudarse |dekasa| éstásémáná↓	Mis vecinos van a mudarse de casa esta semana.
(they) live (to live)	bibén↓ bibír↓	viven (vivir)

equal to, the same as	igwál–à↓	igual a
They live in an apartment just like mine.	bíben │ènùnàpártàmento │igwálàlmíò↓	Viven en un apartamento igual al mío.
expensive	kárò↓	caro

White
Is it very expensive?

ezmuykaro↑

White
¿Es muy caro?

the contrary	èl–kòntráryò↓	el contrario
on the contrary	àl–kòntráryò↓	al contrario
the price	èl–prèşyò↓	el precio
bad	má'l↓ malò↓	mal (malo)

Molina
On the contrary, the price is not bad.

àlkòntráryò↓ èlprèşyo │noestamál↓

Molina
Al contrario, el precio no está mal.

(it) gives (to give)	dá↓ dár↓	da (dar)
to face on	dar–à↓	dar a
the street	là–ka(l)yé↓	la calle
the yard, the court, the patio	èl–pátyò↓	el patio

White
Does it face the street or the patio?

dálaka(l)ye↑oalpátyò↓

White
¿Da a la calle o al patio?

| pretty | bónitô↓ | bonito |
| the view | lá‑bistá↓ | la vista |

Molina
The street, and it has a beautiful view.

dálaká(l)ye |ityéné |múybonitabístá↓

Molina
Da a la calle y tiene muy bonita vista.

| the room | la‑abitáşyon↓ | la habitación |

White
How many rooms does it have?

kwántasabitaşyónes |tyéné↓

White
¿Cuántas habitaciones tiene?

| the living room | lá‑salá↓ | la sala |
| the kitchen | lá‑kóşiná↓ | la cocina |

Molina
A large living room, kitchen and bath.

únásálágránde↑kóşina |ikwártodebányó↓

Molina
Una sala grande, cocina y cuarto de baño.

| the bedroom | él‑dórmitóryó↓ | el dormitorio |

White
Doesn't it have a bedroom?

nótyéne |dórmitóryo↑

White
¿No tiene dormitorio?

Molina
No, but the living room is quite large.

nó↓ pérólásala |ezbastántegrándé↓

Molina
No, pero la sala es bastante grande.

| the sofa | él‑sófá↓ | el sofá |

the bed	lá—kámá↓	la cama
the sofa-bed	él—sófa—kámá↓	el sofá cama
In mine I have a sofa-bed.	énlàmia↑tèngǫunsofakámá↓	En la mía tengo un sofá cama.
the reality	lá—rrẹáliḍáḍ↓	la realidad
it must be, it's probably	débé—sér↓	debe ser
comfortable	komóḍó↓	cómodo

White
Actually the apartment must be very comfortable.

énrrẹáliḍáḍ↑débésér |mùykòmóḍǫ |

èlápártàméntó↓

White
En realidad, debe ser muy cómodo el apartamento.

(you) come (to come)	byénès↓ bénɪ́r↓	vienes (venir)
the night	lá—noché↓	la noche
tonight	éstá—noché↓	esta noche
so	ásí↓	así
(you) see (to see)	bés↓ bér↓	ves (ver)
(I) live (to live)	bibó↓ bibɪ́r↓	vivo (vivir)

Molina
Why don't you come tonight and you can see where I live?

pòrkénobyénes |estanoche |

ɹ̀àsíbez |ḍondebíbó↓

Molina
¿Por qué no vienes esta noche y así ves dónde vivo?

| to leave, to let | dèhár↓ | dejar |
| to leave me | dèharmè↓ | dejarme |

White
O.K. Will you let me off at the hotel?

múybyén↓ kyérez │dèharmę │ènęlótél↑

White
Muy bien, ¿quieres dejarme en el hotel?

to have to	tèner—kè↓	tener que
myself	mé↓	me
to change myself of (to change oneself)	kàmbyármè—dè↓ kàmbyársè↓	cambiarme de (cambiarse)
the clothes, the clothing	là—rrópà↓	la ropa

I have to change my clothes.

tèngo │kèkàmbyárme │derrópà↓

Tengo que cambiarme de ropa.

to come by	pàsár↓	pasar
you	tí↓	ti
at eight (o'clock)	à—làs—ochò↓	a las ocho

Molina
Then I'll take you (to the hotel), and come by for you at eight.

éntonşes │tèⓁyebo │ipásòpòrti │àlas óchò↓

Molina
Entonces te llevo y paso por ti a las ocho.

| the million | èl—mi(l)yón↓ | el millón |
| (I) hope (to hope, expect, wait for) | èsperò↓ èspérár↓ | espero (esperar) |

White
Thanks a million. I'll be waiting
for you.

unmiᴖyondegráşyàs↓ tėspérò↓

White
Un millón de gracias. Te espero.

8.2 DRILLS AND GRAMMAR

8.21 Pattern drills

8.21.1 Present tense forms of regular /—ír/ verbs

A. Presentation of pattern

ILLUSTRATIONS

_____	1	ɹàsíbéz |dondebíbô↓	Y así ves donde *vivo*.
I live on the first floor.	2	bíbo|ėṇėlprimérpísô↓	*Vivo* en el primer piso.
Do you live on the first floor?	3	bíbes |ėṇėlprimérpísot	¿*Vives* en el primer piso?
(you) (fam.) open (to open)		ábrês↓ ábrír↓	abres (abrir)
Why don't you open another agency?	4	pórkénọabres |ótrahenşyà↓	¿Por qué no *abres* otra agencia?
_____	5	subẹobáhà↓	¿*Sube* o baja?
writes (to write)		ėskríbė↓ ėskríbír↓	escribe (escribir)

He writes too much.	6	él eskríbe |démásyadó↓	El *escribe* demasiado.
And so you can see where we live.	7	ḷás ibéz |dóndébibímos↓	Y así ves donde *vivimos*.
(we) write (to write)		éskribímos↓ éskribír↓	escribimos (escribir)
Why do we write so much?	8	pórkeskribímostántó↓	¿Por qué *escribimos* tanto?
_____	9	bíben |énúnápártámentó↓	*Viven* en un apartamento.
Are you going up in the elevator?	10	súben |enelas(ṣ)ensór↑	¿*Suben* en el ascensor?

EXTRAPOLATION

	sg	pl
1	—o	—ímos
2 fam	—es	
2-3	—e	—en

NOTES

a. The pattern for /—ír/ verbs differs from /—ér/ only in the occurrence of /—í/ as the theme vowel in 1 pl forms.

8.21.11   Substitution drills - number substitution

1   èskríbımos |enlạeskwélà↓   èskríbọ |enlạeskwélà↓

2   bíben |léhozɖelşéntrò↓   bíbe |léhozɖelşéntrò↓

3   súbọ |enẹlas(ş)ensór↓   súbımos |enẹlas(ş)ensór↓

4   nọabrẹ |e(0)líbrò↓   nọabren |e(0)líbrò↓

5   bíbımos |(ş)érkaɖẹakí↓   bíbo |şérkaɖẹakí↓

6   nọéskrıbo |múchò↓   nọéskrıbımoz |múchò↓

7   súbén |menos,aórà↓   súbé |menos,aórà↓

---

1 *Escribimos* en la escuela.   Escribo en la escuela

2 *Viven* lejos del centro.   Vive lejos del centro.

3 *Subo* en el ascensor.   Subimos en el ascensor.

4 No *abre* el libro.   No abren el libro.

5 *Vivimos* cerca de aquí.   Vivo cerca de aquí.

6 No *escribo* mucho.   No escribimos mucho.

7 *Suben* menos ahora.   Sube menos ahora.

Person - number substitution

1 yóbibo|léhozdęakíↆ

   àntónyo_____ↆ   bíbe|léhozdęakíↆ

   àlişyaiyó_____ↆ   bíbimoz|léhozdęakíↆ

   ústeđ_____ↆ   bíbe|léhozdęakíↆ

   èｌｙoz_____ↆ   bíben|léhozdęakíↆ

2 éléskríbe|sólǫéninglés↓

   yó_____ↆ   èskríbo|sólǫéninglés↓

---

1 *Yo* vivo lejos de aquí.

   Antonio_____.   Vive lejos de aquí.
   Alicia y yo_____.   Vivimos lejos de aquí.
   Ud. _____.   Vive lejos de aquí.
   Ellos _____.   Viven lejos de aquí.

2 *El* escribe sólo en inglés.

   Yo _____.   Escribo sólo en inglés.

kármen_____↓   èskríbe |sólǫèniŋglé·s↓

nòsótrós_____↓   èskríbimos |sólǫèniŋglé·s↓

ùsteďes_____↓   èskríbèn |sólǫèniŋglé·s↓

3 eǫ̣yos.abren | lạémbàhaďà↓

yó_____↓   àbro | lạémbàhaďà↓

kármen_____↓   àbre | lạémbàhaďà↓

nòsótrós_____↓   àbrimoz | lạémbàhaďà↓

ùsteďes_____↓   àbrèn | lạémbàhaďà↓

Carmen _____.   Escribe sólo en inglés.
    Nosotros_____.   Escribimos sólo en inglés.
    Uds._____.   Escriben sólo en inglés.

3 Ellos abren la Embajada.

    Yo _____.   Abro la Embajada.
    Carmen_____,   Abre la Embajada.
    Nosotros _____.   Abrimos la Embajada.
    Uds. _____.   Abren la Embajada.

8.21.12   Response drill

1 èskríbẹustéd |en̦espan̦yól↑ọenin̦glés↓   èskríbọènin̦glés↓

2 bíben̦ustéd̦es |en̦un̦apartamentó↑ọen̦un̦akásà↓   bíbímos |èn̦ûn̦âkasà↓

3 èskríbelmúchọ↑opókò↓   èskríbépokò↓

[èn̦ûn̦òtél]   4 dóndebíbèn |éⁿⁿyòs↓   biben |en̦un̦otél↓

[èn̦èlṣéntrò↓]5 dóndebíbẹ |ûstéd̦↓   bíbọ |en̦elṣéntrò↓

[tréṣ↓]   6 kwán̦toschékes |èskríbél↓   èskríbetréṣ↓

---

1 ¿Escribe Ud. en español o en inglés?   Escribo en inglés.

2 ¿Viven Uds. en un apartamento o en una casa? Vivimos en una casa.

3 ¿Escribe él mucho o poco?   Escribe poco.

(en un hotel)   4 ¿Dónde viven ellos?   Viven en un hotel.

(en el centro)   5 ¿Dónde vive Ud.?   Vivo en el centro.

(tres)   6 ¿Cuántos cheques escribe él? Escribe tres.

[éspáŋyól↓] 7 éskríben̩ustédes |éníŋglést   nó↓ éskríbimos |én̩espáŋyól↓

[ápártáméntó↓] 8 bíbeꞥyą |én̩únákásat   nó↓ bíbę |én̩únápártáméntó↓

            9 ábrel |ląembáhádat   sí↓ ábreląembahádá↓

           10 bíben̩ustédes |énlás̩áfwérast   sí↓ bíbimos |enlas̩afwérás↓

           11 subenẹꞥyos |én̩ęlás(s)énsórt   sí↓ suben |en̩ęlas(ş)ensór↓

(español)   7 ¿Escriben Uds. en inglés?   No, escribimos en español.

(apartamento) 8 ¿Vive ella en una casa?   No, vive en un apartamento.

               9 ¿Abre él la Embajada?   Sí, abre la Embajada.

              10 ¿Viven Uds. en las afueras?   Sí, vivimos en las afueras.

              11 ¿Suben ellos en el ascensor?   Sí, suben en el ascensor.

8.21.13 Translation drill

1 We live in an old house.

bíbimos |énúnákasabyéhà↓

Vivimos en una casa vieja.

2 They live in a big apartment.

e(l)yozbíben |énúnápàrtámentográndè↓

Ellos viven en un apartamento grande.

3 What time do they open that building?

ákęorabren |ésédifişyò↓

¿A qué hora abren ese edificio?

4 Where do you live?

dondebíbęustéd↓

¿Dónde vive usted?

5 Does he write the ads?

ęskribel |lósánúnşyos↑

¿Escribe él los anuncios?

6 When do you write?

kwandǫeskribęustéd↓

¿Cuándo escribe Ud.?

7 Since when have you all lived there?

dézdękwandobiben |ustédęsái↓

¿Desde cuándo viven Uds. ahí?

8 Does he open the Embassy?

abrel |lạémbàhadá↑

¿Abre él la Embajada?

9 I go up at eight o'clock.

yósubǫ |alas.óchó↓

Yo subo a las ocho.

10 They go up at seven.

e(l)yo(s)suben |ala(s)syété↓

Ellos suben a las siete.

11 They live near a friend (of) mine.

bibenşerka |dęúnámígomió↓

Viven cerca de un amigo mío.

12 I live in the United States.

bíbo |énlós.ęstados.unídós↓

Vivo en los Estados Unidos.

13 I live a long ways from the language school.

bíbolehoz |dèlạęskweladeléŋgwàs↓

Vivo lejos de la escuela de lenguas.

B.   Discussion of pattern

In almost all tense forms other than present tense forms there is no distinction between /—ér/ and /—ír/ theme class verb endings, and they will be referred to as /—ér—ír/ patterns. The important differences are in the theme vowel of the infinitive and the 1 pl form of the present tense.

Below is the complete pattern for regular verbs in the present tense, illustrated with three common verbs:

		abl—ár	kom—ér	bib—ír
1	sg	ábl—o	kóm—o	bíb—o
2	fam	ábl—as	kóm—es	bíb—es
2 - 3	sg	ábl—a	kóm—e	bíb—e
1	pl	abl—ámos	kom—émos	bib—ímos
2 - 3	pl	ábl—an	kóm—en	bíb—en

Note that theme class membership is marked by the presence of a vowel /a, e, i/ in all forms except 1 sg. All 1 sg forms have the ending /—o/ in common. Note also that the person-number endings /—s, —mos, —n/ are present in their appropriate forms regardless of what theme vowel precedes them. Note also that /—ér/ and /—ír/ verbs are distinguished only in 1 pl forms, where distinct /—e—/ and /—i—/ theme vowels appear.

8.21.2   The obligatory contractions

A.   Presentation of pattern

ILLUSTRATIONS

_____	1 kyéropresentárlę ↓ålséŋyórmolínȧ↓	Quiero presentarle *al* señor Molina.
_____	2 dálakáọyeↆǫalpátyò↓	¿Da *a la* calle, o *al* patio?
of the, from the	dél↓	del
Far from the Embassy, or the hotel?	3 léhoz ↓dèlạèmbȧhȧdạↆodèlotél↓	¿Lejos *de la* Embajada, *o del* hotel?
_____	4 ėnėlédifíṣyodèlkámpȯ↓	En el edificio *Del* Campo.

EXTRAPOLATION

	a	de
el	al	del
la	a—la	de—la
los	a—los	de—los
las	a—las	de—las

NOTES

a. The contractions /al/ and /del/ are obligatory on all style levels of Spanish.

b. Many other contractions occur, but they are not obligatory.

8.21.21 Substitution drills - number substitution

1 kyérêmprêséntárlẹ |álsê n̦yór↓

_____sê n̦yorés↓   kyérêmprêséntárlẹ |álô(ș)sê n̦yorés↓

2 lá l̦ y̦ abéd̦elkwártô↓

_____kwártôs↓   lá l̦ y̦ abéd̦eloskwártôs↓

3 lákásạ |ezd̦elo(s)sê n̦yórès↓

_____sê n̦yór↓   lákásạ |ezd̦elsê n̦yór↓

---

1 Quieren presentarle al *señor*.

_____ *señores*.   Quieren presentarle a los señores.

2 La llave del *cuarto*.

_____ *cuartos*.   La llave de los cuartos.

3 La casa es de los *señores*.

_____ señor.   La casa es del señor.

4 kyérǫáblár|delosₐapártaméntòs↓

_____apartaméntò↓   kyérǫáblár|delapartaméntò↓

5 ǫ̃yébenos|alozrrestoránès↓

_____rrestorán↓   ǫ̃yébenos|alrrestorán↓

_____

4 Quiero hablar de los *apartamentos*.

_____ _____ *apartamento*.   Quiero hablar del apartamento.

5 Llévenos a los *restoranes*.

_____*restorán*.   Llévenos al restorán.

Item substitution

1 banalạembạhádạ↓

   _____otél↓   banalotél↓

2 bamosạlşéntró↓

   _____ahénşyà↓   bamosạlahénşyà↓

3 èlótélezdelasenyórà↓

   _____senyór↓   èlótélezdelsenyór↓

---

1 Van a la *Embajada.*

   _____ *hotel.*   Van al hotel.

2 Vamos al *centro.*

   _____ *agencia.*   Vamos a la agencia.

3 El hotel es de la *señora.*

   _____ *señor.*   El hotel es del señor.

4 èlkwárto |dalakáļ̣è↓

_____pátyò↓   èlkwárto |dalpátyò↓

5 kyéròprèséntarlẹ |àlsènyòr↓

_____sènyòritá↓   kyéròprèséntarlẹ |àlásènyòritá↓

_____

4 El cuarto da a la *calle.*

_____*patio.*   El cuarto da al patio.

5 Quiero presentarle al *señor.*

_____*señorita.*   Quiero presentarle a la señorita.

8.21.22   Translation drill

1 They want to go to the restaurant.　　kyérenír |alrrestorán↓　　Quieren ir al restorán.

2 They want to go to the agency.　　kyérenír |alahénşyà↓　　Quieren ir a la agencia.

3 They are going to the same hotel.　　bánàlmizmotél↓　　Van al mismo hotel.

4 This is the key to (of) the house.　　éstąez |lázỹabedelakásà↓　　Esta es la llave de la casa.

5 These are the keys to (of) the apartment.　　éstąęsonḷázỹabez |delapartaméntó↓　　Estas son las llaves del apartamento.

6 Two hundred dollars a (to the) month.　　dòs(ş)yentozdolares |almés↓　　Doscientos dólares al mes.

7 This is Mr. Molina's car (the car of Mr. Molina).　　ésteselawto |delseŋyormolínà↓　　Este es el auto del señor Molina.

8 This is the light bill (bill of the light).　　éstąezlakwenta |delalúş↓　　Esta es la cuenta de la luz.

9 This is the gas bill (bill of the gas).　　éstąezlakwenta |delgás↓　　Esta es la cuenta del gas.

End of Tape 5A

B.   Discussion of pattern

There are many instances of contraction, or telescoping of forms, in Spanish. This is particularly true when two vowels are brought together at word boundaries. The contraction is usually complete if the two vowels involved are the same. For example, in /dóndestá/ the final /—e/ of /dónde/ and the initial /e—/ of /está/ are telescoped in normal pronunciation. A slower pronunciation, however, would be /dónde | está↓/.

The two cases of contraction presented above are selected for special drill because they are obligatory; /de/ and /el/ will always be /del/, no matter how slowly pronounced. The two contractions /al/ and /del/ are the only ones recognized in the writing system - no others, however they are pronounced, are written as contractions. Note that it is the weak-stressed /el/ 'the' which combines with /a/ and /de/ ; the strong-stressed /él/ 'he' does not.

8.22   Replacement drills

A   bíben |ènùnàpàrtàméntò↓

1 _____kásà↓   bíben |ènùnàkásà↓

2 bíbimos_____↓   bíbimos |ènùnàkásà↓

3 _____ésta_____↓   bíbimos |ènestakásà↓

4 _____òtél↓   bíbimos |ènestęotél↓

5 tràbàhamos_____↓   ᴄràbàhamos |ènestęotél↓

6 _____ésę_____↓   tràbàhamos |ènesęotél↓

7 _____èmbàhàɖà↓   tràbàhamos |ènesąembaháɖà↓

A   Viven en un apartamento.

1 _____casa.   Viven en una casa.

2 Vivimos_____.   Vivimos en una casa.

3 _____ esta ____.   Vivimos en esta casa.

4 _____hotel.   Vivimos en este hotel.

5 Trabajamos_____.   Trabajamos en este hotel.

6 _____ese_____.   Trabajamos en ese hotel.

7 _____embajada.   Trabajamos en esa embajada.

B   ėzmúykárȯ↓

1 sȯn_____↓   sȯnmuykárȯs↓

2 ____barátȯs↓   sȯnmuybarátȯs↓

3 ____barátȯ↓   ėzmuybarátȯ↓

4 ____byéhȯ↓   ėzmuybyéhȯ↓

5 ȧȯy_____↓   sȯymuybyéhȯ↓

6 sȯn_____↓   sȯnmuybyéhȯs↓

7 ____bonítȧ↓   ėzmúybonítȧ↓

_____

B   Es muy caro.

1 Son_____.   Son muy caros.

2 _____baratos.   Son muy baratos.

3 _____barato.   Es muy barato.

4 _____viejo.   Es muy viejo.

5 Soy_____.   Soy muy viejo.

6 Son_____.   Son muy viejos.

7 _____bonita.   Es muy bonita.

C élpréşyo |noéstámál↓

1 éstós_____↓   éstóspréşyoz |noéstánmál↓

2 ___kása_____↓   éstákása |noéstámál↓

3 ésá_____↓   ésákása |noéstámál↓

4 ___mwéblez_____↓   ésózmwéblez |noéstánmál↓

5 ___kántidad_____↓   ésákántidad |noéstámál↓

6 éstá_____↓   éstákántidad |noéstámál↓

7 ___imfórmáşyon___↓   éstaimfórmáşyon |noéstamál↓

C   El precio no está mal.

1 Estos_____.   Estos precios no están mal.

2 _____casa_____.   Esta casa no está mal.

3 Esa_____.   Esa casa no está mal.

4 _____muebles_____.   Esos muebles no están mal.

5 _____cantidad_____.   Esa cantidad no está mal.

6 Esta_____.   Esta cantidad no está mal.

7 _____información_____.   Esta información no está mal.

D ityéné |múybonitabístá↓

1 _____bwéna_____↓   ityéné |múybwenabístá↓

2 _____entráđá↓   ityéné |múybwenąentráđá↓

3 _____amígòs↓   ityéné |múybwenos.amígòs↓

4 _téŋgò_____↓   itéŋgò |múybwenos.amígòs↓

5 _____ımformaşyónés↓   itéŋgò |múybwenas.ımformaşyónés↓

6 _____mwéblès↓   itéŋgò |múybwenozmwéblès↓

7 _____máloz_____↓   itéŋgò |múymalozmwéblès↓

D   Y tiene muy bonita vista.

1 _____buena_____.   Y tiene muy buena vista.

2 _____entrada.   Y tiene muy buena entrada.

3 _____amigos.   Y tiene muy buenos amigos.

4 _tengo_____.   Y tengo muy buenos amigos.

5 _____informaciones.   Y tengo muy buenas informaciones.

6 _____muebles.   Y tengo muy buenos muebles.

7 _____malos_____.   Y tengo muy malos muebles.

E   kwántas |ábitáȿyónestyéné↓

1 _____són↓   kwántas |ábitáȿyónessón↓

2 _____kwártos_____↓   kwántoskwárto(s)són↓

3 _____áy↓   kwántoskwártos̞áy↓

4 _____ágwa̬_____↓   kwántagwáy↓

5 _____señyores_____↓   kwánto(s) señyores̞áy↓

6 _____trabáhán↓   kwánto(s) señyores |trabáhán↓

7 _____señyoras_____↓   kwánta(s) señyoras |trabáhán↓

E   ¿Cuántas habitaciones tiene?

1 ¿_____son?   ¿Cuántas habitaciones son?

2 ¿_____cuartos_____?   ¿Cuántos cuartos son?

3 ¿_____hay?   ¿Cuántos cuartos hay?

4 ¿_____agua_____?   ¿Cuánta agua hay?

5 ¿_____señores _____?   ¿Cuántos señores hay?

6 ¿_____trabajan?   ¿Cuántos señores **trabajan**?

7 ¿_____señoras_____?   ¿Cuántas señoras **trabajan**?

F   kyérez |dehármę |eṇ elotél↑

1 pwédez_____↑   pwédez |dehármę |eṇ elotél↑

2 _____Øyebármę_____↑   pwédez |Øyebármę |alotél↑

3 _____kása↑   pwédez |Øyebármę |alakása↑

4 _____alkılárme_____↑   pwédes |alkılárme |lakása↑

5 _____apartamento↑   pwédes |alkılármę |elapartamento↑

6 _____un_____↑   pwédes |alkılármę |uṇapartamento↑

7 kyéres_____↑   kyéres |alkılárme |uṇapartamento↑

_____

F   ¿Quieres dejarme en el hotel?

1 ¿Puedes _____?   ¿Puedes dejarme en el hotel?

2 ¿_____llevarme_____?   ¿Puedes llevarme al hotel?

3 ¿_____ casa?   ¿Puedes llevarme a la casa?

4 ¿_____alquilarme _____?   ¿Puedes alquilarme la casa?

5 ¿_____ apartamento?   ¿Puedes alquilarme el apartamento?

6 ¿_____, un_____?   ¿Puedes alquilarme un apartamento?

7 ¿Quieres _____?   ¿Quieres alquilarme un apartamento?

8.23   Variation drills

A mízbéṣínoz |bánámúdarse |dekásạ|

éstásémáná↓   Mis vecinos van a mudarse de casa
                     esta semana.

1 My friends are going to move   misámígoz |bánámúdarse |dẹápártámẹntọ| Mis amigos van a mudarse de
  to another apartment this   éstásémánả↓   apartamento esta semana.
  week.

2 My neighbors are going to   mízbéṣínoz |bánámúdarse |dekwartọ| Mis vecinos van a mudarse de
  move to another room this   éstásémáná↓   cuarto esta semana.
  week.

3 My neighbors are going to look mízbéṣínoz |bánábúskár |otrakásá↓   Mis vecinos van a buscar otra
  for another house.   casa.

4 My friends are going to rent   misámígoz |bánálkilár |otrakásá↓   Mis amigos van a alquilar otra
  another house.   casa.

5 My friends are going to work   misámígoz |bánátrábáhar |enunahénṣyá↓   Mis amigos van a trabajar en una
  in an agency.   agencia.

6 My (girl) friends are going   misámígaz |bánákómer |enẹlrrestorán↓   Mis amigas van a comer en el
  to eat in the restaurant.   restorán.

7 My (girl) friends are going   misámígaz |bánạéstárákí |maŋyáná↓   Mis amigas van a estar aquí
  to be here tomorrow.   mañana.

B bíben |ènùnàpàrtàmént̬o |igwálalmíò↓   Viven en un apartamento igual al
                                                                   mío.

1 They live in a room just   bíben |ènùnkwárt̬o |igwálalmíò↓   Viven en un cuarto ıgual al mío.
   like mine.

2 They live in a building just   bíben |ènùnèdifíş̬yo̬ |igwálalmíò↓   Viven en un edificio igual al mío.
   like mine.

3 They live in a hotel.   bíben̬en̬un̬otél↓   Viven en un hotel.

4 He lives in the U.S.   bíb̬e |ènlòs̬èstàd̬os̬uníd̬òs↓   Vive en los Estados Unidos.

5 I live in Washington.   bíb̬o̬eŋwáshiŋtòn↓   Vivo en Washington.

6 We live here.   bíbimos̬akí↓   Vivimos aquí.

7 We live there.   bíbimos̬aí↓   Vivimos ahí.

C dálàka(l)ye↑ǫalpátyò↓   ¿Da a la calle o al patio?

1 Does it face the street or   dálàka(l)ye↑ǫalabenídà↓   ¿Da a la calle o a la avenida?
  the avenue?

2 Does it face the avenue or   dálàbènídà↑ǫalpátyò↓   ¿Da a la avenida o al patio?
  the court.

3 Does it face 20th Street or   dálàká(l)yèbeyntè↑ǫalabenídà↓ ¿Da a la Calle Veinte o a la
  the avenue?   avenida?

4 Does it face Fifth Street or dálàká(l)yèṣiŋko↑ǫalaka(l)yeđós↓ ¿Da a la Calle Cinco o a la Calle
  Second St.?   Dos?

5 Does it face the living room dálàsala↑ǫalakoṣínà↓   ¿Da a la sala o a la cocina?
  or the kitchen?

6 Does it face the bedroom or   dáldòrmitóryo↑ǫalkwartođebáɲò↓ ¿Da al dormitorio o al cuarto
  the bathroom?   de baño?

7 Does it face the American   dalạembaháđạ|amerikanat   ¿Da a la Embajada Americana?
  Embassy?

D no̞↓ pér̊ó̊lás̊álą |ézbás̊tánte |grándê̞↓   No, pero la sala es bastante
                                                            grande.

1 No, but the kitchen is   no̞↓ pér̊ó̊lákô̞ș̊ın̞ą |ézbás̊tánte |grándê↓   No, pero la cocina es bastante
  quite large.   grande.

2 No, but the rooms are quite   no̞↓ pér̊ó̊lás̊ą̊bítą̊ș̊yónes |sómbás̊tánte | No, pero las habitaciones son
  large.   grándês↓   bastante grandes.

3 No, but the view is rather   no̞↓ pér̊ó̊lábís̊tą |ézbás̊tánte |bwénà↓   No, pero la vista es bastante
  nice.   buena.

4 No, but the street is   no̞↓ pér̊ó̊láka⒨y̞ę̞ |ézbás̊tánte |bwénà↓   No, pero la calle es bastante
  rather nice.   buena.

5 Yes, and the Embassy is   si̞↓ ílą̊émbàhaɗą |és̊tábás̊tánte |ș̊erkà↓   Sí, y la Embajada está bastante
  quite near.   cerca.

6 Yes, and the restaurant is   si̞↓ ɨ̞élrr̊és̊tòrán |és̊tąș̊erkà↓   Sí, y el restorán está cerca.
  near.

7 Yes, and the apartment is   si̞↓ ɨ̞éląpàrtąment̞ǫ |ézbàrató↓   Sí, y el apartamento es barato.
  inexpensive.

E énlàmía |téŋgǫúnsòfákámà↓   En la mía tengo un sofá cama.

1 In mine I have a bed.   énlàmía |téŋgǫúnàkámà↓   En la mía tengo una cama.

2 In mine I have a table.   énlàmía |téŋgǫúnàmésà↓   En la mía tengo una mesa.

3 In my room I have a desk.   énmikwárto |téŋgǫúnèskritóryò↓   En mi cuarto tengo un escritorio.

4 In the living room I have   énlàsála |téŋgòkwátrosíǫyàs↓   En la sala tengo cuatro sillas.
   four chairs.

5 In the kitchen I have a few   énlàkòṣina |téŋgǫúnàzmònéďàs↓   En la cocina tengo unas monedas.
   coins.

6 In the hotel I have a few   énèlótel |téŋgǫúnòzďolárès↓   En el hotel tengo unos dólares.
   dollars.

7 On the table I have an   énlàmésa |téŋgǫúnṣèniṣérò↓   En la mesa tengo un cenicero.
   ash-tray.

F débèsér |múykómóđǫ |èláṗàrtàméntò↓   Debe ser muy cómodo el aparta-
                                                                        mento.

1 The room must be very   débèsér |múykómóđǫ |èlkwártò↓   Debe ser muy cómodo el cuarto.
   comfortable.

2 The house must be very   débèsér |múykómòđà |làkásà↓   Debe ser muy cómoda la casa.
   comfortable.

3 The hotel must be very good.   débèsér |múybwénǫ |èlótél↓   Debe ser muy bueno el hotel.

4 The car must be very cheap.   débèsér |múybáratǫ |èláwtò↓   Debe ser muy barato el auto.

5 The kitchen must be very   débèsér |múygrándè |làkòṣínà↓   Debe ser muy grande la cocina.
   large.

6 The hotels must be very   débènsér |múybáratòz |lòsǫtélès↓   Deben ser muy baratos los
   cheap.   hoteles.

7 The apartments must be very   débènsér |múybónıtòz |lòsáṗàrtàméntòs↓ Deben ser muy bonitos los
   nice.   apartamentos.

8.24   Review drill - noun-adjective agreement

1   It's a bad pen.   ésúnáplumamálà↓   Es una pluma maia.

     It's a bad book.   ésúnlíbromálò↓   Es un libro malo.

2   It's a good chair.   ésúnásíⁿyabwénà↓   Es una silla buena.

     It's a good desk.   ésúnéskritoryobwénò↓   Es un escritorio bueno.

3   He has an old house.   tyenéunakásabyéhà↓   Tiene una casa vieja.

     He has an old apartment. tyenéunapartamentobyéhò↓ Tiene un apartamento viejo.

4   It's a good pen.   ésúnáplumabwénà↓   Es una pluma buena.

     It's a good book.   ésúnlíbrobwénò↓   Es un libro bueno.

5   It's a good table.   ésúnámesabwénà↓   Es una mesa buena.

     It's a bad desk.   ésúnéskritoryomálò↓   Es un escritorio malo.

6 He has a pretty table.

tyéneunamésabonítà↓

Tiene una mesa bonita.

He has an old desk.

tyéneuneskritoryobyého↓

Tiene un escritorio viejo.

7 He has an expensive house.

tyéneunakásakárà↓

Tiene una casa cara.

He has an expensive apartment.

tyéneunapartamentokáro↓

Tiene un apartamento caro.

8 I live in an inexpensive house.

bibgenunakásabarátà↓

Vivo en una casa barata.

I live in an inexpensive apartment.

bibgenunapartamentobárátò↓

Vivo en un apartamento barato.

9 I live in a comfortable house.

bibgenunakásakómodà↓

Vivo en una casa cómoda.

I live in a comfortable apartment.

bibgenunapartamentokómodò↓

Vivo en un apartamento cómodo.

8.3   CONVERSATION STİMULUS

NARRATIVE 1

1	Jose and Juan take a taxi and go see some apartments.	hóseɪhwan |tómánùntaksɪ | ibánàber |ùnósàpàrtámentôs↓	José y Juan toman un taxi y van a ver unos apartamentos.
2	The taxi costs six pesos, more or less.	èltaksɪ |kwéstàseyspésôz |másòménôs↓	El taxi cuesta seis pesos, más o menos.
3	Jose has only a ten peso bill and Juan some travelers checks.	hôse |tyénésôlo̧umbiɲyetec̣eadyéş↓ ihwan |unoschekezbyahérôs↓	José tiene sólo un billete de a diez y Juan unos cheques viajeros.
4	The driver doesn't have change.	èlchófer |nótyenekámbyô↓	El chofer no tiene cambio.
5	So he takes the ten, six for the trip and four for a tip.	èntonşes |tómaȩlbiɲyete |cȩadyéş↓ seys |pòrèlbyahȩ |ikwatrocȩpropína↓	Entonces toma el billete de a diez; seis por el viaje y cuatro de propina.

DIALOG 1

José, pregúntele al chofer que cuánto le debe.	kwántoleḍébô↓	José: ¿Cuánto le debo?

Chofer, contéstele que son seis pesos.	sònseyspésòs↓	Chofer: Son seis pesos.
José, pregúntele si tiene cambio para diez.	tyenekámbyo |páraɑyęș↑	José: ¿Tiene cambio para diez?
Chofer, contéstele que no, que no tiene.	nó |sę̀ny6r↓ notéŋgò↓	Chofer: No, señor, no tengo.
Juan, dígale que Ud. tiene sólo cheques viajeros.	yosólotengo |chékęzbyàhéròs↓	Juan: Yo sólo tengo cheques viajeros.
José, dígale al chofer que tome los diez, que cuatro de propina.	tomelozɑyéș↓ kwátroɑepropína↓	José: Tome los diez, cuatro de propina.
Chofer, contéstele que un millón de gracias.	ùnmiⒻⓎ ondegráșyàs↓	Chofer: Un millón de gracias.

NARRATIVE 2

1 Jose and Juan talk with the agent, a friend of Jose's.	hòseɪhwán |ablaŋkoṇelahéntè↓ ùnàmɪgoɑehosé↓	José y Juan hablan con el agente, un amigo de José.
2 The three (of them) go together to the Del Campo building.	lòstrezbaŋhuntos |àlèɑifɪșyoɑelkámpò↓	Los tres van juntos al edificio Del Campo.

3 They go in.

pásanaḍelántė↓

Pasan adelante.

4 They like the first apartment
  they see very much.

ėlprimẻrapartamento|kebẻn↑
lėzgustamúchó↓

El primer apartamento que ven
  les gusta mucho.

5 But, gosh!, it's very expensive.

perỏ|kȧrambȧ↓ ėzmuykárỏ↓

Pero ¡caramba!, es muy caro.

6 It costs three hundred a month.

kwéstȧtrès(ș)yentos.almés↓

Cuesta trescientos al mes.

7 And that without including the
  gas and other things.

įeso|sınıŋklwír|élgas|įotras
kósȧs↓

Y eso sin incluir el gas y otras
  cosas.

8 There's another one on the same
  floor, but it doesn't face the
  street.

áyotrọ|ėnėlmızmopísò↓ pėrỏ
noḍa|ạlaká()yė↓

Hay otro en el mismo piso, pero
  no da a la calle.

9 They go see it.

ban̩abérlỏ↓

Van a verlo.

DIALOG 2

Agente, dígales que pasen adelante.

pasen|ȧḍélantė↓

Agente: Pasen adelante.

José, dígale que le gusta mucho
  este apartamento. Pregúntele a
  Juan que qué le parece a él.

mėgustạ|éstẹạpȧrtȧméntò↓ įȧtí↑
keteparéșė|hwán↓

José: Me gusta este apartamento.

¿Y a ti, qué te parece, Juan?

Juan, contéstele que está bastante
bonito, pero que hay que ver
cuánto cuesta.

ésta|bàstantebonítò↓ perǫ|áykèber|
kwàntokwestà↓

Juan: Está bastante bonito, pero
hay que ver cuánto cuesta.

Agente, dígale que trescientos,
sin incluir el gas y otras cosas.

très(ṣ)yéntòs↓ síniŋklwír|êlgás
ȷotraskósàs↓

Agente: Trescientos, sin incluir
el gas y otras cosas.

Juan, dígale que caramba, que muy
caro, que no le conviene. Pregúntele si no tiene algo más barato.

kàrambà↓ muykárò↓ nómekombyénè↓
nótyenę|algomazbarato↑

Juan: ¡Caramba, muy caro! No me
conviene. ¿No tiene algo
más barato?

Agente, contéstele que en este
mismo piso tiene otro, pero
que no da a la calle.

ènéstèmizmo|piso|teŋgótrò↓
pérónoȼa|ạlakáꝶyè↓

Agente: En este mismo piso tengo
otro, pero no da a la
calle.

Juan, pregúntele si pueden verlo.

pòȼemozbérlo↑

Juan: ¿Podemos verlo?

Agente, contéstele que cómo no,
que con mucho gusto.

komonó↓ kònmuchogústò↓

Agente: Cómo no, con mucho
gusto.

NARRATIVE 3

1	This other one costs two hundred and twenty five.	éstęotrokwésta |dós(ş)yéntoz beyntişíŋkò↓	Este otro cuesta doscientos veinticinco.
2	The bath is to the right.	èlbaŋyọ |estaladeréchà↓	El baño está a la derecha.
3	The kitchen isn't very large, but it's convenient.	làkóşinạ |nọezmuygránde |pèrọés kómòdà↓	La cocina no es muy grande, pero es muy cómoda.
4	Jose thinks that the price is reasonable.	àhóse↑lépàreşe |kèlpréşyo | nọestámál↓	A José le parece que el precio no está mal.
5	But he really doesn't like it.	pèrọénrrẹàlidàd↑nólegústà↓	Pero en realidad no le gusta.
6	The furniture looks old, and there isn't much light.	lózmwébles |pàréşènmúybyéhòs↓ ḷáypokalúş↓	Los muebles parecen muy viejos, y hay poca luz.

DIALOG 3

Agente, dígale a Juan que éste cuesta doscientos veinticinco.	ésté |kwéstádós(ṣ)yéntoz| beyntiṣíŋkò↓	Agente: Este cuesta doscientos veinticinco.
Juan, pregúntele dónde está el baño.	dondestaẹlbáŋyò↓	Juan: ¿Dónde está el baño?
Agente, contéstele que ahí a la derecha.	ái|áládérechá↓	Agente: Ahí a la derecha.
Juan, pregúntele que la cocina, dónde está.	iláköṣiná↓ dondestá↓	Juan: Y la cocina, ¿dónde está?
Agente, contéstele que aquí está, que no es muy grande, pero es cómoda.	ákiẹstá↓ nọezmuygrande |perọés kómódá↓	Agente: Aquí está. No es muy grande, pero es cómoda.
Juan, pregúntele a José que qué cree él.	kekreẹstú |hósé↓	Juan: ¿Qué crees tú, José?
José, contéstele que el precio no está mal, pero que en realidad no le gusta mucho.	élpreṣyo |nọestámál↓ pérọèn rreálidád |nomegustamúchò↓	José: El precio no está mal, pero en realidad no me gusta mucho.
Juan, pregúntele que por qué.	pòrké↓	Juan: ¿Por qué?

José, contéstele que los muebles parecen muy viejos, y no hay mucha luz.

lózmwébles |páréşénmúybyéhòs↓

inọaymuchalúş↓

José: Los muebles parecen muy

viejos, y no hay mucha luz.

Juan, dígale a José que sí, que en realidad tiene razón.

sí↓ énrrẹálidad|tyénezrraşón↓

Juan: Sí, en realidad tienes razón.

NARRATIVE 1

1 Mr. Richard Brown lives in this building.

élsèņyórríchàrbrawm |bìben

estèdifíşyò↓

El Sr. Richard Brown vive en

este edificio.

2 He works in the American Embassy.

éltrábahạ |ènlạémbàhadamerikáná↓

El trabaja en la Embajada Americana.

3 He has an apartment on the first floor.

tyénẹ |ùnápàrtámentọ |énélprimerpísò↓

Tiene un apartamento en el primer piso.

4 But he plans to move out this week.

pérópyénsamudarsẹ |éstàsémaná↓

Pero piensa mudarse esta semana.

5 The apartment is small, but comfortable and inexpensive.

élápàrtámentọ |éspékeņyo↑

péròkomodọibarátò↓

El apartamento es pequeño pero

cómodo y barato.

6 Mr. Brown isn't there now.   él sènyorbrawn | noèstaìaórà↓   El Sr. Brown no está ahí ahora.

7 But the agent has the key.   pèroèláhénte | tyénelaǫyábè↓   Pero el agente tiene la llave.

DIALOG 4

José, pregúntele al agente que
en qué piso vive el señor
Richard Brown.

èŋképísóbìbè | èlsèŋyórrícharbráwn↓

José: ¿En qué piso vive el
       Sr. Richard Brown?

Agente, pregúntele si el americano que trabaja en la Embajada.

èlàmèrikano | ketrabáhaer.laembahadà↑

Agente: ¿El americano que trabaja
        en la Embajada?

José, contéstele que sí. Que le
dijeron que vive aquí, pero que
piensa mudarse esta semana.

sí↓ mèdìheroŋ | kebìbęakí↓ pèrókè
pyensa | mudarsestasemánà↓

José: Sí. Me dijeron que vive aquí,

       pero que piensa mudarse
       esta semana.

Agente, dígale que caramba, que
tiene razón, que ahora recuerda.

kàrambá↓ tyénèrràson↓ àora
rrekwérdò↓

Agente: ¡Caramba! Tiene razón,

        ahora recuerdo.

Que él está en el primer piso.

élesta | ęnèlprimérpísò↓

       El está en el primer piso.

Y que tiene un apartamento
pequeño, pero muy cómodo y
barato.

ityene | ùnàpàrtàméntôpèkeŋyo |
pèrômuykómodǫibarátò↓

       Y tiene un apartamento

       pequeño, pero muy cómodo
       y barato.

José, pregúntele si el Sr. Brown
está ahí ahora.

èstaęlsèŋyorbráwn | aìǫorá↑

José: ¿Está el Sr. Brown ahí
      ahora?

Agente, contéstele que no, pero   nó↓ pérọåkítéŋgolaⱪⱪábé↓   Agente: No, pero aquí tengo la
que ahí tiene Ud. la llave.   llave.

                                                                                   End of Tape 5B

Tape 6A

9.1   BASIC SENTENCES.   White goes to Molina's apartment.

John White and Jose Molina arrive at Molina's apartment.

ENGLISH SPELLING	AID TO LISTENING	SPANISH SPELLING
come in (to come in)	pásá↓ pàsár↓	pasa (pasar)
your (yours)	tú↓ tuyó↓	tu (tuyo)
Molina		*Molina*
Come in. Make yourself at home. (1)	pasadelánté↓ éstasentukásá↓	Pasa adelante. Estás en tu casa.
seat (to seat)	syéntá↓ séntár↓	sienta (sentar)
seat yourself (to sit down)	syéntáté↓ séntarsé↓	siéntate (sentarse)
Sit down.	syéntáté↓	Siéntate.
White		*White*
Thanks.	grasyàs↓	Gracias.
like, as	kómó↓	como
Will my apartment be like this one?	basér |miápàrtámento |komoésté↑	¿Va a ser mi apartamento como éste?
just the same (equal)	igwálító↓ igwál↓	igualito (igual)

Molina
Just exactly.   ìgwálìtôↄ↓   *Molina*
                                                                         Igualito.

        all   toↄô↓   todo

        fixed, arranged (to fix,   àrrèglàↄô↓ àrrèglár↓   arreglado (arreglar)
          to arrange)

White   éstǫ|èstátôↄò|múybyèn,arreglàↄô↓ *White*
  This is all very nicely fixed up.   Esto está todo muy bien arreglado.

        yet, still   tôↄàbìà↓   todavía

        to buy   kômprár↓   comprar

Molina   tôↄàbìà|nèşèsítòkômprár|múchaskósàs↓ *Molina*
  I still have to buy a lot of   Todavía necesito comprar muchas
  things.   cosas.

        the soda   là—sóↄà↓   la soda

        the whiskey   èl—wìskì↓   el whiskey

        the whiskey with soda   èl—wìskì—kon—sóↄà↓   el whiskey con soda

  Would you like a whiskey and soda? (2) kyéres|unwìskìkonsóↄa↑   ¿Quieres un whiskey con soda?

        the idea   lạ—iↄéà↓   la idea

White   bwénạiↄéà↓   *White*
  Good idea.   Buena idea.

who   kyén↓   quien

the girl   lá—múchachá↓   la muchacha

the picture   lá—fotó↓   la foto

Who's that girl in the picture?   kyenesesamuchacha|delafótó↓   ¿Quién es esa muchacha de la
                                                                   foto?

how pretty   ké—bonító↓   qué bonito

She sure is pretty.   kebonítá↓   ¡Qué bonita!

the sweetheart, the   lá—nobyá↓   la novia
fiancée

Molina   ezminobyá↓ tyéneskekonoşérlá↓   *Molina*
That's my fiancée. You'll have   Es mi novia. Tienes que
to meet her.   conocerla.

(she) does (to do, to make) aşé↓ aşér↓   hace (hacer)

studying (to study)   estúdyandó↓ estúdyár↓   estudiando (estudiar)

(she) is studying   esta—estudyándó↓   está estudiando

White   keáşé↓ estaestudyando↑   *White*
What does she do? Is she   ¿Qué hace? ¿Está estudiando?
studying?

working (to work)   trábáhandó↓ trábáhár↓   trabajando (trabajar)

301

(she) is working	èsta—trabahándó↓	está trabajando
the secretary	lá—sèkrètaryá↓	la secretaria

Molina
No, she's working as a secretary.

noʻ↓ éstátrabahándo │kòmósékrètaryá↓

Molina
No. Está trabajando como
   secretaria.

the wedding	lá—bóɖá↓	la boda
to have a wedding	téner—bóɖá↓	tener boda
soon	próntó↓	pronto

White
Are we going to have a wedding
   soon?

bamos,aténérbóɖa │próntoʻ↑

White
¿Vamos a tener boda pronto?

(we) have (to have)	émós↓ àbér↓	hemos (haber)
decided (to decide)	dèşiɖiɖó↓ dèşiɖír↓	decidido (decidir)
(we)'ve decided	émoz—ɖeşiɖíɖó↓	hemos decidido
the date	lá—fechá↓	la fecha

Molina
Yes, but we haven't set the date
   yet.

síↆ péró │nóemozɖeşiɖíɖo │laféchá │
tóɖabíá↓

Molina
Sí, pero no hemos decidido la
   fecha todavía.

the man	él—ombré↓	el hombre

White
Boy, this is a good whiskey!

ómbré↓ kébwénọestá|ẹstewískí↓

drinking (to drink)

bébyéndó↓ bébér↓

(you) are drinking

éstaz—bebyéndó↓

What are you drinking?

itú↑ késtazbebyéndó↓

the 'cuba libre'

él—kúbá—líbré↓

Molina
A 'cuba libre'.

úŋkubalíbré↓

to you

té↓

the

ló↓

the of, the matter of[3]

ló—dé↓

your(s)

tuɣó↓

John, what do you say we go see
about your apartment?

hwán↓ kéteparéşe|síbamos.abér|

lódélápártámentotúɣó↓

(we) return (to return)

bólbemós↓ bólbér↓

We'll come back later.

déspwezbolbémós↓

White
¡Hombre! Qué bueno está este
whiskey.

bebiendo (beber)

estás bebiendo

Y tú ¿qué estás bebiendo?

el 'cuba libre'

Molina
Un 'cuba libre'.

te

lo

lo de

tuyo

Juan, ¿qué te parece si vamos a
ver lo del apartamento tuyo?

volvemos (volver)

Después volvemos.

9.10   Notes on the basic sentences

(1) This expression, 'You are in your home', is paralleled by dozens of similar ones. Thus if you admire a man's car, he's likely to say, 'It's yours'. This is a polite formula, of course.

(2) This expression is like many expressions referring to food combinations where in English two components are linked by *and - whiskey and soda, bacon and eggs, chicken and rice* - but in Spanish they are linked by *con - whiskey con soda, huevos con tocino, arroz con pollo.*

(3) The construction /lo—del—apartaménto—túyo/ is an example of a very important grammatical process in Spanish. This process, which will be further explained and drilled in Units 33 and 35, is called 'nominalization.' Stated in simple terms 'nominalization' means the functioning as nouns by items which normally are *not* nouns. Thus /lo/ , usually a special kind of adjective, in this construction functions as a noun and is itself modified by the phrase /del—apartaménto—túyo/. A literal translation of /lo/ is very difficult to devise in English, but it implies 'the matter, the business, the idea previously mentioned.' Thus the construction /lo—del—apartaménto—túyo/ is translated in a roundabout way as 'about your apartment.'

9.2   DRILLS AND GRAMMAR

9.21   Pattern drills

9.21.1   The irregular verb /abér/ and regular /—do/forms: in the present perfect construction

A.   Presentation of pattern

ILLUSTRATIONS

	1	yóya│lọekomído↓	Yo ya lo *he comido.*
I haven't thought about the visa.	2	nọepensadọ│enlabísá↓	No *he pensado* en la visa.
(you) have (to have)		ás↓ àbe·r↓	has (haber)
Have you already eaten it?	3	yalọaskomído↑	¿Ya lo *has comido?*

You haven't been here this week.	4	noásestadoakí |estásémánà↓	No *has estado* aquí esta semana.
(you) have (to have)		á↓ àbér↓	a (haber)
Have you lived on that street?	5	ábibidoustéd |enésaka()ye↑	¿*Ha vivido* usted en esa calle?
Have you waited long?	6	áespéradomuchó↑	¿*Ha esperado* mucho?
_____	7	sí↓ péronoémozdesídido |là fechà |tódàbíá↓	Sí, pero no *hemos decidido* la fecha todavía.
We haven't looked for a house.	8	noémoz |buskadokásà↓	No *hemos buscado* casa.
(you) (pl.) have (to have)		án↓ àbér↓	han (haber)
Have you decided on the date?	9	andesídido |lafécha↑	¿*Han decidido* la fecha?
They haven't straightened up the apartment.	10	noán |arregládo |èlàpàrtàméntó↓	No *han arreglado* el apartamento.

305

EXTRAPOLATION

abér		/—do/ form	
		-ár	-ér, -ír
		-ádo	-ído
sg			
1	é		
2 fam	ás		kom—ído
2 - 3	á(c)	abl—ádo	
pl			bɪb—ído
1	émos		
2 - 3	án		

NOTES

a. The perfect construction consists of a conjugated form of the verb /abér/ plus the /—do/ form of the verb.

b. /—do/ forms in perfect constructions are uninflected (do not change their endings); in other constructions, functioning as modifiers, the /—do/ forms do inflect (change their endings) for number and gender.

c. A variant /áy/ occurs as a distinct form not participating in the present perfect construction.

9.21.11   Substitution drills - person-number substitution

1   yọé |ạprèndíɗòmúchọ |àkíↆ

     karmen_____ↆ   ạprèndíɗòmúchọ |àkíↆ

     kármenɪyó_____ↆ   emos |ạprèndíɗòmúchọ |àkíↆ

     ústeɗ_____ↆ   ạprèndíɗòmúchọ |àkíↆ

     e(l)yos_____ↆ   ánɑprèndíɗòmúchọ |àkíↆ

_____

1   *Yo* he aprendido mucho aquí.

     Carmen————————.   Ha aprendido mucho aquí.

     Carmen y yo ————————.   Hemos aprendido mucho aquí.

     Ud.————————.   Ha aprendido mucho aquí.

     Ellos ————————.   Han aprendido mucho aquí.

2 ȧntónyo |nọaẹŋkontraɗokásả↓

   yó_____↓   nọẹŋkontraɗokásả↓

   kȧrmen |ɹȧntónyo_____↓   nọan |ẹŋkȯntraɗokásả↓

   nȯsótroz_____↓   nọemos |ẹŋkȯntraɗokásả↓

   ústeɗez_____↓   nọan |ẹŋkȯntraɗokásả↓

3 eɾyos.ȧmbibiɗọ |ãɾɥitambyén↓

   ȧntónyọ |iyó_____↓   émȯzbibiɗọ |ãɾɥitambyén↓

   ústeɗ_____↓   ábibiɗọ |ãɾɥitambyén↓

---

2 *Antonio* no ha encontrado casa.

   Yo_____.   No he encontrado casa.

   Carmen y Antonio_____.   No han encontrado casa.

   Nosotros _____.   No hemos encontrado casa.

   Uds._____.   No han encontrado casa.

3 *Ellos* han vivido allí también.

   Antonio y yo_____.   Hemos vivido allí también.

   Ud._____.   Ha vivido allí también.

yo _____↓   ébíbídǫ|ằ໓yitambyén↓

karmen _____↓   ábíbídǫ|ằ໓yitambyén↓

4 àntónyǫipàblǫ|ántrábàhaďopókǒ↓

yo _____↓   étrábàhaďopókǒ↓

karmen _____↓   átrábàhaďopókǒ↓

ústeďes _____↓   ántrábàhaďopókǒ↓

nòsotros _____↓   émǒs|trábàhaďopókǒ↓

Yo _____.   He vivido allí también.

Carmen _____.   Ha vivido allí también.

4 *Antonio* y *Pablo* han trabajado poco.

Yo _____.   He trabajado poco.

Carmen _____.   Ha trabajado poco.

Uds. _____.   Han trabajado poco.

Nosotros _____.   Hemos trabajado poco.

5   nòsótros |émòskômídodemasyádò↓

    lwisa_____↓   ákòmídodemasyádò↓

    yo_____↓   ékòmídodemasyádò↓

    àntonyoipáblo_____↓   áŋkòmídodemasyádò↓

    eólyas_____↓   áŋkòmídodemasyádò↓

---

5   *Nosotros* hemos comido demasiado.

    Luisa_____.   Ha comido demasiado.

    Yo_____.   He comido demasiado.

    Antonio y Pablo _____.   Han comido demasiado.

    Ellas _____.   Han comido demasiado.

Construction substitution

Problem: p<u>rònunsya</u> |muybyén↓

Answer: áprònûnsyado |muybyén↓

Problem: *Pronuncia* muy bien.

Answer: Ha pronunciado muy bien.

1 nobuskokásá↓   nǫebuskadokásá↓

2 trábáhamoz│demásyádó↓   émóstrábáhado│demásyádó↓

3 nodeşidenésó↓   nǫandeşididǫésó↓

4 kreętódó↓   ákréidotódó↓

5 álkilǫunabitaşyón↓   éạlkiladǫunabitaşyón↓

6 súbimos│enelas(ş)ensór↓   émó(s)úbidǫ│enelas(ş)ensór↓

7 komenlasálá↓   ákómidǫ│enlasálá↓

---

1 No *busco* casa.   No he buscado casa.

2 *Trabajamos* demasiado.   Hemos trabajado demasiado.

3 No *deciden* eso.   No han decidido eso.

4 *Cree* todo.   Ha creído todo.

5 *Alquilo* una habitación.   He alquilado una habitación.

6 *Subimos* en el ascensor.   Hemos subido en el ascensor.

7 *Come* en la sala.   Ha comido en la sala.

9.21.12 Response drill

1 ústedes |ánábladot̞o̞aŋkomído↓   émo̞s̞ábladó↓

2 e̞(l)yos |ámbébidot̞o̞antrabaháđó↓   ámbébidó↓

3 el |ábàhadot̞o̞asubído↓   ásúbidó↓

4 ústed |ábladot̞o̞atrabaháđó↓   étràbàhadó↓

[ènúnrrès̞tòrán↓] 5 dóndȩakomíd̞o̞ |é(l)yà↓   ènúnrrès̞tòrán↓

[làsékrètaryà↓]   6 kóŋkyen |abladȩo̞us̞téd↓   kónlàs̞ékrètaryà↓

---

1 ¿Uds. han hablado o han comido?   Hemos hablado.

2 ¿Ellos han bebido o han trabajado?   Han bebido.

3 ¿El ha bajado o ha subido?   Ha subido.

4 ¿Ud. ha hablado o ha trabajado?   He trabajado.

(en un restorán) 5 ¿Dónde ha comido ella?   En un restorán.

(la secretaria)   6 ¿Con quién ha hablado Ud.?   Con la secretaria.

313

[kárô↓]   7   áeŋkòntráɗǫustéɗ | toɗobaráto↑   no↓ éŋkontráɗo|toɗo |muykárô↓

[ápàrtàmentô↓]   8   ánâlkiláɗǫustéɗes |unakása↑   no↓ émos |âlkiláɗǫ |ûnâpàrtâmentô↓

[iŋglés↓]   9   ánâbláɗǫeᶜỵos |enéspaɲol↑   no↓ ánâbláɗǫeᶇiŋglés↓

[bwénà↓]   10   áǫstáɗomala |lasópa↑   no↓ áǫstáɗo |muybwénà↓

                       11   áǫstáɗǫustéɗ |ènsàmfrànşisko↑   si↓ sịestáɗô↓

                       12   ántràbàhàɗǫustéɗez |múcho↑   si↓ émòstràbàhaɗo |ɗèmàsyaɗô↓

                       13   ábibiɗǫel |èmpànáma↑   si↓ sịabibíɗô↓

(caro)   7   ¿Ha encontrado Ud. todo barato?   No, he encontrado todo muy caro.

(apartamento)   8   ¿Han alquilado Uds. una casa?   No, hemos alquilado un apartamento.

(inglés)   9   ¿Han hablado ellos en español?   No, han hablado en inglés.

(buena)   10   ¿Ha estado mala la sopa?   No, ha estado muy buena.

               11   ¿Ha estado Ud. en San Francisco?   Sí, sí he estado.

               12   ¿Han trabajado Uds. mucho?   Sí, hemos trabajado demasiado.

               13   ¿Ha vivido él en Panamá?   Sí, sí ha vivido.

9.21.13   Translation drill

1	They haven't come yet.	é(l)yòz∣ngambeníđó∣tòđàbíá↓	Ellos no han venido todavía.
2	We haven't remembered anything.	ngemoz∣rrèkòrđađó∣náđà↓	No hemos recordado nada.
3	You all have left everything for tomorrow.	ùsteđes∣ándèháđòtóđó∣paramanyáná↓	Uds. han dejado todo para mañana.
4	Have you been in Chile?	ágstađoustéđ∣enchilé↑	¿Ha estado Ud. en Chile?
5	Has he lived in Cuba?	ábibíđoel∣èŋkuba↑	¿Ha vivido él en Cuba?
6	I haven't been in that part of Peru.	ngestáđo∣enesaparté∣đèlpèrú↓	No he estado en esa parte del Perú.
7	We've rented a very pretty house.	emos̞alkiláđo∣ùnàkásà∣múybonítà↓	Hemos alquilado una casa muy bonita.
8	Where has she eaten?	dondęakomíđo∣é(l)yà↓	¿Dónde ha comido ella?
9	They haven't included that in the bill.	é(l)yoz∣ngan̪iŋklwíđo∣ésǫènlàkwéntà↓	Ellos no han incluído eso en la cuenta.
10	She hasn't gone up yet.	é(l)yà∣ngasubíđo∣tòđàbíá↓	Ella no ha subido todavía.
11	I've worked here two years.	etrabaháđo∣akí∣đos̞ányòs↓	He trabajado aquí dos años.

B. Discussion of pattern

The verb /abér/ is extremely irregular. In the present tense it has no stem, appearing only as a set of endings with erratic theme vowels /e-a/ and the regular person-number endings /-s, -mos, -n/.

/abér/ shares with /tenér/ the range of meaning covered by the English verb 'have', though they are not difficult to differentiate: /tenér/ means 'have, hold, possess', while /abér/ is the equivalent of 'have' in sentences like 'I *have* eaten'.

The /-do/ form of the verb can be constructed by adding /-ádo/ (theme /-á-/ plus /-do/) to /-ár/ verbs, and /-ído/ (theme /-í-/ plus /-do/) to /-ér, -ír/ verbs. The /-do/ form is more or less equivalent to the -ed form of English verbs (peeped, begged, headed). Thus the construction equivalents are these:

yo-é terminádo↓

I've finished.

There are a number of irregularly formed /-do/ forms which will be collected and drilled in Unit 44.

In the present perfect construction, as indeed in all verb constructions, only the first verb is inflected (for person, number, tense). Thus /abér/ is inflected, but the /-do/ form is not. (However, see Unit 10 for other constructions the /-do/ forms appear in).

The present perfect construction in Spanish is used, although with much less frequency, in much the same way as the corresponding construction in English.

There is a variant of the 2 - 3 sg /a/ which occurs frequently without an accompanying /-do/ form. This variant, /áy/ 'there is, there are', occurs with no number agreement with the verb, as the double translation 'there is, there are' would suggest.

9.21.2   Possessives - full forms

A.   Presentation of pattern

ILLUSTRATIONS

_____

_____

        our(s)

She's a neighbor of ours.

They're friends of ours.

_____

This is your clothing.

These books, Miss. Are they
   yours?

This car, gentlemen. Is it yours?

        his

Mr. Smith wants a large house; his
   family is coming tomorrow.

#		
1	pòrkénobémos ̣|ạúṇạmịgomịò↓	¿Por qué no vemos a un amigo *mío*?
2	̇ẹlgustọẹzmịò↓	El gusto es *mío*.
	nwéstrò↓	nuestro
3	ẹsunabȩ̣ịnanwéstrạ̀↓	Es una vecina *nuestra*.
4	sóṇạmịgoznwéstròs↓	Son amigos *nuestros*.
5	bámos̩abér ̣|lòdẹ̀lạpạrtạméntotúyò↓	Vamos a ver lo del apartamento *tuyo*.
6	́ẹstạẹz ̣|làrrópatúyạ̀↓	Esta es la ropa *tuya*.
7	́ẹstozlịbròs ̣|sẹ̀ṇyòrítạ̀↓ sónsuyos↑	Estos libros, señorita, ¿son *suyos*?
8	́ẹstȩ̣awtò ̣|sẹ̀ṇyórès↓ ẹ̀(s)suyo↑	Este auto, señores, ¿es *suyo*?
	súyò↓	suyo
9	̇ẹlsẹ̀ṇyórsmị̧ ̣|kyérȩ̣unakásaagrándè↓	El señor Smith quiere una casa grande;
	làfạmịlyasuyạ̀ ̣|byené ̣|mạ̀ṇyánạ̀↓	la familia *suya* viene mañana.

their(s)	súyȯ↓	suyo
We don't know the Quinteros, but we have a book of theirs.	10 nokonoşemos |ȧlȯ(s) sėņyoreskıntérȯ↑ pérȯtėnemos |unlıbrosúyȯ↓	No conocemos a los señores Quintero, pero tenemos un libro *suyo*.

EXTRAPOLATION

Reference:	sg	pl
1	mío(s) —a(s)	nwéstro(s) —a(s)
2 fam	túyo(s) —a(s)	
2 - 3	súyo(s) —a(s)	

NOTES

a. Possessives are a special kind of adjective, and like other adjectives, they agree in number and gender with the noun they modify.

b. There are forms for singular and plural reference, both of which have singular and plural forms independently agreeing with the noun modified.

c. There are different forms that can be correlated to person; the 2 - 3 form /súyo/ is common to singular and plural reference.

9.21.21   Substitution drills - form substitution

1   éstęawtǫezmíò↓

_____súy̨ò↓   éstęawtǫ |e(s)súy̨ò↓

_____nwéstró↓   éstęawtǫeznwéstró↓

2   éstòzmwébles |sonmíòs↓

_____súy̨òs↓   éstòzmwébles |sonsúy̨òs↓

_____nwéstròs↓   éstòzmwébles |so(n)nwéstròs↓

---

1 Este auto es mío.

_____suyo.   Este auto es suyo.

_____nuestro.   Este auto es nuestro.

2 Estos muebles son míos.

_____ suyos.   Estos muebles son suyos.

_____ nuestros.   Estos muebles son nuestros.

319

3 éstákasa̯ezmíà↓

_____súyà↓   éstákasa̯e(s)súyà↓

_____nwéstrà↓   éstákasa̯eznwéstrà↓

4 éstázmònedas |sonmíàs↓

_____súyàs↓   éstázmònedas |sonsúyàs↓

_____nwéstràs↓   éstázmònedas |so(n)nwéstràs↓

---

3 Esta casa es mía.

————— suya.   Esta casa es suya.
————— nuestra.   Esta casa es nuestra.

4 Estas monedas son mías.

——————suyas.   Estas monedas son suyas.
——————nuestras.   Estas monedas son nuestras.

5   éstęótélezmíó↓

_____súyó↓   éstęótéle(s)súyó↓

_____nwéstró↓   éstęóteleznwéstró↓

---

5 Este hotel es mío.

_____suyo.   Este hotel es suyo.

_____nuestro.   Este hotel es nuestro.

Number substitution

1   éstèbìḷỵétezmíǒ↓
    ____bìḷỵétes____↓   éstòzbìḷỵétes |sonmíos↓

2   éstàmònèḍaezmíà↓
    ____mònèḍas____↓   éstàzmònèḍas |sonmíàs↓

3   éstèchéke(s)súyò↓
    ____chékes____↓   éstòschékes |sonsúyòs↓

_____

1 Este *billete* es mío.

   ____billetes____.   Estos billetes son míos.

2 Esta *moneda* es mía.

   ____monedas____.   Estas monedas son mías.

3 Este *cheque* es suyo.

   ____cheques____.   Estos cheques son suyos.

4   ésédifişyọeznwéstró↓
_____édifişyos_____↓

ésósédifişyos│so(n)nwéstrós↓

5   éstázḽyabes │sonsúyàs↓
_____ḽyabe_____↓

éstàḽyabe(s)súyá↓

---

4   Ese *edificio* es nuestro.

___ edificios_____.

Esos edificios son nuestros.

5   Estas *llaves* son suyas.

_____llave_____.

Esta llave es suya.

6 éstàsfótos |so(n)nwéstràs↓

   _____fotǫ_____↓   éstàfótǫ |eznwéstrà↓

7 éstòs(ṣ)ènişéros |sonmíòs↓

   _____ṣènişérǫ_____↓   éstèṣènişérǫ |ezmíó↓

---

6 Estas *fotos* son nuestras.

   _____ foto _____.   Esta foto es nuestra.

7 Estos *ceniceros* son míos.

   _____cenicero_____.   Este cenicero es mío.

                                                        End of Tape 6A

1 ésákasae(s)súyà↓
   __ápártámento__↓

ésęápártámentoes ¡súyó↓

2 éstęótéleznwéstró↓
   __àhenşyą__↓

éstáhenşyąeznwéstrà↓

3 éstózmwebles ¡sonsúyós↓
   __kósas__↓

éstáskósas ¡sonsúyàs↓

4 éstęawtoezmíó↓
   __kásą__↓

éstákasąezmíá↓

---

1 Esa *casa* es suya.
   __apartamento__.

Ese apartamento es suyo.

2 Este *hotel* es nuestro.
   __agencia__.

Esta agencia es nuestra.

3 Estos *muebles* son suyos.
   __cosas__.

Estas cosas son suyas.

4 Este *auto* es mío
   __casa__.

Esta casa es mía.

5 éstázλ̮y̶abes |sonmías↓
   ____péryoðikos____↓   éstòspéryoðikos |sonmíòs↓

6 éstòzlíbros |so(n)nwéstròs↓
   ____sił̮y̶as_____↓   éstà(s)sił̮y̶as |so(n)nwéstràs↓

7 éstàkas̶aezmíà↓
   ____éðifiş̶y̶o____↓   éstèðifiş̶y̶oezmíò↓

---

5 Estas *llaves* son mías.
   ____periódicos_____.   Estos periódicos son míos.

6 Estos *libros* son nuestros.
   ____sillas_____.   Estas sillas son nuestras.

7 Esta *casa* es mía.
   ____edificio_____.   Este edificio es mío.

9.21.22   Response drill

         1   éstèlíbròↆ èzmıosuyóↆ.   é(s)suyóↆ

         2   éstázmónedásↆ sònmıas̟osuyásↆ   sònsuyásↆ

[suyóↆ]   3   dèkyen|es̟es̟elıbróↆ   èzmíóↆ

[suyáↆ]   4   dèkyen|es̟es̟aplumàↆ   èzmıàↆ

[mıósↆ]   5   dèkyen|son̟estozlıbròsↆ   sònsuyósↆ

[suyóↆ]   6   èzmıǫeselıbro↑   nóↆ èzmíóↆ

---

        1 Este libro, ¿es mío o suyo?   Es suyo.

        2 Estas monedas, ¿son mías o suyas?   Son suyas

(suyo)   3 ¿De quién es ese libro?   Es mío.

(suya)   4 ¿De quién es esa pluma?   Es mía.

(míos)   5 ¿De quién son estos libros?   Son suyos.

(suyo)   6 ¿Es mío ese libro?   No, es mío.

[mía↓]	7	é(s) súyąestaplúmá↑
[mías↓]	8	sónsúyas|éstazmonédas↑
	9	é(s)súyọesẹawto↑
	10	sónsúyos|ésozlíbros↑
	11	sónsúyas|ésazmonédas↑
	12	sónmías|éstazmonédas↑
	13	sónmíos|éstozlíbros↑

nó↓ é(s)súyá↓

nó↓ sónsúyás↓

sí↓ ėzmíó↓

sí↓ sónmíós↓

sí↓ sónmíás↓

sí↓ sónsúyás↓

sí↓ sónsúyós↓

(mía)   7 ¿Es suya esta pluma?   No, es suya.

(mías)   8 ¿Son suyas estas monedas?   No, son suyas.

        9 ¿Es suyo ese auto?   Sí, es mío.

  10 ¿Son suyos esos libros?   Sí, son míos.

  11 ¿Son suyas esas monedas?   Sí, son mías.

  12 ¿Son mías estas monedas?   Sí, son suyas.

  13 ¿Son míos estos libros?   Sí, son suyos.

9.21.23   Translation drill

1 These books are ours.	éstoȥlíbros |so(n̄)nwéstròs↓	Estos libros son nuestros.
2 That old house is ours.	ésakasabyehạ |eȥnwéstrà↓	Esa casa vieja es nuestra.
3 This apartment is ours.	éstẹapartaméntọ |eȥnwéstrò↓	Este apartamento es nuestro.
4 Whose (of whom) is this book? Is it yours?	dékyenẹsẹestelíbrò↓ é(s)súyọ↑	¿De quién es este libro? ¿Es suyo?
5 Is that pencil his?	é(s)súyọ |eselápịş↑	¿Es suyo ese lápiz?
6 Is this pencil mine?	éȥmịọ |estelápịş↑	¿Es mío este lápiz?
7 Those books are mine.	ésòȥlíbros |sonmíòs↓	Esos libros son míos.
8 These books are his.	éstòȥlíbros |sonsúᵧòs↓	Estos libros son suyos.
9 These coins are mine.	éstạȥmónedas |sonmíàs↓	Estas monedas son mías.
10 These things are ours.	éstạskósas |so(n̄)nwéstràs↓	Estas cosas son nuestras.
11 That pen is yours.	ésạplumạ |e(s)súyà↓	Esa pluma es suya.

B.   Discussion of pattern

Possessives differ in meaning and association from other adjectives in that they have reference to person and number. No other adjectives have these features of similarity to pronouns and verb forms. Yet the possessives are definitely adjectives, because each form inflects for number and gender to agree with the noun modified. One should not confuse the *number of reference*, which involves selection of one form or another (/míɔ/—/nwéstro/) with the *number of agreement*, which involves the omission or addition of an ending (/mío/ — /míos/). The first choice is a matter of what one wishes to say; the second is a matter of adjective agreement, and given the noun there is no choice in the number and gender of the possessive (or any other adjective). Likewise /líbro—súyo/ can mean 'his book' *or* '*her* book' (or 'your book'). The form /súyo/ does not change to /súya/ when it means 'her,' rather only when it modifies a feminine noun, as /kása—súya/, which can mean '*his* house' *or* 'her house' (or 'your house'). As in the case of any other adjective, the appropriately agreeing form is obligatory.

The possessives usually appear in their full forms in a position immediately after the noun they modify, or after the verb /sér/. Both variant form and a special construction in other positions are presented in Unit 11.

The forms of /súyo/ can refer to the English equivalents 'your (sg or pl), his, her, its, their'. Unless the context clearly indicates another reference, however, the most frequent reference is 'your (sg)'. If the contextual reference is not obvious other constructions are usually used (presented in Unit 13) to avoid any ambiguity. Thus the chart in A above could be modified as follows:

Reference	sg	pl
1	mío	nwéstro
2 fam	túyo	(súyo)
2 for	súyo	
3	(súyo)	(súyo)

When these forms follow a noun they are similar to, and translated by, an English construction consisting of noun plus 'of' plus the long form of the possessive. In the equivalent Spanish construction there is no relator corresponding to 'of'. Thus 'a book of mine' is translated to /un—líbro—mío/ and English speakers have to remember not to translate the English 'of'.

9.22   Replacement drills

A   báser |mి àpártàmento |komǫeste↑

1   _____kása_____↑   báser |mikása |komǫesta↑

2   _____sǔ_____↑   báser |sǔkása |komǫesta↑

3   bán_____↑   bánàser |sùskásas |komǫesta↑

4   _____èskrîtoryo_____↑   báser |sῠèskrîtoryo |komǫeste↑

5   _____èse↑   báser |sῠèskrîtoryo |komǫese↑

6   _____bèşinos_____↑   bánàser |súzbèşinos |komǫese↑

7   _____sèkrètarya_____↑   báser |sùsèkrètarya |komǫesa↑

A   ¿Va a ser mi apartamento como éste?

1   ¿_____casa_____?   ¿Va a ser mi casa como ésta?

2   ¿_____su_____?   ¿Va a ser su casa como ésta?

3   ¿Van_____?   ¿Van a ser sus casas como ésta?

4   ¿_____escritorio_____?   ¿Va a ser su escritorio como éste?

5   ¿_____ése?   ¿Va a ser su escritorio como ése?

6   ¿_____vecinos_____?   ¿Van a ser sus vecinos como ése?

7   ¿_____secretaria_____?   ¿Va a ser su secretaria como ésa?

331

B   tŏđábía |nĕşĕsíto |kŏmprár |muchaskόsàs↓

1 _____únà_____↓   tŏđábía |nĕşĕsíto |kŏmprár |ùnàkόsà↓

2 _____ber_____↓   tŏđábía |nĕşĕsítober |ùnàkόsà↓

3 _____áykĕ_____↓   tŏđábịạ |áykĕber |ùnàkόsà↓

4 _____àşer_____↓   tŏđábịạ |áykĕạşer |ùnàkόsà↓

5 _____trabáhŏ↓   tŏđábịạ |áykĕạşer |untrabáhŏ↓

6 _____mucho_____↓   tŏđábịạ |áykĕạşer |muchotrabáhŏ↓

7 _____pwéđọ_____↓   tŏđábía |pwéđọạşer |muchotrabáhŏ↓

B   Todavía necesito comprar muchas cosas.

1 _____una_____.   Todavía necesito comprar una cosa.

2 _____ver_____.   Todavía necesito ver una cosa.

3 _____hay que_____.   Todavía hay que ver una cosa.

4 _____hacer_____.   Todavía hay que hacer una cosa.

5 _____trabajo.   Todavía hay que hacer un trabajo.

6 _____mucho_____.   Todavía hay que hacer mucho trabajo.

7 _____puedo_____.   **Todavía puedo hacer mucho trabajo.**

C   éstátrábáhando |kómósékrétaryà↓

1 _____ústedés↓   éstátrábáhando |kómoústedés↓

2 _____kón_____↓   éstátrábáhando |kónústedés↓

3 ____áblando_____↓   éstáblando |kónústedés↓

4 éstóy_____↓   éstóyáblando |kónústedés↓

5 _____ústed↓   éstóyáblando |kónústéd↓

6 _____de____↓   éstóyáblando |deústéd↓

7 _____súzbéşinòs↓   éstóyáblando |désúzbéşinòs↓

C   Está trabajando como secretaria.

1 _____ustedes.   Está trabajando como ustedes.

2 _____con _____.   Está trabajando con ustedes.

3 ____hablando_____.   Está hablando con ustedes.

4 Estoy_____.   Estoy hablando con ustedes.

5 _____usted.   Estoy hablando con usted.

6 _____de_____.   Estoy hablando de usted.

7 _____ sus vecinos.   Estoy hablando de sus vecinos.

D bámòs,àtèner |bodaprónto↑

1 bás_____↑   bás,àtèner |bodaprónto↑

2 _____kása____↑   bás,àtèner |kasaprónto↑

3 ___kómprar_____↑   bás,àkómprar |kasaprónto↑

4 _____aóra↑   bás,àkómprar |kasaóra↑

5 bán_____↑   bán,àkómprar |kasaóra↑

6 _____algǫ____↑   bán,àkómprar |algǫaóra↑

7 ___àṣer_____↑   bán,àṣeralgǫ |aóra↑

D ¿Vamos a tener boda pronto?

1 ¿Vas_____?   ¿Vas a tener boda pronto?

2 ¿_____casa____?   ¿Vas a tener casa pronto?

3 ¿____comprar_____?   ¿Vas a comprar casa pronto?

4 ¿_____ahora?   ¿Vas a comprar casa ahora?

5 ¿Van_____?   ¿Van a comprar casa ahora?

6 ¿_____algo____?   ¿Van a comprar algo ahora?

7 ¿_____hacer_____?   ¿Van a hacer algo ahora?

E   noémoz |dèşíđiđo |lafechá | tóđàbíà↓

1 _____nađà_____↓   noémoz |dèşíđiđonađà |tóđàbíà↓

2 _____tràbàhađo_____↓   noémos |tràbàhađonađá |tóđàbíà↓

3 __é_____↓   noé |tràbàhađonađá |tóđàbíà↓

4 _____muchò_____↓   noé |tràbàhađomuchò |tóđàbíà↓

5 ___estúđyađo_____↓   noé |estúđyađomuchò |tóđàbíà↓

6 __àn_____↓   noan |èstúđyađomuchò |tóđàbíà↓

7 ____kòmiđo_____↓   noaŋ |kòmiđomuchò |tóđàbíà↓

E   No hemos decidido la fecha todavía.

1 _____nada_____.   No hemos decidido nada todavía.

2 _____trabajado_____.   No hemos trabajado nada todavía.

3 ___he_____.   No he trabajado nada todavía.

4 _____mucho_____.   No he trabajado mucho todavía.

5 _____estudiado_____.   No he estudiado mucho todavía.

6 ___han_____.   No han estudiado mucho todavía.

7 _____comido_____.   No han comido mucho todavía.

F   kebweṇǫestá |ǫstệwískiↆ

1 _____kásàↆ   kebweṇạèstá |ǫstàkásàↆ

2 _____éstàs___ↆ   kebwenàsèstán |éstàskásàsↆ

3 _____són_____ↆ   kebwenà(s)són |éstàskásàsↆ

4 __malàs_____ↆ   kemalà(s)són |éstàskásàsↆ

5 _____líbrọↆ   kemalǫès |éstèlíbrọↆ

6 _____ésòz_____ↆ   kemalδ(s)són |ésòzlíbròsↆ

7 _____sèkṣyónↆ   kemalạès |ésàsèkṣyónↆ

F   ¡Qué bueno está este whisky!

1 ¡_____casa!   ¡Qué buena está esta casa!

2 ¡_____estas___!   ¡Qué buenas están estas casas!

3 ¡_____ son _____!   ¡Qué buenas son estas casas!

4 ¡___malas_____!   ¡Qué malas son estas casas!

5 ¡_____libro!   ¡Qué malo es este libro!

6 ¡_____esos___!   ¡Qué malos son esos libros!

7 ¡_____ sección!   ¡Qué mala es esa sección!

9.23   Variation drill

A éstasentukásá↓   Estás en tu casa.

1 You're in your bedroom.   éstasentudormitóryó↓   Estás en tu dormitorio

2 You're in your room.   éstasentukwártó↓   Estás en tu cuarto.

3 You're in your hotel.   éstasentuotél↓   Estás en tu hotel.

4 You're in your apartment.   éstasentuapartaméntó↓   Estás en tu apartamento.

5 You're in your building.   éstasentuedifíşyó↓   Estás en tu edificio.

6 You're in your restaurant.   éstasenturrestorán↓   Estás en tu restorán

7 You're in your car.   éstasentuáwtó↓   Estás en tu auto.

B tódọ |èstábyén̯arregláđọ↓   Todo está bien arreglado.

1 The patio looks very neat.   èlpátyọ |èstábyén̯arregláđọ↓   El patio está bien arreglado.

2 The apartment is unoccupied.   èlåpàrtåmentọ |èstáđèsọkùpađọ↓   El apartamento está desocupado.

3 The desk is unoccupied.   èlèskrìtóryọ |èstáđèsọkùpađọ↓   El escritorio está desocupado.

4 The kitchen looks very neat.   làkọ̧ṣin̯ạ |èstábyén̯arregláđạ↓   La cocina está bien arreglada.

5 The house looks very neat.   làkásạ |èstábyén̯arregláđạ↓   La casa está bien arreglada.

6 The rooms are unoccupied.   lòskwártos |èstándèsọkùpađos↓   Los cuartos están desocupados.

7 The houses are unoccupied.   làskásas |èstándèsọkùpađạs↓   Las casas están desocupadas.

C kyéresˌuŋwiski |konsóða↑   ¿Quieres un whisky con soda?

1 Would you like a whisky and   kyéresˌuŋwiski |konˌagwaminerál↑   ¿Quieres un whisky con agua
  sparkling water?   mineral?

2 Would you like a 'cuba libre'?   kyéresǀuŋkubalíbre↑   ¿Quieres un cuba libre?

3 Would you like a ham sandwich?   kyéresǀunsáŋwich |ðehamón↑   ¿Quieres un sandwich de jamón?

4 Would you like a beer?   kyéresǀunaşerbéşa↑   ¿Quieres una cerveza?

5 Would you like a bowl of   kyéresǀunasópa |ðeleçumbrés↓   ¿Quieres una sopa de legumbres?
  vegetable soup?

6 Would you like a pork chop?   kyéresǀunachuléta |ðeşérðo↑   ¿Quieres una chuleta de cerdo?

7 Would you like a tomato salad?   kyéresǀunaensaláða |ðetomáte↑   ¿Quieres una ensalada de tomate?

D kyénes |esamuchácha |delafótó↓   ¿Quién es esa muchacha de la
                                                                     foto?

1 Who is that young lady in   kyénes |esamuchácha |delaseksyoŋkonsulár↓   ¿Quién es esa muchacha de la
   the consular section?
                                                                     sección consular?

2 Who is that young lady from   kyénes |esamuchácha |delaembahádà↓   ¿Quién es esa muchacha de la
   the Embassy?
                                                                     Embajada?

3 Who is that young lady in   kyénes |esamuchácha |delkwártosyété↓   ¿Quién es esa muchacha del
   room seven?
                                                                     cuarto siete?

4 Who is that young lady with   kyénes |esamuchácha |deláwtó↓   ¿Quién es esa muchacha del
   the car?
                                                                     auto?

5 Who is that young lady from   kyénes |esasenyoríta |delahénsyà↓   ¿Quién es esa señorita de la
   the agency?
                                                                     agencia?

6 Who is that gentleman from   kyénes |esesenyór |delprimérpísó↓   ¿Quién es ese señor del primer
   the first floor?
                                                                     piso?

7 Who is that gentleman from   kyénes|esesenyór |delotél↓   ¿Quién es ese señor del hotel?
   the hotel?

E èzmínóbyà↓ tyéneskekonoṣérlà↓   Es mi novia. Tienes que
                                                                           conocerla.

1 It's my girl friend. You'll   èzmínóbyà↓ tyéneskebérlà↓   Es mi novia. Tienes que verla.
  have to see her.

2 It's my friend. You'll have   èzmḷámígà↓ tyéneskebérlà↓   Es mi amiga. Tienes que verla.
  to see her.

3 It's Mrs. Molina. You have   èzlàsêŋyóra|ɗèmólínà↓ tyénes   Es la señora de Molina. Tienes
  to meet her.
                                  kekonoṣérlà↓   que conocerla.

4 It's Miss Molina. I have   èzlàsêŋyóritamolínà↓ teŋgokebérlà↓   Es la señorita Molina. Tengo
  to see her.   que verla.

5 It's the secretary. I have   èzlàsékrètáryà↓ teŋgokẹayuɗárlà↓   Es la secretaria. Tengo que
  to help her.   ayudarla.

6 It's Louise. We'll have   èzlwísà↓ tènemoskesperárlà↓   Es Luisa. Tenemos que
  to wait for her.   esperarla.

7 It's Carmen. We'll have   èskármèn↓ tènemoskeⱪyebárlà↓   Es Carmen. Tenemos que llevarla.
  to take her.

F ké|áşè↓ èstáęstúdyándo↑   ¿Qué hace? ¿Está estudiando?

1 What's she doing? Is she   ké|áşè↓ èstátràbàhándo↑   ¿Qué hace? ¿Está trabajando?
  working?

2 What are you doing? Are   ké|áşè↓ èstáblándo↑   ¿Qué hace? ¿Está hablando?
  you speaking?

3 What are you doing? Are   ké|áşè↓ èstápènsándo↑   ¿Qué hace? ¿Está pensando?
  you thinking?

4 What are you doing? Are   ké|áşè↓ èstábàhándo↑   ¿Qué hace? ¿Está bajando?
  you going down?

5 What are you doing? Are   ké|áşè↓ èstápràktikándo↑   ¿Qué hace? ¿Está practicando?
  you practicing?

6 What are you doing? Are   ké|áşè↓ èstáęspérándo↑   ¿Qué hace? ¿Está esperando?
  you waiting?

7 What are you doing? Are   ké|áşè↓ èstákòmprándo↑   ¿Qué hace? ¿Está comprando?
  you buying something?

9.24   Review drill - adjective position

1 I have little furniture.   téngó|pokozmwéblès↓   Tengo pocos muebles.

   I have expensive furniture.   téngó|mwebleskárôs↓   Tengo muebles caros.

2 I have too many clothes.   téngó |dêmâsyadarrópà↓   Tengo demasiada ropa.

   I have cheap clothes.   téngó|rropabarátà↓   Tengo ropa barata.

3 I have many checks.   téngó|muchoschékès↓   Tengo muchos cheques.

   I have travelers checks.   téngó|chekezbyahérôs↓   Tengo cheques viajeros.

4 I have a lot of clothes.   téngó|mucharrópà↓   Tengo mucha ropa.

   I have American clothes.   téngó|rropamerikánà↓   Tengo ropa americana.

5 I have other furniture.   téngo |ótrozmwéblès↓   Tengo otros muebles.

   I have cheap furniture.   téngó|mweblezbarátôs↓   Tengo muebles baratos.

6 I want a lot of water.   kyéro |muchágwà↓   Quiero mucha agua.

   I want carbonated water.   kyero |agwaminerál↓   Quiero agua mineral.

7 I want enough clothes.   kyéro |bàstánterrópá↓   Quiero bastante ropa.

   I want expensive clothes.   kyérorrópakárá↓   Quiero ropa cara.

8 I'm in the same section.   èstóy |ènlàmízmasekşyón↓   Estoy en la misma sección.

   I'm in the consular section. èstóy |ènlàsèkşyónkonsulár↓ Estoy en la sección consular.

9 There is the same gentleman. ái |ęstáęlmízmoseṇyór↓   Ahí está el mismo señor.

   There is the English gentleman. ái |ęstáęlsèṇyóriṇglés↓   Ahí está el señor inglés.

10 Here there are few young ladies. ákı |aypóka(s)seṇyorítás↓ Aquí hay pocas señoritas.

   Here there are Spanish girls.   ákı |aysèṇyórítàsęspàṇyolàs↓ Aquí hay señoritas españolas.

11 I work with the same young lady. tràbáho |kònlàmízmaseṇyorítá↓ Trabajo con la misma señorita.

   I work with the American girl.   tràbáho |kònlàsèṇyóritamerikáná↓ Trabajo con la señorita americana.

344

9.3   CONVERSATION STIMULUS

NARRATIVE 1

1 Jose has been in his neighbors' apartment.	hôsé|ạ́estáđọ|ênẹ̀lápàrtámén̩to| đẹ́súzbéṣinôs↓	José ha estado en el apartamento de sus vecinos.
2 And it's exactly the same as his.	ịẹ́s̩igwắlítọalsúyọ̀↓	Y es igualito al suyo.
3 Juan wants to see it.	hwaŋkyérebérlồ↓	Juan quiere verlo.
4 Jose says that he can go any day.	hôsédiṣệ↑kelpweđẹir|kwắlkyérđíà↓	José dice que él puede ir cualquier día.
5 Juan wants to go tomorrow.	hwaŋ|kyérẹir|maŋyán̩à↓	Juan quiere ir mañana.
6 Jose's going to talk to his neighbors, then.	hôsébablár|kônsúzbéṣinôs| ên̩tón̩ṣês↓	José va a hablar con sus vecinos, entonces.
7 And he'll let Juan know.	ilẹ̀àbisahwán↓	Y le avisa a Juan.

DIALOG 1

Juan, pregúntele a José si él ha estado en el apartamento de sus vecinos.

tuas.estado̦|ėnėlåpårtåmento|
detuzbe̦çinos↑

Juan: ¿Tú has estado en el apartamento de tus vecinos?

José, contéstele que sí, que es igualito al suyo. Pregúntele que cuándo quiere verlo.

si↓ ės.igwålitǫalmío↓
kwandokyerezbérlô↓

José: Sí, es igualito al mío. ¿Cuándo quieres verlo?

Juan, contéstele que cualquier día, que mañana, si le parece.

kwålkyerdíå↓ måŋyanå|sitėpårę̇ș̇ė↓

Juan: Cualquier día. Mañana, si te parece.

José, dígale que muy bien, que Ud. habla con ellos y le avisa.

muybyén↓ yǫablo|kônę̇l̩yos|itǫabísô↓

José: Muy bien. Yo hablo con ellos y te aviso.

NARRATIVE 2

1 Juan isn't planning to do anything this evening.

hwan|nȯpyensaser|nada̦|éståtárdė↓

Juan no piensa hacer nada esta tarde.

2 Why doesn't he go see where Jose lives, then?

pȯrkenobaber|dóndebibehose|ęntónș̇ės↓

¿Por qué no va a ver dónde vive José, entonces?

3 That way he can see what his apartment is going to be like.

ásıpweɗebér |kómòbásér |syápártàmentȯↆ

Así puede ver cómo va a ser su apartamento.

4 He thinks it might be an excellent idea.

élkreę |kėsùnąiɗeąeks(ş)elénteↆ

El cree que es una idea excelente.

DIALOG 2

José, pregúntele a Juan que qué piensa hacer esta noche.

képyensąşąşér |éstànoché |hwánↆ

José: ¿Qué piensas hacer. esta noche, Juan?

Juan, contéstele que nada, que por qué.

naɗåↆ pòrkeↆ

Juan: Nada, ¿Por qué?

José, pregúntele que por qué no viene a ver dónde Ud. vive?

pòrkénobyénesąbér |ɗóndęyobíbȯↆ

José: ¿Por qué no vienes a ver donde yo vivo?

Juan, contéstele que le parece una idea excelente.

mėpåreşę |ûnąiɗeąeks(ş)élénteↆ

Juan: Me parece una idea excelente.

José, dígale que así puede ver cómo va a ser el apartamento suyo.

ásıpweɗezbér |komòbásér |
èlåpàrtàmentotúyȯↆ

José: Así puedes ver cómo va a ser el apartamento tuyo.

NARRATIVE 3

1 Jose has everything very neat in his apartment.	hósetyénetodo |muybyen |arregladǫ | ènsу̯ápàrtàméntò↓	José tiene todo muy bien arreglado en su apartamento.
2 But he's still got a million things to buy.	pérótòdȧbìa |tyénęûnmíℓℓyònde kósàs|kèkǫmprár↓	Pero todavía tiene un millón de cosas que comprar.
3 He has already talked with his neighbors.	yáblado |kònsûzbèşinòs↓	Ya ha hablado con sus vecinos.
4 They told him that they're going to be home tomorrow afternoon.	lèdíheroŋ |kèbáną̀estárèŋkasa| mànyanaporlatárdè↓	Le dijeron que van a estar en casa mañana por la tarde.
5 Juan says that if the other apartment is like this one, he'll take it.	hwándişe |kèsı̯èlótrǫapartaméntǫ | èskómǫeste↑lótomà↓	Juan dice que si el otro apartamento es como éste, lo toma.

DIALOG 3

Juan, dígale a José que qué bien arreglado tiene todo.	kébyén | árrégládó | tyénèstódó↓	Juan: ¡Qué bien arreglado·tienes todo!
José, dígale que gracias, pero que todavía tiene un millón de cosas que comprar.	graşyás↓ pérótóðábía | téŋgọ ùnmíl0yondekósàs | kèkòmprár↓	José: Gracias, pero todavía tengo un millón de cosas que comprar.
Juan, pregúntele si no ha hablado con sus vecinos todavía.	nọásạ̀bladọ | kòntúzbèşinos | todabía↑	Juan: ¿No has hablado con tus vecinos todavía?
José, contéstele que sí, que le dijeron que van a estar en casa mañana por la tarde.	si↓ mèdiheroŋ | kèbánạ̀estár èŋkasa | mànyanaporlatárdé↓	José: Sí, me dijeron que van a estar en casa mañana por la tarde.
Juan, dígale que está bien, y que si el apartamento de ellos es como éste, Ud. lo toma.	èstabyén↓ sẹ̀èlàpàrtàmento | dẹ̀0yós↑èskómọ̀estè↑lótomó↓	Juan: Está bien. Si el aparta- mento de ellos es como éste, lo tomo.

NARRATIVE 4

1 Carmen is Jose's girl friend.	kármen |ėzlánobyadehosé↓	Carmen es la novia de José.
2 Juan hasn't had the pleasure of meeting her yet.	hwan |nọåtènidọelgústo |dė kònòşerlå |tòdåbíå↓	Juan no ha tenido el gusto de conocerla todavía.
3 Here's a picture of her. She sure is pretty!	åkɹay |ùnåfótò |dẹŵyå↓ kébonítạés↓	Aquí hay una foto de ella. ¡Qué bonita es!
4 Jose and Carmen haven't talked about the wedding yet.	hòseɹkármen |nọanabládò | dèlåbòdå |tòdåbíå↓	José y Carmen no han hablado de la boda todavía.
5 But Jose thinks it's going to be soon.	pérohòsékreẹ |kèbasér |próntò↓	Pero José cree que va a ser pronto.

DIALOG 4

José, pregúntele a Juan si él conoce a Carmen, la novia suya.	túkônoșeșakarmen↑lånóbyamia↑	José: ¿Tú conoces a Carmen, la novia mía?
Juan, contéstele que no, que todavía no ha tenido el gusto.	nó↓ tôðåbia|nọeteniðǫ|elgústô↓	Juan: No, todavía no he tenido el gusto.
José, dígale que aquí hay una foto de ella, y pregúntele si le gusta.	åkɹåy|unafótô|ðéⓁɥå↓ tégústa↑	José: Aquí hay una foto de ella. ¿Te gusta?
Juan, contéstele que sí, hombre, que cómo no, que qué bonita. Y pregúntele que cuándo es la boda.	si|ómbrê↓ kómônó↓ kébonítå↓ kwåndǫezlabóðå↓	Juan: ¡Sí, hombre, cómo no! ¡Qué bonita! ¿Cuándo es la boda?
José, contéstele que todavía no han hablado de eso, pero que Ud. cree que va a ser pronto.	tôðåbıa|nǫemoșabláðô|ðésô↓ pérókreo|kèbaser|prónto↓	José: Todavía no hemos hablado de eso, pero creo que va a ser pronto.

End of Tape 6B

Tape 7A

10.1   BASIC SENTENCES.   Molina explains where he sends his laundry.

    After having spoken with the manager of the house and having rented the furnished apartment for John, the two friends return to Molina's apartment.

ENGLISH SPELLING	AID TO LISTENING	SPANISH SPELLING
the end	èl—fín↓	el fin
so, then, well	èm—fín↓	en fin
ready	lìstó↓	listo
Molina		*Molina*
Well, you're all set.[1]	èmfín↓ yaęstálisto|tóđò↓	En fin. Ya está listo todo.
yourself	té↓	te
yourself (you) change, move (to change, move)	tè—muđás↓ múđarsé↓	te mudas (mudarse)
When will you move?	kwàndo|temúđàs↓	¿Cuándo te mudas?
(they) give (to give)	dàn↓ dár↓	dan (dar)
Friday	èl—byérnès↓	el viernes
myself (I) change, move (to change, move)	mè—muđó↓ múđarsé↓	me mudo (mudarse)

Saturday	èl—sábàdò↓	el sábado

White
If they give me the apartment on Friday, I'll move on Saturday. (2)

siméđan |elapartamento |elbyérnes↑
mêmuđoelsábàđò↓

White
Si me dan el apartamento el viernes,

me mudo el sábado.

| the suitcase | là—màletà↓ | la maleta |

Molina
I can help you with your suitcases.

yotepweđoayuđar |kònlàzmàlétàs↓

Molina
Yo te puedo ayudar con las maletas.

| the that, that which, what (3) | ló—kê↓ | lo que |

| to bother | mòlèstár↓ | molestar |

| not yourself bother (to bother) | nó—te—moléstès↓ mòlèstarsè↓ | no te molestes (molestarse) |

White
I don't have very much. You needn't bother.

éspokò |lòkètéŋgò↓ nótemoléstès↓

White
Es poco lo que tengo. No te molestes.

| (you) send (to send) | mándàs↓ màndár↓ | mandas (mandar) |

| Where do you send your laundry? | dóndemándas |turrópà↓ | ¿Dónde mandas tu ropa? |

| the suit | èl—trahè↓ | el traje |

them (m)   lós↓   los

the cleaner's shop   là—tintórèrìà↓   la tintorería

in front   émfrenté↓   enfrente

Molina

I send my suits to the cleaner's across the street. (4)   lóstrahez │lozmandǫ │álátintórèrìà │ késtáęmfrenté↓   *Molina*

Los trajes los mando a la tintorería que está enfrente.

the shirt   là—kámìsà↓   la camisa

the laundry   là—làbàndèrìà↓   la lavandería

the corner   lạ—èskìnà↓   la esquina

And my shirts to the laundry on the corner. (5)   ilàskámìsas │àlálàbàndèrìadelạeskínà↓   Y las camisas a la lavandería de la esquina.

-self   mízmò↓   mismo

I myself   yo—mízmò↓   yo mismo

them (f)   lás↓   las

I take them over myself. (6)   yomízmolaz◊yébò↓   Yo mismo las llevo.

to clean   limpyár↓   limpiar

White
Who cleans the apartment for you?

kyéntelímpyą |élápártámentó↓

White
¿Quién te limpia el apartamento?

(she) comes (to come)

byéné↓ bénír↓

viene (venir)

all, every

todó↓

todo

Thursday

èl─hwébès↓

el jueves

all the Thursdays, every
  Thursday

tódoz─los─hwébès↓

todos los jueves

Molina
A girl who comes every Thursday. (7)

unamuchácha |kébyéne |tódozloshwébès↓

Molina
Una muchacha que viene todos
  los jueves.

to her

lé↓

le

If you want I'll speak to her. (8)

sikyérest yoleabló↓

Si quieres yo le hablo.

White
Swell.

muybyén↓

White
Muy bien.

late

tárdé↓

tarde

to go myself (to go oneself,
  to leave)

ìrmé↓ ìrsé↓

irme (irse)

Well, it's late. I've got to go.

bwenó↓ yaęstárdé↓ téŋgókęirmé↓

Bueno, ya es tarde. Tengo que
  irme.

before

ántès↓

antes

the swallow, the drink	él—tragó↓	el trago

Molina
Won't you have another drink first? (9)

ántez |nokyéres |ótrotrago↑

Molina
Antes, ¿no quieres otro trago?

White
No, thanks. Tomorrow is a work day.

no↓mucha∍grá∫yàs↓

mànyanáy |ketrabahár↓

White
No, muchas gracias. Mañana hay que trabajar.

grateful (to be grateful)

àgràdé∫idó↓ àgràdé∫ér↓

agradecido (agradecer)

Thanks a lot for everything.

muyagradé∫ido |pòrtodó↓

Muy agradecido por todo.

10.10   Notes on the basic sentences

(1) The utterance in Spanish says, of course, not that *you* are ready but that 'everything' is all ready already. But 'You're all set' is more probably what we would say, since the implication of the English phrase 'Everything is all ready' is that considerable packing has been completed to bring the situation into a state of readiness. The Spanish remark is much more casual in its implication.

(2) The item /mudárse/ *mudarse* also means 'to change clothes.' The context and relative time sequence are all that reveal whether you should consider it as referring to a change of clothes or a change of residence. Thus /memúdǫenmédyą́óra↓/ *Me mudo en media hora* would mean 'I'll change clothes in half an hour,' unless, of course, the moving van were waiting out front and the context unequivocally demanded such an interpretation.

(3) The process of nominalization that is represented in this construction will be dealt with in Units 33 and 35.

(4) The only reason for the particular intonation that appears in the last part of this sentence /késtáęmfréntè↓/ instead of /kèstáęmfrénté↓/ is to show contrast between this cleaner's store and the laundry referred to in the next utterance. The two utterances go together, and the intonation on the first one is not natural unless they do.

(5) Note the equivalence here of English *on* with Spanish *de*. It is almost impossible to state any generalized description of the differences involved here and elsewhere between English and Spanish prepositions.

(6) The form /mísmo/ *mismo* may be added to any subject pronoun or to any noun in this sense of '—self.' It agrees in respect to number and gender with the item it follows.

(7) The names of three days of the week have now appeared. It may be convenient, therefore, to list all seven here together:

Monday	el lunes	Friday	el viernes
Tuesday	el martes	Saturday	el sábado
Wednesday	el miércoles	Sunday	el domingo
Thursday	el jueves		

When listed in series, the article is not attached.

(8) Some speakers, particularly in Madrid, might say /la/ instead of /le/.

(9) Perhaps a more literal and equally possible translation would be, 'Before you go, won't you have another drink?

10.2   DRILLS AND GRAMMAR

10.21   Pattern drills

10.21.1   Personal /a/

A. Presentation of pattern

ILLUSTRATIONS

1   pòrkénobémos|aúnàmigomíò↓   ¿Por qué no vemos *a* un amigo mío?

2   kyéròprèséntarlę|àlàsèŋyóra   Quiero presentarle *a* la señora Molina.
    molínà↓

Are we going to meet the family?	3 bamos,akonoşer ǀ ạláfámilya↑	¿Vamos a conocer a la familia?
(I) see (to see)	beo↓ beŕ↓	veo (ber)
I see the car, but I don't see the chauffer.	4 beọelawto↑peronobeọalchofér↓	Veo el auto, pero no veo al chofer.
anyone	algyèn↓	alguien
Do you see anybody?	5 bes,algyen↑	¿Ves a alguien?
no one	naɗyê↓	nadie
No, I don't see anyone	6 no↓ nobeọanáɗyê↓	No, no veo a nadie.

EXTRAPOLATION

Nonperson noun object	Verb - object
Person noun object	Verb -/a/- object

NOTES

a. When a noun referring to a person occurs as the direct object of a verb, it is marked (preceded) by the relater /a/.

b. A noun direct object is one which can be substituted for the third person direct clitic pronouns previously presented.

10.21.11 Substitution drill - Personal substitution

Problem:

béolakásà↓

_____kármèn↓

Answer:

béọakármèn↓

_____

Problem:

Veo *la casa.*

_____Carmen.

Answer:

Veo a Carmen.

1 búskolakásá↓

_____señóra↓   búskọalaseņóra↓

2 noẹŋkontrámos |elapartaméntó↓

_____hwán↓   noẹŋkontrámos |ahwán↓

3 ŋyébọeláwtó↓

_____lwísà↓   ŋyébọalwísà↓

---

1 Busco *la casa.*

_____señora.   Busco a la señora.

2 No encontramos *el apartamento.*

_____Juan.   No encontramos a Juan.

3 Llevo *el auto.*

_____Luisa.   Llevo a Luisa.

4 búskamos │alasekretáryà↓
   _____eskwélà↓   búskamoz │lặeskwélà↓

5 buskalaseɲórà↓
   _____eɖifíşyó↓   búskặeleɖifíşyó↓

---

4 Buscamos a la *secretaria*.

   _____escuela.   Buscamos la escuela.

5 Busca a la *señora*.

   _____edificio.   Busca el edificio.

10.21.12 **Response drill**

	1 búskálàhénṣyà↑ọàlàsékrétáryà↓	àlàsêkrètáryà↓
	2 búskánlàfóto↑ọàlàmúchàchà↓	àlàmúchàchà↓
[àlàséŋyòrà↓]	3 àkyém |búskànùstédès↓	àlàséŋyòrà↓
[àmáryò↓]	4 àkyém |búskàéⁿyà↓	àmáryò↓
[élòtél↓]	5 kébúskàél↓	élòtél↓
[àlmóṣò↓]	6 búskànùstédès |àlchófér↑	nó↓ àlmóṣò↓

---

	1 ¿Busca la agencia o a la secretaria?	A la secretaria.
	2 ¿Buscan la foto o a la muchacha?	A la muchacha.
(a la señora)	3 ¿A quién buscan Uds.?	A la señora.
(a Mario)	4 ¿A quién busca ella?	A Mario.
(el hotel)	5 ¿Qué busca él?	El hotel.
(al mozo)	6 ¿Buscan Uds. al chofer?	No, al mozo.

[ákármèn↓]   7   búskausted |ahwán↑   nó↓ ákármèn↓

             8   beusted |alasenyoritá↑   sí↓ lábéó↓
             9   beusted |ala(s) senyóras↑   sí↓ lázbéó↓
            10   ᶜyebanustédes |alchofér↑   sí↓ lóᶜyébamòs↓
            11   búskael |alozmoᶊós↑   sí↓ lózbuská↓
            12   benustédes |lakása↑   sí↓ lábemòs↓
            13   benustédes |elotél↑   sí↓ lóbemòs↓

──

       (a Carmen)   7   ¿Busca Ud. a Juan?   No, a Carmen.

                    8   ¿Ve Ud. a la señorita?   Sí, la veo.
                    9   ¿Ve Ud. a las señoras?   Sí, las veo.
                   10   ¿Llevan Uds. al chofer?   Sí, lo llevamos.
                   11   ¿Busca él a los mozos?   Sí, los busca.
                   12   ¿Ven Uds. la casa?   Sí, la vemos.
                   13   ¿Ven Uds. el hotel?   Sí, lo vemos.

10.21.13 Translation drill

1 We see the car, but not the   bémòs̩e̩làwtô↓pèrònòa̩lchofér↓   Vemos el auto pero no al chofer.
   chauffeur.

2 I see the house, but not the   béòlàkàsà↓pèrònòa̩lasȩŋyórà↓   Veo la casa pero no a la señora.
   lady.

3 We see the building, but not   bémos |èlèd̩ifi̩ȩyô↓pèrònòa̩lseŋyór↓   Vemos el edificio pero no al señor.
   the gentleman.

4 They see the desk, but not   bénè̩lèskritóryô↓pèrònòa̩lasekretáryà↓   Ven el escritorio pero no a la
   the secretary.   secretaria.

5 I'm looking for the suitcases   buskó |làzmàlétas↑i̩àlà(s) sȩŋyórastambyén↓   Busco las maletas y a las señoras
   and the ladies also.   también.

6 We're looking for Carmen.   búskamos̩akármèn↓   Buscamos a Carmen.

7 We can't find John.   noȩŋkontrámos |ahwán↓   No encontramos a Juan.

8 We can't find the house.   noȩŋkontrámoz |lakásà↓   No encontramos la casa.

9 I'm looking for the apartment.   búskȩelapartaméntô↓   Busco el apartamento.

B.   Discussion of pattern

Many Spanish verbs can be followed by a noun which is not the subject of the verb, since the usual agreement of person and number between the subject and verb is not necessary, as in /por‑ké‑no‑bémos |la‑kása↓/. If the verb is not /sér/ (as in /mi‑nómbre |és‑hosé↓/ in which case the noun following the verb is identified as the same as the noun preceding), the following noun is usually described as the 'direct object' of the verb.

The direct object is often thought of as in some sense 'receiving' the action of the verb; thus in /bémos‑la‑kása↓/, the 'house' gets seen. There have been many examples of verbs followed by a direct object in previous units, such as /tyéne‑un‑lápiş↑   kyére‑ustéd |ágwa‑minerál↑   yo‑kyéro‑un‑sánwich |de‑hamón↓   bámos‑a‑bér |el‑peryódiko↓/, etc.

When a noun functioning as the direct object of a verb refers to specific person, it is usually marked by the occurrence of the relater /a/ preceding the noun. The resulting phrase usually follows the verb, though it may precede: /por‑ké‑no‑bémos |a‑un‑amígo‑mío↓/

The forms /kyén, álgyen, nádye/ , though they do not necessarily refer to specific persons, are also included in this pattern. (Their participation in the pattern is one reason they can logically be analyzed as nouns, and not pronouns as some analysts have maintained. Also, since /kyén‑kyénes/ has noun-like formation of the plural, and since none of these forms have any *case* designation in the way that the pronouns do, their analysis as a special kind of nouns, not occurring with articles, seems appropriate.)

The /a/ which marks the person noun object may or may not appear after the verb /tenér/ and minimal contrasts of the following types are possible:

/téngomifamílya |enchíle↓/	'My family is in Chile.'
/téngoamifamílya |enchíle↓/	'I sent my family to Chile.'
/téngodós,amígos |akí↓/	'I have two friends here.'
/téngoadós,amígos |akí↓/	'There are two friends of mine with me.'

The /a/ may be missing after other verbs when the reference is not to a specific person:

/neşesítounchofér↓/	'I need a chauffeur.'

10.21.2 Direct clitic pronouns

A. Presentation of pattern

ILLUSTRATIONS

Will you take me to the hotel?	1	mė(l)yėḃalotél↑	¿*Me* lleva al hotel?
———————————	2	(l)yėḃemẹalotél↓	Lléve*me* al hotel.
———————————	3	kyérez |ḋėharmenẹlotél↑	¿Quieres deja*rme* en el hotel?
Will you take us downtown?	4	nóz(l)yėḃalşentro↑	¿*Nos* lleva al centro?
———————————	5	(l)yėḃenosalşéntró↓	Lléve*nos* al centro.
———————————	6	tėsperó↓	*Te* espero.
———————————	7	ạustéḋ |lo(l)yamoḋespwés↓	A usted *lo* llamo después.
———————————	8	ạ̇hwán |lọ̇ạyụḋamcstóḋòs↓	A Juan *lo* ayudamos todos.
———————————	9	komolokyérė↓	¿Cómo *lo* quiere?
———————————	10	lȯsyéntomúchò↓	*Lo* siento mucho.
never		núŋkȧ↓	nunca

We never can see it.

11 núŋka |póďemozbérló↓   Nunca podemos ver*lo.*

12 tyénés |kékónóşerlá↓   Tienes que conocer*la.*

13 lóstráhezlozmandǫ |álá   Los trajes *los* mando a la tintorería.
     tintórérlá↓

14 yomízmó |lázφyébó↓   Yo mismo *las* llevo.

EXTRAPOLATION

	sg	pl
1	me	nos
2 fam	te	
2 - 3	lo	los
	la	las

NOTES

a. Clitic pronouns appear only with verbs, usually immediately preceding them, sometimes immediately following them.

b. Like other pronouns, clitics inflect for person, number, and in 2-3 person forms for gender.

c. A redundant construction /a‑hwán, a‑ustéd, los‑tráhes/, restating the direct object, may be added to the sentence to clarify or emphasize the direct clitic pronoun.

10.21.21 Substitution drills - Form substitution

Problem: bémozlafótó↓

Answer: lábemós↓

1 álkilanelapartaméntó↓   lǫálkilán↓

2 búskamozlos.anúnsyós↓   lózbúskamós↓

3 tyenelaz(l)yábès↓   lástyenè↓

4 komprǎeláwtó↓   lókomprǎ↓

Problem: Vemos *la foto.*

Answer: La vemos.

1 Alquilan *el apartamento.*   Lo alquilan.

2 Buscamos *los anuncios.*   Los buscamos.

3 Tiene *las llaves.*   Las tiene.

4 Compra *el auto.*   Lo compra.

5 ėskrıboloznómbrės↓   lós.ėskrıbȯ↓

6 bemozlạȯ́rȧ↓   lȧbemȯs↓

7 beọelotél↓   lȯbeȯ↓

8 lımpyanlas.abıtaşyónės↓   lȧzlımpyȧn↓

9 Ꝇyebalasóȡȧ↓   lȧꝆyebȧ↓

---

5 Escribo *los nombres.*   Los escribo.

6 Vemos *la hora.*   La vemos.

7 Veo *el hotel.*   Lo veo.

8 Limpian *las habitaciones.*   Las limpian.

9 Lleva *la soda.*   La lleva.

Person- number substitution

1 ånòsotroz↑nòs̜åyuɗahwán↓

ℊeↁↄyoz_____↓   ℊeↁↄyoz↑lòs̜åyuɗahwán↓

åmɪ_____↓   åmɪ↑m̜ℊåyuɗahwán↓

åhòsé_____↓   åhòsé↑lℊåyuɗahwán↓

åkarmen_____↓   åkarmen↑låy̜uɗahwán↓

---

1 A nosotros *nos* ayuda Juan.

A ellos_____.   A ellos los ayuda Juan.

A mí_____.   A mí me ayuda Juan.

A José_____.   A José lo ayuda Juan.

A Carmen_____.   A Carmen la ayuda Juan.

2 àmí↑nómèbuskanáɗyè↓

àⁿòsotroz_____↓   àⁿòsotroz↑nónòzbuskanáɗyè↓

ạeᐧỿaz_____↓   ạeᐧỿaz↑nólàzbuskanáɗyè↓

àlwisa_____↓   àlwisa↑nólàbuskanáɗyè↓

ạel_____↓   ạel↑nólòbuskanáɗyè↓

---

2 A mí no *me* busca nadie.

A nosotros_____.   A nosotros no nos busca nadie.

A ellas_____.   A ellas no las busca nadie.

A Luisa _____.   A Luisa no la busca nadie.

A él_____.   A él no lo busca nadie.

3 ạẹͫyaↃláⓝyebantónyòↄ

åhwan_____ↄ   åhwanↃláⓝyebantónyòↄ

åmı_____ↄ   åmıↃmeⓝyebantónyòↄ

ånósotroz_____ↄ   ånósotrozↃnózⓝyebantónyòↄ

ạẹͫyoz_____ↄ   ạẹͫyozↃlózⓝyebantónyòↄ

---

3   A ella *la* lleva Antonio.

    A Juan_____.   A Juan lo lleva Antonio.

    A mí_____.   A mí me lleva Antonio.

    A nosotros_____.   A nosotros nos lleva Antonio.

    A ellos_____.   A ellos los lleva Antonio.

10.21.22 Translation drill

1   The pen? I don't have it.   láplúma↑ nólaténgò↓   ¿La pluma? No la tengo.

2   The keys? I don't have them.   làzⓁyàbès↑ nólasténgò↓   ¿Las llaves? No las tengo.

3   The bills? You have them.   lòzbiⓁyétes↑ ústeđlostyénè↓   ¿Los billetes? Ud. los tiene.

4   The coins? You have them.   làzmónèđas↑ ústeđlastyénè↓   ¿Las monedas? Ud. las tiene.

5   The information? Here it is.   laimfórmàşyon↑ àkìlàtyénè↓   ¿La información? Aquí la tiene.

6   The date? I don't have it.   làféchà↑ nólaténgò↓   ¿La fecha? No la tengo.

7   The pie? I don't want it.   èlpástel↑ nólokyérò↓   ¿El pastel? No lo quiero.

8   The apartment? I haven't   èlápártàmento↑ nólọẹạlkiláđò↓ ¿El apartamento? No lo he
    rented it.   alquilado.

9   The travelers checks?   lòschékèzbyàheros↑ nólos.emandáđò↓   ¿Los cheques viajeros? No los
    I haven't sent them.   he mandado.

10 The soup? I haven't tried it.   làsópa↑ nólaeprobádó↓   ¿La sopa? No la he probado.

11 She never helps me.   é0yánuŋka |m̥eayúḋà↓   Ella nunca me ayuda.

12 He always takes us there.   élsyémpre |noz0yébàí↓   El siempre nos lleva ahí.

13 They take me downtown.   é0yoz |me0yébanalṣéntró↓   Ellos me llevan al centro.

14 Who's looking for her.   kyénlabúskà↓   ¿Quién la busca?

15 Who's looking for me.   kyénmebúskà↓   ¿Quién me busca?

End of Tape 7A

B. Discussion of pattern

Clitic pronouns are so designated because this term describes their dependence on verbs. They can appear only with (clinging to) verbs, and then in a very close relationship: nothing can ever occur between a clitic and the verb it appears with.

There are three classes of clitic pronouns in Spanish: direct, indirect, and reflexive. All clitics have certain features in common: they are weak-stressed (except for limited patterns in some dialect areas), they are included in the intonation phrase with the verb, and they occur in the same sequence relation with regard to the verb.

Clitics *precede* conjugated verbs (those with person-number endings) except for affirmative command forms which they must follow: not /meꞮyébe̯aloté↓↓/, but /ꞯyébeme̯aloté↓↓/; 'Take me to the hotel'. Clitics can also appear with certain nonconjugated verb forms, the infinitives and the /‒ndo/ forms (see Unit 13); the clitics *follow* these forms: /podémosbérlo↑/ 'Can we see it?' The infinitive and /‒ndo/ forms, however, frequently occur in verb constructions which include conjugated verb forms. In these constructions the clitic may either precede the conjugated verb or follow the nonconjugated verb and apparently the option implies no distinction in meaning: either /mekyéresbér↑/ or /kyéresbérme↑/ 'Do you want to see me?' Note, however, that a clitic cannot appear between the conjugated and nonconjugated verb forms.

Direct clitic pronouns are substitutable in a frame with (can be replaced by) nouns functioning as the direct object of a verb. Direct object nouns are identifiable by the appearance of the relater /a/ before them, if the noun refers to a specific person. Thus /bémos amaría↓/ 'We see Mary' can be restated, once we know the reference, as /labémos↓/'We see her'. Nonperson nouns functioning as a direct object can usually be identified by their position after the verb. Thus /bémoslakása↓/ 'We see the house' can be restated as /labémos↓/'We see it'.

Occasionally a direct object noun and a direct clitic pronoun may both appear with one verb. With person nouns, this 'redundant construction' may occasionally be used for contrast or clarity. The sentence /labémos|amaría↓/ 'We see Mary' may imply 'María, not Carmen'. With nonperson nouns, a redundant construction is less common, but may occur if the noun object precedes the verb in a different intonation phrase separated usually by a terminal-rising juncture: /lostráhes↑ losmándo|alatıntorería↓/ 'The suits, I send to the cleaners'. The intonation phrase division between /tráhes/and /los/ is essential as it is in an English sentence of the same type. Constructions like */lostráheslosmándo↓/ or */losmándolostráhes↓/ do not occur. The last example becomes possible by the addition of a terminal juncture after /mándo↓/ but this gives the second phrase the character of an afterthought: /losmándo↓lostráhes↓/ 'I send them, I mean the suits.' Note, of course, that the personal /a/ does not occur with nonperson direct object nouns.

Direct clitic pronouns are inflected for person and number in all forms and for gender also in 2-3 forms. Note that /lo/ can mean 'you, him, it', /la/ can mean 'you, her, it', and similarly the plurals /los, las/. If any confusion results from this multiple reference possibility, it can be clarified by a redundant phrase. Along with the inflections for person, number, and gender, a few dialects, notably in Central Spain (the dialect usually referred to as 'Castilian'), make an additional distinction in the 2-3 forms, a person-nonperson distinction:

a clitic form /le/ refers to persons (you, him -and with some speakers- her) and /les/ (you all, them), though the forms described above also appear, and are preferred in some constructions. Nonperson objects are always referred to by the clitics /lo, la, los, las /. The difference between Spain and Latin America on this point is shown in the chart below:

		Castilian Spain	General Latin America	Reference	
Person	sg	le–béo (lo–béo) la–béo (le–béo)	lo–béo la–béo	a–él a–é()ya	a–ustéd
	pl	los–béo (les–béo) las–béo (les–béo)	los–béo las–béo	a–é()yos a–é()yas	a–ustédes
Nonperson	sg	lo–béo la–béo		el–líbro la–plúma	
	pl	los–béo las–béo		los–líbros las–plúmas	

A student might do well to notice the similarity and correlation between direct clitic pronouns and definite articles. Both occur normally under weak stress, both frequently occur in a position that precedes the word that they are grammatically most closely associated with (articles before a noun and clitics before a verb), and three of the four forms are identical in form:

	Definite Article	Direct Clitic
m sg	el	lo
f sg	la	
m pl	los	
f pl	las	
neuter	lo	

A probable answer to /tyénelaplúma↑/ is /sí|laténgo↓/, where the form of the article is a direct key to the selection of the form of the clitic.

Spelling conventions recognize the close relationship of verb and clitic when the clitic follows the verb by writing both as one word. Although this same close relationship prevails when the clitic precedes the verb, they are written in the spelling system as two words, that is, with space between the clitic and verb.

10.21.3 /—do/ forms functioning as modifiers
Tape 7B

   A. Presentation of pattern

ILLUSTRATIONS

Joseph: 'Pleased to meet you'.	1	hóse↓ eŋkàntádọ̀ḍ̀ekonoṣérlá↓	José: '*Encantado* de conocerla'.
Mary: 'Pleased to meet you'.	2	màríá↓ eŋkàntádaḍ̀ekonoṣérló↓	María: '*Encantada* de conocerlo'.
————————————	3	ị̀ustéḍ↓ éskásáḍò↑	Y usted, ¿es *casado?*
And you, Mary, are you married?	4	ìtú|màríá↓ éréskásàḍà↑	Y tú, María, ¿eres *casada?*
————————————	5	à,ŷayunamésa|ḍèsókúpàḍà↓	Allá hay una mesa *desocupada.*
————————————	6	solotéŋgo|ḍozḍesokupáḍòs↓	Sólo tengo dos *desocupados.*
————————————	7	kasisyémprẹ|èstámozmuyokupáḍòs↓	Casi siempre estamos muy *ocupados.*

EXTRAPOLATION

—ádo(s)	—ído(s)
—a(s)	—a(s)

NOTES

   a. /—do/ forms, when functioning as modifiers, are inflected for number
   and gender, like other regular fully inflected adjectives.

10.21.31 Substitution drill - Item substitution

1   ái │áyúnàmésa │desokupáḋà↓

_____únạwto_____↓   ái │áyúnạwto │desokupáḋó↓

_____únà(s)síꞶyaz_____↓   ái │áyúnà(s)síꞶyaz│desokupáḋàs↓

2   ésésèꞶyor │eskasáḋò↓

ésàsèꞶyorạ_____↓   ésàsèꞶyorạ │eskasáḋà↓

ésò(s)séꞶyores_____↓   ésò(s)séꞶyores │soꞶkasáḋòs↓

---

1   Ahí hay una mesa *desocupada*.

_____un auto_____.   Ahí hay un auto desocupado.

_____unas sillas_____.   Ahí hay unas sillas desocupadas.

2   Ese señor es *casado*.

Esa señora_____.   Esa señora es casada.

Esos señores_____.   Esos señores son casados.

3 élápártáménto |estálkiláɖó↓

   lákasa _____↓

   lósécifisyos_____↓

           lákasa |estálkiláɖá↓

           lósécifisyos |estanalkiláɖós↓

4 lásala |estárregláɖá↓

   láskamas _____↓

   éldórmitoryo _____↓

           láskamas |estanarregláɖás↓

           éldórmitoryo |estárregláɖó↓

5 lásékrétarya |estaọkupáɖá↓

   lózmoṣos_____↓

   élchófer_____↓

           lózmoṣos |estanokupáɖós↓

           élchófer |estaọkupáɖó↓

---

3 El apartamento está *alquilado*.

   La casa _____ .

   Los edificios _____ .

4 La sala está *arreglada*.

   Las camas _____ .

   El dormitorio _____ .

5 La secretaria está *ocupada*.

   Los mozos _____ .

   El chofer _____ .

La casa está alquilada.

Los edificios están alquilados.

Las camas están arregladas.

El dormitorio está arreglado.

Los mozos están ocupados.

El chofer está ocupado.

10.21.32 Translation drill

1 I have a vacant apartment.	téngǫ ǀúnạ̀pàrtàmén̄to ǀ ᵭesokupáᵭȯ↓	Tengo un apartamento desocupado.
2 That young lady is happy here.	ésàsényȯrı̣tạ ǀ ệstáeŋkàntáᵭạ ǀ àkí↓	Esa señorita está encantada aquí.
3 The secretaries are happy here.	lá(s)sékrétàryas ǀ ệstánệŋkàntáᵭàs ǀ àkí↓	Las secretarias están encantadas aquí.
4 At the language school they're very busy.	̣ẹnlạéskwela ǀ ᵭélé̦ŋgwas↑ẹstánm̄uy okupáᵭȯs↓	En la escuela de lenguas están muy ocupados.
5 The chauffeur is busy.	ẹlchȯfér ǀ estạọkupáᵭȯ↓	El chofer está ocupado.
6 The house is rented.	lákasạ ǀ estạlkiláᵭạ̀↓	La casa está alquilada.
7 I have a vacant house, too.	tàmbyén ǀ téŋgǫ̀ùnàkasạ ǀ ᵭesokupáᵭạ̀↓	También tengo una casa desocupada.
8 She's not single; she's married.	é(ᴵᴵ)yàngẹ(s)soltéráↆ éskàsaᵭạ̀↓	Ella no es soltera. Es casada.
9 They're married.	é(ᴵᴵ)yo(s)soŋkasáᵭȯs↓	Ellos son casados.

10 The rooms are rented.   lóskwártos|éstánálkiladós↓   Los cuartos están alquilados.

11 The apartment is quite fixed up.   élápártámento|éstámuyarregládó↓   El apartamento está muy arreglado.

B. Discussion of pattern

The /—do/ forms, when they appear in constructions other than those with /abér/, are functioning as modifiers. In this function they have full adjective inflections for number and gender. They can appear with nouns (normally following the noun): /únamésa| desokupáda↓/; after certain verbs, most commonly /sér/ or /estár/ but also such verbs as /pareşér/: /éskasádo ustéd↑ estámosokupádos↓ paréşekansádo↓/; in the so-called 'absolute' construction: /enkantádadekonoşér la↓/ or nominalized: /kwáles,elkasádo↓ eldesokupádo|estáen,elşéntro↓/. Usage has established some /—do/ forms as nouns, which now have a single gender form with no gender alternation permitted: /laentráda↓ lakomída↓/. For contrast, compare /unkonoşídomío↓ unakonoşídamía↓/.

10.22   Replacement drills

A   mémuꭉꬲelsábáꭑȯↆ

1 tè_____ↆ   témuꭑas,elsábáꭑȯↆ

2 ____bas_____ↆ   tèbas,elsábáꭑȯↆ

3 _____este____ↆ   tèbas |estesábáꭑȯↆ

4 _____nȯchèↆ   tèbas |estanȯchèↆ

5 mè_____ↆ   mèboy |estanȯchèↆ

6 _____hwébèsↆ   mèboy |estehwébèsↆ

7 _____el_____ↆ   mèboyelhwébèsↆ

_____

A   Me mudo el sábado.

1 Te_____.   Te mudas el sábado.

2 ____vas_____.   Te vas el sábado.

3 _____este_____.   Te vas este sábado.

4 _____noche.   Te vas esta noche.

5 Me _____.   Me voy esta noche.

6 _____jueves.   Me voy este jueves.

7 _____el_____.   Me voy el jueves.

B   dóndemándas |turrópà↓

1 _____kósàs↓   dóndemándas |tuskósàs↓

2 _____ṅyebas_____↓   dónde ṅyebas |tuskósàs↓

3 komo_____↓   komo ṅyebas |tuskósàs↓

4 _____éstas___↓   komo ṅyebas |éstaskósàs↓

5 _____deşídes_____↓   komodeşídes |éstaskósàs↓

6 kyen_____↓   kyendeşídę |éstaskósàs↓

7 _____aşę_____↓   kyen̦aşę |éstaskósàs↓

B   ¿Dónde mandas tu ropa?

1 ¿_____cosas?   ¿Dónde mandas tus cosas?

2 ¿_____llevas_____?   ¿Dónde llevas tus cosas?

3 ¿Cómo_____?   ¿Cómo llevas tus cosas?

4 ¿_____estas____?   ¿Cómo llevas estas cosas?

5 ¿_____decides_____?   ¿Cómo decides estas cosas?

6 ¿Quién_____?   ¿Quién decide estas cosas?

7 ¿_____hace _____?   ¿Quién hace estas cosas?

C   yómízmo |lazⓊyébó↓

1 lánóbyà_____↓

2 _____mándà↓

3 nòsótròz_____↓

4 _____tàmbyen____↓

5 _____aşémòs↓

6 ústeđ_____;

7 ____nuŋka_____↓

lánóbyàmízma |lazⓊyébà↓

lánóbyàmízma |lazmándà↓

nòsótròzmízmoz |lazmandámòs↓

nòsotros |tàmbyenlazmandámòs↓

nòsotros |tàmbyenlas,aşémòs↓

ústeđ |tàmbyenlas,áşè↓

ústeđ |nuŋkalas,áşè↓

C   Yo mismo las llevo.

1 La novia_____.

2 _____ manda.

3 Nosotros_____ .

4 _____también___ __ .

5 _____hacemos.

6 Ud._____ .

7 ____nunca_____.

La novia misma las lleva.

La novia misma las manda.

Nosotros mismos las mandamos.

Nosotros también las mandamos.

Nosotros también las hacemos.

Ud. también las hace.

Ud. nunca las hace.

D   únåmúcháchá |kéƀyéné |todozloshwéƀés↓

1   _____semánås↓   únåmúchacha |kéƀyéné |todazla(s)semánås↓

2   _____práktíkå_____↓   únåmúchacha |képráktíkå |todazla(s)semánås↓

3   ___ombre_____↓   únombre |képráktíkå |todazla(s)semánås↓

4   los_____↓   lósombres |képráktíkán |todazla(s)semánås↓

5   _____díås↓   lósombres |képráktíkán |todozlozdíås↓

6   _____límpyån_____↓   lósombres |kélímpyån |todozlozdíås↓

7   ___moşos_____↓   lózmoşoskélímpyån |todozlozdíås↓

D   Una muchacha que viene todos los jueves.

1   _____ semanas.   Una muchacha que viene todas las semanas.

2   _____practica_____.   Una muchacha que practica todas las semanas.

3   ____hombre_____.   Un hombre que practica todas las semanas.

4   Los_____.   Los hombres que practican todas las semanas.

5   _____ días.   Los hombres que practican todos los días.

6   _____ limpian _____.   Los hombres que limpian todos los días.

7   ___ mozos_____.   Los mozos que limpian todos los días.

E   sikyérez↑yólęáblô↓

1   _____eskríbô↓   sikyérez↑yóleskríbô↓

2   _____nósótroz_____↓   sikyérez↑nósótrozleskribímôs↓

3   _tępáreşe_____↓   sitępáreşe↑nósótrozleskribímôs↓

4   _____tu_____↓   sitępáreşe↑tuleskríbês↓

5   _____ áblás↓   sitępáreşe↑tulęáblás↓

6   _pweđes_____↓   sipweđes↑tulęáblás↓

7   _____díşés↓   sipweđes↑tuleđíşês↓

E   Si quieres, yo le hablo.

1   _____, ____escribo.   Si quieres, yo le escribo.

2   _____, nosotros____.   Si quieres, nosotros le escribimos.

3   _te parece, _____.   Si te parece, nosotros le escribimos.

4   _____, tú_____.   Si te parece, tú le escribes.

5   _____, ____hablas.   Si te parece, tú le hablas.

6   _puedes, _____.   Si puedes, tú le hablas.

7   _____, ____dices.   Si puedes, tú le dices.

F   ántéz↓nókyéres |otrotrágo↑

1 _____kósa↑   ántéz↓nókyéres |otrakósa↑

2 déspwéz_____↑   déspwéz↓nókyéres |otrakósa↑

3 _____aşes_____↑   déspwéz↓nọaşes |otrakósa↑

4 _____esas_____↑   déspwéz↓nọaşes |esaskósas↑

5 éntonşéz_____↑   éntonşéz↓nọaşes |esaskósas↑

6 _____syéntes_____↑   éntonşéz↓nósyentes |esaskósas↑

7 lwegó_____↑   lwegó↓nósyentes |esaskósas↑

F   Antes, ¿no quieres otro trago?

1 _____, ¿_____cosa?   Antes, ¿no quieres otra cosa?

2 Después, ¿_____?   Después, ¿no quieres otra cosa?

3 _____, ¿ _haces_____?   Después, ¿no haces otra cosa?

4 _____, ¿_____esas____?   Después, ¿no haces esas cosas?

5 Entonces, ¿_____?   Entonces, ¿no haces esas cosas?

6 _____, ¿ _sientes_____?   Entonces, ¿no sientes esas cosas?

7 Luego, ¿_____?   Luego, ¿no sientes esas cosas?

10.23   Variation drills

A   èmfín↓ ya̧ȩstálístotóa̧ò↓   En fin, ya está listo todo.

  1 Well, the pie's ready.   èmfín↓ ya̧ȩstálísto̧|elpastél↓   En fin, ya está listo el pastel.

  2 Well, the clothes're ready.   èmfín↓ ya̧ȩstálísta|larrópà↓   En fin, ya está lista la ropa.

  3 Well, the soup's ready.   èmfín↓ ya̧ȩstálísta|lasópà↓   En fin, ya está lista la sopa.

  4 Well, the pork-chops're ready. èmfín↓ ya̧ȩstànlístaz|laschulétàs↓ En fin, ya están listas las chuletas.

  5 Well, the drinks're ready.   èmfín↓ ya̧ȩstànlísto̧z|lostrágòs↓   En fin, ya están listos los tragos.

  6 Well, the hotel's already old. èmfín↓ ya̧ȩstàbyȩho̧elotél↓   En fin, ya está viejo el hotel.

  7 Well, the car's already fixed. èmfín↓ ya̧ȩstàrréglado̧|eláwtò↓   En fin, ya está arreglado el auto.

B   yó|tèpwéo̧a̧yúa̧ar|kònlázmálétàs↓   Yo te puedo ayudar con las maletas.

  1 I can help you with the salad. yó|tèpwéo̧a̧yúa̧ar|kònla̧ensáláa̧à↓   Yo te puedo ayudar con la ensalada.

  2 I can help you with your dessert. yó|tèpwéo̧a̧yúa̧ar|kònèlpóstrè↓   Yo te puedo ayudar con el postre.

  3 I can use 'tú' with you.   yotepweo̧o|tratardetú↓   Yo te puedo tratar de 'tú'.

4 I can rent the house to you.

yótepwéḓǫ|alkilárlakásá↓

Yo te puedo alquilar la casa.

5 I can look for the wine for you.

yótepwéḓo|buskárelbínǫ̀↓

Yo te puedo buscar el vino.

6 I can take you to the wedding.

yótepwéḓo|ꭓyebáralabóḓa̍↓

Yo te puedo llevar a la boda.

7 I can give you an idea, more or less.

yótepwéḓo|ḓarunaiḓeá↓másómḗnǫ̀s↓

Yo te puedo dar una idea, más o menos.

C lóstráhez↑lozmándǫalatintoreríá↓

Los trajes, los mando a la tintorería.

1 I'll send the ashtrays to the living-room.

lós(ş)éníşeroz↑lozmándǫalasálá↓

Los ceniceros, los mando a la sala.

2 I'll send the desks to the consular section.

lóséskritóryoz↑lozmándǫ|ála sékşyoŋkonsulár↓

Los escritorios, los mando a la sección consular.

3 I'll send the books to the school of languages.

lózlíbroz↑lozmándǫ|ála̤ęskwéla ḓeléŋgwàs↓

Los libros, los mando a la escuela de lenguas.

4 I'll send the drinks to the room.

lóstrágoz↑lozmándǫalkwártǫ̀↓

Los tragos, los mando al cuarto

5 I'll send the 'cuba'libres' to the apartment.

lóskúbàlíbrez↑lozmándǫal apartaméntǫ̀↓

Los cuba libres, los mando al apartamento.

6 I'll send the newspapers to the Embassy.

lóspéryóɗikoz↑lozmandǫalǫ
embahádà↓

Los periódicos, los mando a la Embajada.

7 I'll send the shirts to the laundry.

láskámisaz↑lazmandǫalá
labanderíà↓

Las camisas, las mando a la lavandería.

D kyéntelímpyǫ|elapartaméntó↓

¿Quién te limpia el apartamento?

1 Who sends you the newspaper.

kyéntemandǫ|elperyóɗikó↓

¿Quién te manda el periódico?

2 Who buys the shirts for you?

kyéntekómpra|láskamísàs↓

¿Quién te compra las camisas?

3 Who cashes the checks for you?

kyéntekámbya|loschékès↓

¿Quién te cambia los cheques?

4 Who talks to you in Spanish?

kyéntǫablǫ|enǫspaǫyól↓

¿Quién te habla en español?

5 Who takes you downtown?

kyénteɥébalꞩéntró↓

¿Quién te lleva al centro?

6 Who's waiting for you there?

kyéntespéraí↓

¿Quién te espera ahí?

7 Who helps you?

kyéntǫayúɗà↓

¿Quién te ayuda?

E yaẹstárdè↓ téŋgòkẹirmè↓   Ya es tarde. Tengo que irme.

1 It's late. I've got to study.   yaẹstárdè↓ téŋgòkẹstúdyar↓   Ya es tarde. Tengo que estudiar.

2 It's late. I've got to change   yaẹstárdè↓ teŋgo|kẹkàmbyárme   Ya es tarde. Tengo que cambiarme
   clothes.   derrópà↓   de ropa.

3 I've got to move.   teŋgo|kẹmúdarmedekásà↓   Tengo que mudarme de casa.

4 I've got to go back.   teŋgokebolbér↓   Tengo que volver.

5 He's got to go.   tyénekẹír↓   Tiene que ir.

6 We've got to go up.   tẽnemoskesubír↓   Tenemos que subir.

7 They've got to go down.   tyéneŋkebahár↓   Tienen que bajar.

F máŋyanáy|ketrabahár↓   Mañana hay que trabajar.

1 You have to clean tomorrow.   máŋyanáy|kelimpyár↓   Mañana hay que limpiar.

2 You have to return tomorrow.   máŋyanáy|kebolbér↓   Mañana hay que volver.

3 You have to decide soon.   próntọay|kedẹṣidír↓   Pronto hay que decidir.

4 You'll have to bring another   prónto|áyketráerótrȯ↓   Pronto hay que traer otro.
   one soon.

5 You'll have to study on Monday.   é(l)lunes|áykestuḋyár↓   El lunes hay que estudiar.

6. You'll have to practice on Friday.   élbyérnes|áykepraktikár↓   El viernes hay que practicar.

7 You won't nave to work on   élsábado|noȧyketrabahár↓   El sábado no hay que trabajar.
   Saturday.

10.24   Review drill - Theme class in present tense forms

1 He talks and eats a lot.   ábla|ikómemúchȯ↓   Habla y come mucho.

2 He studies and lives here.   éstuḋyą|ıbıbęakí↓   Estudia y vive aquí.

3 He works and lives there.   trȧbahą|ıbıbęaí↓   Trabaja y vive ahí.

4 He works and eats very little.   trȧbahą|ikómėmuypókȯ↓   Trabaja y come muy poco.

5 We study and eat here.   éstuḋyamos|ikómemos,akí↓   Estudiamos y comemos aquí.

6 We work and eat too much.   trȧbȧhamos|ikómemozḋemasyáḋȯ↓   Trabajamos y comemos demasiado.

7 We talk and write a lot.   áblamos|ı̧éskribımozmúchȯ↓   Hablamos y escribimos mucho.

8 We work and live here.   trábáhamos|ibibimos.akí↓   Trabajamos y vivimos aquí.

9 We go down and come up   báhamos|isúbímòzmúypókò↓   Bajamos y subimos muy poco.
   very little.

10 They go down and come   bahan|ɪsubenmúchô↓   Bajan y suben mucho.
   up a lot.

11 They work and live in the   trábahan|ibiben|enlósẹstádọsuní dòs↓   Trabajan y viven en los Estados
   United States.   Unidos.

12 They talk and write very   áblan|ɪẹskríbènmuybyén↓   Hablan y escriben muy bien.
   well.

13 They study and eat very   éstuďyan|ikómènmúypókò↓   Estudian y comen muy poco.
   little.

10.3   CONVERSATION STIMULUS

NARRATIVE 1

1 Juan likes the apartment.   áhwan↑légustạ|elapartaméntò↓   A Juan le gusta el apartamento.

2 He's going to take it.   batomárlò↓   Va a tomarlo.

3 He plans to move this week.   pyénsamuďarsẹ|éstásémaná↓   Piensa mudarse esta semana.

4 But he hasn't decided what day. pèrònọaďeşiďiďo|kéďíá↓   Pero no ha decidido qué día.

5 If the apartment is ready, he'll
   move on Saturday.

si̯ẹlåpårtåméntọẹstálistoↄↄse
muↄạelsábåↄô↓

Si el apartamento está listo, se
muda el sábado.

6 Saturday is a good day.

ẹlsabaↄọ|ẹsừmbʋendíá↓

El sábado es un buen día.

7 You don't have to work.

nọaykẹtrabahár↓

No hay que trabajar.

DIALOG 1

José, pregúntele a Juan que si le gusta
el apartamento.

tégustạelapartamentoↄ

José: ¿Te gusta el apartamento?

Juan, contéstele que sí, que va a
tomarlo, que está muy bonito.

si̯↓bóyåtòmarlô↓ ẹstámuybonítô↓

Juan: Sí, voy a tomarlo. Está
       muy bonito.

José, pregúntele que cuándo piensa
mudarse.

kẉandopyensazmuↄárté↓

José: ¿Cuándo piensas mudarte?

Juan, contéstele que Ud. cree que
esta semana.

kreokéstasemánà↓

Juan: Creo que esta semana.

José, pregúntele si ha decidido qué día.

áↄdẹↄidido|kéↄiáↄ

José: ¿Has decidido qué día?

Juan, contéstele que si el apartamento
está listo, se muda el sábado.

si̯ẹlåpårtåméntọẹstálistoↄ
memuↄọelsábåↄô↓

Juan: Si el apartamento está listo,
       me mudo el sábado.

José, dígale que sí, que el sábado es un buen día. Que no hay que trabajar.

sí↓ èlsábadǫ|èsúmbwendíà↓

nǫaykètrabahár↓

José: Sí, el sábado es un buen día. No hay que trabajar.

NARRATIVE 2

1 It seems that José and Juan are going to be neighbors, then.

párėșe|kèhòsȩ̱hwam|bánásér bèșinòs|èntónșès↓

Parece que José y Juan van a ser vecinos entonces.

2 José can help Juan move his things.

hòsé|pwéđȩ̱àyùđáráhwan|apasar suskósàs↓

José puede ayudar a Juan a pasar sus cosas.

3 What John has isn't much.

nǫezmuchò|lòkètyénèhwán↓

No es mucho lo que tiene Juan.

4 He cau move them himself.

élmizmo|pwéđepasárlàs↓

El mismo puede pasarlas.

5 But Jose's got a car.

pèròhòsé|tyenȩ̱áwtò↓

Pero José tiene auto.

6 It's easier that way.

èzmasfașíl|àsí↓

Es más fácil así.

DIALOG 2

José, dígale a Juan que parece que
Uds. van a ser vecinos, entonces.

páreşe │kèbámòsàsér │bèşınòs↓èntónşès↓

José: Parece que vamos a ser
vecinos, entonces.

Juan, dígale que así parece.

àsıparéşè↓

Juan: Así parece.

José; dígale que Ud. le puede ayudar
a pasar las cosas.

yotepwedọayudar │àpàsárlaskósàs↓

José: Yo te puedo ayudar a pasar
las cosas.

Juan, dígale que no se moleste. Que
Ud. mismo las puede pasar. Que no
es mucho lo que tiene.

notemoléstès↓ yòmızmo │laspwedo
pasár↓ nọezmucho │loketéŋgò↓

Juan: No te molestes. Yo mismo
las puedo pasar. No es
mucho lo que tengo.

José, pero Ud. tiene auto, dígale.
Dígale que es más fácil así.

pèrọyótéŋgọ │awtò↓ èzmasfaşil │àsí↓

José: Pero yo tengo auto. Es más
fácil así.

Juan, dígale que bueno, que muy
agradecido.

bwenò↓ múyạcradeşídò↓

Juan: Bueno, muy agradecido.

NARRATIVE 3

1   Another thing. Where can Juan
take his clothes to be washed?

ótrakósà↓ dóndepwedehwán │ɲyèbár
surrópalabár↓

Otra cosa. ¿Dónde puede Juan
llevar su ropa a lavar?

2 There's a laundry on the corner

   and a cleaner's around the
   corner.

áyúnálábándèriạ|ènlạèskinat
ɹúnátìntóreríalabwélt.àↆ

Hay una lavanderia en la esquina

y una tintorería a la vuelta.

3 But he can't take his clothes
   there himself.

pèrọèlmízmo|nópwèdeↄ̃yebár|sùrropaíↆ

Pero él mismo no puede llevar

su ropa ahí.

4 This is not the United States.

éstónọez|los̺estạdosụnídosↆ

Esto no es los Estados Unidos.

5 The girl who cleans his apartment

   will take them, then.

làmúchacha|kèlímpyàsụàpàrtàmentot
laↄ̃yébạ|èntónṣèsↆ

La muchacha que limpia su apar-

tamento la lleva, entonces.

DIALOG 3

Juan, dígale a José que otra cosa.
Preguntele que dónde puede llevar
la ropa a lavar.

ótrakósà|hòsét dòndepwèdoⁿyebár|
làrropalabárↆ

Juan: Otra cosa, José. ¿Dónde

puedo llevar la ropa a lavar?

José, contéstele que hay una lavandería en la esquina y una tintorería
a la vuelta.

áyúnálábàndèriạ|ènlạèskìnatɹ̀ùnà
tìntórèríalạbwéltàↆ

José: Hay una lavandería en la

esquina y una tintorería a
la vuelta.

Juan, pregúntele que si él mismo la
lleva.

tumizmolaↄ̃yebast

Juan: ¿Tú mismo la llevas?

José, contéstele que no, hombre, que
nunca. Que aquí no estamos en
los Estados Unidos.

no|ombrèↆnuŋkàↆ àkí|nọestámos|
ènlós̺estádósụnídosↆ

José: No, hombre, nunca. Aquí

no estamos en los Estados
Unidos.

Juan, pregúntele que cómo hace   kómọáṣès | ∋ntónṣès↓   Juan: ¿Cómo haces, entonces?
él, entonces.

José, contéstele que la muchacha   lâmúchacha | kèlímpyàmχápàrtàméntồ | José: La muchacha que limpia mi
que limpia su apartamento la
lleva.   lâ0yébầ↓   apartamento la lleva.

                                                                                     End of Tape 7B

Tape 8A

11.1   BASIC SENTENCES.   White interviews a maid.

The woman who cleans Molina's apartment comes to be interviewed by White.

ENGLISH SPELLING	AID TO LISTENING	SPANISH SPELLING
Maid Good afternoon, sir.	bwénastardès |sèŋyór↓	*Sirvienta* Buenas tardes, señor.
White Good afternoon. What can I do for you?	bwénàstardès↓ kedeséà↓	*White* Buenas tardes, ¿qué desea?
the one that	lá—kè↓	la que
Maid I'm the one that cleans Mr. Molina's apartment.	yosóy|làkèlimpya|èlàpàrtàmento| dèlsèŋyórmólinà↓	*Maid* Yo soy la que limpia el aparta-mento del Sr. Molina.
White Oh, yes. Can you clean mine, too?	à↓ múybyén↓ pwedelimpyár|èlmiotambyén↑	*White* ¡Ah! Muy bien. ¿Puede limpiar el mío también?
the yours	èl—suyò↓	el suyo
isn't it?, didn't he?, haven't they?, etc.	nó↑	no

Maid		*Sirvienta*
Yours is bigger, isn't it?	élsúyo |ezmázgrándè↓ nó↑	El suyo es más grande, ¿no?
the (one) of him	él—dé—él↓	el de él
White		*White*
No, it's the same size as his. [1]	nó↓ és.igwal |aldél↓	No, es igual al de él.
the day	él—diá↓	el día
What day can you come on?	kediás |pwédèbénír↓	¿Qué días puede venir?
Maid		*Sirvienta*
On Mondays. [2]	lózlunès↓	Los lunes.
White		*White*
No, on Mondays it's not convenient for me.	nó↓ lózlunez |nomekombyéné↓	No, los lunes no me conviene.
during the afternoon [3]	pòr—là—tardè↓	por la tarde
Can't you come on Friday afternoon?	nópwedebenír |lozbyérnesporlatardé↑	¿No puede venir los viernes por la tarde?
Maid		*Sirvienta*
I think so.	kreokesí↓	Creo que sí.

What do I have to do?	kétengokęaşér↓	¿Qué tengo que hacer?
to sweep	bårrér↓	barrer

White
Sweep the house and dust the furniture. (4)

bårrér│låkasą↑ílímpyárlozmwéblês↓

White
Barrer la casa y limpiar los muebles.

to wash	låbár↓	lavar

Mop up the kitchen and bathroom.

låbár│låkôşina│ɹelbáŋyô↓

Lavar la cocina y el baño.

the sheet	lå—sabånå↓	la sábana
the (pillow) case	lå—fundå↓	la funda
the pillow	lą—ålmwađå↓	la almohada

And change the sheets and pillow-cases.

íkåmbyár│lå(s)sábanas│ílåsfundazdęalmwáđå↓

Y cambiar las sábanas y las fundas de almohada.

to charge	kôbrár↓	cobrar

How much are you going to charge me?

kwántobakôbrármê↓

¿Cuánto va a cobrarme?

mister (5)	dón↓	don

Maid
The same as for Mr. Molina. (6)

lómizmo|kẹadoṇhosél

Sirvienta
Lo mismo que a don José.

the party

lá—fyéstàl

la fiesta

White
And if I have a party....Can
you help me out?

isitengọ|unafyéstàl pwedẹayudarmet

White
Y si tengo una fiesta, ¿puede
ayudarme?

the time

él—tyémpòl

el tiempo

with time, in time enough

kón—tyémpòl

con tiempo

Maid
Certainly, if you let me know
in time.

kláról simẹábisa|kontyémpòl

Sirvienta
Claro, si me avisa con tiempo.

dirty

suṣyól

sucio

White
This place is quite dirty. (7)

estọtéstábástantesúṣyòl

White
Esto está bastante sucio.

to begin

émpéṣárl

empezar

Can you begin this week?

pwedempeṣar|estasemanat

¿Puede empezar esta semana?

Maid
Yes. Then I'll see you Friday.

sil éntonṣestástạélbyérnésl

Sirvienta
Sí. Entonces hasta el viernes.

11.10   Notes on the basic sentences

(1) This sentence of course literally says, 'It's equal to the one of him', contextually 'It's the same as his.' This construction is drilled in Unit 13, section 13.21.3.

(2) Note that with days of the week no word equivalent to English 'on' occurs.

(3) This is given as a unit expression because of the occurrence of the item *por* in the meaning 'during' or 'in', which it regularly has only with time-words like 'morning', 'afternoon', and so on.

(4) Note that this answer is to the question /kéténgokęașér↓/ *¿Qué tengo ꞵue hacer?*, which has the /—r/ form, the infinitive, of *hacer*. Consequently, the answer merely replaces *hacer* with a series of verbs all in the same /—r/ form, much as we would do in English in such a sequence as 'What do I have to do?' 'You have to eat, to wash up,' etc. But notice: the 'have to' must be present in the English answer, though it does not need to be present in the Spanish answer.

(5) The item *don* is used only before the given name, the 'first' name, not the surname. It is translatable by 'mister' except that 'mister' is used only before surnames (though in the South one may hear servants talk about 'Mister Bill' or the like). It is rather formal. *Doña* is the feminine equivalent of *don*.

(6) See (5) above for explanation of why *Mr. Molina* is used to translate *don José*.

(7) *Bastante* occurs more often in this sense of 'rather' or 'quite' than it does in the more literal sense 'enough'.

11.2   DRILLS AND GRAMMAR

11.21   Pattern drills

11.21.1   Possessives - shortened forms

A. Presentation pattern

ILLUSTRATIONS

1 éstezmɪáwtó↓   Este es *mi* auto.

2 ezmɪnóbyá↓   Es *mi* novia.

nwebó↓

———————————————   new   nuevo

Hand me my new books.	3 páseme |mız lıbroznwébòs↓	Páseme *mis* libros nuevos.
_____	4 éstas,entukásá↓	Estás en *tu* casa.
_____	5 dondemándasturrópá↓	¿Dónde mandas *tu* ropa?
Where are your things?	6 dondestántuskósàs↓	¿Dónde están *tus* cosas?
_____	7 éste |baser |suéskritóryò↓	Este va a ser *su* escritorio.
_____	8 bınqusted |kònsúfámılyá↑	¿Vino usted con *su* familia?
his	su↓ suyò↓	su (suyo)
He himself takes his shirts.	9 élmızmo |①yebasuskamísàs↓	El mismo lleva *sus* camisas.
John and his ideas!	10 hwanısusıdéàs↓	¡Juan y *sus* ideas!
our	nwestrò↓	nuestro
They're not our friends.	11 é①yos |noson |nwestros,amígòs↓	Ellos no son *nuestros* amigos.
their	su↓ suyò↓	su (suyo)
The Whites have their house (fixed up) very pretty.	12 lózhwayt |tyenenmuybonità |sú kásá↓	Los White tienen muy bonita *su* casa.

EXTRAPOLATION

Reference	sg	pl
1	mı(s)	[nwestro(s) a(s)]
2 fam	tu(s)	
2 - 3	su(s)	

NOTES

a. All possessives except /nwéstro/ occur in shortened forms when placed before nouns.

b. Gender distinctions are lost in shortened forms, though agreement in number remains.

405

11.21.11 Substitution drills - number substitution

1   éltyéne |mişenişéró↓

    _____şenişéros↓   éltyéne |mı(s)şenişéros↓

2   yótéŋgo |suplúmȧ↓

    _____plúmȧs↓   yótéŋgo |susplúmȧs↓

3   eⱴozbíben |e(n)nwéstroediíşyó↓

    _____ediíşyós↓   eⱴozbíben |e(n)nwéstroseдifíşyós↓

---

1 El tiene mi *cenicero.*

   _____ceniceros.   El tiene mis ceniceros.

2 Yo tengo su *pluma.*

   _____plumas.   Yo tengo sus plumas.

3 Ellos viven en nuestro *edificio.*

   _____edificios.   Ellos viven en nuestros edificios.

4 éꙅ̌askómen |e(n)nwéstrazmésàs↓
    _____mésà↓   éꙅ̌askómen |e(n)nwéstramésà↓

5 éꙅ̌atyéne |mizmalétàs↓
    _____malétà↓   éꙅ̌atyéne |mimalétà↓

6 ténemos |suzlíbròs↓
    _____líbrò↓   ténemos |sulíbrò↓

7 éꙅ̌oz |banamifyéstà↓
    _____fyéstàs↓   éꙅ̌oz |banamisfyéstàs↓

_____

4 Ellas comen en nuestras *mesas*.
    _____ mesa.   Ellas comen en nuestra mesa.

5 Ella tiene mis *maletas*.
    _____ maleta.   Ella tiene mi maleta.

6 Tenemos sus *libros*.
    _____libro.   Tenemos su libro.

7 Ellos van a mi *fiesta*.
    _____ fiestas.   Ellos van a mis fiestas.

1 éstₐezlₐmalétàↆ

        mi   ↆ   éstₐezmimalétàↆ

        su   ↆ   éstₐe(s)sumalétàↆ

        nwéstra_ↆ   éstₐ|eznwéstramalétàↆ

2 éstese̱lkwártòↆ

        mi   ↆ   éstezmikwártòↆ

        su   ↆ   éste(s)sukwártòↆ

        nwéstro_ↆ   éstez|nwéstrokwártòↆ

---

1 Esta es *la* maleta.

       mi   .   Esta es mi maleta.

       su   .   Esta es su maleta.

       nuestra__.   Esta es nuestra maleta.

2 Este es *el* cuarto.

       mi   .   Este es mi cuarto.

       su   .   Este es su cuarto.

       nuestro__.   Este es nuestro cuarto.

3   éstos |sonlozbeşínòs↓

_____ miz _____ ↓

_____ suz _____ ↓

_____ nwestroz___ ↓

éstos |sonmizbeşínòs↓

éstos |sonsuzbeşínòs↓

éstos |so(n)nwestrozbeşínòs↓

----

3 Estos son *los* vecinos.

_____ mis _____ .

_____ sus _____ .

_____ nuestros ___ .

Estos son mis vecinos.

Estos son sus vecinos.

Estos son nuestros vecinos.

11.12.12 Translation drill

1 This is my agency.   éstạezmịahénṣyá↓   Esta es mi agencia.

2 This is our building.   éstẹ |eznwéstrọeḍifíṣyó↓   Este es nuestro edificio.

3 They are my friends.   éꞗyos |sónmisạamígòs↓   Ellos son mis amigos.

4 Our house is vacant.   nwéstrȧkasạ |éstaḍesokupáḍá↓   Nuestra casa está desocupada.

5 These are my suits.   ésto(s)sónmistráhės↓   Estos son mis trajes.

6 Our cleaner's is across   nwéstrȧtịntȯrḗrịạ |estaẹmfréntė↓   Nuestra tintorería está enfrente.
   (the street).

7 Your house is very big.   súkasạ |ėzmúygrándė↓   Su casa es muy grande.

8 I never send my suits   nuŋkamando |mistráhesạí↓   Nunca mando mis trajes ahí.
   there.

9 My car is on the corner.   mịawto |ẹstaẹnlạeskínȧ↓   Mi auto está en la esquina.

10 Someone has my books.   álgyeṅ |tyénemịzlíꞗròs↓   Alguien tiene mis libros.

11 Nobody lives in our house.

náðyebíbȩ |e(n)nwéstrakásà↓

Nadie vive en nuestra casa.

12 Our family is here.

nwéstràfámílyȩ |estakí↓

Nuestra familia está aquí.

13 It's (just) that my Spanish isn't very good.

éskémȩéspáɲyol |nȩezmúybwénò↓

Es que mi español no es muy bueno.

14 We always speak with your (girl) friends a little bit.

syémprȩablamoṣumpóko |konsuṣamígàs↓

Siempre hablamos un poco con sus amigas.

15 Bring me my thirteen dollars.

tráygame |mistréṣeðólàrès↓

Tráigame mis trece dólares.

B. Discussion of pattern

Some adjectives of two or more syllables in Spanish, including the possessives /mío, túyo, súyo/, are subject to shortening when they occur in a position before the nouns they modify. This shortening involves the loss of the final syllable of the adjective. A complete discussion of the patterns of shortening, including all adjectives affected, how much is removed in taking the final syllable off, and what position-agreement requirements control the shortening, are presented in the appendix.

The shortening of possessives is characterized by the loss of their final syllable whether singular or plural and in both gender forms. This shortening in chart form is:

	Full	Shortened
1 sg	mío(s) mía(s)	mɪ(s)
2 fam	túyo(s) túya(s)	tu(s)
2 - 3	súyo(s) súya(s)	su(s)
1 pl	nwéstro(s) nwéstra(s)	————

The full forms always carry a strong stress: the shortened forms may, especially if they appear in a contrastive construction, though they are normally weak stressed. The construction with shortened forms appearing before the noun occurs much more frequently than the construction with full forms appearing after the noun.

The range of possible meaning is the same for /su/ as for /súyo/ , namely all 2-3 forms. Hence / su / may be translated 'your (referring to one or more than one), his, her, its, their'. However, in the absence of contextual evidence to the contrary, it will refer only to 2 sg, that is, meaning 'your' (referring to one person). Thus the chart presented above could be modified as follows:

Reference	sg	pl
1	mi(s)	nwéstro(s) —a(s)
2 fam	tu(s)	[su(s)]
2 for	su(s)	
3	[su(s)]	[su(s)]

11.21.2 The negative particle with verbs

A. Presentation of pattern

ILLUSTRATIONS

_____	1 élpreşyo |no̧estámál↓	El precio *no* está mal.
_____	2 no̧emoz |dȩşidi̧dolaféchá↓	*No* hemos decidido la fecha.
_____	3 pórkenoḇyenes |estanóché↓	¿Por qué *no* vienes esta noche?
_____	4 antez |noḵyeres |otrotrago↑	Antes, ¿*no* quieres otro trago?
_____	5 nomedi̧ga |seṇyormolína̧↓	*No* me diga señor Molina.
_____	6 notemoléstes↓	*No* te molestes.
_____	7 nó↓ estálehós↓	*No*, está lejos.
_____	8 élsuyo̧ |ezmazarandȩ↓ nó↑	El suyo es más grande, ¿*no?*

EXTRAPOLATION

Affirmative—	Verb
Negative—	/nó/ Verb

NOTES

a. Used as a verb modifier, /nó/ appears immediately before the verb, or the verb along with any preposed clitics.

11.21.21 Substitution drill - Construction substitution

Problem:

tengọ̃ámbrè↓

Answer:

nótengọ̃ámbrè↓

1	práktıkam	bastántè↓	nópráktıkam	bastántè↓
2	làsényorạ	ablạespạnyól↓	làsényora	nọablạespạnyól↓
3	mègustạésò↓	nómegustạésò↓

Problem:

Tengo hambre.

Answer:

No tengo hambre.

1	Practican bastante.	No practican bastante
2	La señora habla español.	La señora no habla español.
3	Me gusta eso.	No me gusta eso.

4 èlsábaḍo |èstóyòkúpáḋò↓   èlsábaḍo |nọestóyokupáḋò↓

5 hwan |èstámuyagraḍeşíḋò↓   hwan |nọesta |muyagraḍeşíḋò↓

6 èlhweḅes |tràḅàhamos̩akí↓   èlhweḅez |notraḅahamos̩akí↓

7 làkahạ |èstálạentráḋà↓   làkaha |nọestalạentráḋà↓

8 étràḅàhaḍo |ḍèmásyáḋò↓   nọetrabahaḍo |ḍemasyáḋò↓

9 komenlechúgà↓   nokomenlechúgà↓

---

4 El sábado estoy ocupado.   El sábado no estoy ocupado.

5 Juan está muy agradecido.   Juan no está muy agradecido.

6 El jueves trabajamos aquı.   El jueves no trabajamos aquí.

7 La caja está a la entrada.   La caja no está a la entrada.

8 He trabajado demasiado.   No he trabajado demasiado.

9 Comen lechuga.   No comen lechuga.

11.21.22 Translation drill

1 I don't work on the first floor.	nótrabáhǫ |enelprimerpísô↓	No trabajo en el primer piso.
2 He hasn't been here before.	élnǫaęstádǫaki |ántês↓	El no ha estado aquí antes.
3 Gosh, I don't remember anything.	kárambá↓ nórrěkwérdónadâ↓	¡Caramba! No recuerdo nada.
4 Well, she's not coming.	ěmfíh↓ ěꝍy̨anobyénê↓	En fin, ella no viene.
5 They're not going to move.	nobán |ámúdarsedekásâ↓	No van a mudarse de casa.
6 By the way, I don't remember your name.	áprópósítô↓ nórrekwerdo |sunómbrê↓	A propósito, no recuerdo su nombre.
7 They're not very grateful.	ěꝍy̨ǒznǫestán |múyagradeꜱídôs↓	Ellos no están muy agradecidos.
8 She doesn't sweep very well.	nobárre |muybyén↓	No barre muy bien.
9 They don't clean the whole house.	nólimpyan |todalakásâ↓	No limpian toda la casa.

End of Tape 8A

B. Discussion of pattern

The particle /nó/ is uninflectable, that is, it does not change for person, number, or any other grammatical category. It is most commonly used as a complete sentence followed by a terminal juncture, /↓/ (often marked with a comma in the writing system) answering a query in the negative, or followed by /↑/ after a statement, which means the speaker is asking for corroboration:

/nó↓ estáléhos↓/

/elsúyo|esmásgránde↓nó↑/

When /nó/ appears in an intonation phrase with other words, it is usually placed directly before the verb, or before the verb and any preceding clitic pronouns that accompany it, since the clitics become part of the verb.

In the case of verb phrases, /nó/ comes before the first verb, not between the two as it does in English

/noémosdeşıdído↓/   We haven't decided.

The occurrence of /↓/ between /nó/ and the verb is, of course, of the utmost importance, because it can totally change the meaning of the sentence:

/nó↓ estáléhos↓/   No, it's very far off.

/nóestáléhos↓/   It's not very far off.

Both /nó/'s can occur in a single utterance, like this.

/nó↓ nóestáléhos↓/   No, it's not very far off.

You will note that the first /nó/ translates the English 'no', but the second one, the one which immediately precedes the verb, translates English 'not'. Examine especially these utterances, which are of very high frequency and great utility, answering the question 'Do you have it?'

/nó↓ nóténgo↓/   No, I don't.

/sí↓ síténgo↓/   Yes, I do.

The pattern of negative usage in Spanish includes what in English is called a 'double negative', i. e. the appearance of two negative words in the same construction. 'I don't have nothing' is criticized as socially unacceptable in English, but /nó—téngo—náda/ *No tengo nada* is a normal, regular pattern in Spanish. The general pattern in Spanish is: some negative precedes the verb in a negative sentence. Thus:

/nádye—byéne↓/	/nó—byéne—nádye↓/
/núnka—bóy/	/nó—bóy—núnka↓/

or

Tape 8B

11.22   Replacement drills

A   pwédelımpyár |elmío |tambyén↑

1   _____aóra↑   pwédelımpyár |elmíọ |aóra↑

2   _____kwartọ_____↑   pwédelımpyár |elkwartọ |aóra↑

3   _____mı_____↑   pwédelımpyár |mıkwartọ |aóra↑

4   _____bárrer_____↑   pwédebárrer |mıkwartọ |aóra↑

5   _____este_____↑   pwédebárrer |estekwartọ |aóra↑

6   _____despwés↑   pwédebárrer |estekwarto |despwés↑

7   _____su_____↑   pwédebárrer |sukwarto |despwés↑

A   ¿Puede lımpıar el mío también?

1 ¿_____ahora?   ¿Puede limpiar el mío ahora?

2 ¿_____cuarto___?   ¿Puede limpiar el cuarto ahora?

3 ¿_____mı_____?   ¿Puede limpiar mi cuarto ahora?

4 ¿____barrer_____?   ¿Puede barrer mı cuarto ahora?

5 ¿_____este_____?   ¿Puede barrer este cuarto ahora?

6 ¿_____después?   ¿Puede barrer este cuarto después?

7 ¿_____su_____?   ¿Puede barrer su cuarto después?

B   élsúyǫ |ezmázgrándè↓noↄ

1   lòs_____ↄ   lò(s) súyos |sonmázgrándèz↓noↄ

2   _____bonítàz__ↄ   là(s) súyas |sonmázbonítàz↓noↄ

3   __mías_____ↄ   lázmías |sonmazbonítàz↓noↄ

4   _____ez_____ↄ   làmįą |ezmázbonítà↓noↄ

5   _____súşyò____ↄ   élmįǫ |ezmá(s) súşyò↓noↄ

6   __ótrǫ_____ↄ   élótrǫ |ezmá(s) súşyò↓noↄ

7   làs_____ↄ   làşotras |sonma(s) súşyàs↓noↄ

B   El suyo es más grande, ¿no?

1   Los_____, ¿—?   Los suyos son más grandes, ¿no?

2   _____bonitas, ¿—?   Las suyas son más bonitas, ¿no?

3   __mías_____, ¿—?   Las mías son más bonitas, ¿no?

4   _____es_____, ¿—?   La mía es más bonita, ¿no?

5   _____sucio, ¿—?   El mío es más sucio, ¿no?

6   __otro_____, ¿—?   El otro es más sucio, ¿no?

7   Las_____, ¿—?   Las otras son más sucias, ¿no?

C   kétengokęaşér↓

1   _____komprár↓   ketengokekomprár↓

2   __ay_____↓   kęaykekomprár↓

3   kwantǫ_____↓   kwantǫaykekomprár↓

4   _____tenemos__↓   kwantotenemos |kekomprár↓

5   _____kambyár↓   kwantotenemos |kekambyár↓

6   _____ayke_____↓   kwantǫaykekambyár↓

7   kę_____↓   kęaykekambyár↓

C   ¿Qué tengo que hacer?

1 ¿ _____comprar?   ¿Qué tengo que comprar?

2 ¿____hay_____?   ¿Qué hay que comprar?

3 ¿Cuánto _____?   ¿Cuánto hay que comprar?

4 ¿____tenemos_____?   ¿Cuánto tenemos que comprar?

5 ¿_____cambiar?   ¿Cuánto tenemos que cambiar?

6 ¿____hay que _____?   ¿Cuánto hay que cambiar?

7 ¿Qué_____?   ¿Qué hay que cambiar?

D   kwántobakobrármė↓

1   kwándo_____↓   kwándobakobrármė↓

2   _____ablármė↓   kwándobablármė↓

3   _____bas_____↓   kwándo |bas.ablármė↓

4   _____mudártė↓   kwándo |bas.amudártė↓

5   pórke_____↓   pórke |bas.amudártė↓

6   _____pyensaz_____↓   pórke |pyensazmudártė↓

7   ádonde_____↓   ádonde |pyensazmudártė↓

D   ¿Cuánto va a cobrarme?

1   ¿Cuándo_____?   ¿Cuándo va a cobrarme?

2   ¿_____ hablarme?   ¿Cuándo va a hablarme?

3   ¿_____vas_____?   ¿Cuándo vas a hablarme?

4   ¿_____mudarte?   ¿Cuándo vas a mudarte?

5   ¿Por qué_____?   ¿Por qué vas a mudarte?

6   ¿_____piensas_____?   ¿Por qué piensas mudarte?

7   ¿A dónde_____?   ¿A dónde piensas mudarte?

E   ésto|èstábàstantesúʂyò↓   míkasạ|èstábàstantesúʂyà↓

1   míkasạ_____↓   místrahes|èstámbàstantesúʂyòs↓

2   __trahes_____↓   místrahes|èstánmuysúʂyòs↓

3   _____múy_____↓   místrahes|èstánmuynwébòs↓

4   _____nwébòs↓   místrahes|èstánmuynwébòs↓

5   sùs_____↓   sùstrahes|èstánmuynwébòs↓

6   __kàmísas_____↓   sùskàmisas|èstánmuynwébàs↓

7   _____súʂyàs↓   sùskàmisas|èstánmuysúʂyàs↓

E   Esto está bastante sucio.

1 Mi casa_____.   Mi casa está bastante sucia.

2 ___trajes_____.   Mis trajes están bastante sucios.

3 _____ muy_____.   Mis trajes están muy sucios.

4 _____nuevos.   Mis trajes están muy nuevos.

5 Sus_____.   Sus trajes están muy nuevos.

6 ___camisas_____.   Sus camisas están muy nuevas.

7 _____sucias.   Sus camisas están muy sucias.

F   pwedempeşar │estasemanat

1 pwedes＿＿＿＿＿＿＿＿t   pwedes.empeşar │estasemanat

2 ＿＿＿＿＿＿＿byernest   pwedes.empeşar │estebyernest

3 ＿＿＿trabahar＿＿＿t   pwedestrabahar │estebyernest

4 kyeres＿＿＿＿＿＿t   kyerestrabahar │estebyernest

5 ＿＿＿＿＿＿＿＿diast   kyerestrabahar │estozdiast

6 ＿＿＿＿＿＿＿unoz＿＿t   kyerestrabahar │unozdiast

7 ＿＿＿benir＿＿＿＿t   kyerezbenir │unozdiast

F   ¿Puede empezar esta semana?

1 ¿Puedes＿＿＿＿＿＿＿?   ¿Puedes empezar esta semana?

2 ¿＿＿＿＿＿＿＿viernes?   ¿Puedes empezar este viernes?

3 ¿＿＿trabajar＿＿＿?   ¿Puedes trabajar este viernes?

4 ¿Quieres＿＿＿＿＿?   ¿Quieres trabajar este viernes?

5 ¿＿＿＿＿＿＿dias?   ¿Quieres trabajar estos días?

6 ¿＿＿＿＿＿unos＿?   ¿Quieres trabajar unos días?

7 ¿＿＿venir＿＿＿?   ¿Quieres venir unos días?

11.23   Variation drills

A   kéđias |pweđebenír↓   ¿Qué días puede venir?

1 What days can you clean?   kéđias |pweđelimpyár↓   ¿Qué días puede limpiar?

2 What days can you sweep?   kéđias |pweđebarrér↓   ¿Qué días puede barrer?

3 What days can you wash?   kéđias |pweđelabár↓   ¿Qué días puede lavar?

4 What days can you study?   kéđias |pweđestuđyár↓   ¿Qué días puede estudiar?

5 What days do you want to   kéđias |kyérepraktikár↓   ¿Qué días quiere practicar?
   practice?

6 What days do you want to   kéđias |kyéretrabahár↓   ¿Qué días quiere trabajar?
   work?

7 What days do you want to   kéđias |kyérebolbér↓   ¿Qué días quiere volver?
   return?

B   nópwedebenír |lózbyérnes|porlatárdet   ¿No puede venir los viernes por la tarde?

1   Can't you come Friday evenings?   nópwedebenír |lózbyérnes |porlanóchet   ¿No puede venir los viernes por la noche?

2   Can't you come Monday mornings?   nópwedebenír |lózlunes |porlamañanat   ¿No puede venir los lunes por la mañana?

3   Can't you go at three o'clock?   nópwedeir |alastrést   ¿No puede ir a las tres?

4   Can't you eat at six o'clock?   nópwedekomér |ala(s)séyst   ¿No puede comer a las seis?

5   Don't you want to eat in that restaurant?   nókyerekomér |éneserrestoránt   ¿No quiere comer en ese restorán?

6   Don't you want to come back tomorrow?   nókyerebolbér |mañanat   ¿No quiere volver mañana?

7   Don't you want to speak Spanish?   nókyereablár |españólt   ¿No quiere hablar español?

C tyéne |kebarrérlakásaↃılımpyárlozmwéblès↓   Tiene que barrer la casa y limpiar
                                                                los muebles.

1 You have to sweep the kitchen   tyéne |kebarrérlakoṣına↑ɹelbáɲyò↓   Tiene que barrer la cocina y el
   and the bathroom.   baño.

2 You have to change the sheets   tyéne |kekambyárla(s)sábanas↑   Tiene que cambiar las sábanas y
   and the pillow cases.   ılasfúndàs↓   las fundas.

3 You have to clean the entrance   tyéne |kelımpyárlaentrada↑ɹelpátyò↓   Tiene que limpiar la entrada y
   and the patio.   el patio.

4 I have to study and to work.   téŋòkèstùdyár |ıtrabahár↓   Tengo que estudiar y trabajar.

5 I have to wait for Jose and   téŋo |kèspèráràhòsé |ɹakármèn↓   Tengo que esperar a José y a
   Carmen.   Carmen.

6 We have to see Jose and   ténemos |kèbéràhòsé |ɹàlsèɲyormolínà↓ Tenemos que ver a José y al
   Mr. Molina.   señor Molina.

7 They have to send the suits   tyénèŋ |kèmàndár |lòstrahesⱥala   Tienen que mandar los trajes a la
   to the cleaner's.   tıntorería↓   tintorería.

D siteŋgǫunafyéstá↓pweɖęayuɖarme↑

Si tengo una fiesta, ¿puede ayudarme?

1 If I change the sheets, can you help me?

sikambyola(s)sábánás↓pweɖęayuɖarme↑

Si cambio las sábanas, ¿puede ayudarme?

2 If I sweep the house, can you help me?

sibarrolakásá↓pweɖęayuɖarme↑

Si barro la casa, ¿puede ayudarme?

3 If I wash the kitchen, can you help me?

silabolakoşíná↓pweɖęayuɖarme↑

Si lavo la cocina, ¿puede ayudarme?

4 If I have something to do, can you help me?

siteŋgǫalgokęaşér↓pweɖęayuɖarme↑

Si tengo algo que hacer, ¿puede ayudarme?

5 If you want a house, can you let me know?

siɖésęaunakásá↓pweɖęabisarme↑

Si desea una casa, ¿puede avisarme?

6 If you need a maid, can you let me know?

sinęşésitąunamucháchá↓pweɖęabisarme↑

Si necesita una muchacha, ¿puede avisarme?

7 If I go downtown, can you wait for me?

siboyalşéntró↓pweɖesperarme↑

Si voy al centro, ¿puede esperarme?

E klárô↓símęàbisakontyémpô↓   Claro, si me avisa con tiempo.

1 Sure, if you let me know   klárô↓símęàbisamaɲánà↓   Claro, si me avisa mañana.
  tomorrow.

2 Sure, if you let me know at   klárô↓símęàbisalastrés↓   Claro, si me avisa a las tres.
  three o'clock.

3 Sure, if you let me know at   klárô↓símęàbisą|àlà(s)syétęıkínşè↓   Claro, si me avisa a las siete
  seven fifteen.   y quince.

4 Sure, if you wait for me.   klárô↓símèsperà↓   Claro, si me espera.

5 Sure, if you look for me.   klárô↓símèbuskà↓   Claro, si me busca.

6 Sure, if you take me.   klárô↓símèⓁyebà↓   Claro, si me lleva.

7 Sure, if you speak to me in   klárô↓símęabląenęspaɲól↓   Claro, si me habla en español.
  Spanish.

F èntónşesↂastạelbyérnès↓   Entonces, hasta el viernes.

1 Well, I'll be seeing you   èntónşesↂastạe(l)lúnés↓   Entonces, hasta el lunes.
   Monday.

2 Well, I'll be seeing you   èntónşesↂastạelsábảdò↓   Entonces, hasta el sábado.
   Saturday.

3 Well, I'll be seeing you   èntónşesↂastạelhwébès↓   Entonces, hasta el jueves.
   Thursday.

4 Well, I'll be seeing you   èntónşesↂastamaŋyánả↓   Entonces, hasta mañana.
   tomorrow.

5 Well, I'll see you   èntónşesↂastadespwés↓   Entonces, hasta después.
   afterwards.

6 Well, I'll see you some   èntónşesↂastạotrodíà↓   Entonces, hasta otro día.
   other day.

7 Well, I'll see you later.   èntónşesↂastamastárdè↓   Entonces, hasta más tarde.

11.24   Review drill - Unemphatic 'some, any' from English

1 Give me some soup.   démesópà↓   Déme sopa.

2 Give me some salad.   démensaláɗà↓   Déme ensalada.

3 Give me some water.   deméágwà↓   Déme agua.

4 Give me some wine.   démebínô↓   Déme vino.

5 Give me some pie.   démepastél↓   Déme pastel.

6 Give me some dessert.   démepóstrè↓   Déme postre.

7 Give me some beer.   démeşerbéşà↓   Déme cerveza.

8 Do you have any tomatoes?   tyénetomátes↑   ¿Tiene tomates?

9 Do you have any vegetables?   tyénelegúmbres↑   ¿Tiene legumbres?

10 Do you have any pork chops?   tyénechulétaz |ďeşérďo↑   ¿Tiene chuletas de cerdo?

11 Do you have any beer?   tyéneşerbéşa↑   ¿Tiene cerveza?

12 Do you have any soup?   tyénesopa↑   ¿Tiene sopa?

13 Do you have any coffee?   tyénekafé↑   ¿Tiene café?

11.3   CONVERSATION STIMULUS

NARRATIVE 1

1 The girl who cleans Molina's   lámúchacha |kělɪmpyą |ělápártáméntǒ   La muchacha que limpia el aparta-
   apartment is excellent.   ďěmólɪną |ěsěks(ş)ěléntě↓   mento de Molina es excelente.

2 And she charges very little,   ikóbrámuypókǒ↓ dyéşpesosˌaldíá↓   Y cobra muy poco, diez pesos al
   ten pesos a day.   día.

3 That's a dollar and a quarter,   esǫ |ěsˌundólarďeyntişínkǒ |mássˌóménǒs↓   Eso es un dólar veinticinco, más
   more or less.   o menos.

4 Mr. Molina is going to talk
  with her.

ėlsėŋyórmólina |báblárkonė(l)yá↓

El Sr. Molina va a hablar con ella.

5 He's going to talk with her to
  see if she wants to clean
  Mr. White's apartment also.

báblárkónė(l)yaↄpáråber |síkyérė
limpyar |ėlåpàrtåmentoɗelseŋyor
hwáyt |tåmbyén↓

Va a hablar con ella para ver si
quiere limpiar el apartamento
del Sr. White también.

6 He'll talk with her tomorrow.

måŋyanảblakonė(l)yá↓

Mañana habla con ella.

DIALOG 1

Juan, pregúntele a José que qué
tal es la muchacha que le
limpia su apartamento.

kétál |ezlamuchácha |kėtėlímpyatụ
apartaméntồ |hồsé↓

Juan: ¿Qué tal es la muchacha que te
limpia tu apartamento, José?

José, contéstele que es excelente.
Y que cobra muy poco, diez
pesos al día.

ėşėks(ş)ėléntė↓ ikóbråmuypókồ↓
ɗyeş̧pesos̜ald͟íá↓

José: Es excelente. Y cobra muy
poco, diez pesos al día.

Juan, pregúntele que cuánto es eso
en dólares.

kwántọes̜ės̜ọ |endólárės↓

Juan: ¿Cuánto es eso en dólares?

José, dígale que uno veinticinco,
más o menos.

únobeyntiş̧íŋkồ |más̜.ộménồs↓

José: Uno veinticinco, más o
menos.

Juan, pregúntele que por qué no habla con ella.	pórkeņạáblás |kóņ,é0ɥạ↓	Juan: ¿Por qué no hablas con ella?
José, pregúntele que para qué.	párake↓	José: ¿Para qué?
Juan, dígale que para ver si quiere limpiar el suyo también.	párábér |síkyérèlímpyárèlmió|tàmbyén↓	Juan: Para ver si quiere limpiar el mío también.
José, contéstele que muy bien. Que mañana habla con ella, entonces.	múybyén↓ màņyanàblokoņ,é0ɥạ |èntónşès↓	José: Muy bien, mañana hablo con ella, entonces.

NARRATIVE 2

1 The girl comes to see Mr. White in the afternoon.	làmúchácha |byéņạábér |alseņyórhwáyt| enlatárdè↓	La muchacha viene a ver al Sr. White en la tarde.
2 She's the one who cleans Mr. Molina's apartment.	é0ɥạ |èzlàkélímpyạ |èlàpàrtáménto| dèlsèņyormolínà↓	Ella es la que limpia el apartamento del Sr. Molina.
3 She goes over there on Thursdays.	báíloshwébès↓	Va ahí los jueves.

4 She can't come here on
   Saturdays, only on
   Fridays.

éꞎyanópwéde |bénírákilo(s)sábàdôs↓
sólólózbyérnès↓

Ella no puede venir aquí los
sábados, sólo los viernes.

5 The other days she has to
   go to other homes.

lós,otrozdías |tyénekęir |ąotraskásàs↓

Los otros días tiene que ir a
otras casas.

DIALOG 2

Srta., dígale 'buenas tardes' al
Sr. White, y que dice don José
que aquí necesitan una muchacha.

bwénastárdès↓ díşędónhóse |kęàkí |
néşésitanunamucháchà↓

Srta.: Buenas tardes. Dice don
José que aquí necesitan
una muchacha.

Juan, pregúntele si ella es la
que limpia su (de él) apartamento.

ęsústed |làkélimpyą |elapartaménto
del↑

Juan: ¿Es Ud. la que limpia el
apartamento de él?

Srta., contéstele al señor que sí. Que
Ud. va ahí los jueves.

sí |seꞑyór↓ bóyaíloshwébès↓

Srta.: Sí, señor. Voy ahí los
jueves.

Juan, pregúntele si puede venir
aquí los sábados.

pwédebeníraki |lo(s)sábados↑

Juan: ¿Puede venir aquí los
sábados?

435

Srta., dígale que no, que   nó|seŋyór↓sólólózbyérnès↓   Srta: No, señor, sólo los viernes.
   sólo los viernes. Que los   Los otros días tengo que
   otros días tiene que ir a   lòs,ótrózdías|teŋgokeir|aotraskásàs↓   ir a otras casas.
   otras casas.

Juan, contéstele que está bien.   èstabyén↓   Juan: Está bien.

NARRATIVE 3

1 The girl wants to see the   làmúchacha|kyéreberelapartaméntò↓   La muchacha quiere ver el
   apartment.   apartamento.

2 She wants to see what work   kyéréber|kétrabaho|aykeaşér↓   Quiere ver qué trabajo hay que
   there is to be done.   hacer.

3 She's got to do all the housework. tyénèkeáşer|todoeltrabahodekásà↓   Tiene que hacer todo el trabajo
                                                                              de casa.

4 That is to say, sweep the floors,   èzdèşir↑bàrrérlóspísos↑ làbárèl   Es decir, barrer los pisos, lavar
   wash the bathroom, make the   el baño, hacer la cama....
   bed....   baŋyo↑ àşérlàkama↑

5 But she doesn't have to wash   pèrònotyéne|kèlàbarrópà↓   Pero no tiene que lavar ropa.
   clothes.

6　He sends all his clothes to　　　èlmándàtoₒdalarrópₐ|alalabandería↓　　　El manda toda la ropa a la
　　the laundry.　　　　　　　　　　　　　　　　　　　　　　　　　　　　　lavandería.

DIALOG 3

Srta., pregúntele al señor si　　　pwedₒober|elapartamento|señor↑　　　Srta: ¿Puedo ver el apartamento,
puede ver el apartamento.　　　　　　　　　　　　　　　　　　　　　　　　señor?

Juan, contéstele que sí, cómo　　　sí|kómòno↓ paseₐₐdeIántê↓　　　　　　Juan: Sí, cómo no, pase adelante.
no, que pase adelante.

Srta., pregúntele que qué trabajo　　kétrabahoₐaykₑaₛér↓　　　　　　　　Srta: ¿Qué trabajo hay que hacer?
hay que hacer.

Juan, contéstele que todo el trabajo　tódₒeltrabahodekásà↓ èzdèₛír|　　　Juan: Todo el trabajo de casa. Es
de casa. Que es decir, barrer los　　bàrrérlóspìsos↑ làbárélbañyo↑　　　　decir, barrer los pisos,
pisos, lavar el baño, hacer la　　　àₛérlàkama↑　　　　　　　　　　　　lavar el baño, hacer las
cama....　　　　　　　　　　　　　　　　　　　　　　　　　　　　　　camas....

Srta., pregúntele si tiene que　　　teŋgokelabarropa↑　　　　　　　　　Srta: ¿Tengo que lavar ropa?
lavar ropa.

437

Juan, contéstele que no. Que
la ropa hay que mandarla a
la lavandería.

nó↓ lárrópaykemandárlạ|ala

labanderíá↓

Juan: No. La ropa hay que
        mandarla a la lavandería.

NARRATIVE 4

1 Now, (speaking of) another
   thing.

àorạ↑áblándodẹotrakósá↓

Ahora, hablando de otra cosa.

2 The girl charges ten pesos
   for cleaning Mr. Molina's
   apartment.

lámúchacha|kóbrádyẹspésos|por

limpyar| êlápàrtámentodẹelseŋyormolíná↓

La muchacha cobra diez pesos
   por limpiar el apartamento del
   Sr. Molina.

3 And now she wants to charge
   fourteen for this one.

ḷáora|kyérèkóbrar|kàtorşeporésté↓

Y ahora quiere cobrar catorce por
   éste.

4 But she's right. This one is
   larger.

pèrótyénerraşón↓ éstezmazgrándè↓

Pero tiene razón. Este es más
   grande.

5 She can start tomorrow.
   Tomorrow is Friday.

pwedèempeşármaŋyáná↓ màŋyanạezbyérnès↓

Puede empezar mañana. Mañana
   es viernes.

DIALOG 4

Juan, dígale que ahora, hablando de otra cosa, cuánto cobra ella.	áorᶐ↓áblandodᶒᵩotrakósá↓ kwánto kóbrᶐ̧ustéᵭ↓	Juan: Ahora, hablando de otra cosa, ¿cuánto cobra Ud.?
Srta., contéstele que catorce pesos.	kátorᶈepésós↓	Srta: Catorce pesos.
Juan, pero a don José le cobra diez, dígale.	pérᶐᵭónhóse ∣ lᵉ̇kóbrᶐᵭye'ṣ↓	Juan: Pero a don José le cobra diez.
Srta., dígale que sí, pero que este apartamento es más grande.	sí↓pᵉrᶐᵩéstᶒᶐpártámentᶐ ∣ ᵉ̇zmáz grandᵉ̇↓	Srta: Sí, pero este apartamento es más grande.
Juan, dígale que bueno, que muy bien. Que mañana es viernes. Que si puede empezar mañana.	bwenó↓múybyén↓ mᶐ̇ɲyanᶐᵩezbyérnᵉ̇s↓ pweᵭempeᶊarmaɲyanáᵼ	Juan: Bueno, muy bien. Mañana es viernes. ¿Puede empezar mañana?
Srta., contéstele que sí, y pregúntele que a qué hora?	sí ∣ seɲyór↓ ákᶒorá↓	Srta: Sí, señor. ¿A qué hora?
Juan, dígale que por la tarde, a la una o a las dos.	pórlàtarᵭᵉ̇↓ álᶐ̧una ∣ ᶐalazᵭós↓	Juan: Por la tarde, a la una o a las dos.

12.1   BASIC SENTENCES.   No water in White's apartment.

John comes into Molina's apartment looking upset.

ENGLISH SPELLING	AID TO LISTENING	SPANISH SPELLING
(it) happens (to happen)	pásá↓ pàsár↓	pasa (pasar)
Molina What's the matter, John?	kétepásà | hwán↓	*Molina* ¿Qué te pasa, Juan?
(I) know (to know)	sé↓ sàbér↓	sé (saber)
White I don't know. There's no water in my apartment.	nosé↓ noayagwa | ênmɪ̀àpàrtàméntô↓	*White* No sé. No hay agua en mi apartamento.
don't tell (to tell)	nò—dígàs↓ dèşír↓	no digas (decir)
Molina Don't tell me! Again?	nomedígàs↓ ótràbeş↑	*Molina* ¡No me digas! ¿Otra vez?
to bathe	bànyár↓	bañar
to bathe myself (to bathe oneself) (1)	bànyarmê↓ bànyarsê↓	bañarme (bañarse)
to shave	àfèytár↓	afeitar

to shave myself (to shave oneself)   àféytármè↓ àféytàrsè↓   afeitarme (afeitarse)

And here I am without having bathed or shaved! (2)   iyó|kèstóysìmbàɲyàrme̲isìnafeytármè↓   ¡Y yo que estoy sin bañarme y sin afeitarme!

(I) was (to be)   èstábà↓ èstár↓   estaba (estar)

cleaning myself (to clean oneself) (3)   lìmpyandómè↓ lìmpyàrsè↓   limpiándome (limpiarse)

(I) was cleaning (myself)   èstábà—límpyandòmè↓   estaba limpiándome

the tooth   èl—dyèntè̲↓   el diente

White
I was brushing my teeth.   yo|ęstàbalìmpyándome|lozdyèntès↓   *White*
Yo estaba limpiándome los dientes.

went, was going (to go)   íbà↓ ír↓   iba (ir)

was going to give myself   iba̲—a—dármè↓   iba a darme

the shower   là—ducha↓   la ducha

I was going to take a shower, too.   ibadàrmęunaḍuchà|tàmbyén↓   Iba a darme una ducha también.

the joke   là—bromà↓   la broma

the boy   èl—chìkó↓   el chico

Molina
What a fix, chum!

kebrómà|chíkò↓

Molina
¡Qué broma, chico!

The party is at seven!

làfyestạ|èsạlà(s)syetè↓

La fiesta es a las siete.

scarcely, barely

àpenàs↓

apenas

(we) have (to have)

tènemòs↓ tènèr↓

tenemos (tener)

half

međyò↓

medio

to, in order to

parà↓

para

to dress

bèstír↓

vestir

to dress ourselves (to dress oneself)

bèstírnòs↓ bèstírsè↓

vestirnos (vestirse)

White
We barely have half an hour to get dressed.

àpenas|tènémòzmeđyạórà|páràbèstírnòs↓

White
Apenas tenemos media hora para vestirnos.

the moment

èl-mòmentò↓

el momento

just a minute (4)

ùn-mòmentò↓

un momento

(I) go (to go)

bóy↓ ìr↓

voy (ir)

(it) arrived (to arrive)

ɑyègó↓ ɑyègár↓

llegó (llegar)

Molina

Just a minute. I'm going to see
if the water has come on. (5)

únmoméntò↓ bóyaber|síⁿⁿyėgóęlágwà↓

Molina

Un momento. Voy a ver si llegó
el agua.

Yes, it has. (6)

sí↓ yaáy↓

Sí, ya hay.

the haste

là—prísà↓

la prisa

to hurry myself (to hurry
oneself)

dárme—prísà↓ dárse—prísà↓

darme prisa (darse prisa)

White

I'm going, then. I've got to
hurry.

mèbóyentónșés↓ tėngokeđármeprísà↓

White

Me voy entonces. Tengo que
darme prisa.

listen (to listen)

óyè↓ óìr↓

oye (oir)

at last

pòr—fín↓

por fin

Molina

Hey, who did you finally decide
to take? (7)

óyè↓ pòrfín↑ákyėmbásàⁿⁿyebár↓

Molina

Oye, por fin, ¿a quién vas a llevar?

a little fat (fat)

gòrdító↓ górdó↓

gordito (gordo)

the chubby girl

là—górdità↓

la gordita

the eye glasses

làz—gáfàs↓

las gafas

White

The chubby gal with the glasses.

àlàgórditadelazgáfàs↓

White

A la gordita de las gafas.

to leave, to go out	sålír↓	salir
on leaving	ål—sålír↓	al salir
to call	(l)yåmár↓	llamar

Molina
Fine. I'll call you when I leave. (8)

bwenó↓ ålsålírte(l)yámó↓

Molina
Bueno, al salir te llamo.

12.10   Notes on the basic sentences

(1)   Reflexive verbs such as this one are not discussed and drilled in detail until Unit 24, but it is impossible to so arrange the dialogs that reflexive forms will not appear before then with some frequency. It will therefore be necessary to build up each one before that unit in the rather full form shown here: first the non-reflexive verb, then the reflexive form which appears in the utterance, and finally the reflexive citation form.

(2)   This sentence is unusually difficult to approximate in a translation that reflects adequately both the structure and the meaning. The actual meaning is best paralleled by a translation like 'And I haven't bathed or shaved yet!', but structurally, the *cited* translation is somewhat closer and more subject to variation drill later in this Unit.

(3)   To be examined in detail in Unit 25, this use of certain clitics in a fashion that can only be translated as possessive in English is rather common. Literally, of course, the utterance is roughly this: 'I was cleaning for myself the teeth'.

(4)   The 'just' of 'just a moment' is not stated in the Spanish, nor need it be in the English: 'One moment' would be a satisfactory, though rather formal, translation.

(5)   One of the striking differences between Spanish syntax and English syntax is illustrated in this sentence: the occurrence in Spanish of the Past I form [(l)yegó] *llegó* in a situation where only the English present perfect construction can satisfactorily occur.

(6)   Here the occurrence of the present perfect construction in the English of the preceding utterance requires that the confirmation utterance (whether negative or affirmative—here it happens to be affirmative) continue in the same way. The Spanish does not require continuation in this situation, so that the complete shift, from 'arrived' to 'already there is (some)', is not startling.

(7)   [porfín] *por fin* in this utterance means 'Finally after all that deliberation you were going through' or something similar. The translation is therefore not as literal as 'Hey, who are you finally going to take?'

(8)   The phrase relator [a] *a* in [alsalír] *al salir* does not imply 'when' or 'before' or 'as' in itself; but the context indicates that 'On leaving' is equivalent to 'When I leave', since the more literal 'On leaving' is much too formal an English equivalent.

12.2   DRILLS AND GRAMMAR

12.21   Pattern drills

12.21.1   Subject pronouns

A. Presentation of pattern

ILLUSTRATIONS

_____	1	yókyérọunsaṇẉich |ᵭehamón↓	*Yo* quiero un sandwich de jamón.
_____	2	itu↑ késtazḃebyéndò↓	**Y** *tú* ¿qué estás bebiendo?
_____	3	komọestaụstéᵭ↓	¿Como está *usted?*
He's coming this week.	4	élbyénestasemánà↓	*El* viene esta semana.
She washes very well.	5	e(l)yalàba |múyḃyén↓	*Ella* lava muy bien.
We're American.	6	nòsótros |sómosͺamerikánòs↓	*Nosotros* somos americanos.
We're American (f).	7	nòsótras |sómosͺamerikánàs↓	*Nosotras* somos americanas.
_____	8	keᵭeseanụstéᵭès↓	¿Qué desean *ustedes?*
They're not in the street.	9	e(l)yoz |noͺestánͺenlaká(l)yè↓	*Ellos* no están en la calle.
They(f) want pillow cases.	10	e(l)yaskyérem |fundazᵭẹalmwáᵭà↓	*Ellas* quieren fundas de almohada.

EXTRAPOLATION

	sg		pl	
	m	f	m	f
1	yó		nosótros	nosótras
2 fam	tú			
2 for	ustéd		ustédes	
3	él	é(l)ya	é(l)yos	é(l)yas

NOTES

a. Spanish subject pronouns are usually used only for contrastive emphasis, when the reference of the pronoun is otherwise clear from the context.

b. Spanish /tú/ is the structural equivalent of English 'thou', but is much more frequently used.

c. English has distinct gender forms in 3 sg; Spanish has distinct gender forms in 3 sg *and* pl, and also in 1 pl.

d. English 3 sg 'it', which is neither masculine nor feminine, is very rarely translated in Spanish.

12.21.11 Translation drill

1 She's American, but I'm Spanish.

éᶿyạeṣạmerikánå↓pèrðyósoyespạɲyól↓

Ella es americana, pero yo soy español.

2 I'm single, but he's married.

yósoysoltérò↓pèrọeleskaság̈ò↓

Yo soy soltero, pero él es casado.

3 They're from here, but we're from Chile.

éᶿyo(s)sondẹakí↓pèrðnòsótros |

somozg̈echílè↓

Ellos son de aquí, pero nosotros somos de Chile.

4 She drinks water and I drink whisky and soda.

éᶿyạbébẹagwạt̶iyó|wiskikonsóg̈å↓

Ella bebe agua y yo whisky con soda.

5 He's in the patio, and she's in the kitchen.

élèstáẹnẹlpátyot̶ᶦeᶿyạenlakoṣínå↓

El está en el patio, y ella en la cocina.

6 They're (f) Spanish, and we are too.

éᶿyạ(s)sónẹspạɲyólast̶inósotros

tambyén↓

Ellas son españolas y nosotros también.

7 Are we going, or are they?

bamoznosótrost̶obanéᶿyós↓

¿Vamos nosotros o van ellos?

8 Am I going, or are you all?

bóyyót̶ọbanụstég̈ès↓

¿Voy yo o van Uds.?

9 Are they going, or are we?   báneɑ̨yos↑obámoznosótros↓   ¿Van ellos o vamos nosotros?

10 Who wants ham, you or he?   kyeŋkyérehamón↓ ústeɑ↑ǫél↓   ¿Quién quiere jamón? ¿Ud. o él?

11 Who works in the consular   kyentrábahạ|ênlâsêkşyoŋkonsulár↓   ¿Quién trabaja en la sección
     section, you all or she?   ústeɑes↑ǫéɑyạ↓   consular? ¿Uds. o ella?

12 Who wants something else,   kyendeséạ|álgomás↓ ústeɑ↑ǫéɑyǒs↓   ¿Quién desea algo más? ¿Ud.
     you or they?   o ellos?

13 What does *he* want?   keɑeséạ|él↓   ¿Qué desea él?

14 What do *they* need?   keneşesítan.|éɑyǒs↓   ¿Qué necesitan ellos?

15 What does *she* want?   kekyérẹ|éɑyạ↓   ¿Qué quiere ella?

B. Discussion of pattern

In unit 4 (4.21.1) the concept of person was discussed as it applies to the proper selection of verb forms, and person-number categories were illustrated by English pronouns. The same classification—that of first, second, and third categories, each ocurring in both singular and plural forms, constituting a set of six categories for Spanish verbs-can be used to describe Spanish pronouns. In addition there are distinct gender forms in the 1 pl and 3 sg and pl categories and two 2nd person forms distinguishing formal and familiar.

This means that there are several areas of overlap between pronoun and verb patterns, as the charts below illustrate:

yó	nosótros nosótras
tú	ustédes
ustéd	
él éˆya	éˆyos éˆyas

ábl—o	abl—ámos
ábl—as	
ábl—a	ábl—an

Note that the pattern discrepancies of Spanish, though they exist, are relatively minor compared to English.

I	we
you	
he she it	they

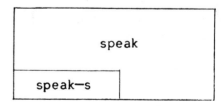

As the chart shows, only the English pronouns which are marked for gender (he, she, it) require a verb form that is different from the name form or infinitive form which all other English pronouns occur with. The Spanish pronoun and verb patterns coincide except for a distinction between 2nd formal and 3rd person forms.

Since verbs in Spanish carry person-number distinctions in their structure, pronouns that carry the same information are frequently considered redundant and unnecessary, and a student's tendency to translate all English pronouns into Spanish pronouns is very conspicuous to a Spanish speaker. Spanish pronouns are usually used only for emphasis or contrast as in /yónolokyéro↓/ 'I don't want it', /ıtú↑ késtásbebyéndo↓/ 'And what are *you* drinking', /yómebóy↓ pérọélsekéda↓/ 'I'm going, but *he's* staying', or when they are needed to distinguish forms, as between /él/ and /ustéd/ with a verb form like / ábla /.

The regional American 'you all' is often used in drills in this book to signal the distinction between /ustéd/ and /ustédes/ that 'you' alone does not show.

Very commonly used abbreviations of *usted* and *ustedes* are *Ud.* and *Uds.*

12.21.2   Pronouns after phrase relators

A. Presentation of pattern

ILLUSTRATIONS

_____	1 ạmi↑ tráygame |sópadelegúmbrès↓	*A mí* tráigame sopa de legumbres.
with me	kónmıgò↓	conmigo
He's going to work with me.	2 batrabahár |konmígò↓	Va a trabajar *conmigo*.
_____	3 pásoportí |ạlàsóchò↓	Paso *por ti* a las ocho.
with you (fam.)	kóntıgò↓	contigo
He's going to work with you.	4 bátrabahár |kontígò↓	Va a trabajar *contigo*.
the letter	lạ—kártạ↓	la carta
The letter is for you.	5 làkártạ |ẹspárạustéd↓	La carta es *para usted*.

—————————————   6 nó↓ésigwál|aldęé1↓   No, es igual al *de él.*

—·—·—·—·—·—·—·—   7 bátrabahár|ko(n)nosótrós↓   Va a trabajar *con nosotros.*

He's going without you all.   8 élbá|sinusté́des↓   El va *sin ustedes.*

Sit down with them.   9 syéntese|koné(l)yós↓   Siéntese *con ellos.*

EXTRAPOLATION

	sg	pl
1	mí	nosótros, —as
2 fam	tí	
2 for	ustéd	ustédes
3	él, é(l)ya	é(l)yos, —as

NOTES

a. Pronouns after phrase relators differ from subject pronouns only in 1 sg and 2 fam sg forms.

b. When the two distinct forms mentioned in (a) occur with the phrase relator /kon/ , the special combinations /konmígo/ and /kontígo/ appear.

12.21.21 Response drill

1	éstǫesparamí†ǫparǫustéd↓	pàrǫustéd↓
2	ésǫezdé(0)yạ†ǫdél↓	del↓
3	éstǫezdé(0)yạs†ǫdenosótrǫs↓	dènǫsótrǫs↓
4	lǫzmwébles |sómparanosótrǫs↑	
	ǫpárạé(0)yǫs↓	pàrạé(0)yǫs↓

[nòsótrǫs↓]	5	kǫ̀ŋkyém |banέ(0)yǫs↓	kǫ̀(n)nǫsótrǫs↓
[é(0)yạ↓]	6	kǫ̀ŋkyém |baél↓	kǫ̀nέ(0)yạ↓
[él↓]	7	pàrạkyén |esẹéstasí(0)yạ↓	pàrạél↓

	1	¿Esto es para mí o para Ud.?	Para Ud.
	2	¿Eso es de ella o de él?	De él.
	3	¿Esto es de ellas o de nosotros?	De nosotros.
	4	¿Los muebles son para nosotros o para ellos?	Para ellos.
(nosotros)	5	¿Con quién van ellos?	Con nosotros.
(ella)	6	¿Con quién va él?	Con ella.
(él)	7	¿Para quién es esta silla?	Para él.

[eⁿyás↓]　8　lázmónedás↓ sómpáránósótrós↑　　　　　nó↓ párąeⁿyás↓

[él↓]　9　ustedba|koneⁿyos↑　　　　　　　　　nó↓ kónel↓

[eⁿyá↓]　10　esteskritóryo|esparąel↑　　　　　　nó↓ párąeⁿyá↓

　　11　estabitaşyon|esparąusted↑　　　　　sí↓ párámí↓

　　12　estekwarto|esparanosótrós↑　　　　sí↓ páránósótrós↓

　　13　eⁿyabakonmigo↑　　　　　　　　sí↓ kónųsted↓

(ellas)　8　Las monedas, ¿son para nosotros?　　　No, para ellas.

(él)　9　¿Ud. va con ellos?　　　　　　　No, con él.

(ella)　10　¿Este escritorio es para él?　　　　No, para ella.

　11　¿Esta habitación es para Ud.?　　　Sí, para mí.

　12　¿Este cuarto es para nosotros?　　Sí, para nosotros.

　13　¿Ella va conmigo?　　　　　　Sí, con Ud.

12.21.22 Translation drill

1 She's going with me.   e(l)yabakonmıgó↓   Ella va conmigo.

2 This sandwich is for me.   éstésaŋwich |esparamí↓   Este sandwich es para mí.

3 After them, John eats.   dèspwezde(l)yos |kómehwán↓   Después de ellos, come Juan.

4 They live near us.   é(l)yozbíben |şerkadenosótrós↓   Ellos viven cerca de nosotros.

5 He doesn't work with me.   el |nótrabahakonmígó↓   El no trabaja conmigo.

6 Carmen lives with us.   kármem |bíbeko(n)nosótrós↓   Carmen vive con nosotros.

7 John lives with them.   hwam |bíbekon(e)(l)yós↓   Juan vive con ellos.

8 The sheets are for us.   là(s)sábanas |sómparanosótrós↓   Las sábanas son para nosotros.

9 There's eleven dollars for   áyonşedolares |párausted↑idyeş | Hay once dólares para Ud. y diez
   you and ten for us.   paranosótrós↓   para nosotros.

10 There's two hundred dollars   áydós(ş)yentozdolares |páramí↑   Hay doscientos dólares para mí
   for me and two hundred   idós(ş)yentos |paraé(l)yós↓   y doscientos para ellos.
   for them.

11 There's nine dollars for him   áynwebedolares |paraél↑ikwatro | Hay nueve dólares para él y cuatro
   and four for her.   paraé(l)yà↓   para ella.

B. Discussion of pattern

The forms of pronouns that are used after phrase relators are essentially subject pronouns, except that /mí/ and /tí/ replace /yó/ and /tú/ in the pattern. The subject and phrase-relator pronouns can be classed as nonclitic, in contrast to the clitic pronouns that can appear only with verbs. Thus the nonclitic pronouns can be charted as follows:

	Subject	Phrase relator
1 sg	yó	mí
2 fam sg	tú	tí
2 for sg	ustéd	
3 sg	él, éⁿya	
1 pl	nosótros, —as	
2 pl	ustédes	
3 pl	é(l)yos, —as	

The significance of the relation of the subject and phrase relator function in essentially a single set of forms can be seen by comparing Spanish and English usage. The Spanish classification of nonclitic and clitic case forms is partly paralleled by the English pattern of subject and object case forms. However, as the following chart shows, there is an area of overlap in appearance after a phrase relator. In the examples, /él/ is nonclitic, /lo/ is clitic; 'he' is subject-form, and 'him' is object-form.

Subject of verb	Object of phrase relator	Object of verb
élestákí↓	ésparaél↓	nópwédobérlo↓
He's here.	It's for *him*.	I can't see *him*.

455

More will be said about the concept of 'nominalization' in the next discussion of pattern and elsewhere. The concept assumes, in substance, that a form that is not a noun behaves as if it were. An interesting example of 'pronoun nominalization' occurs in Unit 6 in the sentence /kéleparés sinostratámosdetú↓/ , where a subject pronoun appears after a phrase relator: /tú/ appears where we might expect /tí/ . In this case /tú/ has been nominalized, it is behaving as a noun, a form which has no case forms: nouns do not change in form when used as subject of a verb or object of a phrase relator.

12.21.3 Components of phrases

A. Presentation of pattern

ILLUSTRATIONS

—————————————	1 bínọusted |konsufamílya↑	¿Vino usted *con su familia?*
—————————————	2 bátrabahár |ko(n)nosótròs↓	Va a trabajar *con nosotros.*
By talking so much, you don't learn anything.	3 kònằ̱lartánto↑ngaprendeznáδà↓	*Con hablar* tanto, no aprendes nada.
—————————————	4 siniŋklwírluṣ |ằgwa |nigás↓	*Sin incluir* luz, agua, ni gas.
What do you do after studying?	5 kẹaṣez |δéspwezdestuδyár↓	¿Qué haces *después de estudiar?*
Before translating, repeat.	6 ántez |δètràδụ̱ṣir |repítà↓	*Antes de traducir,* repita.

EXTRAPOLATION

phrase relator	noun pronoun nominalized form

NOTES

a. Phrase relators introduce nominal forms.

b. The infinitive is the nominalized form of verbs that normally occurs after phrase relators.

12.21.31 Translation drill

1 He always studies before
   going out.

   élsyémprestúḏyą|ántezḏesalír↓

   El siempre estudia antes de salir.

2 She always cleans after
   eating.

   éḽyásyémprelímpya|ḏespwézḏekomér↓

   Ella siempre limpia después de
   comer.

3 I'm going downtown before
   eating lunch.

   bóyálşentrǫ|ántezḏęalmorşár↓

   Voy al centro antes de almorzar.

4 We're going after eating.

   nósótrozḃámoz|ḏéspwézḏekomér↓

   Nosotros vamos después de comer.

5 Repeat this before writing
   it (down).

   rrépitąéstǫ↑ántezḏeskribírló↓

   Repita esto antes de escribirlo.

6 I don't have time for
   studying.

   nótęŋgctyémpó|parạęstuḏyár↓

   No tengo tiempo para estudiar.

7 She always comes without
   calling.

   éḽyásyémprebyéne|sinḽyamár↓

   Ella siempre viene sin llamar.

8 You can't learn without
   studying.

   nópweḏęaprendér|sinęstuḏyár↓

   No puede aprender sin estudiar.

9 Two hundred a month without
   including the electricity.

   dós(ş)yéntos|álméstsininklwírlalúş↓

   Doscientos al mes sin incluir
   la luz.

10 Because of (for) talking so
   much, you don't learn.

pòráblártánto |ngápréndè↓

Por hablar tanto no aprende.

11 She charges four dollars for
   sweeping the whole house.

éłyákobra |kwátrodólares↑pórbárrér |
todalakásà↓

Ella cobra cuatro dólares por
barrer toda la casa.

12 I don't like the idea of
   going now.

nomegustalaidea |deiraórà↓

No me gusta la idea de ir ahora.

13 What do you think of the idea
   of buying the house?

kéleparęelaidea |dèkòmprárlakásà↓

¿Qué le parece la idea de comprar
la casa?

End of Tape 9A

B. Discussion of pattern

   A phrase is a subordinate construction consisting of a phrase relator and its object (plus any modifiers of the object). The phrase
normally modifies some other item (noun, verb, etc.) in an utterance, though it may stand alone as in /atrabahár↓/ 'Let's get to work'.

   The term 'preposition' is often employed to designate phrase relators. In the structural discussions in this text it has been omitted
in favor of the term 'phrase relator' to help point up structural and distributional parallels with analogous forms such as clause relators
(see appendix).

   The object of a phrase relator is a nominal form: either a noun , a pronoun, or a nominalized form. 'Nominalization' means the selection and appearance of an item from another form-class (an adjective, modifier, verb, etc.) in a function that is normally occupied by a noun.
A nominalized form may be the subject of a sentence /elbyéhoestákí↓/ 'The *old man* is here', the object of a verb /béqún
amerikáno↓/ 'I see one *American*' or the object of a phrase relator /ástalwégo↓/ 'See you *later*'. It may be modified by adjectives /elótrobyého↓/ 'The *other* old man', which agree in number and gender with the nominalized form /losótrosbyéhos↓/
'The *other* old men.' In short, nominalized forms are functionally nouns, even though they do not have the defining morphological characteristics of nouns(inflection for gender only).

   The form of the verb which is most readily nominalized is the infinitive, and this is the form which follows phrase relators. The
equivalent English construction very often shows an '—ing' form of the verb where the Spanish infinitive occurs, and the tendency to follow

the English pattern is responsible for many mistakes of English speakers learning Spanish. Thus, /konablártánto↑.../ and /sınınklwírlúş↑.../ are equivalent to 'By talking so much....' and 'without including electricity....'

The regular exception to this generalization is the English phrase relator 'to', which takes the infinitive form, just as in Spanish. The Spanish equivalent to English 'to' is / a, pára, de, ke/, and other phrase relators, varying in different constructions. Note the following correspondences:

/bánatrabahár↓/	They're going *to work.*
/téngǫúnąóra|párakomér↓/	I have an hour *to eat.*
/ésfáşıl|denkontrár↑/	Is it easy *to find?*
/tyéneskekonoşérla↓/	You have *to meet* her.

In all cases the Spanish construction is always *'phrase relator* plus *infinitive'.* In English, it is *'to* plus *infinitive',* but *'any other phrase relator* plus −*ing-form.'*

In most cases the Spanish infinitive immediately follows the phrase relator. Sometimes, however, the nominalized infinitive can be modified by an adjective such as the definite article, as in /alsalír\|te()yámo↓/, though /a/ is normally translated 'to', in this construction it is not: 'On leaving (when I leave), I'll call you.'

Many phrase relators are single words. Often, however, a verb modifier may itself be modified by a phrase in a construction which appears to include a compound phrase relator. In the utterance /elotél\|estáşérka↓/, the form /şérka/ is a verb modifier. In /elotél\|estáşérka\|dęakí↓/, the phrase /dęakí/ modifies /şérka/. It is nevertheless convenient sometimes to consider /şérkade/ as a kind of compound phrase relator which takes the nominalized modifier /akí/ as its object.

The phrase relators so far introduced into this text include: /a, ásta, de, désde, en, ke, kómo, kon, ménos, pára, por, sin/. Compounds include: /ántes—de, despwés—de, léhos—de, şérka—de/.

Tape 9B

12.21.4 Statement intonation patterns - normal and contrastive statements

A. Presentation of pattern

ILLUSTRATION

It's near.		1	éstaşérká↓		1 2 1 1↓ Está cerca.
———————			no↓ éstálehós↓		21 1 2 3 1↓ No, está lejos.
———————		2	ézmuykáró↓		1 2 11↓ Es muy caro.
———————			álkòntraryò↓		1 3 1↓ Al contrario.
———————		3	tantogústò↓		2 1 1↓ Tanto gusto.
———————			élgustoezmió↓		1 2 31↓ El gusto es mío.

EXTRAPOLATION

Statement	
Uncolored	Contrastive
/1211↓/	/1231↓/

NOTES

a. The uncolored Spanish pattern resembles an English pattern that is often associated with expressions of disinterest or boredom.

b. The contrastive (or emphatic) pattern resembles an English uncolored pattern.

12.21.41 Substitution drills

    Problem:

            éstoyeŋkolómbyà↓

    Answer:

            éstoyeŋkolombyà↓

            Problem:
                    1 2   1 1 ↓
                    Estoy en Colombia.

            Answer:
                    1 2   3 1 ↓
                    Estoy en Colombia.

1   tràbahọẹŋkarákàs↓   tràbahọẹŋkarakàs↓

2   isóyɗechílè↓   isóyɗechɪlè↓

3   kòmemozmúchò↓   kòmemozmuchò↓

4   èstaọkupáɗò↓   èstaọkupaɗò↓

5   prònunşyastóɗò↓   prònunşyastoɗò↓

6   èŋkòntramoskásà↓   èŋkòntramoskasà↓

```
    1 2      1 1↓                    1 2      3 1↓
1 Trabajo en Caracas.            Trabajo en Caracas.

    1 2      11 ↓                   1 2      31↓
2 Y soy de Chile.                Y soy de Chile.

    1 2      1 1↓                   1 2      3 1↓
3 Comemos mucho.                 Comemos mucho.

    1 2      1 1↓                   1 2      31↓
4 Está ocupado.                  Está ocupado.

    1 2      1 1↓                   1 2      3 1↓
5 Pronuncias todo.               Pronuncias todo.

    1     2    1 1 ↓               1    2    3 1↓
6 Encontramos casa.              Encontramos casa.
```

7 ȧlkílámos̬ȩlkwártȯ↓   ȧlkílámos̬ȩlkwartȯ↓

8 ȩstuḏyampókȯ↓   ȩstuḏyampokȯ↓

9 ȩmpȩ̇s̬amozmaŋyánȧ↓   ȩmpȩ̇s̬amozmaŋyanȧ↓

10 nȩ̇s̬ȩ̇sit̬aunlíbrȯ↓   nȩ̇s̬ȩ̇sit̬aunlıbrȯ↓

11 prȯ̇bamos̬ȩlpóstrȩ̇↓   prȯ̇bamos̬ȩlpostrȩ̇↓

```
   1    2      1 1↓
7 Alquilamos el cuarto.
```

```
   1  2    1 1↓
8 Estudian poco.
```

```
   1    2      1 1↓
9 Empezamos mañana.
```

```
    1   2     1 1↓
10 Necesita un libro.
```

```
    1 2      1  1↓
11 Probamos el postre.
```

```
   1    2      3 1↓
Alquilamos el cuarto.
```

```
   1 2     3 1↓
Estudian poco.
```

```
   1   2     3 1↓
Empezamos mañana.
```

```
   1   2     3 1↓
Necesita un libro.
```

```
   1 2     3 1↓
Probamos el postre.
```

12.21.42 Response drill

Problem 1:

deｄondesｨustéd↓

Answer:

sóydechilé↓

Problem 2:

deｄonde↑

Answer:

dechilé↓

Problem 1:

¿De dónde es Ud.?

Answer: 1   21 ↓
Soy de Chile.

Problem 2:

¿De dónde?

Answer: 1   31 ↓
De Chile.

[dóṣè↓] 1 kwántoskwártos.áy↓   áydoṣè↓

kwántos↑   doṣè↓

[à͡yɪ↓] 2 dóndestaᴖlíᴅró↓   ̇estaᴖyɪ↓

dónde↑   àᴖyɪ↓

(doce) 1 ¿Cuántos cuartos hay?   1 2 1↓
                                                     Hay doce.

¿Cuántos?   3 1↓
                                                     Doce.

(allí) 2 ¿Dónde está el libro?   1 2 11↓
                                                     Está allí.

¿Dónde?   1 31↓
                                                     Allí.

[byahè↓]   3 pàràkes,estechékè↓   pàraélbyahé↓

                               pàràke↑   pàraélbyahé↓

[ámbrè↓]   4 kétyénè↓   teŋgoámbrè↓

                                  ké↑   ambrè↓

[ẏıskıkonsóɗà↓] 5 kékyérè↓   ẏıskıkonsóɗà↓

                               kòŋké↑   kónsoɗà↓

---

                                                                    1   2 1 ↓
(viaje)   3 ¿Para qué es este cheque?   Para el viaje.

                                                                    1   3 1 ↓
            ¿Para qué?   Para el viaje.

                                                                    2   1   1 ↓
(hambre)   4 ¿Qué tiene?   Tengo hambre.
                                                                    3   1 ↓
            ¿Qué?   Hambre.
                                                                    2   2 1 ↓
(whisky con soda) 5 ¿Qué quiere?   Whisky con soda.
                                                                    1   3 1 ↓
            ¿Con qué?   Con soda.

[ènlåtìntórèrìà↓]   6   dóndetrabahąélↄ   ènlåtìntórèrìàↄ

                        dóndeↁ   ènlåtìntórèrìàↄ

[ènèlèskritóryò↓]   7   dóndestálaplúmà↓   ènèlèskritóryò↓

                        dóndeↁ   ènèlèskritóryò↓

[båmòsàkòmér↓]   8   pàràⲥondebán↓   båmòsàkómér↓

                        pàràⲥondeↁ   àkòmér↓

(en la tintorería)   6   ¿Dónde trabaja él?

                         ¿Dónde?

(en el escritorio)   7   ¿Dónde está la pluma?

                         ¿Dónde?

(vamos a comer)   8   ¿Para dónde van?

                         ¿Para dónde?

| 1 | 21↓ |
En la tintorería.

1   31↓
En la tintorería.

1   2 1↓
En el escritorio.

1   3 1↓
En el escritorio.

1   21↓
Vamos a comer.

1   31↓
A comer.

[àtràbàhár↓]   9   aḋondebán↓   àtràbàhár↓

                     aḋonde↑   àtràbàhár↓

[ótràkàmisà↓] 10   kekyéré↓   ótràkàmisà↓

                     ké↑   ótrakamisà↓

[ènlàkóṣinà↓] 11   dondȩaȩstáḋó↓   ènlàkóṣinà↓

                     donde↑   ènlàkóṣinà↓

(a trabajar)   9 ¿Adónde van? | 1   21 ↓ |
                                                    | A trabajar. |

               ¿Adónde? | 1   31 ↓ |
                                                    | A trabajar. |

(otra camisa) 10 ¿Qué quiere? | 1   21 ↓ |
                                                    | Otra camisa. |

               ¿Qué? | 2   31 ↓ |
                                                    | Otra camisa. |

(en la cocina) 11 ¿Dónde ha estado? | 1   21 ↓ |
                                                    | En la cocina. |

               ¿Dónde? | 1   31 ↓ |
                                                    | En la cocina. |

469

B. Discussion of pattern

Intonation patterns are arrangements of stress $/\acute{\ }\ \dot{\ }/$, pitch $/1$, 2 , $3/$, and terminal junctures $/|$, $\uparrow$, $\downarrow/$. These patterns are different in English and Spanish, first of all because the number of available counters in the systems of the two languages is different: Spanish has two stresses, English four; Spanish has three pitches, English four.

In this text intonation patterns have been shown by $/\acute{\ }/$ and $/\dot{\ }/$ placed at varying heights over each syllable to represent pitch. This is an effective pedagogical device to present these patterns. However, Spanish intonations can most efficiently be described by marking all real or potential pitch changes, followed by the terminal juncture. It has been determined that normally the points of potential pitch change in any single phrase are all strong stressed syllables plus the first and last syllables, when these are weak stressed. Thus the intonation pattern of $/\grave{e}sta\acute{s}\acute{e}rk\acute{a}\downarrow/$, $/t\grave{e}nemoslab\acute{i}sa\downarrow/$ can be abstracted as $/1211\downarrow/$ for both sentences, even though the formula has to account for a different number of syllables in each case. The sentences can then be rewritten $/\overset{1}{e}st\overset{2}{a}\overset{1}{s}\overset{1}{e}rka\downarrow/$, $/\overset{1}{t}e\overset{2}{n}\overset{1}{e}moslab\overset{1}{i}sa\downarrow/$, writing the significant numbers above each appropriate syllable and marking only strong stress.

When the first syllable is strong - stressed, the first number of the pattern formula does not actually occur: $/ty\acute{e}nen\acute{o}tr\grave{o}\downarrow/$, $/d\acute{o}ndest\acute{a}m\grave{o}s\downarrow/$ or $/ty\overset{2}{e}ne\overset{1}{n}\overset{1}{o}tr\grave{o}\downarrow/$, $/d\overset{2}{o}ndest\overset{1}{a}m\overset{1}{o}s\downarrow/$. When the last syllable is strong stressed, both numbers are written over the last vowel, since a glide in this position can be significant; $/\grave{e}stak\acute{i}\downarrow/$, $/\grave{e}st\acute{a}k\imath\downarrow/$ then are written $/\overset{1}{e}st\overset{2}{a}k\overset{11}{i}\downarrow/$, $/\overset{1}{e}st\overset{2}{a}k\overset{31}{i}\downarrow/$ The last $/1/$ on the first sentence may seem to be superfluous, but is needed in the analysis to contrast with the last $/1/$ on the second sentence, which cannot be omitted; $/\grave{e}stak\imath\downarrow/$ can occur, analyzed as $/\overset{1}{e}st\overset{2}{a}k\overset{33}{i}\downarrow/$, where final $/3/$ is significantly and minimally different from final $/1/$ of the previous sentence.

The two patterns drilled in this section, $/1211\downarrow/$ and $/1231\downarrow/$, are important because they resemble English patterns which have very different meanings. A pattern very much like $/1211\downarrow/$, unlike the Spanish normal, uncolored connotation, means disinterested or discourteous: $/\overset{2}{W}h\overset{1}{a}t's$ for $\overset{1}{d}inner$ $/$, $/\overset{2}{W}h\overset{1}{y}$ $n\overset{1}{o}t$ $/$, and unless a student realizes that it has no such meaning in Spanish, he will avoid using it, even though he may be unaware of his aversion to the pattern.

On the other hand, $/1231\downarrow/$, which is contrastive in Spanish, used only for special emphasis, is very similar to a pattern that means normal or uncolored in English. Thus the pattern of $/\overset{2}{\text{I}}\text{'m }\overset{\wedge}{\text{goíng }}\overset{31}{\text{hóme}}\overset{\downarrow}{/}$, $/\overset{2}{\text{Hé}}\text{'s frôm }\overset{3}{\text{Kánsas}}\overset{1}{}\overset{\downarrow}{/}$, if transferred to Spanish $/\overset{2}{\text{bó}}\text{yak}\overset{3}{\text{ás}}\overset{1}{\text{a}}\downarrow/$ $/\overset{2}{\text{é}}\text{sdek}\overset{3}{\text{á}}\text{ns}\overset{1}{\text{as}}\downarrow/$ is likely to sound over-insistent in Spanish where $/1231\downarrow/$ means emphatic.

One other feature related to intonation that needs to be brought to the attention of students, since it is notably different in the structure of the two languages, is rhythm. Rhythm is syllable-centered in Spanish, phrase-centered in English. This means that the recurring tempo unit in Spanish is the syllable — each is of approximately the same length; in English the recurring tempo unit is the phrase, and also each is of approximately the same length. But Spanish phrases and English syllables are of differing lengths, and English phrases usually arrange syllables so that two long (stronger stressed) do not occur together nor more than two short (weaker stressed) occur in uninterrupted sequence. Imposing the English pattern of alternate long and short syllables on Spanish produces a distortion which will immediately come to the attention of any Spanish speaker, even though he may not be able to explain exactly what it is that 'sounds funny'. This feature of rhythm was discussed with illustrations in section 1.22.4.

One of the important purposes of this and of subsequent intonation drills is to bring the patterns that are involved to the awareness of the learner. In some cases the patterns are similar to English patterns; in some cases they are very different. It is most important that the student master the differences, but in all cases the manipulation of the patterns, with the proper correlation to the meaning significance of their use, is valuable practice.

12.22   Replacement drills

A nósé↓ noáyágwa|enmiapartaméntó↓

1	__pwéáó_____↓	nópwéáó↓ noáyágwa|enmiapartaméntó↓
2	_____el_____↓	nópwéáó↓ noáyágwa|enelapartaméntó↓
3	_____kásá↓	nópwéáó↓ noáyágwa|enlakásá↓
4	_____nááye_____↓	nópwéáó↓ noáynááye|enlakásá↓
5	__kréó_____↓	nókréó↓ noáynááye|enlakásá↓
6	_____akéȳa____↓	nókréó↓ noáynááye|enakéȳakásá↓
7	_____otél↓	nókréó↓ noáynááye|enakelotél↓

A   No sé, no hay agua en mi apartamento.

1	—puedo,_____.	No puedo, no hay agua en mi apartamento.
2	_____,_____el_____.	No puedo, no hay agua en el apartamento.
3	_____casa.	No puedo, no hay agua en la casa.
4	_____,___nadie_____.	No puedo, no hay nadie en la casa.
5	__creo,_____.	No creo, no hay nadie en la casa.
6	_____,_____aquella_____.	No creo, no hay nadie en aquella casa.
7	_____,_____hotel.	No creo, no hay nadie en aquel hotel.

B y̦o̦estaba|limpyandomelozd̦yéntės↓

1 _____rrópá↓   y̦o̦estaba|limpyandomelarrópá↓

2 _____komprandome_____↓   y̦o̦estaba|komprandomelarrópá↓

3 _____áwtô↓   y̦o̦estaba|komprandomeláwtô↓

4 _____un____↓   y̦o̦estaba|komprandom̦un̦áwtô↓

5 _____mwéblės↓   y̦o̦estaba|komprandom̦un̦ozmwéblės↓

6 _____așyendom̦_____↓   y̦o̦estaba̦|așyendom̦un̦ozmwéblės↓

7 _____trágós↓   y̦o̦estaba̦|așyendom̦un̦ostrágós↓

B   Yo estaba limpiándome los dientes.

1 _____ropa.   Yo estaba limpiándome la ropa.

2 _____comprándome_____.   Yo estaba comprándome la ropa.

3 _____auto.   Yo estaba comprándome el auto.

4 _____un____.   Yo estaba comprándome un auto.

5 _____muebles.   Yo estaba comprándome unos muebles.

6 _____haciéndome_____.   Yo estaba haciéndome unos muebles.

7 _____ tragos.   Yo estaba haciéndome unos tragos.

C ápenastenémoz |méđyaóra |parabestírnòs↓

1 _____bañyárnòs↓   ápenastenémoz |méđyaóra |parabañyárnòs↓

2 _____una_____↓   ápenastenémos |unaóra |parabañyárnòs↓

3 syémpre_____↓   syémpretenémos |unaóra |parabañyárnòs↓

4 _____afeytárnòs↓   syémpretenémos |unaóra |parafeytárnòs↓

5 _____momento_____↓   syémpretenémos |unmomento |parafeytárnòs↓

6 núŋka_____↓   núŋkatenémos |unmomento |parafeytárnòs↓

7 áora_____↓   áoratenémos |unmomento |parafeytárnòs↓

C   Apenas tenemos media hora para vestirnos.

1 _____bañarnos.   Apenas tenemos media hora para bañarnos.

2 _____una _____ .   Apenas tenemos una hora para bañarnos.

3 Siempre_____ .   Siempre tenemos una hora para bañarnos.

4 _____ afeitarnos.   Siempre tenemos una hora para afeitarnos.

5 _____momento_____ ,   Siempre tenemos un momento para afeitarnos.

6 Nunca_____ .   Nunca tenemos un momento para afeitarnos.

7 Ahora_____ .   Ahora tenemos un momento para afeitarnos.

D mèbóy |entónşès↓ téngokedårmeprísà↓

1 _____komér↓   mèbóy |entónşès↓ téngokekomér↓

2 _____áyke_____↓   mèbóy |entónşès↓ áykekomér↓

3 _____trabahár↓   mèbóy |entónşès↓ áyketrabahár↓

4 _____ténemoske_____↓   mèbóy |entónşès↓ ténemosketrabahár↓

5 _____bestírnòs↓   mèbóy |entónşès↓ ténemoskebestírnòs↓

6 _____estudyár↓   mèbóy |entónşès↓ ténemoskestudyár↓

7 _____téngoke_____↓   mèbóy |entónşès↓ téngokestudyár↓

D   Me voy entonces, tengo que darme prisa.

1 _____,_____comer.   Me voy entonces, tengo que comer.

2 _____,hay que_____.   Me voy entonces, hay que comer.

3 _____,_____trabajar.   Me voy entonces, hay que trabajar.

4 _____,tenemos que____.   Me voy entonces, tenemos que trabajar.

5 _____,_____vestirnos.   Me voy entonces, tenemos que vestirnos.

6 _____,_____estudiar.   Me voy entonces, tenemos que estudiar.

7 _____,tengo que_____.   Me voy entonces, tengo que estudiar.

E óyè↓ pòrfín |àkyémbas.aⓁyebár↓

1 _____ Ⓛyamár↓   óyè↓ pòrfín |àkyémbas.aⓁyamár↓

2 _____ èntonşes_____↓   óyè↓ èntonşes |àkyémbas.aⓁyamár↓

3 _____kwàndo_____↓   óyè↓ èntonşes |kwàndobas.aⓁyamár↓

4 _____trabahár↓   óyè↓ èntonşes |kwàndobas.atrabahár↓

5 _____dónde_____↓   óyè↓ èntonşez |dóndebas.atrabahár↓

6 chikò_____↓   chikò↓ èntonşez |dóndebas.atrabahár↓

7 _____kòŋkyem_____↓   chikò↓ èntonşes |kòŋkyémbas.atrabahár↓

E Oye, ¿por fin a quién vas a llevar?

1 ___, ¿_____llamar?   Oye, ¿por fin a quién vas a llamar?

2 ___, ¿entonces_____?   Oye, ¿entonces a quién vas a llamar?

3 ___, ¿_____cuándo_____?   Oye, ¿entonces cuándo vas a llamar?

4 ___, ¿_____trabajar?   Oye, ¿entonces cuándo vas a trabajar?

5 ___, ¿_____dónde_____?   Oye, ¿entonces dónde vas a trabajar?

6 Chico, ¿_____?   Chico, ¿entonces dónde vas a trabajar?

7 ___, ¿_____con quién_____?   Chico, ¿entonces con quién vas a trabajar?

F   bwenò↓ àlsálìrteⓎámó↓

1   oyè_____↓   oyè↓ àlsálìrteⓎámó↓

2   _____Ⓨégar_____↓   oyè↓ àlⓎégarteⓎámó↓

3   _____ayúdò↓   oyè↓ àlⓎégarteayúdò↓

4   éntonşes_____↓   éntonşes↑ àlⓎégarteayúdò↓

5   _____abísò↓   éntonşes↑ àlⓎégarteabísò↓

6   _____émpèşar_____↓   éntonşes↑ àlémpèşarteabísò↓

7. byén_____↓   byén↓ àlémpèşarteabísò↓

F   Bueno, al salir te llamo.

1 Oye, _____.   Oye, al salir te llamo.

2 ___ , ____llegar_____.   Oye, al llegar te llamo.

3 ___ , _____ayudo.   Oye, al llegar te ayudo.

4 Entonces, _____.   Entonces, al llegar te ayudo .

5 _____,_____aviso.   Entonces, al llegar te aviso.

6 _____,empezar_____.   Entonces, al empezar te aviso.

7 Bien, _____.   Bien, al empezar te aviso.

12.23   Variation drills

A kétepásà|hwán↓   ¿Qué te pasa, Juan?

1 What's the matter, Jose?   kétepásà|hòsé↓   ¿Qué te pasa, José?

2 What do you think of it,   kéteparéşè|hòsé↓   ¿Qué te parece, José?
   Jose?

3 What do you think of it,   kéteparéşè|chíkò↓   ¿Qué te parece, chico?
   boy?

4 What do you like, Carmen?   kétegústà|kármèn↓   ¿Qué te gusta, Carmen?

5 What do you want, Carmen?   kekyérès|kármèn↓   ¿Qué quieres, Carmen?

6 What are you writing,   késkríbès|kármèn↓   ¿Qué escribes, Carmen?
   Carmen?

7 What are you studying,   kestúdyàs|kármèn↓   ¿Qué estudias, Carmen?
   Carmen?

B iyó|kėstóysimbȧŋyȧrmę|isinȧfeytȧrmė↓   ¡Y yo que estoy sin bañarme y sin
                                                             afeitarme!

1 And here I am without having   iyó|kėstóysinlimpyȧrme|lozḍyéntės↓   ¡Y yo que estoy sin limpiarme los
   brushed my teeth!   dientes!

2 And here I am without having   iyó|kėstóysiŋkámbyȧrme|ḍerrópå↓   ¡Y yo que estoy sin cambiarme de
   changed my clothes!   ropa!

3 And here I am without having   iyó|kėstóysintrȧbáhár↓   ¡Y yo que estoy sin trabajar!
   worked!

4 And here I am without having   iyó|kėstóysiŋkòmér↓   ¡Y yo que estoy sin comer!
   eaten!

5 And here I am without having   iyó|kėstóysinȧlmòrṣár↓   ¡Y yo que estoy sin almorzar!
   had lunch!

6 And here's John without any   ihwȧŋ|kėstásindolȧrės↓   ¡Y Juan que está sin dólares!
   dollars!

7 And here's John without a car.   ihwȧŋ|kėstásinȧwtó↓   ¡Y Juan que está sin auto!

C íbàdármęûnàdúchà|tàmbyén↓   Iba a darme una ducha también.

1 I was going to clean my teeth.   íbàlìmpyármè|lôzdyéntès↓   Iba a limpiarme los dientes.

2 I was going to change my shirt.   íbàkàmbyármè|làkàmìsà↓   Iba a cambiarme la camisa.

3 I was going to sit there.   íbàsèntármęàî↓   Iba a sentarme ahí.

4 I was going to move.   íbàmùdármè|dèkasà↓   Iba a mudarme de casa.

5 I was going to hire a taxi.   íbàlkìlár|ûntàksî↓   Iba a alquilar un taxi.

6 I was going to wait for Jose.   íbạèspèrár|àhòsé↓   Iba a esperar a José.

7 I was going to practice   íbàpràktìkár|èspàŋyól↓   Iba a practicar español.
   Spanish.

D   ilȧfyestą|ęşȧlȧ(s̩)syėtėↆ   Y la fiesta es a las siete.

1 And the party is nine o'clock.   ilȧfyestą|ęşȧlȧznwebėↆ   Y la fiesta es a las nueve.

2 And the party is tomorrow.   ilȧfyestą|ęzmȧŋyanȧↆ   Y la fiesta es mañana.

3 And the party is later.   ilȧfyestą|ęzd̯ęspwės̩ↆ   Y la fiesta es después.

4 And the party is before.   ilȧfyestą|ęs̩ȧntęs̩ↆ   Y la fiesta es antes.

5 And the party is in my apartment.   ilȧfyestą|ęs̩ęnmı̧ȧpȧrtȧmentȯↆ   Y la fiesta es en mi apartamento.

6 And there'll be whiskey at the   ilȧfyestą|ęskȯŋwiskı́ↆ   Y la fiesta es con whisky.
  party.

7 And there'll be 'cuba libre' at   ilȧfyestą|ęskȯŋkúbȧlıbrėↆ   Y la fiesta es con cuba libre.
  the party.

E únmoméntò↓ bóyabér |siṅyḗgoẹlágwà↓   Un momento, voy a ver si llegó
                                                                   el agua.

1 Just a minute, I'll see if the   únmoméntò↓ bóyabér |siṅyḗgoẹláwtò↓   Un momento, voy a ver si llegó
   the car has arrived.   el auto.

2 Just a minute, I'll see if my   únmoméntò↓ bóyabér |siṅyḗgómibẹsínò↓   Un momento, voy a ver si llegó
   neighbor has arrived.   mi vecino.

3 Just a minute, I'll see if   únmoméntò↓ bóyabér |siṅyḗgo |làsẹṅyòríta   Un momento, voy a ver si llegó
   Miss Molina has arrived.   molínà↓   la señorita Molina.

4 Just a minute, I'll see if the   únmoméntò↓ bóyabér |siṅyḗgoẹltáksi↓   Un momento, voy a ver si llegó
   taxi has arrived.   el taxi.

5 Just a minute, I'll see if the   únmoméntò↓ bóyabér |siṅyḗgo |làkélimpyạ   Un momento, voy a ver si llegó
   lady who cleans the apartment   elapartaméntò↓   la que limpia el apartamento.
   has arrived.

6 Just a minute, I'll see if the   únmoméntò↓ bóyabér |siṅyḗgo | Un momento, voy a ver si llegó
   wash-woman has arrived.   làkélabalarrópà↓   la que lava la ropa.

7 Just a minute, I'll see if the   únmoméntò↓ bóyabér |siṅyḗgo |là   Un momento, voy a ver si llegó
   girl who studies Spanish   kèstudyạespaṅyól↓   la que estudia español.
   has arrived.

F làgórdita |delazgáfàs↓   La gordita de las gafas.

1 The chubby girl at the cashier's   làgórdita |delakáhà↓   La gordita de la caja.
  desk.

2 The young lady at the cleaners'.   làsènyòrita |delatintorería↓   La señorita de la tintorería.

3 The young lady who has the car.   làsènyòrita|deláwtò↓   La señorita del auto.

4 The girl at the hotel.   làmúchacha |delotél↓   La muchacha del hotel.

5 The lady on the first floor.   làsènyora |delprimerpísó↓   La señora del primer piso.

6 The gentleman in the ad.   èlsènyor|delanúnşyò↓   El señor del anuncio.

7 The man in the elevator.   èlombre|delas(ş)ensór↓   El hombre del ascensor.

12.24   Review drill -Adjective agreement in remote position

1	The house is pretty.	làkasًaezbonítàↆ	La casa es bonita.
2	The school is good.	làéskwelًaezbwénàↆ	La escuela es buena.
3	The books are expensive.	lózlìbro(s)soŋkáròsↆ	Los libros son caros.
4	The agency is no good.	làhenًsyًaezmálàↆ	La agencia es mala.
5	The apartments are comfortable.	lòsàpàrtámèntos |soŋkómòċòsↆ	Los apartamentos son cómodos.
6	The secretary is pretty.	làsèkrétaryًaezbonítàↆ	La secretaria es bonita.
7	The lady is Spanish.	làsèŋyoraً |esۑespaŋyólàↆ	La señora es española.
8	The cars are American.	lòsۑawtos |sónۑamerıkánòsↆ	Los autos son americanos.
9	The suitcases are expensive.	làzmáletas |soŋkáràsↆ	Las maletas son caras.
10	The buildings are pretty.	lòsèċifıṣyos |sombonítòsↆ	Los edificios son bonitos.
11	The shirts are cheap.	làskámısas |sombarátàsↆ	Las camisas son baratas.
12	The furniture is no good.	lòzmwébles |sonmálòsↆ	Los muebles son malos.
13	The ladies are English.	là(s)sèŋyoras |sonıŋglésàsↆ	Las señoras son inglesas.

NARRATIVE 1

1 Tonight there's a party at the Harris' (home).

éstànochẹↄ̂áyúnàfyèstạ̀|ènlà kasaↄeloshárris↓

Esta noche hay una fiesta en la casa de los Harris.

2 Jose and Juan are going (to go).

hósẹɪhwàm|bànạírↄ̂↓

José y Juan van a ir.

3 They have to be there at seven.

tyénenkestáraↄↄyi|ạ̀la(s)syétè↓

Tienen que estar allí a las siete.

4 Juan is going to take that chubby girl.

hwàm|baↄↄyebár|akeↄↄyagorↄítà↓

Juan va a llevar a aquella gordita.

5 She isn't very pretty, but he likes her very much.

nọ̀ezmuybonítà↓ pérọàeↄↄleↄusta múchó↓

No es muy bonita, pero a él le gusta mucho.

6 Jose is going to take his fiancée.

hóse|baↄↄyebàrasunóbyà↓

José va a llevar a su novia.

7 He's going to come by for Juan at six-thirty.

élbapasárporhwàn|àlà(s)séys ɪméↄyà↓

El va a pasar por Juan a las seis y media.

8 Then they'll pick up the girls.

lwego†pasamporlaschíkas↓

Luego pasan por las chicas.

9 Jose doesn't want another
   drink, now.

hóse |nokyere |ótrotrágo |aóra↓

José no quiere otro trago ahora.

10 He's got to leave.

tyéneke̦ırsè↓

Tiene que irse.

11 He barely has time to shave
   and dress.

ápenastyenetyémpo |pàràféytàrse̦
ıbestírsè↓

Apenas tiene tiempo para
afeitarse y vestirse.

DIALOG 1

José, dígale a Juan que esta
noche hay una fiesta en la
casa de los Harris, que si
recuerda.

éstànoche̦ |ayunafyésta̦ |ènlàkásà
de̦lósharris↓ rrékwerdas†

José: Esta noche hay una fiesta
en la casa de los Harris,
¿recuerdas?

Juan, contéstele que sí, que
cómo no. Pregúntele que
a qué hora hay que estar allí.

sí↓ kómòno†↓ àke̦oraykestaraⓞyí↓

Juan: Sí, cómo no. ¿A qué hora
hay que estar allí?

José, contéstele que a las
siete, y pregúntele si va a
a llevar a alguien.

àlà(s)syétè↓ básàⓞye̦baralgyen†

José: A las siete. ¿Vas a llevar
a alguien?

Juan, dígale que sí, que a la gordita. Que no es muy bonita pero que a Ud. le gusta mucho. Y pregúntele que a quién va a llevar él.

sí↓ àlàgòrɖìtà↓ nọẹʐmuybonita|

pérọàmimegustamúchó↓

itú↓ àkyèmbasàɲẹbár↓

Juan: Sí, a la gordita. No es muy bonita pero a mí me gusta mucho. Y tú, ¿a quién vas a llevar?

José, contéstele que a su novia. Dígale que si quiere, Ud. pasa por él a las seis y media y luego pasan por las chicas.

àminóbyà↓ sikyéres|pásoportí↑

àlà(s)séys, iméɖyà↓ ilwego|pasamos

porlaschíkàs↓

José: A mi novia. Si quieres, paso por ti a las seis y media y luego pasamos por las chica

Juan, dígale que muy bien, y pregúntele si no quiere otro trago.

múybyén↓ nókyéresọtrotrágò↑

Juan: Muy bien. ¿No quieres otro trago?

José, contéstele que no, gracias, que Ud. ya se va. Que apenas tiene tiempo para afeitarse y vestirse. Que adiós.

nográşyàs↓ yamebóy↓ ápenas

tengotyempo|pàráféytarmẹibestírmè↓

àɖyós↓

José: No, gracias, ya me voy. Apenas tengo tiempo para afeitarme y vestirme. Adiós.

NARRATIVE 2

1 Juan isn't ready yet.

hwa(n)nọestalístó|tóɖàbíà↓

Juan no está listo todavía.

2 He doesn't look like an American.

nó|pàreşẹamerikánó↓

No parece americano.

3 It's already twenty to seven.

yásónlà(s)syéte|ménózbeyntè↓

Ya son las siete menos veinte.

4 And they've got to go pick up   ḷáykẹpásar |pórlàschikás↓   Y hay que pasar por las chicas.
  the girls.

5 Juan says there's (plenty of)   hwan |diṣekẹaytyémpó↓   Juan dice que hay tiempo.
  time.

6 Here it's not like in the United   àkínọes |kómọènlòṣèstádòs̩únidós↓   Aquí no es como en los Estados
  States.   Unidos.

7 One's got to arrive late to   áykéṇyẹgártarɗẹ |àlàsfyéstàs↓   Hay que llegar tarde a las fiestas.
  parties.

8 'But the party is at an American   pèrólàfyestạ |ésèŋkásàɗẹàmèrikanóz | Pero la fiesta es en casa de
  home', says José.   ɗíṣéhósé↓   americanos —dice José.

9 It's the same as being in the   èzlómizmo |kestàrenlos̩estados   Es lo mismo que estar en los
  United States.   uníɗòs↓   Estados Unidos.

10 Jose's right. Juan's going to   hósétyenerraṣón↓ hwam |baɗarse   José tiene razón. Juan va a
   hurry, then.   prísạ |èntónṣès↓   darse prisa, entonces.

11 He'll be ready in a minute.   ènṇunmomentọ↑estalístò↓   En un momento está listo.

Juan, dígale a José que qué tal,   ketál |hósé↓ pasaɗelántè↓   Juan: ¿Qué tal José? Pasa
  que pase adelante, y dígale que   nọéstoylìstò |tóɗàbíà↓   adelante. No estoy
  Ud. no está listo todavía.   listo todavía.

José, dígale a José que
Dígale que no parece americano. Que ya son las siete
menos veinte. Y que hay que
pasar por las chicas.

ke↑ nopareṣes |ámérikanȯ↓

ɥásȯnlá(s)syete |ménȯzbeynte↑

ḷáykėpásar |pórḷáschikás↓

José: ¿¡Qué!? No pareces americano. Ya son las siete menos
veinte. Y hay que pasar
por las chicas.

Juan, dígale que hay tiempo, hombre,
que hay tiempo. Que aquí no es
como en los Estados Unidos. Que
aquí hay que llegar tarde a las
fiestas.

aytyémpọ |ómbré↓ áytyempȯ↓

ȧkínọes |komọenlos.estaḋos.unídȯs↓

ȧki↑áykė(l)ɥȩgártarḋẹ |ȧlȧsfyéstȧs↓

Juan: Hay tiempo, hombre, hay tiempo.
Aquí no es como en los Estados Unidos. Aquí hay que
llegar tarde a las fiestas.

José, dígale que sí, pero que la
fiesta es en casa de americanos. Que es lo mismo que estar
en los Estados Unidos.

si |pėrȯláfyestạ |és.ẹŋkásȧḋẹ

ȧmėrikanȯs↓ ėzlȯmizmo |

kėstár |ėnlós.ėstáḋós.únidȯs↓

José: Sí, pero la fiesta es en casa
de americanos. Es lo mismo
que estar en los Estados
Unidos.

Juan, dígale que tiene razón, que
Ud. va a darse prisa, entonces.
Y que en un momento está listo.

tyénezrraṣón↓ boyaḋarmeprísạ |

ėntónṣés↓ ėnụnmomentọ |estȯylístȯ↓

Juan: Tienes razón. Voy a darme
prisa, entonces. En un momento estoy listo.

NARRATIVE 3

1 Juan has to bathe, shave, and get
dressed, that's all.

hwán |tyénėkėbáŋyársẹ↑ áféytarsẹ

ibestírsé↓ esọestóḋȯ↓

Juan tiene que bañarse, afeitarse, y
vestirse, eso es todo.

2 But, gosh! What's wrong now?
There isn't any water.

perȯ |káṙambȧ↓ képasaórȧ↓

nọayágwȧ↓

Pero ¡caramba! ¿Qué pasa ahora?
No hay agua.

3 He can't shave or bathe.

nópwéḋẹȧfėytàrse |nıbaŋyársé↓

No puede afeitarse ni bañarse.

4 They'll *never* get to the party.

nóbáná↑yéɣár |nuŋkạ |áláfyéstá↓

No van a llegar nunca a la fiesta.

5 Jose can do one thing, then.

hóse |pwéɗẹạ̧ę̧erunakósạ |éntónˌe̢s↓

José puede hacer una cosa, entonces.

6 He can go pick up the girls first.

pwéɗépásár |pórláschikàs |priméró↓

Puede pasar por las chicas primero.

7 And then he'll come by for Juan.

ilwéɣo |pasaporhwán↓

Y luego pasa por Juan.

8 If Juan isn't ready then, Jose won't wait.

sihwan |noẹstálistọ |entónˌ̧es↑
hóse |noẹspérá↓

Si Juan no está listo entonces, José no espera.

DIALOG 3

José, pregúntele a Juan que qué tiene que hacer.

kétyeneskẹạ̧ę̧ér↓

José: ¿Qué tienes que hacer?

Juan, contéstele que tiene que bañarse, afeitarse y vestirse, que eso es todo. Pero ahora diga: ¡Ay, caramba!

téŋgókébáɲyarmẹ↑áféytarmẹibestírmè↓
esọestóɗó↓ áy↓ kárambá↓

Juan: Tengo que bañarme, afeitarme y vestirme, eso es todo..... ¡Ay, caramba!

José, pregúntele que qué le pasa ahora.

kétepásaorá↓

José: ¿Qué te pasa ahora?

Juan, contéstele que Ud. no puede bañarse ni afeitarse. Que no hay agua.	nópwéɖóbáŋyarme |nɪafeytármé↓ nọayágwá↓	Juan: No puedo bañarme ni afeitarme. No hay agua.
José, dígale que ¡no puede ser! Que Uds. no van a llegar nunca a la fiesta.	nopweɖesér↓ nóbamos |ảⓞyẹgárnuŋkạ | ảlảfyéstả↓	José: ¡No puede ser! No vamos a llegar nunca a la fiesta.
Juan, pregúntele que por qué no hace una cosa.	pórkenọaşesụnakósả↓	Juan: ¿Por qué no haces una cosa?
José, pregúntele que qué cosa.	kekósả↓	José: ¿Qué cosa?
Juan, dígale que por qué no pasa por las chicas primero y luego pasan por usted.	pórkenopasas |pórlàschikas |primero↑ ilwegopasampormí↓	Juan: ¿Por qué no pasas por las chicas primero y luego pasan por mí?
José, dígale que está bien, pero si él no está listo entonces, que Ud. no espera, que lo siente mucho.	ẻstabyén↓ pérósinọẹstảzlistọ | ẻntonşes↑ noẹspéró↓ lòsyéntomúchó↓	José: Está bien, pero si no estás listo entonces, no espero, lo siento mucho.

End of Tape 9B

Tape 10A

13.1   BASIC SENTENCES.   White and Molina go to a party.

After being introduced to Carmen, Jose's fiancée, and meeting his own date, John goes with the others to the party which a Latin American official is giving in honor of the newly arrived Americans.

ENGLISH SPELLING	AID TO LISTENING	SPANISH SPELLING
often	å—mė́nud̯ó↓	a menudo
White Hey, do they throw these parties here very often? (1)	óyė↓ dán |ėstasfyéstas͵akı |múyåmėnud̯o↑	*White* Oye, ¿dan estas fiestas aquí muy a menudo?
from time to time	dė̇—bė̇ş—eṇ—kwándó↓	de vez en cuando
Molina No, just every now and then. Why?	nó↓ sólo |d̯ėbė̇ş͵eŋkwándó↓ pórké↓	*Molina* No, sólo de vez en cuando, ¿por qué?
terrific	ėstúpendó↓	estupendo
White I think this one's terrific.	ésta |mėpåréşė |ėstúpendå↓	*White* Esta me parece estupenda.
to fix	fihár↓	fijar
fix yourself, notice (to pay attention)	fihátė↓ fiharsė↓	fíjate (fijarse)
dancing (to dance)	båylandó↓ båylár↓	bailando (bailar)

brunette	mòrénò↓	moreno
Look how that brunette's dancing!	fíhate |kómǫestábaylándǫ |ésàmòrénà↓	¡Fíjate cómo está bailando esa morena!
the care	èl—kwiɗaɗò↓	el cuidado
don't go (to go)	nò—ɓayàs↓ ìr↓	no vayas (ir)
to put in	mè̦tér↓	meter
the paw	là—patà↓	la pata
to put your foot in your mouth	mè̦ter—la—pátà↓	meter la pata

Molina
Careful. Don't go making any cracks!

kwiɗaɗò↓ nòɓayas \|ametérlapátà↓

Molina
¡Cuidado, no vayas a meter la pata!

the daughter	lǫ—íhà↓	la hija
the owner of the house	èl—sèŋyor—de—la—kásà↓	el señor de la casa

That's the daughter of our host.

ézlǫíha \|ɗèlsèŋyórɗèlákasà↓

Es la hija del señor de la casa.

look (to look)	mirà↓ mirár↓	mira (mirar)
(I) believed (to believe)	krè̦íà↓ krè̦ér↓	creía (creer)
(they) were, were being (to be) [2]	eràn↓ sèr↓	eran (ser)
quiet	tràŋkilò↓	tranquilo

Carmen
Say! I thought Americans were
  more reserved. (3)

  mırá↓ yokreía|kélós,ámérikanos|
  éránmástráŋkilós↓

  that way

  pór─ái↓

  the colonel

  él─kóronél↓

Molina
That man going that way is
  Colonel Harris.

  esekepasa|pórái↑ és,élkóronélhárris↓

  come (to come)

  bén↓ benír↓

Come on over and I'll introduce you.(4)

  bén↑itélópresentó↓

  the goblet

  lá─kopá↓

White
Let's take our drinks. (5)

  bamos,aʎyebárnoz|laskópás↓

  yours

  lá─túyá↓

Here's yours.

  ákityénezlatúyá↓

  to confuse

  kómfúndír↓

  don't yourself confuse
    (to confuse oneself)

  nó─te─komfúndás↓ kómfúndírsé↓

Carmen
Mira. Yo creía que los americanos eran más tranquilos.

  por ahí

  el coronel

Molina
Ese que pasa por ahí, es el
  Coronel Harris.

  ven (venir)

  Ven y te lo presento.

  la copa

White
Vamos a llevarnos las copas.

  la tuya

  Aquí tienes la tuya.

  confundir

  no te confundas
    (confundirse)

| hers | lá‑de‑éọyàↆ | la de ella |
| Carmen's | lá‑dé‑karmènↆ | la de Carmen |

Molina
Don't get them mixed; that's hers, Carmen's.

notekomfúndàsↆ ėzládeọ̀yàↆ

ládékarmènↆ

Molina
No te confundas. Es la de ella, la de Carmen.

White
Oh, sorry.

áↆsíↆ pėrdónↆ

White
Ah, sí, perdón.

| the girl | lá‑chikàↆ | la chica |
| at once, right away | ėn‑ségidàↆ | en seguida |

| Will you girls excuse us? | bwenó|chíkàsↆ kómpėrmisóↆ | Bueno, chicas. Con permiso. |
| We'll be right back. | ėnségida|bolbémòsↆ | En seguida volvemos. |

13.10   Notes on the basic sentences

(1) 'Hey' is not a very good translation of /óye/ *oye*, but neither is anything else. /óye/ is an attention‑attracter whose equivalent in English is usually some sort of gesture, such as raised eye‑brows, an upward lift of the head to call for attention — something to indicate that a remark of importance, however slight, is to be made.

(2) Note that the verb form here, an irregular Past II form (to be dealt with in Unit 18), is indicated as being Past II rather than Past I by the presence of *two translations:* simple past, 'were', and what may be called *durative past*. 'were being'.

(3) /míra/ *mira*, like the equivalent given here, 'Say', is essentially an empty exclamation of mild surprise. It may also be used like *oye* as an attention‑attracter to be sure the audience is paying attention to what one is about to say.

(4) The occurrence of two clitics in succession will be treated in Unit 20; for the moment, be certain you realize that /telo presénto↓/ *te lo presento* means 'I'll present him to you' and *not* 'I'll present you to him'.

(5) The reflexive clitics will be treated in Unit 24. Literally this sentence means 'Let's take the cups for ourselves' – i.e., 'which belong to us.'

13.2 DRILLS AND GRAMMAR

13.21 Pattern drills

13.21.1 /—ndo/ forms and the present progressive construction

A. Presentation of pattern

ILLUSTRATIONS

I'm thinking about that.	1	éstoy│pènsandǫen̬ésó↓	*Estoy pensando* en eso.
I'm not drinking as much now.	2	nǫéstoybebyendo│tántǫaórà↓	No *estoy bebiendo* tanto ahora.
_____	3	itú↓ kęęstazbebyéndó↓	Y tú, ¿ qué *estás bebiendo?*
You're finally translating.	4	pòrfın│estastraḍuşyéndó↓	Por fin *estás traduciendo.*
_____	5	éstaęstuḍyando↑	¿*Está estudiando?*
_____	6	éstátrábáhando│kómósèkrétaryà↓	*Está trabajando* como secretaria.

We're waiting for that moment.	7	èstámòs,éspérandǫ	esemoméntò↓	*Estamos esperando* ese momento.
We're just now arriving.	8	yaęstámoz	⌒yęǵándò↓	Ya *estamos llegando.*
How long have you been living here?	9	dézɖ̇ėkwandǫ	estambibyéndǫakí↓	¿Desde cuándo *están viviendo* aquí?
How those brunettes are dancing!	10	kómǫęstámbaylándǫ	esazmorénàs↓	¡Cómo *están bailando* esas morenas!

EXTRAPOLATION

	estár	/—ndo/ form	
		—ár	—ér, —ír
		—ándo	—yéndo
sg			
1	estóy		
2 fam	estás		kom—yéndo
2–3	está	abl—ándo	
pl 1	estámos		bib—yéndo
2–3	están		

NOTES

a. The progressive construction consists of a conjugated form of the verb /estár/ plus the /—ndo/ form of the verb.

b. /—ndo/ forms are invariable, that is, they never inflect for number, gender, etc.

13.21.11 Substitution drills - Person-number substitution

1 éO̯yos |éstámbúskando |apartaméntó↓

   yo_____↓   éstóybúskando |apartaméntó↓

   hwan_____↓   éstábúskando |apartaméntó↓

   karmen̯iyó_____↓   éstamoz |búskando |apartaméntó↓

   ústedes_____↓   éstámbúskando |apartaméntó↓

2 yó |estóytrábáhando |aóra↓

   nósotros_____↓   éstámóstrábáhando |aóra↓

   tú_____↓   éstástrábáhando |aóra↓

---

1 *Ellos* están buscando apartamento.

   Yo_____.   Estoy buscando apartamento.

   Juan_____.   Está buscando apartamento.

   Carmen y yo_____.   Estamos buscando apartamento.

   Uds. _____.   Están buscando apartamento.

2 *Yo* estoy trabajando ahora.

   Nosotros_____.   Estamos trabajando ahora.

   Tú_____.   Estás trabajando ahora.

úste∂_____↓   éstátrábáhandǫ|aórá↓

karmen_____↓   éstátrábáhandǫ|aórá↓

3 karmen|éstáprɛndyéndomúchó↓

   yo_____↓   éstoy|áprɛ̀ndyéndomúchó↓

   úste∂es_____↓   éstan|áprɛ̀ndyéndomúchó↓

   tu_____↓   éstas|áprɛ̀ndyéndomúchó↓

   nósotros_____↓   éstamos|áprɛ̀ndyéndomúchó↓

Ud._____.   Está trabajando ahora.

Carmen_____.   Está trabajando ahora.

3 *Carmen* está aprendiendo mucho.

   Yo_____.   Estoy aprendiendo mucho.

   Uds._____.   Están aprendiendo mucho.

   Tú_____.   Estás aprendiendo mucho.

   Nosotros_____.   Estamos aprendiendo mucho.

4 hwan̪ikármen |estaŋkomyéndó↓

   el_____↓   éstakomyéndó↓

   yo_____↓   éstoykomyéndó↓

   eʎas_____↓   éstaŋkomyéndó↓

   ústed_____↓   éstakomyéndó↓

5 hwan̪estaęskribyéndó↓

   eʎos_____↓   éstan |eskribyéndó↓

   eliyo_____↓   éstamos |eskribyéndó↓

   karmen̪ihwan_____↓   éstan |eskribyéndó↓

   yo_____↓   éstoy |eskribyéndó↓

---

4 *Juan y Carmen* están comiendo.

   El_____ .   Está comiendo.

   Yo_____ .   Estoy comiendo.

   Ellas_____ .   Están comiendo.

   Ud._____ .   Está comiendo.

5 *Juan* está escribiendo.

   Ellos_____ .   Están escribiendo.

   El y yo_____ .   Estamos escribiendo.

   Carmen y Juan_____ .   Están escribiendo.

   Yo_____ .   Estoy escribiendo.

Construction substitution

1 tomọágwà↓	èstóytómandọágwà↓
2 prónunşyazbyén↓	èstásprónúnşyandobyén↓
3 limpyanẹldormitóryó↓	èstánlimpyandọ|eldormitóryó↓
4 bibimos.enlas,afwérás↓	èstamoz|bibyendọenlas,afwérás↓
5 éskribọenlasálà↓	èstóyéskribyendọenlasálà↓
6 beben|agwaminerál↓	èstámbébyendọ|agwaminerál↓
7 komepókó↓	èstákómyendopókó↓

---

1 *Tomo* agua.	Estoy tomando agua.
2 *Pronuncias* bien.	Estás pronunciando bien.
3 *Limpian* el dormitorio.	Están limpiando el dormitorio.
4 *Vivimos* en las afueras.	Estamos viviendo en las afueras.
5 *Escribo* en la sala.	Estoy escribiendo en la sala.
6 *Beben* agua mineral.	Están bebiendo agua mineral.
7 *Come* poco.	Está comiendo poco.

13.21.12 Response drill

1 éstánústedes |trábáhando↑ǫestudyándó↓   èstámós,èstúdyandó↓

2 éstán,é(l)yǫzbáhandǫ↑osubyéndó↓   èstánsúbyendó↓

3 ésta,é(l)yàlábandǫ↑olimpyándó↓   èstálimpyandó↓

4 éstáųstédbébyendǫ↑okomyéndó↓   èstóykómyendó↓

[bébyéndó↓]   5 késtaşyéndǫél↓   èstábébyéndó↓

[trábáhandó↓]   6 késtanaşyéndǫé(l)yós↓   èstántrábáhandó↓

[éskribyéndó↓] 7 késtaşyéndǫustéd↓   èstóyéskribyéndó↓

---

1 ¿Están Uds. trabajando o estudiando?   Estamos estudiando.

2 ¿Están ellos bajando o subiendo?   Están subiendo.

3 ¿Está ella lavando o limpiando?   Está limpiando.

4 ¿Está Ud. bebiendo o comiendo?   Estoy comiendo.

(bebiendo)   5 ¿Qué está haciendo él?   Está bebiendo.

(trabajando)   6 ¿Qué están haciendo ellos?   Están trabajando.

(escribiendo)   7 ¿Qué está haciendo Ud.?   Estoy escribiendo.

[kómyéndó↓]   8 éstánųstédézbébyendo↑   no↓ éstámóskómyéndó↓

[trábáhandó↓]   9 éstáně().yás.éstúdyando↑   no↓ éstántrábáhandó↓

                10 éstáųstédálmórşandó↑   sı↓ éstóyálmórşandó↓

                11 éstaél|áb1ándǫespáņyol↑   sı↓ éstáblandǫespaņyól↓

                12 éstastú|aprándyéndómúcho↑   sı↓ éstoy|aprendyendomúchó↓

                13 éstábárryéndǫe().yá↑   sı↓ éstábárryéndó↓

(comiendo)   8 ¿Están Uds. bebiendo?   No, estamos comiendo.

(trabajando) 9 ¿Están ellas estudiando?   No, están trabajando.

             10 ¿Está Ud. almorzando?   Sí, estoy almorzando.

             11 ¿Está él hablando español?   Sí, está hablando español.

             12 ¿Estás tú aprendiendo mucho?   Sí, estoy aprendiendo mucho.

             13 ¿Está barriendo ella?   Sí, está barriendo.

13.21.13 Translation drill

1 I'm working at the Embassy.

éstóytrábàhandǫ |enlǫembahádà↓

Estoy trabajando en la Embajada.

2 We're living downtown.

estámózbibyéndǫ |enelşéntró↓

Estamos viviendo en el centro.

3 They're writing now.

estáṇeskribyéndǫ |aórá↓

Están escribiendo ahora.

4 I'm looking at the glasses.

éstóybyéndolazgáfàs↓

Estoy viendo las gafas.

5 Who's calling?

kyeṇesta(l)yamándó↓

¿Quién está llamando?

6 Where're you living?

dondestabibyéndó↓

¿Dónde está viviendo?

7 What are you all learning?

kestaṇaprendyéndó↓

¿Qué están aprendiendo?

8 What time are they arriving (these days)?

àkęorǫ |están(l)yegándó↓

¿A qué hora están llegando?

9 The girl is making (fixing) the beds.

làmúchachǫ |éstárréglandolaskámàs↓

La muchacha está arreglando las camas.

10 We're speaking less English.

éstámós,áblando |menosıŋglés↓

Estamos hablando menos inglés.

11 I'm not giving (any) tips (these days).

nǫéstóydando |propínàs↓

No estoy dando propinas.

12 They're always studying.   syémprę |éstanȩstuḓyándȯↆ   Siempre están estudiando.

13 He's going up in the elevator.   ȩstásúḃyéndǫ |enȩlas(s̹)ensórↆ   Está subiendo en el ascensor.

B. Discussion of pattern

The progressive construction in Spanish is closely paralleled by a similar construction in English, composed of a form of the verb *be* plus the *–ing* form of a verb: 'I'm going, he's going,' etc.

In Spanish the progressive construction consists of a form of the verb /estár/ and the /⌐ndo/ form of a verb, arranged together in a close construction which only rarely admits the appearance of any form intervening between them. In the comparable English construction, the relationship of the constituents is not so close; 'He's just now ating' in Spanish would be /yáȩstákomyéndoↆ/, rather then */estáyá komyéndoↆ/.

The English *–ing* form can be made plural, as in 'his comings and goings', but the /⌐ndo/ form in Spanish is invariable —it never changes or inflects for number, gender, etc. Analytically the /⌐ndo/ form is classed as a verb element in verb constructions, or as a verb modifier, a function class of words which typically do not inflect: /estudyándomúcho |sȩapréndemúchoↆ/.

While /estár/ is most frequently the conjugated verb that appears in the construction 'verb plus /⌐ndo/', others, such as /andár, /benír, (l)yegár, ír, segír/ , appear with /⌐ndo/ forms with different but related meanings. Thus:

/están—aprendyéndoↆ/   'They're learning'.

/bán—aprendyéndoↆ/   'They're beginning to learn'.

/ándan—aprendyéndoↆ/   'They're (out) learning'.

/sígen—aprendyéndoↆ/   'They're still learning'.

Usually the Spanish construction appears in contexts where the same English construction would be appropriate. One important exception is the use of the progressive construction in English with reference to future time. It's quite normal in English to say 'He's coming tonight', but in Spanish */estábınyéndǫ|éstanóche↓/would never occur (simple present would); the construction is limited to present or customary actions.

13.21.2 Possessive constructions with /de/

A. Presentation of pattern

ILLUSTRATIONS

This is our part.	1 éstąezlaparte|denosótrós↓	Esta es la parte *de nosotros*.
Pardón, is this your book?	2 pérdoné↓ ésestelibro|dęustéd↑	Perdone, ¿es éste el libro *de usted*?
Come in; that's your table.	3 adélanté↓ ákeǿyąezlamésa|dęustédés↓	Adelante; aquélla es la mesa *de ustedes*.
His car is excellent.	4 éláwtódel|es.eks(ş)elénté↓	El auto *de él* es excelente.
small	pékeŋyó↓	pequeño
Her room is very small.	5 élkwártódeǿyą|ézmuypekéŋyó↓	El cuarto *de ella* es muy pequeño.
Their furniture is expensive.	6 lózmwéblézdeǿyos|soŋkárós↓	Los muebles *de ellos* son caros.

Please hand me their (f) glasses (goblets).	7 pòrfàbór↓ pàsèmèlàskópàzdé(l)yàs↓	Por favor, páseme las copas *de ellas*.
_____	8 èlàpàrtámèntò |dèlsèɲyórmòlínà↓	El apartamento *del señor* Molina.
_____	9 èzlaiha |dèlsèɲyórdèlàkásà↓	Es la hija *del señor* de la casa.

EXTRAPOLATION

Possessives	
Forms	**Constructions**
la—kása—mía (c) la—kása—nwéstra	_____ (a) la—kása—de—nosótros (b)
la—kása—túya	_____ (a)
la—kása—súya	la—kása—de—ustéd la—kása—de—ustédes la—kása—de—él la—kása—de—é(l)ya la—kása—de—é(l)yos la—kása—de—é(l)yas

NOTES

a. Possessive constructions equivalent to /mío/ and /túyo/ do not occur.

b. The phrase /de—nosótros/ as part of a possessive construction occurs more frequently than /nwéstro/ in certain dialect areas.

c. For /la—kása—mía/ etc., read also /el—líbro—mío/, /las—kásas—mías/, and /los—líbros—míos/.

507

13.21.21 Substitution drill — Construction substitution

Problem:

ésａｅｚlamígasúyà↓   [dｅｅ́1↓]

éstａｅ(s)sukwéntá↓   [dｅùstéａ↓]

Answer:

ésａｅｚlamígａｄél↓

éstａ|ｅｚlakwéntａｄｅustéａ↓

Problem:

Esa es la amiga *suya*. (de él)

Esta es *su* cuenta.   (de Ud.)

Answer:

Esa es la amiga de él.

Esta es la cuenta de Ud.

1 éstaezlarrópasúyá↓   [dęústedés↓]   éstạ|ezlarrópadęustédés↓

2 élápártámentosuyǫ|ezgrándé↓   [deꝊyá↓]   élápártámentodeꝊyạ|ezgrándé↓

3 lánobyasuyạ|ezbonítá↓   [dęústed↓]   lánobyadęusted|ezbonítá↓

4 éstạe(s)sumalétá↓   [dęústedés↓]   éstạ|ezlamaletadęustédés↓

5 esạe(s)sufamílyá↓   [deꝊyá↓]   esạ|ezlafamílyadeꝊyá↓

---

1 Esta es la ropa *suya*. (de Uds.)   Esta es la ropa de Uds.

2 El apartamento *suyo* es grande. (de ella)   El apartamento de ella es grande.

3 La novia *suya* es bonita. (de Ud.)   La novia de Ud. es bonita.

4 Esta es *su* maleta. (de Uds.)   Esta es la maleta de Uds.

5 Esa es *su* familia. (de ella)   Esa es la familia de ella.

6 éstas |so(n)nwéstrasfótòs↓   [dénósótrós↓]   éstas |sònlásfótozdenosótrós↓

7 syámìgaeskasádà↓   [dél↓]   lámígàdeleskasádà↓

8 súsàmigo(s)sonsoltérós↓   [deⁿyá↓]   lósàmígozdeⁿya |sonsoltérós↓

9 sútaksi |estaladeréchà↓   [deⁿyós↓]   éltáksideⁿyos|estaladeréchà↓

---

6 Estas son *nuestras* fotos. (de nosotros)   Estas son las fotos de nosotros.

7 *Su* amiga es casada. (de él)   La amiga de él es casada.

8 *Sus* amigos son solteros. (de ella)   Los amigos de ella son solteros.

9 *Su* taxi está a la derecha. (de ellos)   El taxi de ellos está a la derecha.

13.21.22 Translation drill

1 Their apartment is nice.

élápártámento |deⓁyas |ezⱠonító↓

El apartamento de ellas es bonito.

2 Her family is very large.

láfámilya |deⓁya |ézmuygránde↓

La familia de ella es muy grande.

3 His room (number) is fifteen.

élkwártódel |eselkínṣe↓

El cuarto de él es el quince.

4 All your friends are Americans.

todoz |los̩amigozdⓔusteⱠes |son
amerikánós↓

Todos los amigos de Uds. son
americanos.

5 Your suitcases are very good.

lázmáletaz |dⓔustẹⱠ |sónmuyⱠwénás↓

Las maletas de Ud. son muy buenas.

6 His girl friend is Spanish.

lánóⱠyadel |es̩espaŋyólá↓

La novia de él es española.

7 We can't find her house.

noeŋkontrámoz |lákasadéⓁyá↓

No encontramos la casa de ella.

8 Their bedroom is small.

éldórmitóryodeⓁyos |espekéŋyó↓

El dormitorio de ellos es pequeño.

9 You should see his car.

áykéⱠer |élawtodél↓

Hay que ver el auto de él.

End of Tape 10A

B. Discussion of pattern

A possessive construction is a phrase which consists of the phrase relator /de/ plus a noun or a pronoun. This phrase appears immediately after a noun (or sometimes after the verb /sér/) and indicates the possessor or owner of the modified noun.

In units 9 and 11 possessive forms were presented. In the present extrapolation the full forms are listed along with the equivalent possessive constructions which occur. As can be seen in the chart, the 2-3 form /súya/ is listed as the equivalent of at least six constructions. The fact that /súya/ can be the equivalent of six different constructions implies that the constructions give the more definite information. The phrases /de-ustéd, de-él/ etc. are used when the context does not supply all the information needed to identify the reference of the possessive. Since /súyo – su/ most often means /de-ustéd/, the constructions /de-ustédes, de-él, de-élya, de-élyos, de-élyas/ are more frequently used to refer to 'yours, his, hers, theirs' than is /súyo – su/ with these meanings.

The construction /de-nosótros/ is not used extensively in some dialects, but in others, as in Chile, it is used to the almost complete exclusion of /nwéstro/ .

Tape 10B

13.21.3 Nominalized possessive constructions

A. Presentation of pattern

ILLUSTRATIONS

———————	1 él̩mi̩o̩eshwán↓	*El mío* es Juan.
Can you clean ours too?	2 pwéd̩elimpyar│elnwéstrotambyén↑	¿Puede limpiar *el nuestro* también?
———————	3 ák̩ityénezlatúy̩a↓	Aquí tienes *la tuya*.
———————	4 élsuyo̩ezmazgrándè↓ no↑	*El suyo* es más grande¿no?

each		kádá↓	cada

| Every (man) to his own (taste). | 5 | kádaụno│konlosúyó↓ | Cada uno con *lo suyo*. |

| In ours there isn't much activity. | 6 | <u>énládénósótroz</u>│ņọaymúchomobımyéntó↓ | En *la de nosotros* no hay mucho movimiento. |

| Yours is bigger, isn't it? | 7 | <u>éldeụstéd</u>│ezmazgrándè↓ nó↑ | *El de usted* es más grande, ¿no? |

| In yours there's almost no activity. | 8 | <u>énlázdeụstedes</u>│kásinọaymobımyéntó↓ | En *las de ustedes* casi no hay movimiento. |

| _____ | 9 | nó↓ ésigwálaldél↓ | No, es igual *al de él*. |

| _____ | 10 | ézlá<u>dé()yá↓ láde</u>karmén↓ | Es *la de ella, la de Carmen*. |

| No, it's just like theirs (m). | 11 | nó↓ ésigwálalde<u>()yós↓</u> | No, es igual *al de ellos*. |

| They're theirs, the girls'. | 12 | sónlázde()yás↓ <u>lázdeláschıkás↓</u> | Son *las de ellas, las de las chicas*. |

EXTRAPOLATION

Possessive forms and constructions		Nominalized [a]	
la‑kása‑mía [c] la‑kása‑nwéstra	_____ [b] la‑kása‑de‑nosótros	la‑mía [c] la‑nwéstra	_____ [b] la‑de‑nosótros
la‑kása‑túya	_____ [b]	la‑túya	_____ [b]
la‑kása‑súya	la‑kása‑de‑ustéd la‑kása‑de‑ustédes	la‑súya	la‑de‑ustéd la‑de‑ustédes
	la‑kása‑de‑él la‑kása‑de‑é(l)ya la‑kása‑de‑é(l)yos la‑kása‑de‑é(l)yas		la‑de‑él la‑de‑é(l)ya la‑de‑é(l)yos la‑de‑é(l)yas
		lo‑súyo	

NOTES

a. Nominalization of these constructions is accomplished by omitting the noun.

b. Combinations which do not occur are marked by a dash.

c. For /la‑kása‑mía/ , /la‑mía/ , etc., read also /el‑mío/ , /las‑mías/ , /los‑míos/ etc.

13.21.31 Substitution drill — Construction substitution

Problem:

láz(l)yábézmɪaz |noe̯stan̪akíↆ

Answer:

lázmɪaz |noe̯stan̪akíↆ

1 lákasasuya̯ |éstaşérkàↆ   làsuya̯estaşérkàↆ

2 èlápártámen̪tosuyo |tyénéɗozbáɲyòsↆ   élsuyo |tyénéɗozbáɲyòsↆ

Problem:

Las llaves mías no están aquí.

Answer:

Las mías no están aquí.

1 *La casa suya* está cerca.   La suya está cerca.

2 *El apartamento suyo* tiene dos baños.   El suyo tiene dos baños.

3 lánobyamía |ŋǫézbonítá↓   lámía |ŋǫézbonítá↓

4 lá(s)síļya⊕súyas⊧éstanalạışkyérđá↓   lá⊕súyas⊧éstanalạışkyérđá↓

5 élsófasúyǫ |eskómóđó↓   élsúyǫeskómóđó↓

6 lạíhátuyạ |ézmúybonítá↓   látuyạ |ézmúybonítá↓

7 lóʒmweblestúyos |sónmúybonítós↓   lóstúyos |sónmúybonítós↓

---

3 *La novia mía* no es bonita.   La mía no es bonita.

4 *Las sillas suyas* están a la izquierda.   Las suyas están a la izquierda.

5 *El sofá suyo* es cómodo.   El suyo es cómodo.

6 *La hija tuya* es muy bonita.   La tuya es muy bonita.

7 *Los muebles tuyos* son muy bonitos.   Los tuyos son muy bonitos.

13.21.32 Translation drill

1 There's *my* car; and there's *yours*, too.	ái̠e̠stá |e̠lawtomío↓ i̠éldeu̠ste̠de̠stambyén↓	Ahí está el auto mío y el de Uds. también.
2 *My* family isn't large. What about *yours?*	láfámi̠lyamía |no̠ezgrándé↓ iláde̠u̠ste̠d↑	La familia mía no es grande. ¿Y la de Ud.?
3 This is our table. (Which is) theirs?	ésta̠eznwéstramésá↓ iláde(l)yos↑	Esta es nuestra mesa. ¿Y la de ellos?
4 This is John's check. (Which is) hers?	éste̠ |és.élcheke̠de̠hwán↓ i̠élde(l)ya↑	Este es el cheque de Juan. ¿Y el de ella?
5 My daughter is single. What about theirs?	la̠íhámi̠a̠e(s)soltérá↓ iláde(l)yos↑	La hija mía es soltera. ¿Y la de ellos?
6 Carmen's family arrives on Friday. What about yours?	láfámi̠lya̠de̠kármen |(l)ye̠ga̠e̠lbyérnés↓ iláde̠u̠ste̠de̠s↑	La familia de Carmen llega el viernes. ¿Y la de Uds.?
7 *My* friends are arriving on Saturday. What about *yours?*	lós.ámi̠gozmíoz |(l)ye̠ga̠ne̠lsába̠d̠o̠↓ ilózde̠u̠ste̠d↑	Los amigos mios llegan el sábado. ¿Y los de Ud.?
8 John's apartment doesn't have (any) gas. Does hers?	élápártámento̠de̠hwan |nótye̠ne̠gás↓ i̠élde(l)ya↑	El apartamento de Juan no tiene gas. ¿Y el de ella?
9 *My* girl friend is staying at the American Hotel. Where's *yours* staying?	lánobyamia̠ |ésta̠e̠ne̠lote̠lamerikáno̠↓ ilátuya↑	La novia mía está en el Hotel Americano. ¿Y la tuya?

B. Discussion of pattern

Possessive forms (full forms only) as well as possessive constructions can occur nominalized. These nominalized constructions serve to make a second reference to a noun which has just been mentioned or is readily understood from the context.

The nominalization can be viewed as the simple omission of the noun from the construction. Thus /el—líbro—mío/ becomes /el—mío/, where /mío/ , now nominalized, is the head of the phrase. Note that the English equivalent 'mine' never occurs preceded by 'the'. In the possessive construction /el—líbro—de—ustéd/, the nominalized version is /el—de—ustéd/, where /el/ is the nominalized form, modified by the phrase /de—ustéd/.

One nominalized possessive, /lo—súyo/, may but usually does not occur as a possessive form; that is, it usually appears only nominalized. This is not surprising , since the neuter /lo—súyo/ cannot modify a noun, there being no neuter nouns in Spanish. Thus /tódos |bán̠a traér |losúyo↓/ probably refers to a group of things thought of as a composite whole, translating 'They're all going to bring their own stuff.'

13.21.4   Question intonation patterns — Information questions

A. Presentation of pattern

ILLUSTRATIONS

1   kes̠ésó↓

    2 1 1↓
    ¿Qué es eso?

    kes̠esó↓

    2 3 1↓
    ¿Qué es eso?

2   dondestalakáhá↓

    2   2   11↓
    ¿Dónde está la caja?

    dondestalakahá↓

    2   2   31↓
    ¿Dónde está la caja?

518

_____   3 ákomǫestaęlkámbyò↓

                                                                    1 2   2   1 1↓
                                                                    ¿A cómo está el cambio?

_____   ákomǫestaęlkambyò↓

                                                                    1 2   2   3 1↓
                                                                    ¿A cómo está el cambio?

EXTRAPOLATION

Information question uncolored	Information question emphatic
/1211↓/	/1231↓/

NOTES

a. The intonation patterns of information questions parallel those of statements.

13.21.41 Substitution drill — pattern substitution

Problem:

àdóndebámós↓

Answer:

àdondebamós↓

Problem:

1 2   1 1↓
¿A dónde vamos?

Answer:

1 2   3 1↓
¿A dónde vamos?

1   párákétrabahámós↓   párákétrabahamós↓

2   dédondebyénén↓   dédondebyenén↓

3   dédondérés↓   dédonderés↓

4   pórkestúdyán↓   pórkestudyán↓

5   ikwándoloarréglán↓   ikwándoloarreglán↓

---

1 2 1 1↓		1 2 3 1↓
1 ¿Para qué trabajamos?		¿Para qué trabajamos?
1 2 1 1↓		1 2 3 1↓
2 ¿De dónde vienen?		¿De dónde vienen?
1 2 1 1↓		1 2 3 1↓
3 ¿De dónde eres?		¿De dónde eres?
1 2 1 1↓		1 2 3 1↓
4 ¿Por qué estudian?		¿Por qué estudian?
1 2 1 1↓		1 2 3 1↓
5 ¿Y cuándo lo arréglan?		¿Y cuándo lo arreglan?

6 idondelozmándás↓   idóndelozmandás↓

7 ikómolokyérès↓   ikómolokyerés↓

8 ikwandolo̞alkílán↓   ikwandolo̞alkɪlán↓

9 ikwandolobémós↓   ikwandolobemós↓

10 idondekómén↓   idóndekomén↓

11 ikwantodebémós↓   ikwantodebemós↓

```
     1 2    1 1↓
6 ¿Y dónde los mandas?
```

```
     1 2    1 1↓
7 ¿Y cómo lo quieres?
```

```
     1 2      11↓
8 ¿Y cuándo lo alquilan?
```

```
     1 2    1 1↓
9 ¿Y cuándo lo vemos?
```

```
     1 2    1 1↓
10 ¿Y dónde comen?
```

```
     1 2    1 1↓
11 ¿Y cuánto debemos?
```

```
     1 2     3 1↓
¿Y dónde los mandas?
```

```
     1 2     3 1↓
¿Y cómo lo quieres?
```

```
     1 2      31↓
¿Y cuándo lo alquilan?
```

```
     1 2     3 1↓
¿Y cuándo lo vemos?
```

```
     1 2     3 1↓
¿Y dónde comen?
```

```
     1 2     3 1↓
¿Y cuánto debemos?
```

B.   Discussion of pattern

Information questions are those which cannot be answered by a simple yes or no, but rather must be answered by a statement. Information questions normally begin with a question word, equivalent to 'who, what, when, why, where,' etc. in English.

The intonation patterns appropriate for information questions are the same ones used for statements:/1211↓/is normal, and /1231↓/ adds special emphasis, or in some cases adds the idea of politeness. When a contrast is additionally implied by the occurrence of /entónşes↓/ after an information question, the /1231↓/ pattern is almost compulsory:

```
    1    2      3 1  1  1   1
/paraké trabahámos |entónşes↓/
```
What are we working for, then?

```
  1  2   3 1  1   1   1
/ded ónd éres |entónşes↓/
```
Where're you from, then?

Since these questions very often begin with the stressed syllable of the question word, the first number of the intonation pattern formula is often lost.

13.22   Replacement drills

A   dán |estasfyéstas.akɪ |amenúdo↑

1 _____ debéşeŋkwándo↑   dán |estasfyéstas.akɪ |debéşeŋkwándo↑

2 _____ aɪ _____ ↑   dán |estasfyéstas.aɪ |debéşeŋkwándo↑

3 _____ trágos _____ ↑   dán |estostrágos.aɪ |debéşeŋkwándo↑

4 ___ esos _____ ↑   dán |esostrágos.aɪ |debéşeŋkwándo↑

5 aşen _____ ↑   aşen |esostrágos.aɪ |debéşeŋkwándo↑

6 _____ trabaho _____ ↑   aşen |esetrabahoaɪ |debéşeŋkwándo↑

7 _____ syémpre↑   aşen |esetrabahoaɪ |syémpre↑

A   ¿Dan estas fiestas aquí a menudo?

1 ¿_____ de vez en cuando?   ¿Dan estas fiestas aquí de vez en cuando?

2 ¿_____ ahí _____ ?   ¿Dan estas fiestas ahí de vez en cuando?

3 ¿_____ tragos _____ ?   ¿Dan estos tragos ahí de vez en cuando?

4 ¿___ esos _____ ?   ¿Dan esos tragos ahí de vez en cuando?

5 ¿Hacen _____ ?   ¿Hacen esos tragos ahí de vez en cuando?

6 ¿_____ trabajo _____ ?   ¿Hacen ese trabajo ahí de vez en cuando?

7 ¿_____ siempre?   ¿Hacen ese trabajo ahí siempre?

B   ésta |mépáréşéstúpéndâↆ

1   éstaz_____ↆ   ésⴱaz |mépáréşénॖéstúpéndásↆ

2   _____bwenásↆ   éstaz |mépáréşémbwenásↆ

3   éste_____ↆ   éste |mépáréşébwenóↆ

4   _____malóↆ   éste |mépáréşémalóↆ

5   ákéˆya_____ↆ   ákéˆya |mépáréşémaláↆ

6   _____ éks(ş)élentésↆ ákéˆyaz |mépáréşénॖéks(ş)élentésↆ

7   ákel_____ↆ   ákél |mépáréşéks(ş)élentèↆ

B   Esta me parece estupenda.

1   Estas_____.   Estas me parecen estupendas.

2   _____buenas.   Estas me parecen buenas.

3   Este_____.   Este me parece bueno.

4   _____malo.   Este me parece malo.

5   Aquélla_____.   Aquélla me parece mala.

6   _____excelentes.   Aquéllas me parecen excelentes.

7   Aquél_____.   Aquél me parece excelente.

525

C   fíhate |kómo̞estábaylándo̞ |esamo̞réná↓

1 _____chíkás↓   fíhate |kómo̞estámbaylándo̞ |esaschíkás↓

2 _____ake̞(l)y̞as____↓   fíhate |kómo̞estámbaylándo̞ |ake̞(l)y̞aschíkás↓

3 _____bebyéndo̞_____↓   fíhate |kómo̞estámbebyéndo̞ |ake̞(l)y̞aschíkás↓

4 _____se̞ny̞ór↓   fíhate |kómo̞estabebyéndo̞ |akélse̞ny̞ór↓

5 _____ablándo̞_____↓   fíhate |kómo̞establándo̞ |akélse̞ny̞ór↓

6 _____ko̞ŋkyén_____↓   fíhate |ko̞ŋkyén,establándo̞ |akélse̞ny̞ór↓

7 _____se̞ny̞órés↓   fíhate |ko̞ŋkyén,estan,ablándo̞ |ake̞(l)y̞o̞(s)se̞ny̞órés↓

C   Fíjate cómo está bailando esa morena.

1 _____chicas.   Fíjate cómo están bailando esas chicas.

2 _____aquellas__.   Fíjate cómo están bailando aquellas chicas.

3 _____bebiendo_____.   Fíjate cómo están bebiendo aquellas chicas.

4 _____señor.   Fíjate cómo está bebiendo aquel señor.

5 _____hablando_____.   Fíjate cómo está hablando aquel señor.

6 _____con quién_____.   Fíjate con quién está hablando aquel señor.

7 _____señores.   Fíjate con quién están hablando aquellos señores.

D   ézlaiha |delséɲyordelakásá↓

1 ____ihaz _____ ↓   sònlás,ihaz |délsèɲyordelakásá↓

2 _____ séɲyora____ ↓   sònlás,ihaz |délásèɲyoradelakásá↓

3 ____ámigo _____ ↓   és,élámigo |délásèɲyoradelakásá↓

4 ____otro _____ ↓   és,otroamigo |délásèɲyoradelakásá↓

5 sómòs _____ ↓   sómòs,otros |àmigoz |délásèɲyoradelakásá↓

6 _____ séɲyorez ____ ↓   sómòs,otros |amigoz |délò(s)séɲyorezdelakásá↓

7 sóy _____ ↓   sóyotroamigo |délò(s)séɲyorezdelakásá↓

D   Es la hija del señor de la casa.

1 ____hijas _____ .   Son las hijas del señor de la casa.

2 _____ señora _____ .   Son las hijas de la señora de la casa.

3 ____amigo _____ . .   Es el amigo de la señora de la casa.

4 ____otro _____ .   Es otro amigo de la señora de la casa.

5 Somos _____ .   Somos otros amigos de la señora de la casa.

6 _____ señores _____ .   Somos otros amigos de los señores de la casa.

7 Soy _____ .   Soy otro amigo de los señores de la casa.

E ésekepása |pòrá↑és̬élkórónelhárris↓

1 _____séɲyóra_____↓   ésakepása |pòrá↑ézlàséɲyorahárris↓

2 _____míá↓   ésakepása |pòrá↑ézlàséɲyoramíá↓

3 _____ámıgo_____↓   ésekepása |pòrá↑és̬élámıgomíó↓

4 ákeⓁyos_____↓   ákeⓁyos |kepásan |pòrá↑sónlósámıgozmíós↓

5 _____únós_____↓   ákeⓁyos |kepásan |pòrá↑sónùnós̬àmıgozmíós↓

6 _____súyòs↓   ákeⓁyos |kepásan |pòrá↑sónùnós̬àmıgoⒺsúyòs↓

7 _____ámıga_____↓   ákeⓁya |kepása |pòrá↑és̬ùnàmıgasúyà↓

E   Ese que pasa por ahí es el Coronel Harris.

1 _____señora_____,   Esa que pasa por ahí es la señora Harris.

2 _____ mía.   Esa que pasa por ahí es la señora mía.

3 _____amıgo_____.   Ese que pasa por ahí es el amigo mío.

4 Aquéllos_____.   Aquéllos que pasan por ahí son los amigos
                                      míos.

5 _____unos_____.   Aquéllos que pasan por ahí son unos amigos
                                      míos.

6 _____ suyos .   Aquéllos que pasan por ahí son unos amigos
                                      suyos.

7 _____amıga_____.   Aquélla que pasa por ahí es una amiga suya.

F   ákɪtyénezlatúyà↓

1 _____ túyò↓   ákɪtyénes̬eltúyò↓

2 __ęsta_____ ↓   ákięstaęltúyò↓

3 _____ mías↓   ákięstanlazmías↓

4 áɪ_____ ↓   áięstanlazmías↓

5 _____ótraz__ ↓   áięstan|otrazmías↓

6 _____ nwéstrôs↓   áięstan|otroznwéstrôs↓

7 _____ęl_____ ↓   áięstaęlnwéstrò↓

F   Aquí tienes la tuya.

1 _____ tuyo.   Aquí tienes el tuyo.

2 _____está_____ .   Aquí está el tuyo.

3 _____ mías.   Aquí están las mías.

4 Ahí_____ .   Ahí están las mías.

5 _____ otras__ .   Ahí están otras mías.

6 _____ nuestros.   Ahí están otros nuestros.

7 _____ el _____ .   Ahí está el nuestro.

13.23   Variation drills

A   nó↓ sólodebeşeŋkwándó↓ porké↓   No, sólo de vez en cuando.
                                            ¿Por qué?

1 No, just on Sundays. Why?   nó↓ sólolozdomíngós↓ porké↓   No, sólo los domingos. ¿Por qué?

2 No, just on Fridays. Why?   nó↓ sólolozbyérnés↓ porké↓   No, sólo los viernes. ¿Por qué?

3 No, just on Saturdays. Why?   nó↓ sólolo(s)sábádós↓ porké↓   No, sólo los sábados. ¿Por qué?

4 No, just in the morning. Why? nó↓ sóloenlamaɲyáná↓ porké↓   No, sólo en la mañana. ¿Por qué?

5 No, just at night. Why?   nó↓ sóloenlanóchè↓ porké↓   No, sólo en la noche. ¿Por qué?

6 No, just in the afternoon. Why? nó↓ sóloenlatárdè↓ porké↓   No, sólo en la tarde. ¿Por qué?

7 No, just in the room. Why?   nó↓ sóloeɲelkwártó↓ porké↓   No, sólo en el cuarto. ¿Por qué?

B kwiḋaḋó↓ nóbayas |àmétérlapátà↓   ¡Cuidado, no vayas a meter la pata!

1 Careful, don't go eat that!   kwiḋaḋó↓ nóbayas |àkómerésô↓   ¡Cuidado, no vayas a comer eso!

2 Careful, don't go see that!   kwiḋaḋó↓ nóbayas |àberésô↓   ¡Cuidado, no vayas a ver eso!

3 Careful, don't go drink that!   kwiḋaḋó↓ nóbayas |àbéberésô↓   ¡Cuidado, nc vayas a beber eso!

4 Careful, don't go do that!   kwiḋaḋó↓ nóbayas |àşerésó↓   ¡Cuidado, no vayas a hacer eso!

5 Careful, don't go say that!   kwiḋaḋó↓ nóbayas |àḋèşirésó↓   ¡Cuidado, no vayas a decir eso!

6 Careful, don't go buy that!   kwiḋaḋó↓ nóbayas |àkómprarésô↓   ¡Cuidado, no vayas a comprar eso!

7 Careful, don't go try that!   kwiḋaḋó↓ nóbayas |àpróbarésó↓   ¡Cuidado, no vayas a probar eso!

C mírá↓ yókreía|kèlôs̥ámèrikános|éránmástráŋkilôs↓

Mira, yo creía que los americanos eran más tranquilos.

1 Say, I thought (the) apartments were more expensive.

mírá↓ yókreía|kèlôs̥ápàrtámèntos| éránmáskarôs↓

Mira, yo creía que los apartamentos eran más caros.

2 Say, I thought (the) hotels were more expensive.

mírá↓ yókreía|kèlôs̥óteles|érán máskarôs↓

Mira, yo creía que los hoteles eran más caros.

3 Say, I thought (the) restaurants were less expensive.

mírá↓ yókreía|kèlôzrrèstôranes| éránmázbàratôs↓

Mira, yo creía que los restoranes eran más baratos.

4 Say, I thought (the) houses were cheaper.

mírá↓ yókreía|kèláskasas|érán mázbàratàs↓

Mira, yo creía que las casas eran más baratas.

5 Say, I thought the rooms were bigger.

mírá↓ yókreía|kèlôskwártos|érán mázgrándés↓

Mira, yo creía que los cuartos eran más grandes.

6 Say, I thought the embassy was prettier.

mírá↓ yókreía|kèlaèmbàhàd̥a|érà mázbónitá↓

Mira, yo creía que la embajada era más bonita.

7 Say, I thought the downtown was nicer.

mírá↓ yókreía|kèls̥éntro|érà mázbónitó↓

Mira, yo creía que el centro era más bonito.

D   bámos | aȷ̌ebárnozlaskópàs↓   Vamos a llevarnos las copas.

1 Let's take our chair.   bámos | aȷ̌ebárnozlasíȷ̌à↓   Vamos a llevarnos la silla.

2 Let's take our pen.   bámos | aȷ̌ebárnozlaplúmà↓   Vamos a llevarnos la pluma.

3 Let's take our newspaper.   bámos | aȷ̌ebárnos̩elperyódikò↓   Vamos a llevarnos el periódico.

4 Let's take our car.   bámos | aȷ̌ebárnos̩eláwtò↓   Vamos a llevarnos el auto.

5 Let's take our shirts.   bámos | aȷ̌ebárnozlaskamísàs↓   Vamos a llevarnos las camisas.

6 Let's take our suits.   bámos | aȷ̌ebárnozlostráhès↓   Vamos a llevarnos los trajes.

7 Let's take our furniture.   bámos | aȷ̌ebárnozlozmwéblès↓   Vamos a llevarnos los muebles.

E nótekomfúndàs↓ ézládeÓyá↓

   ládékarmén↓

No te confundas. Es la de ella, la de
Carmen.

1 Don't get them mixed. That's
  hers, Bertha's.

nótekomfúndàs↓ ézládeÓyá↓ ládébertá↓

No te confundas. Es la de ella, la de
Berta.

2 Don't get them mixed. That's
  his, Jose's.

nótekomfúndàs↓ ézládél↓ ládéhòsé↓

No te confundas. Es la de él, la de
José.

3 Don't get them mixed.
  That's John's.

nótekomfúndàs↓ ézládéhwàn↓

No te confundas. Es la de Juan.

4 Don't get them mixed. That's
  (m) hers.

nótekomfúndàs↓ és̩éldeÓyá↓

No te confundas. Es el de ella.

5 Don't get them mixed. That's
  (m) theirs (f).

nótekomfúndàs↓ és̩éldeÓyás↓

No te confundas. Es el de ellas.

6 Don't get them mixed. That's
  (m) theirs (m).

nótekomfúndàs↓ és̩éldeÓyós↓

No te confundas. Es el de ellos.

7 Don't get them mixed. They're (m)
  theirs.

nótekomfúndàs↓ sónlòzdeÓyós↓

No te confundas. Son los de ellos.

F bwénȯ|chíkȧs↓ kȯmpȧrmísȯ↓

   énségidȧbolbémȯs↓

1	Will you girls excuse us? We'll be back tomorrow.	bwénȯ|chíkȧs↓ kȯmpȧrmísȯ↓ máɲyanabolbémȯs↓

Bueno, chicas. Con permiso. En
seguida volvemos.

1 Will you girls excuse us?
  We'll be back tomorrow.

bwénȯ|chíkȧs↓ kȯmpȧrmísȯ↓

máɲyanabolbémȯs↓

Bueno, chicas. Con permiso.
Mañana volvemos.

2 Will you girls excuse us?
  We'll be back Monday.

bwénȯ|chíkȧs↓ kȯmpȧrmísȯ↓

élune⁻bolbémȯs↓

Bueno, chicas. Con permiso.
El lunes volvemos.

3 Will you girls excuse us?
  We'll be back some other
  day.

bwénȯ|chíkȧs↓ kȯmpȧrmísȯ↓ ótro

diabolbémȯs↓

Bueno, chicas. Con permiso.
Otro día volvemos.

4 Will you boys excuse us?
  We'll be back later.

bwénȯ|mùcháchȯs↓ kȯmpȧrmísȯ↓

déspwézbolbémȯs↓

Bueno, muchachos. Con permiso.
Después volvemos.

5 Well gentlemen, we'll be
  back tonight.

bwénȯ|sèɲyórès↓ éstànochebolbémȯs↓

Bueno, señores. Esta noche
volvemos.

6 Well ladies, we'll be back
  this afternoon.

bwénȯ|sèɲyórȧs↓ éstàtardebolbémȯs↓

Bueno, señoras. Esta tarde
volvemos.

7 Well Charles, we'll be back
  in the morning.

bwénȯ|kárlós↓ ènlàmáɲyanabolbémȯs↓

Bueno, Carlos. Mañana volvemos.

13.24   Review drill — placement of negative particle

1 I'm not married.   nosóykasádȯ↓   No soy casado.

2 I'm not single.   nosóysoltérȯ↓   No soy soltero.

3 I'm not Spanish.   nosóyespaŋyól↓   No soy español.

4 I'm not American.   nosóyamerıkánȯ↓   No soy americano.

5 I'm not English.   nosóyıŋglés↓   No soy inglés.

6 I'm not ready.   noȩstóylístȯ↓   No estoy listo.

7 I'm not fat (now).   noȩstóygórdȯ↓   No estoy gordo.

8 I'm not comfortable.   noȩstóykómȯdȯ↓   No estoy cómodo.

9 I'm not busy.   noȩstóyokupádȯ↓   No estoy ocupado.

10 I'm not helping.   noȩstóyayudándȯ↓   No estoy ayudando

11 I'm not studying.   noȩstóyestudyándȯ↓   No estoy estudiando.

12 I'm not learning.   noȩstóyaprendyéndȯ↓   No estoy aprendiendo.

13 I'm not writing.   noȩstóyeskrıbyéndȯ↓   No estoy escribiendo.

13.3   CONVERSATION STIMULUS

NARRATIVE 1

1 This is not Juan's glass.

ésta |noézlakópaďehwán↓

Esta no es la copa de Juan.

2 If it isn't Juan's, it must be
   Jose's.

sinoézlaďehwan↑debesérlaďehosé↓

Si no es la de Juan, debe ser la de
José.

3 Yes, it's his.

sí↓ ézlaďe'l↓

Sí, es la de él.

4 Juan is drinking 'cuba libre.'

hwan |éstábébyendo |kúbalíbré↓

Juan está bebiendo cuba libre.

5 He isn't dancing.

noęstabaylándô↓

No está bailando.

6 He's waiting for his little
   chubby girl.

éstáęspérando |asuɡordítá↓

Está esperando a su gordita.

7 She's in the kitchen helping the
   hostess fix some drinks.

e(l)yaęstaęnlakoşína↓ayúďando |

álásényoraďelakasa |ašerunostráɡôs↓

Ella está en la cocina, ayudando a
la señora de la casa a hacer unos
tragos.

DIALOG 1

José, pregúntele a Juan
 si ésta es su copa o la de
 él.

ésₑestatukópₐ↑olamíà↓

José: ¿Es ésta tu copa o la
 mía?

Juan, contéstele que debe ser
 la de él. Que Ud. está bebiendo cuba libre.

debesérlatúyà↓ yoₑstóybeↄyéndo |
kubalíↄré↓

Juan: Debe ser la tuya. Yo
 estoy bebiendo cuba
 libre.

José, pregúntele a Juan que
 por qué no está bailando.

pórkenₒesta↗baylándò↓

José: ¿Por qué no estás
 bailando?

Juan, contéstele que Ud. está
 esperando a su gordita.

èstóyéspérandₒamₗgordítà↓

Juan: Estoy esperando a mi
 gordita.

José, pregúntele que dónde
 está ella.

dóndestaℰℓyà↓

José: ¿Dónde está ella?

Juan, contéstele que está en
 la cocina ayudando a la
 señora de la casa a hacer
 unos tragos.

èstáₑnlákóṣₗnₐ↓àyúↄando | àlàséɳyórà
ↄèlàkasₐ |aṣérunostrágós↓

Juan: Está en la cocina ayudando
 a la señora de la casa a
 hacer unos tragos.

NARRATIVE 2

1 There's a brunette dancing
 in front of Juan and Jose.

áyúnàmóréna |báylándọ |émfréntė

déhwanįhosé↓

Hay una morena bailando enfrente
 de Juan y José.

2 She's Colonel Harris' secretary.

èzlásèkrétàrya |délkòrónélhárris↓

Es la secretaria del Coronel
 Harris.

3 Juan likes her. He thinks she's
 terrific.

àhwanlegústà↓ lèpàrę̀ẹestupéndà↓

A Juan le gusta. Le parece
 estupenda.

4 Jose doesn't know her very
 well.

hósè |nolakonóṣè |mùybyén↓

José no la conoce muy bien.

5 But she's a friend of Carmen's,
 Jose's fiancée.

pérọẹ́ỵa |èṣàmígaḍèkarmén↓

lànobyaḍehosé↓

Pero ella es amiga de Carmen,
 la novia de José.

6 Her name is Cecilia.

súnombres(ṣ)eṣílyà↓

Su nombre es Cecilia.

7 Juan wants to meet her.

hwaŋkyerekonoṣérlà↓

Juan quiere conocerla.

8 But he can't now.

pérọàora |nopwéḍè↓

Pero ahora no puede.

9 He's waiting for his little
 chubby girl.

èstáẹspérandọ |asugoṛḍítà↓

Está esperando a su gordita.

| 10 Shhh...Careful... Here she comes. | shh\| kwiďaďó↓ ȧkıbyéné↓ | ¡Shhh!...cuidado...aquí viene. |

DIALOG 2

| Juan, pregúntele a José que quién es esa morena que está bailando enfrente de Uds. | kyen̩.es̩.es̩amoréna \|kėṡtȧbaylándo̩ \| émfrenteḑenosótrôs↓ | Juan: ¿Quién es esa morena que está bailando enfrente de nosotros? |

| José, contéstele que es la secretaria del Coronel Harris. Pregúntele que por qué, que si le gusta. | ėzlȧsėkrėtárya \|ďélkórónelhárris↓ pórkė↓ tėguṡta↑ | José: Es la secretaria del Coronel Harris. ¿Por qué? ¿te gusta? |

| Juan, contéstele que le parece estupenda. Pregúntele si él la conoce. | mėpárȩşȩ \|ėṡtúpendȧ↓ túlȧkȯnos̩es↑ | Juan: Me parece estupenda. ¿Tú la conoces? |

| José, dígale que no muy bien. Pero que Carmen es amiga de ella. Pregúntele a Carmen si no es así. | nomuybyém↓pérókarmen \|es̩.amigaďé(l)yȧ↓ no̩és̩.ás̩ı \|karmen↑ | José: No muy bien. Pero Carmen es amiga de ella. ¿No es así, Carmen? |

| Carmen, pregúntele a José que quién. | kyen↑ | Carmen: ¿Quién? |

José, dígale que Cecilia, la morena que está bailando enfrente de Uds.	ṣėṣılyå↓ lámórena|kėstáƀåylandǫ| ėmfréntedenosótrȯs↓	José: Cecilia, la morena que está bailando enfrente de nosotros.
Carmen, contéstele que claro, que ella y Ud. son muy buenas amigas. Pregúntele a Juan que si quiere conocerla.	kláró↓ eʎyaıyo|sómózmúyƀwenas amígás↓ kyerekonoṣerla|hwan↑	Carmen: Claro, ella y yo somos muy buenas amigas. ¿Quiere conocerla, Juan?
Juan, contéstele que sí, pero que ahora no puede. Dígale que está esperando a su gordita.	sí↓ pérǫåoranopwéđó↓ éstóy ėspérandǫamıgorđítá↓	Juan: Sí, pero ahora no puedo. Estoy esperando a mi gordita.
José, dígale a Juan que Ud. lo siente mucho.	lósyentomúchó↓	José: Lo siento mucho.
Juan, dígale que Ud. también. Ahora dígale que 'shh... que cuidado...que aquí viene.	yótambyén↓ sh|kwiđáđǫ↓ ákıƀyéné↓	Juan: Yo también. Shh... cuidado...aquí viene.
Carmen, dígale a José que no vaya a meter la pata.	nóƀáyas|ameterlapátá|hósé↓	Carmen: No vayas a meter la pata, José.

NARRATIVE 3

1 The little fat gal's name is Luz.

èlnómbre |dèlágórdita̧ |ezlúş↓

El nombre de la gordita es Luz.

2 Luz wants to know what Juan, Jose, and Carmen are talking about.

luşkyéresabér |dèkéstánab̧lándo |

hwán |hósȩı̧kármèn↓

Luz quiere saber de qué están hablando Juan, José y Carmen.

3 They're talking about...the party, says Juan. He think's it's very nice.

éstan̨ab̧lándode | láfyéstà |dí̧şė

hwán↓ lépárȩşe |késtámuybonítá↓

Están hablando de ...la fiesta, dice Juan. Le parece que está muy bonita.

4 And it's really terrific.

i̧énrrȩálidad↑éstá̧ȩstúpéndà↓

Y en realidad está estupenda.

5 Juan wants to dance this one with Luz.

hwaŋ |kyérébáyláresta |konlúş↓

Juan quiere bailar ésta con Luz.

6 They'll be back right away.

ènségidab̧wélbèn↓

En seguida vuelven.

DIALOG 3

Luz, dígales 'hola' a ellos. Pregúnteles si Ud. puede saber de qué
están hablando.

ólà↓ pweɖosabér |dèkestánͺablándo↑

Luz: Hola. ¿Puedo saber de qué
están hablando?

Juan, contéstele que están hablando
de...la fiesta. Dígale que está
bonita, que si no le parece.

èstámòsͺàblándoɖe| làfyestà↓
èstábònità↓ nòtéparèşe↑

Juan: Estamos hablando de...la
fiesta. Está bonita, ¿no te
parece?

Luz, contéstele que sí, que en
realidad está estupenda.

si↓ ènrreàliɖaɖ |éstáͅestúpendà↓

Luz: Sí, en realidad está estupenda.

Juan, pregúntele si quiere bailar ésta.

kyerezbaylaresta↑

Juan: ¿Quieres bailar ésta?

Luz, dígale que encantada.

èŋkàntaɖà↓

Luz: Encantada.

Juan, dígales a José y a Carmen que
con permiso. Que en seguida
vuelven.

kòmpérmisò↓ ènsègiɖabolbémòs↓

Juan: Con permiso. En seguida
volvemos.

End of Tape 10B

14.1   BASIC SENTENCES.   Colonel Harris talks about his family's arrival.

Colonel Harris is speaking to Molina and White after the introductions.

ENGLISH SPELLING	AID TO LISTENING	SPANISH SPELLING
satisfied, contented	kóntèntò↓	contento
White Are you enjoying it here, Colonel? (1)	èstàkontentọakı̇́ǀkoronél↑	*White* ¿Está contento aquí, coronel?
Harris Yes, very much so.	sı́↓ muy ǀkóntént̀ò↓	*Harris* Sí, muy contento.
besides	ádémàs↓	además
Besides, my family arrives tomorrow.	ádémàs↑ màŋyàna ǀ(0)yégàmifàmı̀lyà↓	Además, mañana llega mi familia.
(they) come (to come)	byénén↓ bènı̇́r↓	vienen (venir)
the boat	él→barkó↓	el barco
by boat	êm→barkô↓	en barco
White Are they coming by boat?	byénènèmbárkó↑	*White* ¿Vienen en barco?

(they're) go(ing) to come	bánabenír↓	van a venir
the plane	él—ábyon↓	el avión
by plane	pór—ábyon↓	por avión

Harris
No, they're coming by plane.

nó↓ bánabénir |póràbyon↓

Harris
No, van a venir por avión.

the mother-in-law	lá—swegrá↓	la suegra
to make dizzy	máréar↓	marear
herself (she) gets seasick (to get seasick)	sé—máreá↓ márearsé↓	se marea (marearse)

My mother-in-law gets seasick in a ship.

miswégra |sémáreₐembárkó↓

Mi suegra se marea en barco.

White
Oh, your mother-in-law's coming too?

á↓ byéne |súswegratambyén↑

White
Ah, ¿viene su suegra también?

| the wife | lá—ęsposá↓ | la esposa |
| the child | él—niŋyó↓ | el niño |

Harris
Yes, she's coming with my wife and
the children. (2)

sí↓ byéne |kónmięsposą |
ikónlózniŋyós↓

Harris
Sí, viene con mi esposa y con
los niños.

| the son | él—ihó↓ | el hijo |

White

How many children do you have?

kwȧntos̬i̱hȯs |tyénė↓

White

¿Cuántos hijos tiene?

the male

ė̇l→bȧrȯ́n↓

el varón

the (small) girl

lȧ→ni̱ŋyȧ↓

la niña

Harris

Three, two boys and a girl.

tré·s↓ dȯzbarȯ́nes |i̱unaníŋyȧ↓

Harris

Tres. Dos varones y una niña.

Molina

Do you have a house yet? (3)

i̱atyénekasȧ↑

Molina

¿Ya tiene casa?

Bellavista

bė̇ȯ̇yȧbistȧ↓

Bellavista

behind

dė̇trȧ·s↓

detrás

in back of, behind, beyond

dė̇traz→dė̇↓

detrás de

the park

ė̇l→parkė̇↓

el parque

Harris

Yes, in Bellavista, on the other side of the park.

si̱↓ ėmbė̇ȯ̇yȧbista |dė̇trazdelpárkė̇↓

Harris

Sí, en Bellavista detrás del parque.

really (real)

rrę̇alméntė̇↓ rrę̇a·l↓

realmente (real)

(it) is worth (to be worth)

balė̇↓ bȧlė́r↓

vale (valer)

the sorrow, grief

lȧ→pénȧ↓

la pena

(it) is worthwhile

bale→la→pénȧ↓

vale la pena

the section (of a town)

ė̇l→barryȯ̇↓

el barrio

Molina It's really worthwhile to live in that section.	reálménte |balelapénatbibir |én,ésébárryó↓	*Molina* Realmente vale la pena vivir en ese barrio.
It's very quiet.	ezmúytraŋkílö↓	Es muy tranquilo.
above	sóbré↓	sobre
above all, especially	sóbré—tó̃o↓	sobre todo
Harris And it's an especially good place for kids.	isóbrétóotbwénoparaloznínyös↓	*Harris* Y sobre todo, bueno para los niños.
the sister	la̧—érmaná↓	la hermana
Molina A married sister of mine lives there.	úna̧érmánámía |kásaoa̧ |bíbȩa̧0̧y i↓	*Molina* Una hermana mía casada vive allí.
the airport	él—a̧éropwertó↓	el aeropuerto
(you're) go(ing) to go	bá—a̧—ir↓	va a ir
What time are you going to the airport?	ákȩora |baírustéo |ála̧éropwertó↓	¿A qué hora va a ir usted al aeropuerto?
Harris At one.	ála̧uná↓	*Harris* A la una.

the order	lá—ordén↓	la orden
at your service	à—sús—ordénès↓	a sus órdenes

Molina
Let me know if I can help you.

éstoy│àsús,ordenes│páráyúdárlé↓

Molina
Estoy a sus órdenes para
ayudarle.

the car	él—karró↓	el carro
the disposition	lá—disposisyón↓	la disposición
at your disposal	à—sú—disposisyón↓	a su disposición

My car is at your disposal.

mikarro│éstasudisposisyón↓

Mi carro está a su disposición.

look (to look)

miré↓ mirár↓

mire (mirar)

Harris
Thanks, Molina. Look, the girls
are waiting for you all.

grasyàz│mólíná↓ miré│làzmúchachaz│
lós,éstán,éspérandó↓

Harris
Gracias, Molina. Mire, las mucha-
chas los están esperando.

(we're) go(ing) to talk

bámós—ą—áblár↓

vamos a hablar

Molina
So long. We'll talk later. (4)

ástálwegó↓ bamos,ablardespwés↓

Molina
Hasta luego. Vamos a hablar
después.

14.10   Notes on the basic sentences

(1) The translation of /konténto/ *contento* in this sentence is far from literal, but there is no very satisfactory literal translation possible. It does not mean 'contented' or 'satisfied' or even 'happy' in the sense that English speakers would mean in a sentence like 'Are you happy?', which implies something like 'Well, you *were* having problems; have things straightened out now?' The sentence just means, 'Are things going smoothly, is life treating you right?'

(2) Note that English does not normally repeat the preposition before a double object; Spanish does: cf. 'with my wife and the children' and *con mi esposa y con los niños*.

(3) The word /yá/ *ya* has been seen in Spanish utterances that have received a variety of translations into English: 'already,' 'still', 'yet', 'right away', etc. A list of those equivalents that it is most likely to have may be useful:

'already' as in *Ya está aquí.* 'He's already here'.

'yet' as in *¿Ya está aquí?* 'Is he here yet?'

'right away' as in *Ya voy.* 'I'm coming right away'.

'now' as in *Ya estamos llegando.* 'We're arriving now'.

'any longer' as in *Ya no.* 'Not any longer'.

(4) It should be noted that /bámos.ablár/ *vamos a hablar* could mean 'Let's talk' instead of 'We'll talk.' That is, the form /bámos.a____r/ *vamos a -r* is also used in the hortatory sense. It will be examined more closely and drilled in Unit 28.

14.2   DRILLS AND GRAMMAR

14.21   Pattern drills

14.21.1   Present tense forms of the irregular verbs /ír, dár, bér/

   A.   Presentation of pattern

ILLUSTRATIONS

_____	1	mébóy │èntónşés↓	Me *voy*, entonces.
Are you going to the party?	2	básalafyéstá↑	¿*Vas* a la fiesta?
_____	3	kómolebá↓	¿Cómo le *va*?
Let's go that way.	4	bámosporaí↓	*Vamos* por ahí.
Are they going downtown?	5	bánalşéntro↑	¿*Van* al centro?
_____	6	lédoytrés↓ únodepropíná↓	Le *doy* tres, uno de propina.
How much are you giving him, then?	7	kwántoledás │èntónşés↓	¿Cuánto le *das*, entonces?
_____	8	dalakáłye↑ọalpátyò↓	¿*Da* a la calle. o al patio?

We'll give you (an) hour and a half.   9   lédamos |oraiméḍyà↓   Le *damos* hora y media.

                                       10   simédan |elapartaméntó↓   Si me *dan* el apartamento.

It's just that I don't see too well.   11   és |kénobeomuybyén↓   Es que no *veo* muy bien.

Who do you see?   12   àsibez |dondebíbó↓   Así *ves* donde vivo.

                                       13   àkyémbeustéd↓   ¿A quién *ve* usted?

                                       14   pórkenobemos |aunamigomíó↓   ¿Por qué no *vemos* a un amigo mío?

Do you all see that brunette?   15   ben |aesamoréna↑   ¿*Ven* a esa morena?

EXTRAPOLATION

		ír	dár	bér
sg	1	b—óy	d—óy	bé—o
	2 fam	b—ás	d—ás	b—és
	2 – 3	b—á	d—á	b—é
pl				
	1	b—ámos	d—ámos	b—émos
	2 – 3	b—án	d—án	b—én

NOTES

a. These verbs are irregular in their 1 sg forms.

b. /ír/ has a stem /b—/ appearing in the present tense.

c. The monosyllabic forms are stressed on their endings.

14.21.11 Substitution drills - number substitution

1 damospropínà↓   doypropína↓

2 beolosanúnşyòs↓   bemozlosanúnşyòs↓

3 bamosalatıntorería↓   boyalatıntorería↓

4 doydemasyáďò↓   damozdemasyáďò↓

5 benelperyóďikò↓   belperyóďikò↓

6 boyenáwtò↓   bamosenáwtò↓

---

1 Damos propina.   Doy propina.

2 Veo los anuncios.   Vemos los anuncios.

3 Vamos a la tintorería.   Voy a la tintorería.

4 Doy demasiado.   Damos demasiado.

5 Ven el periódico.   Ve el periódico.

6 Voy en auto.   Vamos en auto.

7   dámpermísó↓   dápermísó↓

8   bémozlastáşàs↓   béolastáşàs↓

9   bálabóđà↓   bànalabóđà↓

10   dánchékès↓   dáchékès↓

11   bámpróntò↓   bápróntò↓

---

7 Dan permiso.   Da permiso.

8 Vemos las tazas.   Veo las tazas.

9 Va a la boda.   Van a la boda.

10 Dan cheques.   Da cheques.

11 Van pronto.   Va pronto.

Person - number substitution

1 yoḋoy|larrópabyéhả↓
   máría_____↓   dalarrópabyéhả↓
   hwaṇiyo_____↓   damozlarrópabyéhả↓
   ústeḋez_____↓   danlarrópabyéhả↓
   tu_____↓   dazlarrópabyéhả↓

2 hwán|nóbelosanún̦yós↓
   ústeḋez_____↓   nóbenlosanún̦yós↓
   yó_____↓   nóbeolosanún̦yós↓

_____

1 *Yo* doy la ropa vieja.

   María _____.   Da la ropa vieja.
   Juan y yo_____.   Damos la ropa vieja.
   Uds._____.   Dan la ropa vieja.
   Tú _____.   Das la ropa vieja.

2 *Juan* no ve los anuncios.

   Uds._____.   No ven los anuncios.
   Yo_____.   No veo los anuncios.

```
    máriaikármen_____↓              nobenlosanúnsyós↓
    eȴyoz_____↓              nobenlosanúnsyós↓


3   nósótroz |bámoseStanóché↓
      eȴya_____↓              baeStanóché↓
      yo_____↓              boyeStanóché↓
      hwanikármem_____↓              baneStanóché↓
      ústed_____↓              baeStanóché↓
```

María y Carmen_____.   No ven los anuncios.

Ellos_____.   No ven los anuncios.

3 *Nosotros* vamos esta noche.

   Ella_____.   Va esta noche.

   Yo_____.   Voy esta noche.

   Juan y Carmen_____.   Van esta noche.

   Ud._____.   Va esta noche.

4 eḷyoz |dánmuchaspropínás↓

   ústeđ_____↓   dámuchaspropínás↓

   máriaıhwan_____↓   dánmuchaspropínás↓

   yo_____↓   dóymuchaspropínás↓

   eḷya_____↓   dámuchaspropínás↓

---

4 *Ellos* dan muchas propinas.

   Ud._____.   Da muchas propinas.

   María y Juan_____.   Dan muchas propinas.

   Yo_____.   Doy muchas propinas.

   Ella_____.   Da muchas propinas.

5 yo |béómuybyén↓
    ántonyo_____↓   bémuybyén↓
    tú_____↓   bézmuybyén↓
    ústed₁antonyo____↓   bénmuybyén↓
    nósotroz_____↓   bémózmuybyén↓

---

5 *Yo* veo muy bien.

    Antonio_____.   Ve muy bien.
    Tú_____.   Ves muy bien.
    Ud. y Antonio__.   Ven muy bien.
    Nosotros_____.   Vemos muy bien.

14.21.12 Response drill

	1	baýustedalşéntrot̯ǫasukásá↓	bóyàlşéntró↓
	2	ben̥ustedez│losanunşyostolasfótós↓	bémózlàsfotós↓
	3	banę(l)yos│aorat̯ǫestanóché↓	bánạaorá↓
	4	beél│losperyodıkostolozlíbrós↓	bélózlıbrós↓
[lòsánunşyós↓]	5	kebeụstéd↓	beolosanúnşyós↓
[ya↓]	6	kwandobanustédés↓	bamozụá↓
[làsékrétáryà↓]	7	àkyembenę́(l)yós↓	benalasekretáryà↓
[àláskwátró↓]	8	àkęorabaél↓	balaskwátró↓

---

	1 ¿Va Ud. al centro o a su casa?	Voy al centro.
	2 ¿Ven Uds. los anuncios o las fotos?	Vemos las fotos.
	3 ¿Van ellos ahora o esta noche?	Van ahora.
	4 ¿Ve él los periódicos o los libros?	Ve los libros.
(los anuncios)	5 ¿Qué ve Ud.?	Veo los anuncios.
(ya)	6 ¿Cuándo van Uds.?	Vamos ya.
(la secretaria)	7 ¿A quién ven ellos?	Ven a la secretaria.
(a las cuatro)	8 ¿A qué hora va él?	Va a las cuatro.

[álás,ochó↓] 9 baysteɗ|alaznwebe↑   no↓ bóyálás,ochó↓
[álá(s)seys↓] 10 banustedes|alas(ş)iŋko↑   no↓ bámós,álá(s)seys↓
[lós,ánunşyós↓] 11 ben,e()yoz|lasfotos↑   no↓ bénlós,ánunşyós↓

12 danustedez|lostrahezbyehos↑   si↓ lózɗamós↓
13 daysteɗ|laskamisazbyéhas↑   si↓ lázɗoy↓
14 dael|muchaspropinas↑   si↓ dámuchás↓
15 dane()yoz|larrópabyéha↑   si↓ láɗan↓

(a las ocho)   9 ¿Va Ud. a las nueve?   No, voy a las ocho.
(a las seis)   10 ¿Van Uds. a las cinco?   No, vamos a las seis.
(los anuncios) 11 ¿Ven ellos las fotos?   No, ven los anuncios.

               12 ¿Dan Uds. los trajes viejos? Sí, los damos.
               13 ¿Da Ud. las camisas viejas?   Sí, las doy.
               14 ¿Da él muchas propinas?   Sí, da muchas.
               15 ¿Dan ellos la ropa vieja?   Sí, la dan.

14.21.13 Translation drill

1	I'm not going now.	yónoḅoyaórá↓	Yo no voy ahora.
2	She's going to the wedding.	é(l)yaḅálaḅódá↓	Ella va a la boda.
3	They never give anything.	é(l)yóznuŋka ǀda(n)nádá↓	Ellos nunca dan nada.
4	Let's go right away.	bamosensegídá↓	Vamos en seguida.
5	Why aren't you (all) going?	pórke ǀnoḅanustédés↓	¿Por qué no van Uds.?
6	I always look at the ads.	syémpre ǀḅeoloșanúnş̦yós↓	Siempre veo los anuncios.
7	From time to time I go to that restaurant.	débeş̦eŋkwandoțboyạeserrestorán↓	De vez en cuando voy a ese restorán.
8	How many ladies are going?	kwánta(s)señyorazbán↓	¿Cuántas señoras van?
9	I'm giving all my old clothes.	yódoy ǀtodamirropabyéhá↓	Yo doy toda mi ropa vieja.
10	He doesn't give many tips.	él ǀnoda ǀmuchaspropínás↓	El no da muchas propinas.
11	We give too many tips.	damoz ǀdémásyadaspropínás↓	Damos demasiadas propinas.

End of Tape 11A

B Discussion of pattern

The verb /ír/ is irregular in having a special stem /b—/ in the present tense. This stem is further irregular in that it conjugates not like an /—ír/ verb, but rather like a regular /—ár/ verb except for the added final /—y/ in /bóy/

The verb /dár/ is irregular only in having a final /—y/ on the 1 sg form. /dóy/ shares this irregularity with /bóy/. /sóy/, and /estóy/.

The verb /bér/ has its regular stem /b—/ in all forms except 1 sg where the stem /be—/ occurs in /béo/

All of these verbs have monosyllabic conjugated forms except in 1 pl /bámos/, /dámos/, and /bémos/, and in 1 sg /béo/. As monosyllables their lexical stress appears on their endings rather than on a preceding syllable.

Tape 11B

14.21.2 The periphrastic future construction

A. Presentation of pattern

ILLUSTRATIONS

1   boyabér |siǫyegoęlágwa↓   *Voy a ver si llegó el agua.*

I'm going to talk later.

2   boyablár |despwés↓   *Voy a hablar después.*

3   basabibír |enelotél↑   *¿Vas a vivir en el hotel?*

4   akyémbasaǫyebár↓   *¿A quién vas a llevar?*

5   kwantobakobrármé↓   *¿Cuánto va a cobrarme?*

561

6 batrabahár |ko(n)nosótrós↓   *Va a trabajar con nosotros.*

7 bamos.atenér |bodaprónto↑   *¿Vamos a tener boda pronto?*

8 bamos.abér |elperyódikó↓   *Vamos a ver el periódico.*

9 banakambyarse |dekásá↓   *Van a cambiarse de casa.*

10 no↓ banabenir |porabyón↓   *No, van a venir por avión.*

EXTRAPOLATION

	ír	a	/—Vr/		
			−ár	−ér	−ír
sg					
1	bóy				
2 fam	bás				
2 – 3	bá	a	abl−ár	kom−ér	bıb−ír
pl 1	bámos				
2 – 3	bán				

NOTES

a. The periphrastic future construction consists of a conjugated form of the verb /ír/ plus the phrase relator /a/ plus the infinitive form of the verb.

b. Before an infinitive beginning with the vowel /a/, or after the form /bá/, the phrase relator /a/ regularly fails to occur in actual pronunciation.

14.21.21   Substitution drills - Person-number substitution

1   yoboyatraduşír↓

    ústed_____↓   batraduşír↓

    hwaniyó_____↓   bamos.atraduşír↓

    eǫyoz_____↓   banatraduşír↓

    karmem_____↓   batraduşír↓

2   nósotroz |bámós.átrábáharaí↓

    eǫyoz_____↓   bánátrábáharaí↓

    yo_____↓   bóyátrábáharaí↓

---

1   *Yo* voy a traducir.

    Ud._____.   Va a traducir.

    Juan y yo_____.   Vamos a traducir.

    Ellos_____.   Van a traducir.

    Carmen_____.   Va a traducir.

2   *Nosotros* vamos a trabajar ahí.

    Ellos_____.   Van a trabajar ahí.

    Yo_____.   Voy a trabajar ahí.

lwísaɪantónyo_____↓   bánàtràbàharáí↓
tu_____↓   bás,àtràbàharáí↓

3 eⱺya |bákòmérdespwés↓

   yo_____↓   bóyàkòmérdespwés↓

   lwísaɪantónyo_____↓   bánàkòmérdespwés↓

   lwísaɪyo_____↓   bámósàkòmérdespwés↓

   ústedez_____↓   bánàkòmérdespwés↓

_____

Luisa y Antonio_____.   Van a trabajar ahí.

Tú_____.   Vas a trabajar ahí.

3 *Ella* va a comer después.

   Yo_____.   Voy a comer después.

   Luisa y Antonio_____.   Van a comer después.

   Luisa y yo_____.   Vamos a comer después.

   Uds._____.   Van a comer después.

Construction substitution

1 komobastánté↓   bóyákòmerbastánté↓

2 tómamozbínó↓   bámósàtómarbínó↓

3 suben |en̪elas(ṣ)ensór↓   bánásúbir |en̪elas(ṣ)ensór↓

4 baylaí↓   bábáylaraí↓

5 bibọemfrénté↓   bóyábibiremfrénté↓

6 mandanlostráhés↓   bánámándarlostráhés↓

7 èstúdyamosenelkwártó↓   bámósạéstúdyar |enelkwártó↓

---

1 Como bastante.   Voy a comer bastante.

2 Tomamos vino.   Vamos a tomar vino.

3 Suben en el ascensor.   Van a subir en el ascensor.

4 Baila ahí.   Va a bailar ahí.

5 Vivo enfrente.   Voy a vivir enfrente.

6 Mandan los trajes.   Van a mandar los trajes.

7 Estudiamos en el cuarto.   Vamos a estudiar en el cuarto.

14.21.22 Response drill

1 baustéd |atrabahár↑o aestudyár↓   bóyàtràbàhár↓

2 banustedes |aeskribir↑o asalír↓   bámós̩às̩àlír↓

3 baeOya |alabár↑o abarrér↓   bábàrrér↓

[àeskribír↓]   4 kéban |aserEOyós↓   bánaeskribír↓

[àestúbyár↓]   5 kébaserustéd↓   bóyaestúdyár↓

[àbèbér↓]   6 kéban |aserustédès↓   bámós̩àbèbér↓

[úntráhè↓]   7 kébas |akomprártú↓   boyakomprárúntráhè↓

---

1 ¿Va Ud. a trabajar o a estudiar?   Voy a trabajar.

2 ¿Van Uds. a escribir o a salir?   Vamos a salir.

3 ¿Va ella a lavar o a barrer?   Va a barrer.

(a escribir)   4 ¿Qué van a hacer ellos?   Van a escribir.

(a estudiar)   5 ¿Qué va a hacer Ud.?   Voy a estudiar.

(a beber)   6 ¿Qué van a hacer Uds.?   Vamos a beber.

(un traje)   7 ¿Qué vas a comprar tú?   Voy a comprar un traje.

[lóschékès↓]   8   kebánakambyárustéđès↓   bámósakámbyar |loschékès↓

[áɛstúđyár↓]   9   básálírél↑   nó↓ báɛstúđyár↓
[ásálír↓]   10   bánaɛskribírustéđes↑   nó↓ bámósásálír↓

              11   bákòmeré[ya |póstre↑   sí↓ é[ya |bákòmérpóstrè↓
              12   bánákómerustéđes |pastél↑   sí↓ bamosakomérpastél↓
              13   bá[yèbárusteđ |eláwto↑   sí↓ boya[yebárló↓

(los cheques)   8 ¿Qué van a cambiar Uds.?   Vamos a cambiar los cheques.

(a estudiar)   9 ¿Va a salir él?   No, va a estudiar.
(a salir)   10 ¿Van a escribir Uds.?   No, vamos a salir.

               11 ¿Va a comer ella postre?   Sí, ella va a comer postre.
               12 ¿Van a comer Uds. pastel?   Sí, vamos a comer pastel.
               13 ¿Va a llevar Ud. el auto?   Sí, voy a llevarlo.

14.21.23 Translation drill

1 We're going to repeat that.   bámósárrépétírésò↓   Vamos a repetir eso.

2 I'm going to shave.   boyafeytármé↓   Voy a afeitarme.

3 What're you going to do?   kebaşerustéɑ↓   ¿Qué va a hacer Ud.?

4 Where are you going to work?   dondebatrabahár↓   ¿Dónde va a trabajar?

5 I'm going to take a bath.   bóyábáŋyarmé↓   Voy a bañarme.

6 He's not going to stick his   el |nobameter |lapátạotrabéş↓   El no va a meter la pata otra
   foot (in his mouth) again.   vez.

7 They're going to practice   ban |ápráktikarmás↓   Van a practicar más.
   (some) more.

8 They're going to look for   ban |ábúskarkásà↓   Van a buscar casa.
   a house.

9 We're going to take (make)   bamos |ạşerumbyáhé↓   Vamos a hacer un viaje.
   a trip.

B. Presentation of pattern

The periphrastic future construction has three component forms: (1) a conjugated form of the verb /ír/ , (2) the phrase relator /a/ , and (3) an infinitive. These elements are usually not separated by any other forms, though sometimes a pronoun subject will appear after the form of /ír/.

As the name *periphrastic* indicates, this construction is a roundabout way of expressing future time. Spanish has a future tense which will be presented in Unit 53, but the periphrastic future construction seems to occur more frequently than the future tense in most dialects. It is a rather close equivalent of the 'to be going to....' construction in English.

This double English construction, combining both present progressive and periphrastic future constructions, has no exact parallel in Spanish, though its function is performed by the Spanish periphrastic future.

The periphrastic construction frequently brings into immediate sequence two and sometimes three /a/ phonemes. The normal phonetic pattern of reduction to a single /a/ in normal conversation may appear to be an omission of the relator /a/. Thus /bá-a-komér/ becomes /bákomér/ and /bá-a-ablár/ becomes /báblár/. The relator becomes quickly evident again when /bán/ is substituted for /bá/: /bánakomér/ , /bánablár/, showing that the reduction is purely phonological.

The periphrastic future construction in its 1 pl form can express future time (or intention) as in /bámos—a—estudyár |ésta—nóche↓/ 'We're going to study tonight', or it can express what might be called a hortatory construction, where the speaker exhorts others to accompany him in an action. Thus /bámos—a—komér↓/ appearing in its affirmative form can mean 'We're going to eat' or 'Let's eat'.

14.21.3   Question intonation patterns — Yes-no questions

A. Presentation of pattern

ILLUSTRATIONS

You like the room.	1	légust̯aelkwártȯ↓	1 2 1 1↓ Le gusta el cuarto.
_____		légust̯aelkwárto↑	1 2 2 2↑ ¿Le gusta el cuarto?

————   2   èstaléhòs↓   1 2 1 1↓
                                                                   Está lejos.
Is it far?   èstálèhòs↑   1 2 22↑
                                                                    ¿Está lejos?

————   3   ézmuykáró↓   1   2 1 1↓
                                                                   Es muy caro.
Is it very expensive?   ézmúykáro↑   1   2 22↑
                                                                    ¿Es muy caro?

EXTRAPOLATION

Statement	Yes-no question
/1211↓/	/1222↑/

NOTES

a. One frequent Spanish yes-no question pattern is /1222↑/,
   similar to a common English pattern, but not ending as high
   as the English pattern does.

14.21.31 Substitution drill — pattern substitution

Problem:

       trábahanmúchó↓

Answer:

       trábahanmúcho↑

1 álkilanelkwártó↓   álkilanelkwárto↑

2 légustaelpréşyó↓   légustaelpreşyo↑

$$/1211\!\downarrow/ \quad > \quad /1222\!\uparrow/$$

Problem: 1 2   1 1↓
            Trabajan mucho.

Answer: 1 2   2 2↑
           ¿Trabajan mucho?

        1 2   1 1↓   1 2   2 2↑
1 Alquilan el cuarto.   ¿Alquilan el cuarto?

         1 2   1 1↓   1 2   2 2↑
2 Le gusta el precio.   ¿Le gusta el precio?

3 súbimos̬aórá↓   súbimos̬aora↑

4 éstamwebláđó↓   éstamwebladó↑

5 kómpramos̬eláwtó↓   kómpramos̬elawto↑

6 déseálgó↓   déseálgo↑

7 tómamos̬untáksi↓   tómamos̬untaksi↑

8 álmórşamoshúntós↓   álmórşamoshuntos↑

---

        1 2   1 1 ↓   1 2   2 2 ↑
3 Subimos ahora.   ¿Subimos ahora?

        1 2   1 1 ↓   1 2   2 2 ↑
4 Está amueblado.   ¿Está amueblado?

        1 2   1 1 ↓   1 2   2 2 ↑
5 Compramos el auto.   ¿Compramos el auto?

        1 2 1 1 ↓   1 2 2 2 ↑
6 Desea algo.   ¿Desea algo?

        1 2   1 1 ↓   1 2   2 2 ↑
7 Tomamos un taxi.   ¿Tomamos un taxi?

        1   2   1 1 ↓   1   2   2 2 ↑
8 Almorzamos juntos.   ¿Almorzamos juntos?

9   lépàreşekáró↓   lépàreşekaro↑

10   búskamos.ótró↓   búskamos.otro↑

11   kómpramo(s)sábánàs↓   kómpramo(s)sábanas↑

```
      1   2    1 1↓                                1   2    22 ↑
 9  Le parece caro.                              ¿Le parece caro?

      1   2    1 1↓                                1   2    22 ↑
10  Buscamos otro.                               ¿Buscamos otro?

      1   2    1  1↓                               1   2    2 2↑
11  Compramos sábanas.                           ¿Compramos sábanas?
```

B. Presentation of pattern

   The most common intonation pattern that occurs with yes-no questions, particularly when the questioner does not anticipate whether the answer will be 'yes' or 'no', is /1222↑/.

   This pattern will give English speakers relatively little difficulty since it is very similar to an English pattern with the same meaning. The English pattern, however, ends somewhat higher, and this extra height might be interpreted as insistence or annoyance in Spanish.

```
         2   2    2    2                                     2    2    3
Thus /nó—tyéne—ótro↑/ Don't you have another?' is normal and /nó—tyéne—ótro↑/ could mean 'Don't you have just one more?'
```

14.22   Replacement drills

A   éstákónténtoakí |koronél↑

1 _____señyorés↑   éstáŋkóntentos |akí |señyorés↑

2 _____aora_____ ↑   éstáŋkóntentos |aora |señyorés↑

3 ___ókúpados_____ ↑   éstánókúpados |aora |señyorés↑

4 _____señyoritas↑   éstánókúpadas |aora |señyoritas↑

5 ___désókúpadas_____ ↑   éstándésókúpadas |aora |señyoritas↑

6 _____hosé↑   éstádésókúpado |aora |hosé↑

7 _____kármen↑   éstádésókúpada |aora |kármen↑

A   ¿Está contento aquí, Coronel?

1 ¿_____ señores?   ¿Están contentos aquí, señores?

2 ¿_____ahora,_____?   ¿Están contentos ahora, señores?

3 ¿___ocupados_____?   ¿Están ocupados ahora, señores?

4 ¿_____señoritas?   ¿Están ocupadas ahora, señoritas?

5 ¿___desocupadas_____?   ¿Están desocupadas ahora, señoritas?

6 ¿_____José?   ¿Está desocupado ahora, José?

7 ¿_____Carmen?   ¿Está desocupada ahora, Carmen?

B   ádémas↑ mȧŋyana |ɔ̨ɥégȧmifȧmilyá↓

1 _____ȧmigȯs↓   ádémas↑ mȧŋyana |ɔ̨ɥégȧnmisȧmigȯs↓

2 _____sús_____↓   ádémas↑ mȧŋyana |ɔ̨ɥégȧnsúsȧmigȯs↓

3 _____byénén_____↓   ádémas↑ mȧŋyana |byénénsúsȧmigȯs↓

4 _____élhwebez_____↓   ádémas↑ élhwebez |byénénsúsȧmigȯs↓

5 _____ȧkȩ̨ɥȯs___↓   ádémas↑ élhwebez |byenen |ȧkȩ̨ɥȯsȧmigȯs↓

6 _____mȯrénȧ↓   ádémas↑ élhwebez |byénȩ̨ȧkȩ̨ɥȧmȯrénȧ↓

7 _____séŋyor↓   ádémas↑ élhwebez |byénȩ̨ȧkélséŋyor↓

B   Además, mañana llega mi familia.

1 _____, _____amigos.   Además, mañana llegan mis amigos.

2 _____, _____sus_____.   Además, mañana llegan sus amigos.

3 _____, _____vienen_____.   Además, mañana vienen sus amigos.

4 _____, el jueves_____.   Además, el jueves vienen sus amigos.

5 _____, _____aquellos__.   Además, el jueves vienen aquellos amigos.

6 _____, _____morena.   Además, el jueves viene aquella morena.

7 _____, _____señor.   Además, el jueves viene aquel señor.

C   kwántosᵢhòstyéné↓

1 _____niŋyas___↓   kwántaznìŋyastyéné↓

2 _____áy↓   kwántaznìŋyasáy↓

3 _____tyempọ___↓   kwántotyempọáy↓

4 _____kyérės↓   kwántotyempokyérės↓

5 _____agwa_____↓   kwántagwakyérės↓

6 _____bébés↓   kwántagwabébés↓

7 _____tragoz___↓   kwántostragozbébės↓

C   ¿Cuántos hijos tiene?

1 ¿_____niñas _____?   ¿Cuántas niñas tiene?

2 ¿_____hay?   ¿Cuántas niñas hay?

3 ¿_____tiempo___?   ¿Cuánto tiempo hay?

4 ¿_____quieres?   ¿Cuánto tiempo quieres?

5 ¿_____agua_____?   ¿Cuánta agua quieres?

6 ¿_____bebes?   ¿Cuánta agua bebes?

7 ¿_____tragos_____?   ¿Cuántos tragos bebes?

D   únąérmanamía |kásaơa |bibęaⁿy í↓

1 ___érmanaz_____↓   únás.érmanazmías |kásaơaz |bibenaⁿy í↓

2 _____suyas_____↓   únásérmana⁽s⁾suyas |kásaơaz |bibenaⁿy í↓

3 ___iho_____↓   únihosuyo |kásaơo |bibęaⁿy í↓

4 _____sóltero_____↓   únihosuyo |sóltero |bibęaⁿy í↓

5 _____trábaha___↓   únihosuyo |sóltero |trábahaⁿy í↓

6 _____mio_____↓   únihomio |sóltero |trábahaⁿy í↓

7 ___ámigoz_____↓   únós.ámigozmíos |sólteros |trábahanaⁿy í↓

D   Una hermana mía casada vive allí.

1 ____hermanas_____.   Unas hermanas mías casadas viven allí.

2 _____ suyas_____.   Unas hermanas suyas casadas viven allí.

3 ____hijo_____.   Un hijo suyo casado vive allí.

4 _____ soltero_____.   Un hijo suyo soltero vive allí.

5 _____trabaja___. Un hijo suyo soltero trabaja allí.

6 _____mío_____.   Un hijo mío soltero trabaja allí.

7 ____amigos_____.   Unos amigos míos solteros trabajan allí.

E   ákęora |baɪrusteɗ |alʒeropwértôↄ

1 _____fyéstá↓   ákęora |baɪrusteɗ |alafyéstá↓

2 _____nosotros_____↓   ákęora |bamosₐaɪrnosótros |alafyéstá↓

3 kóŋkyem_____↓   kóŋkyem |bamosₐaɪrnosótros |alafyéstá↓

4 _____yo_____↓   kóŋkyem |boyaɪryó |ʒlafyéstá↓

5 pórke_____↓   pórke |boyaɪryó |ʒlafyéstá↓

6 _____benɪr_____↓   pórke |boyabenɪryó |ʒlafyéstá↓

7 _____ȩⱡⱡos_____↓   pórke |banₐbenɪreȡⱡos |alafyéstá↓

E   ¿A qué hora va a ir usted al aeropuerto?

1 ¿_____fiesta?   ¿A qué hora va a ir usted a la fiesta?

2 ¿_____nosotros _____?   ¿A qué hora vamos a ir nosotros a la fiesta?

3 ¿Con quién_____?   ¿Con quién vamos a ir nosotros a la fiesta?

4 ¿_____yo _____?   ¿Con quién voy a ir yo a la fiesta?

5 ¿Por qué_____?   ¿Por qué voy a ir yo a la fiesta?

6 ¿_____venir_____?   ¿Por qué voy a venir yo a la fiesta?

7 ¿_____ellos_____?   ¿Por qué van a venir ellos a la fiesta?

F   ástálwegó↓ bamos.ablarḍespwés↓

1   muybyén_____↓   múybyén↓ bamos.ablarḍespwés↓

2   _____aórà↓   múybyén↓ bamos.ablaraórá↓

3   _____estuḍyar____↓   múybyén↓ bamos.aestuḍyaraórá↓

4   _____boy_____↓   múybyén↓ boyaestuḍyaraórá↓

5   áḍyós_____↓   áḍyós↓ boyaestuḍyaraórá↓

6   _____teŋgoke_____↓   áḍyós↓ teŋgokestuḍyaraórá↓

7   _____ayke_____↓   áḍyós↓ aykestuḍyaraórá↓

F   Hasta luego, vamos a hablar después.

1 Muy bien,_____.   Muy bien, vamos a hablar después.

2 _____,_____ahora·   Muy bien, vamos a hablar ahora.

3 _____,_____ estudiar_____.   Muy bien, vamos a estudiar ahora.

4 _____,___voy_____ ₀   Muy bien, voy a estudiar ahora.

5 Adiós,_____.   Adiós, voy a estudiar ahora.

6 _____, tengo que_____ ₀   Adiós, tengo que estudiar ahora.

7 _____, hay que_____.   Adiós, hay que estudiar ahora.

14.23		Variation drills

A	byénenembárkot					¿Vienen en barco?

    1	Are they coming by car?		byénenenáwtot					¿Vienen en auto?

    2	Are they coming by plane?		byénenenabyónt					¿Vienen en avión?

    3	Are they coming in the
       evening?		byénenenlanóchet					¿Vienen en la noche?

    4	Are they coming in the
       morning?		byénenenlamaŋyánat					¿Vienen en la mañana?

    5	Are they coming in the
       afternoon?		byénenenlatárdet					¿Vienen en la tarde?

    6	Are they coming right
       away?		byénenensegídat					¿Vienen en seguida?

    7	Are they coming some
       other day?		byénenotrodíat					¿Vienen otro día?

B nó↓ bánábénír |pórábyón↓   No, van a venir por avión.

1 No, they're coming by boat.   nó↓ bánábénír |pórbárkó↓   No, van a venir por barco.

2 No, they're coming by car.   nó↓ bánábénír |pórawtó↓   No, van a venir por auto.

3 No, they're coming in the   nó↓ bánábénír |pórlánóché↓   No, van a venir por la noche.
  evening.

4 No, they're coming in the   nó↓ bánábénír |pórlámáŋyáná↓   No, van a venir por la mañana.
  morning.

5 No, they're coming in the   nó↓ bánábénír |pórlátárdé↓   No, van a venir por la tarde.
  afternoon.

6 Yes, they're coming for you.   sí↓ bánábénír |porustéd↓   Sí, van a venir por usted.

7 Yes, they're coming for me.   sí↓ bánábénír |pormí↓   Sí, van a venir por mí.

C   trés↓ dózḃarónes |ɹunanínyà↓   Tres. Dos varones y una niña.

1 Four. Three boys and a girl.   kwátró↓ trézḃarónes |ɹunanínyà↓   Cuatro. Tres varones y una niña.

2 Five. One boy and four girls.   ṣiŋkó↓ úmbarón |ikwátroníŋyàs↓   Cinco. Un varón y cuatro niñas.

3 Three. The wife, the mother-in-law   trés↓ lạésposa |láswegra |ɹelnínyó↓   Tres. La esposa, la suegra y el
  and the child.   niño.

4 Six. The wife and five children.   séys↓ lạésposạ |iṣiŋkọíhòs↓   Seis. La esposa y cinco hijos.

5 Two. Mr. and Mrs. Molina.   dós↓ élséŋyor |iláséŋyorademolíná↓   Dos. El señor y la señora de
                                                                                              Molına.

6 Two. John and Joseph.   dós↓ hwánɹhosé↓   Dos. Juan y José.

7 Three. Mr. Molina, Joseph and   trés↓ élséŋyórmólına |hóseɹyó↓   Tres. El señor Molina, José y yo.
  myself.

D bálélápená |bibírénésébárryó↓   Vale la pena vivir en ese barrio.

1 That's a good building to live in.   bálélápená |bibír |énésédifíşyó↓   Vale la pena vivir en ese edificio.

2 This is a good section to live in.   bálélápená |bibír |énéstébárryó↓   Vale la pena vivir en este barrio.

3 This is a good restaurant to come
   to for dinner.   bálélápená |kômér |énéstérréstórán↓   Vale la pena comer en este
                                                                                        restorán.

4 It's worth while to study in this
   school.   bálélápená |éstúdyár |énéstaéskwélá↓   Vale la pena estudiar en esta
                                                                                        escuela.

5 It's worth while to work in that
   school.   bálélápená |trábáhár |énésaéskwélá↓   Vale la pena trabajar en esa
                                                                                        escuela.

6 It's not worth the trouble to speak
   any more.   nóbalelapéna |áblármás↓   No vale la pena hablar más.

7 It's not worth the trouble going
   there.   nóbalelapéna |íradyá↓   No vale la pena ir allá.

E mikárrọ|estásudisposisyón↓   Mi carro está a su disposición.

1 You're welcome to my house.   mikása|estásudisposisyón↓   Mi casa está a su disposición.

2 You're welcome to my apartment.   miąpártámentọ|estásudisposisyón↓   Mi apartamento está a su disposición.

3 You're welcome to my room.   mikwártọ|estásudisposisyón↓   Mi cuarto está a su disposición.

4 You're welcome to my plane.   miąbyón|estásudisposisyón↓   Mi avión está a su disposición.

5 You're welcome to use my shower.   midúchą|estásudisposisyón↓   Mi ducha está a su disposición.

6 You're welcome to use our
  kitchen.   nwéstrąkóęiną|estásudisposisyón↓   Nuestra cocina está a su disposición.

7 You're welcome to use our
  living-room.   nwéstrąsálą|estásudisposisyón↓   Nuestra sala está a su disposición.

F   lázmúchachaz |lós,éstan,esperándó↓   Las muchachas los están esperando.

1 The young ladies are waiting   lá(s)séɲyóritaz |lós,éstan,esperándó↓   Las señoritas los están esperando.
  for you.

2 The ladies are waiting for you.   lá(s)séɲyoraz |lós,éstan,esperándó↓   Las señoras los están esperando.

3 The boys are waiting for you.   lózmúchachoz |lós,éstan,esperándó↓   Los muchachos los están esperando.

4 The gentlemen are waiting for us.   ló(s)séɲyorez |nós,éstan,esperándó↓   Los señores nos están esperando.

5 They're waiting for us.   eﬗyoz |nós,éstan,esperándó↓   Ellos nos están esperando.

6 Mary and Joseph are waiting   márịạịhose |méstan,esperándó↓   María y José me están esperando.
  for me.

7 The American girls are waiting   lás,ạmérikanaz |méstan,esperándó↓   Las americanas me están esperando.
  for me.

14.24   Review drill – Theme class in /–do/ forms of verbs

1 I've talked and eaten a lot.	éàbladǫ ǀikómidomúchó↓	He hablado y comido mucho.
2 I've gone up and down a lot.	ébàhadǫǀisùbidomúchó↓	He bajado y subido mucho.
3 I've studied and translated very little.	éstùdyadǫǀitràdùșido ǀmúypókò↓	He estudiado y traducido muy poco.
4 I've danced and gone out very little.	ébàyladǫǀisàlido ǀmúypókò↓	He bailado y salido muy poco.
5 I've studied and learned a little.	éstùdyado ǀɹàpréndidǫ ǀumpókò↓	He estudiado y aprendido un poco.
6 I've washed and swept everything.	élàbadǫǀibàrridotódò↓	He lavado y barrido todo.
7 I've eaten and drunk too much	éàlmòrșadǫǀibébidodemasyádò↓	He almorzado y bebido demasiado.
8 I've taken and brought back the car.	éꝋyèbadǫǀitràidǫeláwtò↓	He llevado y traído el auto.
9 I've arranged and swept the room.	éàrrégladǫǀibàrridǫelkwártò↓	He arreglado y barrido el cuarto.
10 I've bought and brought everything	ékómpradǫǀitràidotódò↓	He comprado y traído todo.
11 I've worked and lived there	étràbàhadǫǀibibidǫaí↓	He trabajado y vivido ahí

586

14.3   CONVERSATION STIMULUS

NARRATIVE 1

1 Jose introduces Colonel Harris to his fiancée.

hóselepreséntạ |èlkórónelharris |
asunóbyá↓

José le presenta el Coronel Harris a su novia.

2 The Colonel arrived Monday from the States.

èlkórónel(l)yegó |ę(l)lunez |ḑèlós
èstaḑosunídós↓

El Coronel llegó el lunes de los Estados Unidos.

3 He's going to be here a long time.

el |báẹstáráki |muchotyémpó↓

El va a estar aquí mucho tiempo.

4 He's going to work with the Embassy.

bátrábàhar |konlạembahá¢á↓

Va a trabajar con la Embajada.

DIALOG 1

José, dígale al Coronel que quiere presentarle a su novia, la señorita Del Valle. A Carmen dígale Carmen, el Coronel Harris.

kórónél↓ kyéróprèséntárlẹ |ami
nobya |làséŋyóritaḑelbá(l)ẏè↓
karmén↓ èlkórónelhárris↓

José: Coronel, quiero presentarle a mi novia, la señorita Del Valle. Carmen, el Coronel Harris.

Coronel, dígale a la señorita que tanto gusto.

tantogústó |séŋyórítá↓

Coronel: Tanto gusto, señorita.

Carmen, dígale al Coronel que
encantada.

éŋkàntáđá↓

Carmen: Encantada.

José, dígale a Carmen que el
Coronel llegó el lunes de los
Estados Unidos.

élkórónel |(l)yègóę(l)lunez |đélòs
éstađosuníđòs↓

José: El Coronel llegó el lunes
de los Estados Unidos.

Carmen, diga 'ah, ¿sí?', y pregúntele al Coronel si va a estar aquí
mucho tiempo.

a|sî↑ baęstárakí |muchotyempo↑

Carmen: Ah, ¿sí? ¿Va a estar
aquí mucho tiempo?

Coronel, contéstele que Ud. cree
que sí. Que va a trabajar con
la Embajada.

kreokesí↓ bóyátrábáhar |kón
laęmbáhađá↓

Coronel: Creo que sí. Voy a
trabajar con la Embaja-
da.

NARRATIVE 2

1 The Colonel's family is arriving
tomorrow.

láfámilya |đélkórónel |(l)yéga
maŋyáná↓

La familia del Coronel llega
mañana.

2 The airport, isn't it quite a
distance?

élaęrópwertó↓ noęstá |múylehos↑

El aeropuerto, ¿no está muy lejos?

3 it's half an hour from here by
car, more or less.

está |amęđyaęoraęakí |ęnáwtó |
más,óménòs↓

Está a media hora de aquí en auto,
más o menos.

4 But he doesn't know how he's
going to (do) manage.

pérǫel |nosábe |komobaşér↓

Pero él no sabe cómo va a hacer.

5 He's got so many things to do.

tyéné|tántaskósaskęaşér↓

Tiene tantas cosas que hacer.

6 Jose says his car is at the
Colonel's disposal.

hósedışe|kesúkarrǫ|éstálà

dispósişyon|delkoronél↓

José dice que su carro está a
la disposición del coronel.

7 'Thanks a million', says the
Colonel.

únmiQyondegráşyàz|dίşélkόrόnél↓

Un millón de gracias -dice el
Coronel.

8 Jose isn't going to be at the
Embassy tomorrow. Tomorrow
is Saturday.

hόse|nobaęstár|enlęembahádà|

máŋyáná↓ máŋyanąe(s)sábàdò↓

José no va a estar en la Embajada
mañana. Mañana es sábado.

9 But the Colonel can call him at
home.

pérǫélkόrόnel|pwédéⁿẏámarlǫ

alakásá↓

Pero el Coronel puede llamarlo a
la casa.

10 The Colonel says that if he needs
him, he'll call him.

élkόrόneldışe|késilόnęşésíta|

loQẏ ámà↓

El Coronel dice que si lo necesita,
lo llama.

DIALOG 2

Carmen, pregúntele al Coronel si
vino con su familia.

bĭnǫustéd|kǫnsufámilyat

Carmen. ¿Vino usted con su familia?

Coronel, contéstele que no. Que su
familia llega mañana. Pregúntele
a José, a propósito, si el aeropuerto
está muy lejos.

nό↓ mifámilya|ⁿẏegamaŋyáná↓

áprópósitό|hόsé↓ éstamuylehos|

eląeropwértot

No. Mi familia llega mañana. A propósito, José ¿está muy lejos el
aeropuerto?

José, contestele que no, que
a media hora de aquí en auto,
más o menos.

nó↓ áme₫yₐóra₫ₑaki |ₑnáwtô |

más.óménós↓

José: No, a media hora de aquí
en auto, más o menos.

Coronel, dígale que Ud. no sabe
como va a hacer. Que tiene
tantas cosas que hacer mañana.

nóse |komoḃoyaşér↓ téŋgó |tántas

kosaskₑaşér |màŋyáná↓

Coronel: No sé cómo voy a hacer.
Tengo tantas cosas
que hacer mañana.

José, dígale que su carro está a
la disposición de él.

mikárrₒ |ₑstású₫ispósişyón↓

José: Mi carro está a su disposición.

Coronel, dígale que un millón de
gracias. Pregúntele si él va a
estar en la Embajada mañana.

únmiⱡyondegráşyás↓ úste₫ba

ₑstar |enlₐembaha₫a |maŋyaná↑

Coronel: Un millón de gracias.
¿Usted va a estar en
la Embajada mañana?

José, dígale que no, que mañana
es sábado. Pero puede llamarlo
a su casa, dígale.

nó↓ màŋyanₐe(s)sáḃa₫ó↓ pérₒ

pwe₫e |ⱡyámármₑàmikásá↓

José: No, mañana es sábado. Pero
puede llamarme a mi casa.

Coronel, dígale que muy bien, que
si lo necesita lo llama. Y que
muchas gracias.

múybyén↓ silónₑşésito |loⱡyámó↓

muchazgráşyás↓

Coronel: Muy bien. Si lo necesito,
lo llamo. Muchas
gracias.

NARRATIVE 3

1 His wife, three children and
  his mother-in-law are
  coming.

byénênsûsêŋyorat tresíhos |
ısuswégrá↓

Vienen su señora, tres hijos y su
suegra.

2 His whole family.

toḍasufamílyá↓

Toda su familia.

3 He's going to have to rent a
  house.

báténer |kẹálkilarunakásá↓

Va a tener que alquilar una casa.

4 But he doesn't know if it's
  worth the trouble.

pérọel |nosabe |sıbalelapéná↓

Pero él no sabe si vale la pena.

5 They say that houses here
  cost a lot.

dışeŋ |kẹláskasas,akı |kwestan
múchó↓

Dicen que las casas aquí cuestan
mucho.

6 But Carmen lives in the
  Bellavista section.

pérókarmem |bıbenẹelbarryo
be(l)yabístá↓

Pero Carmen vive en el barrio
Bellavista.

7 And the houses there are very
  nice and inexpensive.

ıláskasas,a(l)yı |sônmuybonitas
ıbarátás↓

Y las casas allí son muy bonitas
y baratas

8 The Colonel is going to talk to
  his wife (about it) to see what
  she says.

élkórónel |báblárkónsụésposa |
pàrábér |kedış é(l)yà↓

El Coronel va a hablar con su
esposa para ver qué dice ella.

DIALOG 3

Carmen, pregúntele al Coronel
si viene toda su familia.

byenetoḍasufamilya↑

Carmen ¿Viene toda su familia?

Coronel, contéstele que sí, que
su señora y tres hijos. Que
también viene su suegra.

sí↓ miséņyorạ|itrésḭhòs↓
támbyembyenemiswégrạ↓

Coronel Sí, mi señora y tres
hijos. También viene
mi suegra.

Carmen, dígale que entonces va
a tener que alquilar una casa.

éntonșez↑bátènér|kẹàlkilár
únàkasạ↓

Carmen: Entonces va a tener que
alquilar una casa.

Coronel, dígale que Ud. no sabe
si vale la pena. Que dicen que
aquí las casas cuestan mucho.

nosé|sibàlelapénạ↓ dișeņkẹakı|
laskasaskwestanmuchó↓

Coronel: No sé si vale la pena.
Dicen que aquí las
casas cuestan mucho.

Carmen, dígale que en el barrio
Bellavista, donde Ud. vive,
hay casas muy baratas y bonitas

énélbárryóbé(l)yàbɪsta|ḍóndèyo
bibọ↑áykásáz|muybaratasɪbonítàs↓

Carmen En el barrio Bellavista.
donde yo vivo, hay
casas muy baratas y
bonitas

Coronel, dígale que Ud. va a hablar
con su esposa para ver qué dice
ella.

boyablár|kónmɪésposa|párábér|ke
dɪșé(l)yá↓

Coronel Voy a hablar con mi
esposa para ver qué
dice ella

End of Tape 11B

592

15.1   BASIC SENTENCES. Mrs. Harris goes through customs.

Mr. and Mrs. Harris and Molina are going to the customs office while the mother-in-law and children stay behind and wait for them.

ENGLISH SPELLING	AID TO LISTENING	SPANISH SPELLING
rigorous, strict	rrigúrosó↓	riguroso
the customs office	la̯—ádwaná↓	la aduana
Mrs. Harris		**Sra. Harris**
Are they very strict at the customs office here?	sonmuyrrigurosos│enladwanakí↑	¿Son muy rigurosos en la aduana aquí?
sure	séguró↓	seguro
Molina		**Molina**
No, I'm sure that they won't bother you.	no↓ éstóységuro│dekȩa̯ustȩd│nolaba̯n̯a molestár↓	No. Estoy seguro de que a usted no la van a molestar.
the baggage	él—ékipahé↓	el equipaje
Mrs. Harris		**Sra. Harris**
Right here. My baggage is here now.	ákí↓séŋyór↓ ya̯ȩstakí│mȩ̯ekipáhé↓	Aquí, señor. Ya está aquí mi equipaje.
which	kwál↓	cuál
Clerk		**Empleado**
Which is it?	kwalés↓	¿Cuál es?
green	berdé↓	verde

the trunk	èl→baúl↓	el baúl
Mrs. Harris It's these green suitcases and this small trunk. (1)	son|estaᴣmaletaᴣberdes↑ᴣéstèbaúl pekéɲyò↓	*Sra. Harris* Son estas maletas verdes y este baúl pequeño.
have (to have)	tèŋgà↓ tènér↓	tenga (tener)
the kindness, goodness	là→bòndàd↓	la bondad
be so kind as to, please	teŋga→la→bondáꝺ→ꝺè↓	tenga la bondad de
Clerk Please open the trunk first.	teŋgalabondáꝺ|ꝺeábrirelbaúl|priméró↓	*Empleado* Tenga la bondad de abrir el baúl primero.
This thing — what is it?	éstò↓ ke|és↓	Esto, ¿qué es?
the gift	èl→rréɡalò↓	el regalo
to declare	dèklàrár↓	declarar
Mrs. Harris It's some gifts. Everything's declared.	sónᴜnòᴣrrégalós↓ tòꝺoestaꝺeklaráꝺò↓	*Sra. Harris* Son unos regalos. Todo está declarado.
the list	là→listà↓	la lista
Clerk Oh, yes. Here it is on the list.	a|sí↓ àkiᶒstaᶒnlalístà↓	*Empleado* Ah, sí. Aquí está en la lista.
the overnight case, handbag	èl→màlètín↓	el maletín

(for) me

mé↓

me

to examine, inspect

rrėbisár↓

revisar

Mrs. Harris
This handbag, aren't you going to check it? (2)

éstemaletín↓ nómelobarrebisar↑

Sra. Harris
Èste maletín, ¿no me lo va a revisar?

necessary

nėsėsáryó↓

necesario

Clerk
No ma'am, it's not necessary.

nosenyórà↓ nọezneses̬áryó↓

Empleado
No señora, no es necesario.

to you (it) lacks (to lack)

lé—faltà↓ fáltár↓

le falta (faltar)

Molina
Are you missing anything, Mrs. Harris?

nólefaltanáḋa|senyóra↑

Molina
¿No le falta nada, señora?

complete

kómpletó↓

completo

Mrs. Harris
No, everything's here.

nó↓ todoẹstakomplétó↓

Sra. Harris
No. Todo está completo.

(Later, in the lobby)

to take care of, assist

àtèndér↓

atender

the immigration

la—inmiɡráṣyon↓

la inmigración

Molina
Did they take good care of you in Immigration? (3)

láṇàtèndiḋobyen|eninmiɡraṣyon↑

Molina
¿La han atendido bien en Inmigración?

to complain myself (to complain oneself)	kếharmê�↓ kếharsê↓	quejarme (quejarse)
Mrs. Harris I can't complain.	yó|nómếpwédokếhár↓	*Sra. Harris* Yo no me puedo quejar.
kind, nice, courteous	á̇mablế↓	amable
They've been very nice to me.	kònmigọ́↑ànsídòmuyamáblês↓	Conmigo han sido muy amables.
for us	nós↓	nos
that (he) may carry (to carry)	kê̇-ʎyébé↓ ʎyébár↓	que lleve (llevar)
Harris I'll go look for a taxi and someone to carry the suitcases for us.	bóyàbúskárúntaksí↑ ḭ̀alçyen|kénóẓⁿʎyeḇe la̠maḷétàs↓	*Harris* Voy a buscar un taxi y a alguien que nos lleve las maletas.
(I) said (to say)	dihé↓ dé̇ṣír↓	dije (decir)
last night	á̇noché↓	anoche
the car	él-kòché↓	el coche
to fit	ká̇bér↓	caber
Molina As I said last night, there's room in my car for all of us *and* the luggage.	kómoledíhḛ̀ánoché↑ ènmikóche| kàbémóstoḍos|ḭ̀eḷekipáhế↓	*Molina* Como le dije anoche, en mi coche cabemos todos y el equipaje.
great (large)	gran↓ grándê↓	gran (grande)
the help	la̠-áyuḍa̠↓	la ayuda

to us	nós↓	nos
to lend, to provide	préstár↓	prestar

Harris
You're being a great help to us. Thanks a lot, Molina.

nòs̩ès̩tap̩res̩tándo |únáqránayúd̩à↓

muchaz̩gráşyáz |mòlínà↓

Harris
Nos está prestando una gran ayuda. Muchas gracias, Molina.

15.10 Notes on the basic sentences

(1) It is perhaps worth calling to your attention the fact that in this Spanish utterance the number of the verb (plural) rigorously agrees with the number of the subject (plural) even though the subject is positioned *after* the verb. In English the 'logical' subject is plural, but the grammatical subject is *it*, which is singular and requires the singular verb form *is*. The same situation occurs below, 'It's some gifts'.

(2) The occurrence of both direct and indirect clitics in the same phrase will be examined closely in Unit 20. In the meanwhile all that need be pointed out is that the indirect clitic is the first of the two. Note, however, that no equivalent to the indirect /me/ appears in the English translation.

(3) Notice that the Spanish present perfect construction /án—atend́ido/ is translated by the English past tense '*did* they take good care of' in this sentence. This is a not infrequent translation pattern.

15.2   DRILLS AND GRAMMAR

15.21   Pattern drills

15.21.1   Indirect clitic pronouns - one object

A. Presentation of pattern

ILLUSTRATIONS

_____	1	sí↓ mégustà↓	Sí, *me* gusta.
_____	2	mèkòmbyénemás |èlprimérò↓	*Me* conviene más el primero.
_____	3	kétepásà↓	¿Qué *te* pasa?

What do you need (lack)?	4 kétefáltà↓	¿Qué *te* falta?
_____	5 léǥustaelkwàrto↑	¿*Le* gusta el cuarto?
_____	6 kómolebá↓	¿Cómo *le* va?
We like the room.	7 nózǥustaelkwártò↓	*Nos* gusta el cuarto.
It looks small to us.	8 nóspàreşepekéꞃyó↓	*Nos* parece pequeño.
What do you all think?	9 kélesparéşè↓	¿Qué *les* parece?
Does it look all right to you?	10 léspàreşebyén↑	¿*Les* parece bien?

EXTRAPOLATION

	sg	pl
1	me	nos
2 fam	te	
2 - 3	le	les

NOTES

a. Indirect clitic pronouns inflect for person and number, but not for gender.

15.21.11 Substitution drill - Number substitution

1	mégustalakásà↓	nózgustalakásà↓
2	nósfaltanlaskamísàs↓	méfaltanlaskamísàs↓
3	lézgustạeleḏifísyò↓	légustạeleḏifísyò↓
4	léfaltạundólàr↓	lésfaltạundólàr↓
5	nózgustanlazlegúmbrès↓	mégustanlazlegúmbrès↓
6	léskómbyénemașelótró↓	lékómbyénemașelótró↓
7	mèḅamuybyén↓	nózḅamuybyén↓

1	*Me* gusta la casa.	Nos gusta la casa.
2	*Nos* faltan las camisas.	Me faltan las camisas.
3	*Les* gusta el edificio.	Le gusta el edificio.
4	*Le* falta un dólar.	Les falta un dólar.
5	*Nos* gustan las legumbres.	Me gustan las legumbres.
6	*Les* conviene más el otro.	Le conviene más el otro.
7	*Me* va muy bien.	Nos va muy bien.

15.21.12 Response drill

1 légústálášérbeša↑ọelkuḅalíbrè↓   mèǫústàlàšèrḅèšà↓

2 lézçústạélápártámentọ↑olakásà↓   nóžǫústạélápártàmentò↓

3 léfáltàlàsópạ↑olạensaláḋà↓   lèfáltàlàsópà↓

4 lézbábyen↑omál↓   léžbábyen↓

[grándè↓] 5 ketepareše̩|elạerẹopwértò↓   mèpàreše̩ɑrándè↓

[pékéɲò↓] 6 kelespareše̩|eleḋifíšyó↓   nóspàreše̩epekéɲò↓

[bàratòs↓] 7 kelespareše̩n|lostráhés↓   lèspàreše̩embarátós↓

[doše̩↓]   8 kwánta(s)semánaz|lefáltàn↓   mèfaltandóše̩↓

---

1 ¿Le gusta la cerveza o el cuba libre?   Me gusta la cerveza.

2 ¿Les gusta el apartamento o la casa?   Nos gusta el apartamento.

3 ¿Le falta la sopa o la ensalada?   Le falta la sopa.

4 ¿Les va bien o mal?   Les va bien.

(grande)   5 ¿Qué te parece el aereopuerto?   Me parece grande.

(pequeño) 6 ¿Qué les parece el edificio?   Nos parece pequeño.

(baratos) 7 ¿Qué les parecen los trajes?   Les parecen baratos.

(doce)   8 ¿Cuántas semanas le faltan?   Me faltan doce.

[múybyén↓] 9 kómolezbá↓   nôzbámúybyén↓

[èlàbyón↓] 10 lèzgústa̧elbárko↑   no↓ lèzgústa̧èlàbyón↓
[làkàsà↓] 11 lègústa̧elapartaménto↑   no↓ lègústàlàkàsà↓
 [bwénà↓] 12 tèpàreşemala|lalabanderia↑   no↓ mèpàréşèbwená↓

        13 lègústa|la̧eskwélaɗeleŋgwas↑   sí↓ mègústàmuchò↓
        14 lèspàreşebyén|ala(s)syéte↑   sí↓ nòspàreşebyén↓
        15 lèbabyenaki↑   sí↓ lèbámúybyén↓

(muy bien)   9 ¿Cómo les va?   Nos va muy bien.

(el avión)   10 ¿Les gusta el barco?   No, les gusta el avión.
(la casa)   11 ¿Le gusta el apartamento?   No, le gusta la casa.
(buena)   12 ¿Te parece mala la lavandería?   No, me parece buena.

             13 ¿Le gusta la escuela de lenguas?   Sí, me gusta mucho.
             14 ¿Les parece bien a las siete?   Sí, nos parece bien.
             15 ¿Le va bien aquí?   Sí, le va muy bien.

601

15.21.13 Translation drill

1 The suits seem inexpensive to us.	lóstrahez |nóspáréşémbàratòs↓	Los trajes nos parecen baratos.
2 He likes this suburb very much.	léĝústàmucho |èstèὲárryò↓	Le gusta mucho este barrio.
3 I don't like that name.	nomegustạ |esenómbrè↓	No me gusta ese nombre.
4 Does she need (lack) anything.	lèfáltàlgo↑	¿Le falta algo?
5 Don't you like the house?	nolegustàlakàsa↑	¿No le gusta la casa?
6 On the contrary, I like it very much.	àlkòntraryò↓ mèĝústàmuchò↓	Al contrario, me gusta mucho.
7 Besides, it seems inexpensive to us.	àđèmas↑ nóspàreşebaráta↓	Además, nos parece barata.
8 We're thirteen dollars short.	nósfáltan |treşe⁺ólàrès↓	Nos faltan trece dólares.
9 How's it going with you all?	komolerὲá↓	¿Cómo les va?
10 What do they think of the laundry on the corner?	kélespàreşe |lalaɓanderia |đelạeskína↓	¿Qué les parece la lavandería de la esquina?
11 Does she like the new building?	léĝustạele⁺ifişyonwèὲo↑	¿Le gusta el edificio nuevo?
12 It doesn't suit me, it's too expensive.	nɔmekomɓyéné↓ é⁻muykázó↓	No me conviene, es muy caro.
13 Does the other one suit you?	lékómɓyénelotro↑	¿Le conviene el otro?

B. Discussion of pattern

As stated in Unit 10, clitics are pronoun forms which occur with verbs. Clitics are of three kinds, direct (presented in Unit 10), indirect (presented here), and reflexive (to be presented in Unit 24).

The selection of the clitic depends on the verb it accompanies. Some verbs may appear only with direct clitics, some only with indirect, some only with reflexive, and some with various combinations. There is some overlap; some verbs may appear with direct or indirect (/lo‑ayúdo/vs/le‑ayúdo/, /lo‑espéro/ vs /le‑espéro/,/lo‑(l)yámo/vs/le‑(l)yámo/), and some verbs have a different semantic content when used with direct or indirect clitics (/páselo↓/'Pass it' vs /ké‑le‑pása↓/'What's the matter with him').

The presentation in this section has been of constructions where a single clitic, an indirect, appears with a verb. The clitic will often be translated by 'to —'; for example, /mé/= 'to me', though sometimes the English sentence must be rearranged for this to be true: /legústaelkwárto↑/='Does the room please you?' or 'Is the room pleasing to you?' or more freely, 'Do you like the room?'

15.21.2 Indirect clitic pronouns - two objects (indirect clitic pronoun object and direct noun object)

A. Presentation of pattern

ILLUSTRATIONS

_____	1 médiheroŋ|késériandós↓	*Me* dijeron que serían dos.
Will you lend me your pencil?	2 méprestas|tulápis↑	¿*Me* prestas tu lápiz?
_____	3 kyéntelimpya|elapartaméntó↓	¿Quién *te* limpia el apartamento?
Who sends you the newspapers?	4 kyéntemanda|losperyódikós↓	¿Quién *te* manda los periódicos?
_____	5 lédoytrés↓ unodepropína↓	*Le* doy tres, uno de propina.
What has Mario brought you?	6 keleatraidomáryó↓	¿Qué *le* ha traído Mario?

_____	7 álgyen |kénóź⌢yeƀelazmalétàs↓	Alguien que *nos* lleve las maletas.
They told us it would be two.	8 nóźđiheron |kèsèriandós↓	*Nos* dijeron que serían dos.
Who cleans your apartment for you?	9 kyénlezlímpyạ |elapartaméntò↓	¿Quién *les* limpia el apartamento?
Someone to carry the suitcases for them.	10 álọyen |kèlèź⌢yeƀelazmalétàs↓	Alguien que *les* lleve las maletas.

EXTRAPOLATION

	sg	pl
1	me	nos
2 fam	te	
2 - 3	le	les

NOTES

a. This is a repetition of the forms presented in the preceding drill point, appearing here in a different construction.

15.21.21 Substitution drill - Item translation substitution

Problem:

    hwán |mémandalospery6díkós↓

(her)
_____

Answer:

    hwán |lémandalospery6díkós↓

_____

Problem:

    Juan *me* manda los periódicos.

(her)   _____

Answer:

    Juan le manda los periódicos.

1   élnostráȩlarrópà↓

(him)   _____↓   é()letráȩlarrópà↓

(me)   _____↓   élmetráȩlarrópà↓

(her)   _____↓   é(l)letráȩlarrópà↓

(them)   _____↓   é(l)lestráȩlarrópà↓

(you)   _____↓   é(l)letráȩlarrópà↓

1 El *nos* trae la ropa.

(him)   _____   El le trae la ropa.
(me)   _____   El me trae la ropa.
(her)   _____   El le trae la ropa.
(them)   _____   El les trae la ropa.
(you)   _____   El le trae la ropa.

2   éⁿyale̲s̲ˏeskriᵇe|loznómbrès↓

(us)   _____↓   éⁿyanosˏeskriᵇe|loznómbrès↓

(him) _____↓   éⁿyaleskriᵇe|loznómbrès↓

(me)   _____↓   éⁿyameskriᵇe|loznómbrès↓

(you) _____↓   éⁿyaleskriᵇe|loznómbrès↓

(them) _____↓   éⁿyalesˏeskriᵇe|loznómbrès↓

---

2 Ella *les* escribe los nombres.

(us)   _____   Ella nos escribe los nombres.
(him) _____   Ella le escribe los nombres.
(me)   _____   Ella me escribe los nombres.
(you) _____   Ella le escribe los nombres.
(them) _____   Ella les escribe los nombres.

3 éⁿyoz |leↄampermísò↓

(them) _____↓   éⁿyoz |lezↄampermísò↓

(me) _____↓   éⁿyoz |meↄampermísò↓

(her) _____↓   éⁿyoz |leↄampermísò↓

(us) _____↓   éⁿyoz |nozↄampermísò↓

(you pl) _____↓   éⁿyoz |lezↄampermísò↓

---

3 Ellos *le* dan permiso.

(them) _____   Ellos les dan permiso.
(me) _____   Ellos me dan permiso.
(her) _____   Ellos le dan permiso.
(us) _____   Ellos nos dan permiso.
(you pl) _____   Ellos les dan permiso.

4 meánrrébisado|lazmalétàs↓

(her)	_____↓	leánrrébisado|lazmalétàs↓
(us)	_____↓	nòs̠ánrrébisado|lazmalétàs↓
(him)	_____↓	leánrrébisado|lazmalétàs↓
(them)	_____↓	lés̠ánrrébisado|lazmalétàs↓
(you)	_____↓	leánrrébisado|lazmalétàs↓

---

4 *Me* han revisado las maletas.

(her)	_____	Le han revisado las maletas.
(us)	_____	Nos han revisado las maletas.
(him)	_____	Le han revisado las maletas.
(them)	_____	Les han revisado las maletas.
(you)	_____	Le han revisado las maletas.

5   lwísa|lézlabalaskamísàs↓

(me)   _____ ↓   lwísa|mèlabalaskamísàs↓

(him)   _____ ↓   lwísa|lélabalaskamísàs↓

(us)   _____ ↓   lwísa|nózlabalaskamísàs↓

(you)   _____ ↓   lwísa|lélabalaskamísàs↓

(them) _____ ↓   lwísa|lézlabalaskamísàs↓

---

5 Luisa *les* lava las camisas.

(me)   _____   Luisa me lava las camisas.
(him)   _____   Luisa le lava las camisas.
(us)   _____   Luisa nos lava las camisas.
(you)   _____   Luisa le lava las camisas.
(them) _____   Luisa les lava las camisas.

15.21.22 Translation drills - Paired sentences

1 When do you send them the newspapers?

   When do you send the newspapers to them?

kwándo │lézmándaustéð │losperyóðikòs↓

¿Cuándo les manda Ud. los periódicos?

2 What have you sent them?

   What have you sent to them?

kéles‚amandáðo │ustéða‿éᵑyòs↓

¿Qué les ha mandado Ud. a ellos?

3 She never sends us anything.

   She never sends anything to us.

éᵐya │nuŋkanozmandanáðà↓

Ella nunca nos manda nada.

4 What has John brought you all?

   What has John brought to you all?

kélesatraíðo │hwaṇaustéðès↓

¿Qué les ha traído Juan a Uds.?

5 My sister always brings me a new shirt.

   My sister always brings a new shirt to me.

miérmana │syémpremetrae │únákámisanwéɐà↓

Mi hermana siempre me trae una camisa nueva.

6 My mother-in-law always gives me wine.

   My mother-in-law always gives wine to me.

miswégra │syémpremeðabíno↓

Mi suegra siempre me da vino.

7 I've given him my pen.   yóléđáᵗo |miplumaél↓   Yo le he dado mi pluma a él.

   I've given my pen to him.

8 The Molinas haven't rented him the   lóᵇmólína |nólęaṇalkiláđǫ |elapartaméntó↓   Los Molina no le han alquilado el
   apartment.   apartamento .

   The Molinas haven't rented the apartment
   to him.

9 I write her very little.   yóleskríbomuypókǫ |áéⁱyà↓   Yo le escribo muy poco a ella.

   I write very little to her.

10 My girl friend writes me a lot.   minóbya |mèskríbemúchǒ↓   Mi novia me escribe mucho.

    My girl friend writes a lot to me.

11 When are you going to write him.   kwàndolebáęskribír |ùstéđ↓   ¿Cuándo le va a escribir Ud?

    When are you going to write to him.   End of Tape 12A

Sentence translations

Tape 12B

1 When does he give us their names?	kwándonozda |loznómbrezdé(l)yós↓		¿Cuándo nos da los nombres de ellos?
2 Are you going to help her work?	ústéd |lébáyúdaratrabahar↑		¿Ud. le va a ayudar a trabajar?
3 Is she going to rent you (all) the house?	lézbálkilárlakása↑		¿Les va a alquilar la casa?
4 I don't owe him anything.	yónoledebonáda↓		Yo no le debo nada.
5 How much do you owe me?	kwántomedebęustéd		¿Cuánto me debe Ud.?
6 The Harrises always speak to us in English.	lóshárris |syémpre |nos̩ablanęnįnglés↓		Los Harris siempre nos hablan en inglés.
7 The Garcías haven't rented the apartment to him.	lózgárşia |nolęan̩alkilado |elapartaméntó↓		Los García no le han alquilado el apartamento.
8 They're going to write to me.	é(l)yoz |meban̩aeskribír↓		Ellos me van a escribir.
9 Why don't you write to them.	pórkęnoles̩eskríbę |ústéd↓		¿Por qué no les escribe Ud.?

10 The girl cleans the furniture for them.   lámúchacha|lézlímpyalozmwéblès↓   La muchacha les limpia los muebles.

11 The chauffer always carries the suitcases   élchófer|syémpre|nôzⓎebalazmalétàs↓   El chofer siempre nos lleva las maletas.
    for us.

12 My wife doesn't wash my (the) shirts   mįésposa|nomelabalaskamísàs↓   Mi esposa no me lava las camisas.
    for me.

13 Nobody sweeps the apartment for them.   nadye|leʔtˑarrelapartaméntó↓   Nadie les barre el apartamento.

14 Mr. Miranda has bought the furniture   élséɲyormiranda|nôsákômpradolozmwéblès↓   El Sr. Miranda nos ha comprado los
    from us.   muebles.

15 I have bought the sofa bed from them.   yoles.ekómprado|elsofakámà↓   Yo les he comprado el sofá-cama.

16 A man has bought the house from them.   únséɲyor|lésákómprado|lákasaéⓎós↓   Un señor les ha comprado la casa a ellos.

B. Discussion of pattern

     In the earlier drill sections on indirect clitics, one indirect clitic appeared as the single pronoun object of the verb. In the present drill section, two objects appear. They could both be clitics, but since complicating changes occur among the clitics when two appear together, a drill on such combined sequences is reserved for a later unit (Unit 20). In this section one pronoun object (expressed by an indirect clitic) and one noun object appear, controlled by the same verb.

     Notice that the indirect relationship of Spanish is expressed in English with object pronouns in two positions: alone after a verb: 'He writes us a letter every day'; or with the relater 'to': 'He sent the book to us'. Notice also that the indirect clitic construction in Spanish translates several English relaters other than 'to'; they seem to mean quite different things in English, though they are classified as similar by their common participation in the Spanish indirect clitic construction: /metráelos líbros↓/ 'He brings the books *to* me'; /meʔyéba │lamalétaↆ/ 'He carries the suitcase *for* me'; /mekómpra │elkárro↓/ 'He's buying the car *from* me'. *To, for*, and *from* can all be translated by the Spanish indirect clitic.

15.21.3 Question intonation patterns — Yes questions

    A. Presentation of pattern

ILLUSTRATIONS

_____	1 tyenɐunlapiş↑	2 2 2↑ ¿Tiene un lápiz?
_____	tyenɐunlapiş │	2 3 1│ ¿Tiene un lápiz?
_____	2 póḋemozḃerlo↑	1 2 2 2↑ ¿Podemos verlo?
_____	póḋemozḃerló │	1 2 3 1│ ¿Podemos verlo?
_____	3 ėʒmuykaro↑	1 2 2 2↑ ¿Es muy caro?
_____	ėʒmuykaró │	1 2 3 1│ ¿Es muy caro?

EXTRAPOLATION

Yes-no question	Yes question
/1222↑/	/1231 │/

    a. The /1231 │/ pattern signals, in appropriate contexts, a yes-no question in which a 'yes' answer is more or less expected. Note that it differs from the emphatic or contrasting statement pattern of units 12 and 13 (/1231↓/) only in the extent and abruptness of the final fade-out. This difference is transcribed by / │/ vs /↓/

615

15.21.31 Substitution drill - pattern substitution

Problem:

      lépàreʂebarato↑

Answer:

      lépàreʂebaratò|

1 éstalabwelta↑   éstalabweltà|

2 légustalaiↄea↑   légustalaiↄeà|

3 éstaↄesokupaↄo↑   éstaↄesokupaↄò|

4 nèʂèsitalmwaↄas↑   nèʂèsitalmwaↄás|

Problem: 1 2   2 2↑
¿Le parece barato?

Answer: 1 2   3 1|
¿Le parece barato?

         1 2   2 2↑   1 2   3 1|
1 Está a la vuelta?   ¿Está a la vuelta?

         1 2   22↑   1 2   31|
2 ¿Le gusta la idea?   ¿Le gusta la idea?

         1 2   2 2↑   1 2   3 1|
3 ¿Está desocupado?   ¿Está desocupado?

         1 2   2 2↑   1 2   3 1|
4 ¿Necesita almohadas?   ¿Necesita almohadas?

5 tòđàbìahuntòs↑   tòđàbìahuntòs|

6 syempretrabàhandò↑   syémpretrabàhandò|

7 éstaęnlakasà↑   éstaęnlakasà|

8 ènlꞵémbàhađamerikànà↑   ènlꞵémbàhađamerikànà|

9 ènlàbénidanwebè↑   ènlàbénidanwebè|

```
    1  2  2 2↑                                    1  2  3 1 |
5 ¿Todavía juntos?                          ¿Todavía juntos?
    2       2 2↑                                   2      3 1 |
6 ¿Siempre trabajando?                   ¿Siempre trabajando?
    1 2    2 2↑                                  1 2    3 1 |
7 ¿Está en la casa?                          ¿Está en la casa?
    1    2    2 2↑                               1    2    3 1 |
8 ¿En la Embajada Americana?          ¿En la Embajada Americana?
    1    2  2 2↑                                 1    2  3 1 |
9 ¿En la Avenida Nueve?                   ¿En la Avenida Nueve?
```

10 ityéngambré↑   ityéngambré|

11 ibébebinó↑   ibébebinó|

---

                1 2   2 2↑   1 2   3 1 |
10 ¿Y tiene hambre?   ¿Y tiene hambre?

              1 2   22↑   1 2   31 |
11 ¿Y bebe vino?   ¿Y bebe vino?

B. Discussion of pattern

A yes-no question, particularly in an informal situation, to which a 'yes' answer is more or less expected, is frequently uttered with the intonation pattern /1231 |/.

The statement of /1231 |/ on a question anticipating a 'yes' answer can have additional meaning. For instance /tyéngunlápiş |/ may really mean, 'Can I borrow a pencil' if uttered in an appropriate context, such as with the hand of the speaker extended toward the person addressed.

As a generalization, however, it is not inappropriate to say that 'yes' is the anticipated reply to such a question.

15.22   Replacement drills

A   sónmuyrrıgúrosos |enladwanat   sónmuyrrıgúrosos |enesadwanat

1 _____ esa ___t   sónmuyrrıgúrosos |enesakasat

2 _____ kasat   sónmuyamables |enesakasat

3 _____ amables _____ t   sónmuytraŋkilos |enesakasat

4 _____ traŋkilos _____ t   sónmuysuşyos |enesakasat

5 _____ suşyos _____ t   sónmuysuşyos |enesosotelest

6 _____ ótelest   sónmuysuşyos |enakelotelt

7 _____ akél ___t

A   ¿Son muy rigurosos en la aduana?

1 ¿ _____ esa ___?   ¿Son muy rigurosos en esa aduana?

2 ¿ _____ casa?   ¿Son muy rigurosos en esa casa?

3 ¿ _____ amables _____ ?   ¿Son muy amables en esa casa?

4 ¿ _____ tranquilos _____ ?   ¿Son muy tranquilos en esa casa?

5 ¿ _____ sucios _____ ?   ¿Son muy sucios en esa casa?

6 ¿ _____ hoteles?   ¿Son muy sucios en esos hoteles?

7 ¿ _____ aquel___?   ¿Son muy sucios en aquel hotel?

B   yáẹstákí|mịẹkipáhè↓   yáẹstánakí|mizbaúlès↓

1 _____ baúlès↓   yáẹstánaᶜyí|mizbaúlès↓

2 _____ aᶜyí _____↓   yáẹstáᶜyí|subaúl↓

3 _____ su _____↓   yáẹstánaᶜyí|suskósàs↓

4 _____ kósás↓   tóḍàbịạ|estánaᶜyí|suskósàs↓

5 tóḍàbịạ _____↓   tóḍàbịạ|estánaᶜyí|ẹsaskósàs↓

6 _____ ésas ____↓   tóḍàbịạ|estánaᶜyí|ẹsozmaletínès↓

7 _____ maletínès↓

B   Ya está aquí mi equipaje.

1 _____ baúles.   Ya están aquí mis baúles.

2 _____ allí _____.   Ya están allí mis baúles.

3 _____ su ____.   Ya está allí su baúl.

4 _____ cosas.   Ya están allí sus cosas.

5 Todavía _____.   Todavía están allí sus cosas.

6 _____ esas ____.   Todavía están allí esas cosas.

7 _____ maletines.   Todavía están allí esos maletines.

C   són |unazmalétazbérdès↓   es |unamalétabérdè↓

1   és_____↓   es |umbaulbérdè↓

2   _____baul_____↓   es |umbaulpekéɲò↓

3   _____pekéɲò↓   es |estebaulpekéɲò↓

4   __este_____↓   es |estebaulpekéɲò↓

5   _____mesas_____↓   són |estazmesaspekéɲàs↓

6   __otraz_____↓   són |otrazmesaspekéɲàs↓

7   ay_____↓   ay |otrazmesaspekéɲàs↓

C   Son unas maletas verdes.

1 Es_____ .   Es una maleta verde.

2 _____baúl_____ .   Es un baúl verde.

3 _____pequeño.   Es un baúl pequeño.

4 ___ este_____ .   Es este baúl pequeño.

5 _____ mesas_____ .   Son estas mesas pequeñas.

6 ___ otras_____ .   Son otras mesas pequeñas.

7 Hay_____ .   Hay otras mesas pequeñas.

621

D   ákięstálalístá↓

1 _____ęsta__↓   ákięsta |ęstalístá↓

2 _____maletínęs↓   ákięstán |ęstozmaletínęs↓

3 _____loz_____↓   ákięstán |lozmaletínęs↓

4 _áy_____↓   ákiay |unozmaletínęs↓

5 _____kósás↓   ákiay |unaskósás↓

6 ___ótras_____↓   ákiay |otraskósás↓

7 _____ómbręs↓   ákiay |otrosómbręs↓

D   Aquí está la lista.

1 _____ esta__.   Aquí está esta lista.

2 _____ maletines.   Aquí están estos maletines.

3 _____ los_____.   Aquí están los maletines.

4 __ hay _____.   Aquí hay unos maletines.

5 _____ cosas.   Aquí hay unas cosas.

6 ___otras_____.   Aquí hay otras cosas.

7 _____ hombres.   Aquí hay otros hombres.

E   toḍọestákomplétò↓   toḍọestaḍesokupáḍò↓

1   _____ ḍesokupáḍò↓   lázmesas |estándesokupáḍàs↓

2   lázmesas _____ ↓   lámesạestalístà↓

3   _____ lístà↓   élséŋyorestalístò↓

4   élséŋyor _____ ↓   ló(s)séŋyores |estaŋkonténtòs↓

5   _____ konténtòs↓   nósotros |estámoskonténtòs↓

6   nósotros _____ ↓   yọẹstoykonténtò↓

7   ẹstoy _____ ↓

_____

E   Todo está completo.

1   _____ desocupado.   Todo está desocupado.

2   Las mesas _____ .   Las mesas están desocupadas.

3   _____ lista.   La mesa está lista.

4   El señor _____ .   El señor está listo.

5   _____ contentos.   Los señores están contentos.

6   Nosotros _____ .   Nosotros estamos contentos.

7   ____ estoy _____ .   Yo estoy contento.

623

F   boyabuskaruntáksi↓

1   ____traer_____↓   boyatraeruntáksi↓

2   _____ líbròs↓   boyatraerunozlíbròs↓

3   bamos_____↓   bamos|atraerunozlíbròs↓

4   ____ komprar_____↓   bamos|akomprarunozlíbròs↓

5   _____esoz____↓   bamos|akomprar|esozlíbròs↓

6   _____ kósàs↓   bamos|akomprar|esaskósàs↓

7   ténemos|ke_____↓   ténemos|kekomprar|esaskósàs↓

F   Voy a buscar un taxi.

1 ____ traer_____.   Voy a traer un taxi.

2 _____ libros.   Voy a traer unos libros.

3 Vamos _____.   Vamos a traer unos libros.

4 ____ comprar ____.   Vamos a comprar unos libros.

5 _____ esos__.   Vamos a comprar esos libros.

6 _____cosas.   Vamos a comprar esas cosas.

7 Tenemos que _____.   Tenemos que comprar esas cosas.

15.23   Variation drills

A   ėstóysėgúro |dėkęáustę∂ |nolobánamolestár↓

Estoy seguro de que a usted no lo van a
molestar.

1 I'm sure they're not going to send *you.*

ėstóysėgúro |dėkęáustę∂ |nolobánamandár↓

Estoy seguro de que a usted no lo van a
mandar.

2 I'm sure they're not going to wait for
   him.

ėstóysėgúro |dėkęáel |nolobánaęsperár↓

Estoy seguro de que a él no lo van a
esperar.

3 I'm sure they're not going to take *her.*

ėstóysėgúro |dėkęáe()ya |nolabána()yebár↓

Estoy seguro de que a ella no la van a
llevar.

4 He's sure they're going to need *me.*

ėstásėgúro |dėkęámí |mebánanęęsitár↓

Está seguro de que a mí me van a
necesitar.

5 He's sure they're going to need *them.*

ėstásėgúro |dėkęáe()yoz |lozbánanęęsitár↓

Está seguro de que a ellos los van a
necesitar.

6 We're sure they're going to send John
   and Jose.

ėstámó(s)sėgúroz |dėkęáhwan |įahosé |lozbán
amandár↓

Estamos seguros de que a Juan y a José
los van a mandar.

7 We're sure they're going to send Mary
   and Carmen.

ėstámó(s)sėgúroz |dėkęámáría |įakármen |laz
bánamandár↓

Estamos seguros de que a María y a
Carmen las van a mandar.

B   téngalabondáđ |đęábrírelbaúl |priméró↓   Tenga la bondad de abrir el baúl primero.

  1 Please open the green suitcase.   téngalabondáđ |đęábrír |lamalétabérđè↓   Tenga la bondad de abrir la maleta verde.

  2 Please dress right away.   téngalabondáđ |đébéstirsenseǫíđà↓   Tenga la bondad de vestirse en seguida.

  3 Please wait a moment.   téngalabondáđ |đéspérarunmoméntó↓   Tenga la bondad de esperar un momento.

  4 Please wait around the corner.   téngalabondáđ |đéspéraralabwéltà↓   Tenga la bondad de esperar a la vuelta.

  5 Please speak English.   téngalabondáđ |đęáblaringlés↓   Tenga la bondad de hablar inglés.

  6 Please come alone.   téngalabondáđ |đébènirsóló↓   Tenga la bondad de venir solo.

  7 Please come (pl.) together.   ténganlabondáđ |đébènirhúntòs↓   Tengan la bondad de venir juntos.

C   sónúnòzrrègálòs↓ tođǫestađeklaráđò↓   Son unos regalos. Todo está declarado.

  1 They're some books. Everything's   sónúnózlibròs↓ tođǫestakompráđò↓   Son unos libros. Todo está comprado.
    bought.

  2 They're some shirts. Everything's   sónúnáskàmisás↓ tođǫestalabáđò↓   Son unas camisas. Todo está lavado.
    washed.

3 It's whisky. It's in the declaration.

èzwiski↓ éstáḍéklàraḍò↓

Es whiskey. Está declarado.

4 The shirt is washed.

làkàmis̯a̯està́labáḍà↓

La camisa está lavada.

5 The car is fixed.

èlawt̯o̯està́rregláḍò↓

El auto está arreglado.

6 The rooms are rented.

lòskwartos |èstàn̯a̯lkiláḍòs↓

Los cuartos están alquilados.

7 The shirts are washed.

làskàmisas |èstàn̯labáḍàs↓

Las camisas están lavadas.

D   lán̯a̯tèndiḍobyén |en̯inmigra̯şyon↑

¿La han atendido bien en inmigración?

1 Have they taken good care of you (f) in the hotel?

lán̯a̯tèndiḍobyén |en̯e̯lotél↑

¿La han atendido bien en el hotel?

2 Have they included you (m) in the list?

lo̯ánin̯klwiḍo̯ |en̯lalista↑

¿Lo han incluído en la lista?

3 Have they seen much of Washington?

án̯kónóş̯iḍomucho̯ |en̯washin̯ton↑

¿Han conocido mucho en Washington?

4 Have you (pl) eaten in that restaurant?

án̯kómiḍo̯ |en̯eserrestorán↑

¿Han comido en ese restorán?

5 Have you (pl) learned much Spanish?

án̯a̯préndiḍo |mucho̯espanyól↑

¿Han aprendido mucho español?

6 Have you (sg) waited a long time?　　áẹspéraḋo|múchotyémpo↑　　　　　¿Ha esperado mucho tiempo?

7 Have you (sg) spoken with them?　　áblaḋo|konẹ́ṇyos↑　　　　　　¿Ha hablado con ellos?

E   kònmiọọ↑ànsíḋómúyamáblès↓　　　　　　　　　Conmigo han sido muy amables.

1 They've been very nice to you (fam).　　kòntiọọ↑ànsíḋómuyamáblès↓　　　Contigo han sido muy amables.

2 They've been very nice to you (form).　　kònústeḋt↑ànsíḋómuyamáblès↓　　Con usted han sido muy amables.

3 They've been very nice to him.　　kònẹlt↑ànsíḋómuyamáblès↓　　　　　Con él han sido muy amables.

4 He's been very nice to her.　　kònẹṇyạt↑àsíḋómuyamáblé↓　　　　Con ella ha sido muy amable.

5 He hasn't spoken with us.　　kò(ṇ)nósótroz↑nọabláḋò↓　　　　　Con nosotros no ha hablado.

6 He hasn't worked with us.　　kó(ṇ)nósótroz↑nọatrabaháḋò↓　　　Con nosotros no ha trabajado.

7 He hasn't been out with us.　　kó(ṇ)nósótroz↑nọasalíḋò↓　　　　Con nosotros no ha salido.

F nòs̠és̠tàprèstándǫ |únàgránạyúɖà↓   Nos está prestando una gran ayuda.

1 He's waiting for us in the rear of the   nòs̠és̠tàẹspèrándǫ |dètráz̠ɖèlèɖifíṣyò↓   Nos está esperando detrás del edificio.
   building.

2 He's waiting for us in the park.   nòs̠és̠tàẹspèrándǫ |en̥elpárkè↓   Nos está esperando en el parque.

3 The lady is speaking to you (fam).   tès̠tàblándolasèŋyórà↓   Te está hablando la señora.

4 He's fixing the car for you (fam).   tès̠tàrrèɋlándǫęláwtò↓   Te está arreglando el auto.

5 He's sending me two hundred dollars a   mès̠tàmandándo |ɖos(ṣ)yèntoz̠ɖólares |àlmés↓   Me está mandando doscientos dólares al
   month.   mes.

6 He's giving me twenty dollars a week.   mès̠tàɖándo |bèyntèɖólares |àlàsèmánà↓   Me está dando veinte dólares a la semana.

7 It's bothering me a lot.   mès̠tàmolès̠tándomúchò↓   Me está molestando mucho.

                                                                                                        629

15.24   Review drill — Possessive constructions

1   Juan's sister is here.   laèrmána |dèhwán |estákí↓   La hermana de Juan está aquí.

2   Antonio's wife is here.   laèspósa |dęàntónyo |ęstákí↓   La esposa de Antonio está aquí.

3   Carmen's mother-in-law is here.   láswegra |dèkármen |estákí↓   La suegra de Carmen está aquí.

4   Antonio's son is here.   éliho |dęàntónyo |ęstákí↓   El hijo de Antonio está aquí.

5   Carmen's cup is here.   látaşa |dèkármen |estákí↓   La taza de Carmen está aquí.

6   Antonio's girl is here.   làniŋya |dęàntónyo |ęstákí↓   La niña de Antonio está aquí.

7   Antonio's boy is here.   élniŋyo |dęàntónyo |ęstákí↓   El niño de Antonio está aquí.

8   Carmen's friend is here.   lámiga |dèkármen |estákí↓   La amiga de Carmen está aquí.

9   Carmen's things are here.   láskósaz |dèkármen |estanakí↓   Las cosas de Carmen están aquí.

10 Jose's furniture is here.   lózmwéblez |dèhóse |ęstanakí↓   Los muebles de José están aquí.

11 Juan's desk is here.   éléskritóryo |dèhwán |estákí↓   El escritorio de Juan está aquí.

15.3   CONVERSATION STIMULUS

NARRATIVE 1

1 The immigration people have taken good
  care of Colonel Harris' family.

ló(s)sènyórez |dèlàinmiç̧rás̩yon↑ànàtèndido

muybyén |àlàfàmílyà |dèlkòrónélhárris↓

Los señores de la inmigración han atendido
muy bien a la familia del coronel Harris.

2 They've been very nice to them.

ánsido |muyamáblès |kòné⌢yos↓

Han sido muy amables con ellos.

3 Mrs. Harris' name is Jean.

èlnombre |dèlàsènyóraharris |ezy̧ín↓

El nombre de la señora Harris es Jean.

4 Jean has to go to customs now.

y̧in |tyénèkȩ̀ir |àlàdwanàórà↓

Jean tiene que ir a la aduana ahora.

5 The colonel thinks that they are very
  strict there.

èkòrónel↑krȩekeson |muyrrıç̧urósòs |àí↓

El coronel cree que son muy rigurosos ahí.

6 But he isn't sure.

pèrónọestasegúrò↓

Pero no está seguro.

7 Jean has the list of all the things she's
  bringing.

y̧in |tyénèlàlistà |dètoḏazlaskósàsketráè↓

Jean tiene la lista de todas las cosas que
trae.

8 The colonel can't go in.

èlkòrónel |nopweḏepasár↓

El coronel no puede pasar.

9 He'll wait for them here.

àkiloşespérà↓

Aquí los espera.

DIALOG 1

Coronel, pregúntele a Jean si la han
atendido bien en inmigración.

téánátendidobyen |eninmigrașyon |yint

Coronel: ¿Te han atendido bien en
inmigración, Jean?

Jean, contéstele que sí, que los señores
ahí han sido muy amables con ustedes.

sit ló(s)senyores |aitánsidómuyamáblés |
kó(n)nòsótròs↓

Jean : Sí, los señores ahí han sido muy
amables con nosotros.

Coronel, dígale que ahora tiene que ir a
la aduana.

àora |tyénéskeiraladwáná↓

Coronel: Ahora tienes que ir a la aduana.

Jean, dígale que sí, y pregúntele si son
muy rigurosos ahí.

sit sónmuyrrigurosos |ait

Jean: Sí. ¿Son muy rigurosos ahí?

Coronel, contéstele que Ud. cree que sí,
que no está seguro. Pregúntele si tiene
la lista de todas las cosas que trae.

kreokesí↓ nóęstoysegúrò↓
tyenezlalista |detodaslaskosas |ketraest

Coronel: Creo que sí, no estoy seguro.
¿Tienes la lista de todas las
cosas que traes?

Jean, contéstele que sí, que aquí está.
Que todo está declarado. Pregúntele
si no viene con Uds.

sit ákięstá↓ todo |estadeklarádò↓
nòbyenesko(n)nosotrost

Jean: Sí, aquí está. Todo está declarado.
¿No vienes con nosotros?

Coronel, contéstele que no, que Ud. no
puede pasar. Que aquí los espera.

no↓ yonopwedopasár↓ ákiloșespérò↓

Coronel: No, yo no puedo pasar. Aquí
los espero.

NARRATIVE 2

1 They're ready now.	yaę̇stanlístȯs↓	Ya están listos.
2 Jean looks very happy.	yın |páré̦sę̇múykonténtá↓	Jean parece muy contenta.
3 And why shouldn't she? They didn't charge her anything.	ipórkenó↓ nólę̇áŋkȯbra̦donadá↓	¿Y por qué no? No le han cobrado nada.
4 She doesn't know why.	ó͡yá |nosabeporké↓	Ella no sabe por qué.
5 They didn't tell her.	noledihérón↓	No le dijeron.
6 And she isn't going to ask them.	i̦é͡ya |nobapreguntárlės↓	Y ella no va a preguntarles.
7 The colonel (just) can't believe it!	élkȯrónel |nópwedekreérló↓	¡El coronel no puede creerlo!
8 He thought they were very strict here.	élkreia |kéránmuyrrigurósȯs |ȧkí↓	El creía que eran muy rigurosos aquí.

DIALOG 2

Jean, dígale a su esposo que ya están
listos ustedes.

yá |ẹstámózlistós↓

Jean: Ya estamos listos.

Coronel, dígale que ella parece muy
contenta. Que por qué.

páreșez |muy |kóntentá↓ pórké↓

Coronel: Pareces muy contenta. ¿Por
qué?

Jean, contéstele que no le han cobrado
nada.

nó |mẹaŋkòbraḍonaḍá↓

Jean: No me han cobrado nada.

Coronel, dígale que no puede creerlo.
Que por qué.

nópweḍokreérló↓ pórké↓

Coronel: No puedo creerlo, ¿por qué?

Jean, contéstele que Ud. no sabe por qué.
Que no le dijeron, y que Ud. no va a
preguntarles.

nó |sé |pórké↓ nomeḍiheron |iyónobóy |
apreguntárlès↓

Jean: No sé por qué. No me dijeron y
yo no voy a preguntarles.

Coronel, dígale que estupendo. Y que
Ud. creía que eran rigurosos aquí.

ẹstúpendó↓ iyokreía |kéranrrigúrosós | akí↓

Coronel: ¡Estupendo! Y yo creía que eran
rigurosos aquí.

NARRATIVE 3

1 A friend of the colonel's is going to
take them in his car.

únamigo |ḍélkórónel |báⁿyèbarlos‚ensukárró↓

Un amigo del coronel va a llevarlos en
su carro.

2 But with so much baggage there won't
be room for all.

pérókóntanto |ẹkipahe |nobanakaber |tóḍòs↓

Pero con tanto equipaje no van a caber
todos.

3 They'll make two trips, then.

áşèndozbyáhès |èntónşès↓

Hacen dos viajes, entonces.

4 But good gosh! Just a moment!

pérókàrambà↓ únmoméntò↓

¡Pero caramba!, ¡un momento!

5 Something's wrong.

álgopásà↓

Algo pasa.

6 Jean's missing the suitcase with the gifts.

àyìn |lèfálta |làmáletakonlozrregálòs↓

A Jean le falta la maleta con los regalos.

7 She may have left it in the customs (office).

pwéđę |àbèrlà |đèhađǫ |ènlàdwanà↓

Puede haberla dejado en la aduana.

8 She's going to go look for it there.

báìr |àbúskàrlaí↓

Va a ir a buscarla ahí.

DIALOG 3

Coronel, dígale a su esposa que listos, entonces, y que un amigo suyo va a llevarlos a Uds. en su carro.

lìstòs |èntónşès↓ únàmìǫomío | báʸyèbàrnos |ensukárrò↓

Coronel: Listos, entonces. Un amigo mío va a llevarnos en su carro.

Jean, dígale que con tanto equipaje no van a caber todos.

kóntantǫekìpahe |nòbàmosąkabér |tóđòs↓

Jean: Con tanto equipaje no vamos a caber todos.

635

Coronel, dígale que hacen dos viajes,
entonces.

àṣemozⱸozḃyáhés |èntónṣès↓

Coronel: Hacemos dos viajes, entonces.

Jean, dígale que ¡ay, caramba! que un
momento.

ay |kàrambà↓ unmoméntò↓

Jean: ¡Ay, caramba! Un momento.

Coronel, pregúntele que qué le pasa.

ketepásà↓

Coronel: ¿Qué te pasa?

Jean, contéstele que le falta la maleta
con los regalos.

mèfálta |làmàléta |kònlòzrrègàlòs↓

Jean: Me falta la maleta con los regalos.

Coronel, dígale que debe haberla dejado
en la aduana.

debes |àbérla |ⱸehàⱸo |ènlàⱸwanà↓

Coronel: Debes haberla dejado en la
aduana.

Jean, dígale que puede ser. Que Ud. va
a ir a buscarla ahí.

pweⱸesér↓ boyⱥir |àbúskarlaí↓

Jean: Puede ser. Voy a ir a buscarla ahí.

End of Tape 12B

AI.1   Vocabulary

Units 1-15

The following vocabulary list includes all words presented in Units 1-15. The entries are in a respelling which makes it possible to find any item for which the pronunciation is known without being acquainted with the irregularities of the Spanish spelling system.

The first indentations under the main entry are constructions in which the entry item (or a variant form of the entry item) appears, which are felt to be idiomatic from the point of view of English translation.

The second indentations under the main entry consist of inflected forms which are irregular or which have not been treated yet in the drills or discussion.

Main entries are alphabetized according to the English alphabet with the following modifications: /(l)y/ follows /ly/, /ny/ follows /ny/, and /ş/ follows /s/ . The respelling used in the vocabulary is the same as that used in the extrapolations and discussions, technically referred to as a 'phonemic transcription.' This differs from the respelling in the 'aid to listening' column of the basic sentences only in omitting certain details of pronunciation which can also be determined by the position of the 'phoneme' in a sequence of sounds (for example, the phoneme /d/ is [d] initially in an utterance, or after /n/ or /l/ ; it is [đ] elsewhere; both are listed /d/ in the vocabulary.)

Nouns are identified for gender class membership by their appearance with the appropriate form of the definite article. A few nouns which ordinarily do not appear with articles (as some names of persons and places, names of the months, and some indefinites) are identified by empty parentheses instead of by articles.

Adjectives are identified by one of two ways. Those which have two gender endings are listed in their masculine form, with the feminine ending following: /byého , —a/. Those which have a common gender (both masculine and feminine agreement by a single form) are shown with a zero following: /gránde, —∅/.

Verbs can be identified by the /—Vr/ (i.e. /—ár, —ér, —ír/) ending and the English translation 'to _____.' Forms of irregular verbs and unfamiliar forms are given (as described above) at the second indentation after the main entry. Second person verb forms are formal unless marked (fam) for familiar. Command forms appear without an indicated subject. Verb forms which are so irregular as to alphabetize differently from the main entry of the infinitive are cross-referenced.

Clitic pronouns are marked by a following dash, which indicates their dependence on accompanying verbs in an utterance: /les—/ . Other pronouns are not marked, but can be identified by their English translations.

The second column gives the traditional Spanish orthography of the main entries, in parentheses.

The third column gives the English translations of all the entry items.

The fourth (right hand) column gives the unit and section of the first appearance of each entry. Thus 10.1 indicates the item first appears in the basic dialogs of Unit 10; 10.2, in an illustration drill of the drills and grammar section in Unit 10.

In Unit 16 and after, new vocabulary also appears in the reading selections, so 16.4 would indicate that the first appearance was in the readings section, and a second reference of 21.1 would indicate a subsequent entry in the basic dialogs. Two 'first' entries are necessary because an 'active' knowledge is presumed for all items presented in basic sentences and drills, and only a 'passive' knowledge or recognition is presumed for items presented in readings. So, items presented in the readings are not used in drills until or unless they appear later in basic dialogs.

The following abreviations are used:

(f)	feminine
(fam)	familiar
(n)	neuter
(pl)	plural
(sg)	singular

/a/

a	(a)	to	1.1
		at	2.1
a⇀kómo⇀está⇀(el⇀kámbyo)		what's the rate (of exchange)	3.1
al		to the	1.1
a⇀la⇀bwélta		around the corner	5.1
al⇀kontráryo		on the contrary	8.1
al-(més)		per (month)	7.1

	a—menúdo		often	13.1
	a—propósıto		by the way	4.1
	a—su—dısposısyón		at your disposal	14.1
	a—sus—órdenes		at your service	14.1
	á	(ah)	oh	4.1
	á (see abér)			
la	abenída	(avenida)	avenue	3.1
	abér	(haber)	there to be	1.1
			to have	6.1
	á		(you) have	9.2
	án		(you) have (pl)	9.2
	ás		(you) have (fam)	9.2
	áy		there is, there are	1.1
	é		(I) have	6.1
	émos		(we) have	9.1
	áy—ke		it's necessary to	3.1
	nó—áy—de—ké		don't give it a thought	1.1
	abısár	(avisar)	to notify	5.1
la	abıtaşyón	(habitación)	room	8.1
	ablár	(hablar)	to speak, to talk	4.1
	abrír	(abrir)	to open	8.2
el	abyón	(avión)	plane	14.1
	por—abyón		by plane	14.1
	adelánte	(adelante)	straight ahead, forward; come (on) in	2.1
	pasár—adelánte		to come in	9.1

/ade/

	además	(además)	besides	14.1
	admɪnɪstratíbo, —a	(administrativo)	administrative	4.1
la	adwána	(aduana)	customs office	15.1
	adyós	(adiós)	goodbye	1.1
el	ạeropwérto	(aeropuerto)	airport	14.1
	afeytár	(afeitar)	to shave	12.1
	afeytárse		to shave oneself	12.1
las	afwéras	(afueras)	outskirts	7.1
	agradeşér	(agradecer)	to be grateful	10.1
	agradeşído, —a	(agradecido)	grateful	10.1
	múy—agradeşído—por—tódo		thanks a lot for everything	10.1
el	ágwa (f)	(agua)	water	3.1
la	ahénşya	(agencia)	agency	7.1
el	ahénte	(agente)	agent	7.1
	aí	(ahí)	there	2.1
	por—aí		that way	13.1
	akél	(aquél)	that (over there)	7.2
	aké()ya (f)		that (over there)	7.2
	aké()yos, —as		those	7.2
	akí	(aquí)	here	3.1
	akí—tyéne		here you are	3.1
			here is (are)	7.1
	álgo	(algo)	anything, something	3.1
	álgo—más		anything else	3.1
( )	álgyen	(alguien)	anyone	10.2
	alkɪlár	(alquilar)	to rent	7.1

	almorşár	(almorzar)	to lunch	5.1
la	almwáda	(almohada)	pillow	11.1
	aƟyí	(allí)	there (in that place)	6.1
	amáble, —∅	(amable)	kind, nice, courteous	15.1
el	ámbre (f)	(hambre)	hunger	5.1
	tenér—ámbre		to be hungry	5.1
	amerıkáno, —a	(americano)	American	2.1
el	amígo	(amigo)	friend	7.1
	amwebládo, —a	(amueblado)	furnished	7.1
	amweblár	(amueblar)	to furnish	7.1
	án (see abér)			
	anóche	(anoche)	last night	15.1
	ántes	(antes)	before	10.1
el	anúnşyo	(anuncio)	advertisement	7.1
	aóra	(ahora)	now	3.1
	aóra—mísmo		right now	3.1
	por—aóra		right now	7.1
el	apartaménto	(apartamento)	apartment	6.1
	apénas	(apenas)	scarcely, barely	12.1
	aprendér	(aprender)	to learn	4.1
	arregládo, —a	(arreglado)	fixed, arranged	9.1
	arreglár	(arreglar)	to fix, to arrange	9.1
	ás (see abér)			
	así	(así)	so	8.1
el	as(ş)ensór	(ascensor)	elevator	3.1

/ast/

	ásta	(hasta)	until	1.1
	ásta—lwégo		so long	1.1
	ásta—maŋyána		see you tomorrow	1.1
	aşér	(hacer)	to do, to make	9.1
	atendér	(atender)	to take care of, to assist	15.1
el	áwto	(auto)	car	7.1
	áy (see abér)			
	ayér	(ayer)	yesterday	4.1
la	ayúda	(ayuda)	help	15.1
	ayudár	(ayudar)	to help	6.1

/ b /

	bá (see ír)			
	bahár	(bajar)	to go down	2.1
	balér	(valer)	to be worth	14.1
	balér—la—péna		to be worthwhile	14.1
	bámos (see ír)			
	bán (see ír)			
	baŋyár	(bañar)	to bathe	12.1
	baŋyárse		to bathe oneself	12.1
el	bányo	(baño)	bathroom	2.1
	baráto, —a	(barato)	cheap, inexpensive	5.1
el	bárko	(barco)	boat	14.1
	em—bárko		by boat	14.1
el	barón	(varón)	male	14.1
	barrér	(barrer)	to sweep	11.1

el	bárryo	(barrio)	section (of town)	14.1
	bás (see ír)			
	bastánte, ⟶∅	(bastante)	enough, quite (a bit)	5.1
el	baúl	(baúl)	trunk	15.1
	báyas (see ír)			
	baylár	(bailar)	to dance	13.1
	bé (see bér)			
	beámos (see bér)			
	bebér	(beber)	to drink	9.1
( )	beⓁyabísta	(Bellavista)	Bellavista	14.1
	bén (see benír, bér)			
	benír	(venir)	to come	5.1
	bén		come (fam)	13.1
	bíno		(you) came	5.1
	byéne		(she) comes	10.1
	byénen		(they) come	14.1
	byénes		(you) come (fam)	8.1
	béo (see bér)			
	bér	(ver)	to see	6.1
	bé		(you) see	14.2
	beámos		let's see	6.1
	bén		(you) see (pl)	14.2
	béo		(I) see	10.2
	bés		(you) see (fam)	14.2
	bérde, ⟶∅	(verde)	green	15.1

	bés (see bér)			
	bestír	(vestir)	to dress	12.1
	bestírse		to dress oneself	12.1
la	béş	(vez)	time	2.1
	de—béş—en—kwándo		from time to time	13.1
	ótra—béş		again	2.1
el	beşíno	(vecino)	neighbor	8.1
	béynte, —∅	(veinte)	twenty	2.1
	bıbír	(vivir)	to live	6.1
el	bıⓁyéte	(billete)	bill	3.1
	bíno (see benír)			
el	bíno	(vino)	wine	6.1
la	bísta	(vista)	view	8.1
la	bóda	(boda)	wedding	9.1
	bolbér	(volver)	to return	9.1
la	bondád	(bondad)	kindness, goodness	15.1
	tenér—la—bondád—de		to be so kind as to, please	15.1
	boníto, —a	(bonito)	pretty	8.1
	bóy (see ír)			
la	bróma	(broma)	joke	12.1
	ké—bróma		what a fix	12.1
	buskár	(buscar)	to look for	6.1
la	bwélta	(vuelta)	turn	5.1
	a—la—bwélta		around the corner	5.1
	bwéno, —a	(bueno)	good	1.1

			OK	4.1
	bwén		good	5.1
	bwénos—días		good morning	1.1
	bwénas—nóches		good evening	1.1
	bwénas—tárdes		good afternoon	1.1
el	byáhe	(viaje)	trip	4.1
	byahéro, —a	(viajero)	traveler	3.1
	byého, —a	(viejo)	old	7.1
	byén	(bien)	well, fine	1.1
	está—byén		that's O.K., OK	1.1
	byéne (see benír)			
	byénen (see benír)			
	byénes (see benír)			
el	byérnes	(viernes)	Friday	10.1

/ch/

el	chéke	(cheque)	check	3.1
la	chíka	(chica)	girl	13.1
el	chíko	(chico)	boy	12.1
el	chofér	(chofer)	chauffeur	4.1
la	chuléta	(chuleta)	chop	6.1

/dan/   /d/

dá(n) (see dár)			
dár	(dar)	to give	2.1
dá		(it) gives	8.1
dán		(they) give	10.1
dás		(you) give (fam)	14.2
dé		give	2.1
dóy		(I) give	4.1
dár-a-(la-káⓞye)		to face on (the street)	8.1
dárse-prísa		to hurry (oneself)	12.1
dárse-una-dúcha		to take a shower	12.1
dás (see dár)			
de	(de)	of, from	1.1
de-béş-en-kwándo		from time to time	13.1
del		of the, from the	8.2
de-náda		you're welcome	1.1
lo-de		the matter of, about	9.1
dé (see dár)			
debér	(deber)	to owe, must, ought	4.1
débe(n)-sér		must be, probably is (are)	8.1
dehár	(dejar)	to leave, to let	8.1
deklarár	(declarar)	to declare	15.1
demasyádo,' —a	(demasiado)	too much	7.1
demasyádos, —as		too many	7.1
la derécha	(derecha)	right	2.1
désde	(desde)	since	4.1
désde-kwándo		since when (how long)	4.1

	deseár	(desear)	to wish	6.1
	desokupádo, —a	(desocupado)	empty, unoccupied	6.1
	desokupár	(desocupar)	to vacate, to empty	6.1
	despwés	(después)	later	3.1
	deşɪdír	(decidir)	to decide	9.1
	deşír	(decir)	to say, to tell	2.1
	díga		say	4.1
	dígas		tell (fam)	12.1
	díhe		(I) said	15.1
	dɪhéron		(they) told	4.1
	díşe		(you) say	2.1
	deşírse		to say itself, to be said	2.1
	kerér—deşír		to mean	2.1
	detrás	(detrás)	behind	14.1
	detrás—de		in back of, behind, beyond	14.1
el	día	(día)	day	1.1
	bwénos—días		good morning	1.1
	díga (see deşír)			
	dígas (see deşír)			
	díhe (see deşír)			
	dɪhéron (see deşír)			
	dɪspensár	(dispensar)	to excuse	1.1
la	dɪsposɪşyón	(disposición)	disposition	14.1
	a—su—dɪsposɪşyón		at your disposal	14.1

/dɪş/

	díşe (see deşír)			
el	dólar	(dólar)	dollar	3.1
el	domíngo	(domingo)	Sunday	10.1
	dón	(don)	mister	11.1
	dónde	(dónde)	where	2.1
el	dormɪtóryo	(dormitorio)	bedroom	8.1
	dós, ‑∅	(dos)	two	2.1
	dóşe, ‑∅	(doce)	twelve	2.1
	dóy (see dár)			
la	dúcha	(ducha)	shower	12.1
	dárse‑una‑dúcha		to take a shower	12.1
el	dyénte	(diente)	tooth	12.1
	lɪmpyárse‑los‑dyéntes		to brush one's teeth	12.1
	dyéş, ‑∅	(diez)	ten	2.1

/e/

	é (see abér)			
el	edɪfíşyo	(edificio)	building	7.1
el	ekɪpáhe	(equipaje)	baggage	15.1
	eks(ş)elénte, ‑∅	(excelente)	excellent	4.1
el		(el)	the	1.1
	la		the (f)	1.1
	los, las		the (pl)	2.1
	al		to the	1.1

	él	(él)	he	4.2
	é0ya		she	4.2
	é0yos, (é0yas)		they	4.2
la	embaháda	(embajada)	embassy	2.1
	emfrénte	(enfrente)	in front (across the street)	10.1
	émos (see abér)			
	empeşár	(empezar)	to begin	11.1
el	empleádo	(empleado)	clerk	15.1
	en	(en)	in	2.1
			on	3.1
			at	4.1
	em-bárko		by boat	14.1
	en-rrealidád		actually	8.1
	en-segída		at once, right away	13.1
	enkantádo, —a	(encantado)	enchanted	1.1
	enkantádo-de-konoşérla		delighted to meet you	1.1
	enkantár	(encantar)	to enchant	1.1
	enkontrár	(encontrar)	to find	6.1
la	ensaláda	(ensalada)	salad	6.1
	entónşes	(entonces)	then	3.1
la	entráda	(entrada)	entrance	3.1
	éran (see sér)			
	éres (see sér)			
la	ermána	(hermana)	sister	14.1

/es/

	és (see sér)			
	ése, —a'	(ese)	that	7.1
la	eskína	(esquina)	corner	10.1
	eskrıbír	(escribir)	to write	8.2
el	eskrıtóryo	(escritorio)	desk	5.1
la	eskwéla	(escuela)	school	4.1
	éso (n)	(eso)	that	2.1
el	espaŋyól	(español)	(the) Spanish (language)	2.1
	esperár	(esperar)	to hope, expect, wait for	8.1
la	espósa	(esposa)	wife	14.1
	está (see estár)			
el	estádo	(estado)	state	4.1
los	estádos—unídos	(Estados Unidos)	United States	4.1
	están (see estár)			
	estár	(estar)	to be	1.1
	está		(you) are	1.1
	están		(they) are	2.1
	estás		(you) are (fam)	4.2
	estóy		(I) am	1.1
	está—byén		that's O.K., O.K.	1.1
	estás—en—tu—kása		make yourself at home	9.1
	estás (see estár)			
	éste, —a	(este)	this	3.1
	ésta—nóche		tonight	8.1
	ésto (n)	(esto)	this	2.1
	estóy (see estár)			

| | estudyár | (estudiar) | to study | 9.1 |
| | estupéndo, —a | (estupendo) | terrific | 13.1 |

/f/

el	fabór	(favor)	favor	2.1
	por—fabór		please	2.1
	faltár	(faltar)	to lack	15.1
la	famílya	(familia)	family	5.1
	fáṣıl, —∅	(fácil)	easy	6.1
la	fécha	(fecha)	date	9.1
	fıhár	(fijar)	to fix	13.1
	fıhárse		to pay attention	13.1
el	fín	(fin)	end	10.1
	em—fín		so, then, well	10.1
	por—fín		at last	12.1
la	fóto	(foto)	picture	9.1
la	fúnda	(funda)	the (pillow) case	11.1
la	fyésta	(fiesta)	party	11.1

/g/

| las | gáfas | (gafas) | eye glasses | 12.1 |
| el | gás | (gas) | gas | 7.1 |

/gor/

	górdo, —a	(gordo)	fat	12.1
	gordíto, —a		a little fat	12.1
	gránde, —∅	(grande)	big, great	7.1
	grán		great, large	15.1
	gráṣyas	(gracias)	thanks	1.1
	múchas—gráṣyas		thanks a lot	1.1
	gustár	(gustar)	to please	3.1
el	gústo	(gusto)	pleasure	1.1
	múcho—gústo—(de—konoṣérlo)		glad to meet you	1.1
	tánto—gústo—de—konoṣérlo		I'm very glad to know (meet) you	4.1

/h/

el	hamón	(jamón)	ham	6.1
( )	hosé	(José)	Joseph, Joe	4.1
	húntos, —as	(juntos)	together	5.1
( )	hwán	(Juan)	John	4.1
el	hwébes	(jueves)	Thursday	10.1

/ı/

	ı	(y)	and	1.1
	íba (see ír)			
la	ıdéa	(idea)	idea	9.1

	ɪgwál, —∅	(igual)	equal	1.1
	ɪgwál—a		the same as	8.1
	ɪgwálménte		equally; same here	1.1
	ɪgwalíto, —a		just the same	9.1
la	íha	(hija)	daughter	13.1
el	ího	(hijo)	son	14.1
la	ɪmformaşyón	(información)	information	3.1
el	ɪnglés	(inglés)	(the) English (language)	2.1
	ɪnklwír	(incluir)	to include	7.1
la	ɪnmɪgraşyón	(inmigración)	immigration	15.1
	ír	(ir)	to go	1.1
	bá		(it) goes	1.1
	bámos		let's go, (we) go	5.1
	bán		(they) go	8.1
	bás		(you) go (fam)	6.1
	báyas		go (fam)	13.1
	bóy		(I) go	12.1
	íba		(I) went, was going	12.1
	írse		to leave	10.1
	kómo—le—bá		how are you getting along	1.1
la	ɪşkyérda	(izquierda)	left	2.1

	kabér	(caber)	to fit	15.1
	káda, —∅	(cada)	each	13.2
la	káha	(caja)	box, cashier's desk	3.1
el	kahéro	(cajero)	cashier	3.1
la	kál̥ye	(calle)	street	8.1
la	káma	(cama)	bed	8.1
	kambyár	(cambiar)	to change, exchange	3.1
	kambyárse		to change (oneself)	8.1
	kambyárse—(de—rrópa)		to change (clothes)	8.1
el	kámbyo	(cambio)	change, exchange	3.1
la	kamísa	(camisa)	shirt	10.1
el	kámpo	(campo)	field, country	7.1
la	kantɪdád	(cantidad)	amount, quantity	7.1
	karámba	(caramba)	gosh	8.1
( )	kármen	(Carmen)	Carmen	13.1
	káro, —a	(caro)	expensive	8.1
el	kárro	(carro)	car	14.1
la	kárta	(carta)	letter	12.2
la	kása	(casa)	house	8.1
	el—señyór—de—la—kása		the owner of the house	13.1
	estás—en—tu—kása		make yourself at home	9.1
	kasádo, —a	(casado)	married	5.1
	kasár	(casar)	to marry	5.1
	kásɪ	(casi)	almost	4.1

katórşe, —∅	(catorce)	fourteen	2.1
ke	(que)	that	3.1
		who	7.1
áy—ke		it's necessary to	3.1
lo—ke		the that, that which, what	10.1
tenér—ke		to have to	8.1
ké, —∅	(qué)	what	1.1
		how	9.1
ké—bróma		what a fix	12.1
ké—le—paréşe		what do you say	6.1
ké—óra—és		what time is it	5.1
ké—tál		how goes it	1.1
		how	4.1
ké—te—pása		what's the matter	12.1
nó—áy—de—ké		don't give it a thought	1.1
por—ké		why	7.1
kehár			
kehárse	(quejarse)	to complain	15.1
kerér	(querer)	to want	1.1
kyére		(it) wants	2.1
kyéren		(you) want (pl)	6.1
kyéres		(you) want (fam)	6.1
kyéro		(I) want	1.1
kerér—deşír		to mean	2.1
kínşe, —∅	(quince)	fifteen	2.1

/kla/

	kláro, —a	(claro)	clear	7.1
	kláro		of course	7.1
	kobrár	(cobrar)	to charge	11.1
el	kóche	(coche)	car	15.1
( )	kolón	(Colón)	Columbus	3.1
	kombenír	(convenir)	to suit	7.1
	kombyéne		(it) suits	7.1
	komér	(comer)	to eat	6.1
	komfundír	(confundir)	to confuse	13.1
	komfundírse		to be confused	13.1
	komo	(como)	like, as	9.1
	kómo	(cómo)	how	1.1
	a—kómo—está—el—kámbyo		what's the rate of exchange	3.1
	kómo—le—bá		how are you getting along	1.1
	kómo—nó		certainly	1.1
	kómodo, —a	(cómodo)	comfortable	8.1
	kompléto, —a	(completo)	complete	15.1
	komprár	(comprar)	to buy	9.1
	kón	(con)	with	1.1
	kom—permíso		excuse me	1.1
	konmígo		with me	12.2
	kontígo		with you (fam)	12.2
	kon—tyémpo		in time	11.1
	konoşér	(conocer)	to meet, get acquainted, to know	1.1
	enkantádo—de—konoşérla		delighted to meet you	1.1

	múcho-gústo-de-konoşérla		glad to meet you	1.1
	tánto-gústo-de-konoşérlo		I'm very glad to know you	4.1
	konsulár, -∅	(consular)	consular	4.1
	konténto, -a	(contento)	satisfied, contented	14.1
el	kontráryo	(contrario)	contrary	8.1
	al-kontráryo		on the contrary	8.1
la	kópa	(copa)	goblet	13.1
el	koronél	(coronel)	colonel	13.1
la	kósa	(cosa)	thing	4.1
	kostár	(costar)	to cost	3.1
	kwésta		(it) costs	3.1
la	koşína	(cocina)	kitchen	8.1
	kreér	(creer)	to believe	6.1
	kreér-ke-sí		to think so	6.1
el	kúba-líbre	(cuba libre)	cuba libre	9.1
	kwál, -∅	(cuál)	which (one)	15.1
	kwalkyéra, -∅	(cualquiera)	whatever	5.1
	kwalkyér		whatever	5.1
	kwándo	(cuando)	when	4.1
		(cuándo)	when	4.1
	de-béş-en-kwándo		from time to time	13.1
	désde-kwándo		since when (how long)	4.1
	kwánto, -a	(cuánto)	how much	2.1
	kwántos, -as		how many	3.1
el	kwárto	(cuarto)	room	3.1
el	kwárto	(cuarto)	quarter	5.1

/kwa/

	kwátro, –∅	(cuatro)	four	2.1
la	kwénta	(cuenta)	check, bill	6.1
	kwésta (see kostár)			
el	kwɪdádo	(cuidado)	care	13.1
			(be) careful	13.1
	kyén	(quién)	who	9.1
	kyére (see kerér)			
	kyéren (see kerér)			
	kyéres (see kerér)			
	kyéro (see kerér)			

/l/

	la(–) (see el, lo–)			
la	labandería	(lavandería)	laundry	10.1
	labár	(lavar)	to wash	11.1
el	lápɪş	(lápiz)	pencil	2.1
	le–	(le)	(to) you	1.1
			(to) him	4.1
			(to) her	10.1
la	lechúga	(lechuga)	lettuce	6.1
la	legúmbre	(legumbre)	vegetable	6.1
	léhos	(lejos)	far	3.1
la	léngwa	(lengua)	language, tongue	4.1
el	líbro	(libro)	book	2.1

	lımpyár	(limpiar)	to clean	10.1
	lımpyárse		to clean oneself	12.1
	lımpyárse-los-dyéntes		to brush one's teeth	12.1
la	lísta	(lista)	list	15.1
	lísto, —a	(listo)	ready	10.1
	lo (n)	(lo)	the	9.1
	lo-de		the matter of, about	9.1
	lo-ke		the that, that which, what	10.1
	lo—, la—	(lo, la)	you	1.1
			it	1.1
			him (her)	4.1
	los-, las_		them	10.1
	los, las (see el)			
el	lúnes	(lunes)	Monday	10.1
la	lúş	(luz)	light	7.1
	lwégo	(luego)	then, later	1.1
	asta-lwégo		so long	1.1

/ʎy/

la	ʎyábe	(llave)	key	7.1
	ʎyamár	(llamar)	to call	12.1
	ʎyebár	(llevar)	to take, carry	2.1
	ʎyegár	(llegar)	to arrive	12.1

/m/

la	maléta	(maleta)	suitcase	10.1
el	maletín	(maletín)	overnight case, handbag	15.1

/mal/

	málo, —a	(malo)	bad	8.1
	mál		bad	8.1
	mandár	(mandar)	to send	10.1
la	manṣána	(manzana)	apple	6.1
	maŋyána	(mañana)	tomorrow	1.1
	asta—maŋyána		see you tomorrow	1.1
	mareár	(marear)	to make dizzy	14.1
	mareárse		to get seasick	14.1
el	mártes	(martes)	Tuesday	10.1
	más	(más)	more	3.1
	álgo—más		anything else	3.1
	me—	(me)	me	1.1
			(to) me	2.1
			myself	8.1
	médyo, —a	(medio)	half	12.1
	ménos	(menos)	less	3.1
el	menú	(menú)	menu	6.1
	menúdo	(menudo)		
	a—menúdo		often	13.1
el	més	(mes)	month	7.1
	al—més		per month	7.1
la	mésa	(mesa)	table	2.1
el	meséro	(mesero)	waiter	6.1
	metér	(meter)	to put in	13.1
	metér—la—páta		to put your foot in your mouth	13.1

	mı, —∅	(mi)	my	4.1
	mí	(mí)	me	6.1
	konmígo		with me	12.2
el	mı(l)yón	(millón)	million	8.1
	mınerál, —∅	(mineral)	mineral	3.1
	mío, —a	(mío)	mine (my)	4.1
	mı, —∅		my	4.1
	mırár	(mirar)	to look	13.1
	mísmo, —a	(mismo)	same	3.1
			-self	10.1
	aóra—mísmo		right now	3.1
el	mobımyénto	(movimiento)	movement, activity	4.1
	molestár	(molestar)	to bother	10.1
	molestárse		to bother	10.1
el	moménto	(momento)	moment	12.1
	un—moménto		just a minute	12.1
la	monéda	(moneda)	coin, change	3.1
el	móşo	(mozo)	porter	3.1
			waiter	6.1
	moréno, —a	(moreno)	brunette	13.1
la	muchácha	(muchacha)	girl	9.1
	múcho, —a	(mucho)	much, a lot, lots	1.1
	múchos, —as		many	1.1
	múchas—gráşyas		thanks a lot	1.1
	múcho—gústo—(de—konoşérlo)		glad to meet you	1.1

/much/

			very much	5.1
	muchísimo, —a		very much	5.1
	mudár	(mudar)	to move	8.1
	mudárse		to change, to move	10.1
	mudárse—de—kása		to move (one's residence)	8.1
	múy	(muy)	very	1.1
el	mwéble	(mueble)	(piece of) furniture	7.1
	sɪn—mwébles		unfurnished	7.1
el	myérkoles	(miércoles)	Wednesday	10.1

/n/

	náda	(nada)	nothing	1.1
	de—náda		you're welcome	1.1
( )	nádye	(nadie)	no one	10.2
	neşesáryo, —a	(necesario)	necessary	15.1
	neşesɪtár	(necesitar)	to need	3.1
	nɪ	(ni)	nor, (or)	7.1
la	níŋya	(niña)	(small) girl	14.1
el	nɪŋyo	(niño)	child	14.1
	nó	(no)	no, not	1.1
		(¿no?)	isn't it, didn't he, etc.	11.1
	kómo—nó		certainly	1.1
	nó—áy—de—ké		don't give it a thought	1.1
la	nóbya	(novia)	sweetheart, fiancée	9.1
la	nóche	(noche)	night, evening	1.1

/onş/

	bwénas—nóches		good evening	1.1
	ésta—nóche		tonight	8.1
el	nómbre	(nombre)	name	4.1
	nos—	(nos)	us	2.1
			ourselves	6.1
			to us	15.1
	nosótros	(nosotros)	we, us	4.1
	nosótras		we, us (f)	12.2
	núnka	(nunca)	never	10.2
	nwébe, —ø	(nueve)	nine	2.1
	nwébo, —a	(nuevo)	new	11.1
	nwéstro, —a	(nuestro)	our(s)	9.2

/o/

	o	(o)	or	2.1
	ócho, —ø	(ocho)	eight	2.1
el	ofışyál	(oficial)	officer	4.1
	oír	(oír)	to listen	12.1
	óye		listen (fam)	12.1
	okupádo, —a	(ocupado)	busy	4.1
	okupár	(ocupar)	to occupy	4.1
	óla	(hola)	hello, hi	1.1
el	ómbre	(hombre)	man	9.1
	ónşe, —ø	(once)	eleven	2.1

/ora/

la	óra	(hora)	hour	5.1
	ké—óra—és		what time is it	5.1
la	órden	(orden)	order	14.1
	a—sus—órdenes		at your service	14.1
el	otél	(hotel)	hotel	2.1
	ótro, —a	(otro)	another	2.1
	ótra—béş		again	2.1
	óye (see oír)			

/p/

	pára	(para)	for	6.1
			to, in order to	12.1
	pareşér	(parecer)	to seem	5.1
	ké—le—paréşe		what do you say	6.1
	le—paréşe—byén		OK with you	5.1
el	párke	(parque)	park	14.1
la	párte	(parte)	part	5.1
	pasár	(pasar)	to pass, to hand	2.1
			to come by	8.1
			to come in	9.1
			to happen	12.1
	ké—te—pása		what's the matter	12.1
	pasár—adelánte		to come in	9.1
el	pastél	(pastel)	pie	6.1
la	páta	(pata)	paw	13.1

	metér—la—páta		to put your foot in your mouth	13.1
el	pátyo	(patio)	yard, court, patio	8.1
	pekéɲyo, —a	(pequeño)	small	13.2
la	péna	(pena)	sorrow, grief	14.1
	balér—la—péna		to be worthwhile	14.1
	pensár	(pensar)	to think, plan	6.1
	pyénso		(I) think	6.1
el	perdón	(perdón)	pardon; excuse me	2.1
el	permíso	(permiso)	permission	1.1
	kom—permíso		excuse me	1.1
	péro	(pero)	but	4.1
el	peryódıko	(periódico)	newspaper	7.1
el	péso	(peso)	peso	3.1
el	píso	(piso)	floor	3.1
la	plúma	(pluma)	pen	2.1
	podér	(poder)	to be able	3.1
	pwéde		(you) can	3.1
	pwédo		(I) can	6.1
	póko, —a	(poco)	little	4.1
	por	(por)	for, in exchange for	2.1
			during	11.1
	por—abyón		by plane	14.1
	por—aí		that way	13.1
	por—aóra		right now	7.1
	por—fabór		please	2.1

665

/por/

	por—fín		at last	12.1
	por—ké		why	7.1
	por—la—tárde		during the afternoon	11.1
el	póstre	(postre)	dessert	6.1
	praktıkár	(practicar)	to practice	4.1
	presentár	(presentar)	to present	1.1
	prestár	(prestar)	to lend, to provide	15.1
el	préşyo	(precio)	price	8.1
	prıméro, —a	(primero)	first	3.1
	prımér		first	3.1
la	prísa	(prisa)	haste	12.1
	dárse—prísa		to hurry oneself	12.1
	probár	(probar)	to try, to taste	6.1
	prónto	(pronto)	soon	9.1
	pronunşyár	(pronunciar)	to pronounce	4.1
la	propína	(propina)	tip	4.1
el	propósıto	(propósito)	purpose	4.1
	a—propósıto		by the way	4.1
	pwéde (see podér)			
	pwéden (see podér)			
	pwédo (see podér)			
	pyénso (see pensár)			

/r/

la	rraşón	(razón)	reason	6.1
	tenér—rraşón		to be right	6.1
	rréal, —∅	(real)	real	14.1
	rréalménte		really	14.1
la	rrealıdád	(realidad)	reality	8.1
	en—rrealıdád		actually	8.1
	rrebısár	(revisar)	to examine, inspect	15.1
el	rregálo	(regalo)	gift	15.1
	rrekordár	(recordar)	to remember	8.1
	rrekwérdo		(I) remember	8.1
	rrepetír	(repetir)	to repeat	2.1
	rrepíta		repeat, say it again	2.1
el	rrestorán	(restorán)	restaurant	5.1
	rrıguróso, —a	(riguroso)	rigorous, strict	15.1
la	rrópa	(ropa)	clothes, clothing	8.1

/s/

el	sábado	(sábado)	Saturday	10.1
la	sábana	(sábana)	sheet	11.1
	sabér	(saber)	to know	12.1
	sé		(I) know	12.1
la	sála	(sala)	living room	8.1
	salír	(salir)	to leave, to go out	12.1
el	sánwıch	(sandwich)	sandwich	6.1

/se/

	se—	(se)	-self (3rd person, sg and pl)	2.1
	sé (see sabér)			
	segída			
	en—segída		at once, right away	13.1
	segúro, —a	(seguro)	sure	15.1
la	sekretárya	(secretaria)	secretary	9.1
la	sekṣyón	(sección)	section	4.1
la	semána	(semana)	week	8.1
	sentár	(sentar)	to seat	2.1
	syénta		seat (fam)	9.1
	syénte		seat	2.1
	sentárse		to sit down	2.1
	sentír	(sentir)	to regret, to feel	1.1
	syénto		(I) feel	1.1
	sentírlo—múcho		to be very sorry	1.1
el	seɲyór	(señor)	sir, mister	1.1
	el—seɲyór—de—la—kása		the owner of the house	13.1
la	seɲyóra	(señora)	madam, Mrs.	1.1
la	seɲyoríta	(señorita)	miss	1.1
	sér	(ser)	to be	2.1
	éran		(they) were	13.1
	éres		(you) are (fam)	5.2
	és		(it) is	2.1
	sómos		(we) are	5.2

	són		(they) are	4.1
	sóy		(I) am	5.1
	débe(n)—sér		must be, probably is (are)	8.1
	séys, —∅	(seis)	six	2.1
	sı	(si)	if	6.1
	sí	(sí)	yes	2.1
	kręér—ke—sí		to think so	6.1
la	síⓁya	(silla)	chair	2.1
	sín	(sin)	without	7.1
	sın—mwébles		urfurnished	7.1
la	sırbyénta	(sirvienta)	maid	11.1
	sóbre	(sobre)	above	14.1
	sóbre—tódo		above all, especially	14.1
la	sóda	(soda)	soda	9.1
el	sofá	(sofá)	sofa	8.1
el	sofá—káma	(sofá cama)	sofa-bed	8.1
	sólo	(sólo)	only	7.1
	soltéro, —a	(soltero)	unmarried (bachelor)	5.1
	sómos (see sér)			
	són (see sér)			
la	sópa	(sopa)	soup	6.1
	sóy (see sér)			
	sú, —∅	(su)	your (sg and pl)	5.1
			his, their	11.2
	subír	(subir)	to go up	2.1

/suṣ/

	súṣyo, —a	(sucio)	dirty	11.1
	súyo, —a	(suyo)	your(s) (sg and pl)	5.1
			his, their(s)	9.2
	sú, —∅		your (sg and pl)	5.1
			his, their	11.2
la	swégra	(suegra)	mother-in-law	14.1
	syémpre	(siempre)	always	4.1
	syénta (see sentár)			
	syénte (see sentár)			
	syénto (see sentír)			
	syéte, —∅	(siete)	seven	2.1

/ṣ/

el	ṣenıṣéro	(cenicero)	ashtray	2.1
el	ṣéntro	(centro)	center (of town), downtown	2.1
la	ṣerbéṣa	(cerveza)	beer	6.1
el	ṣérdo	(cerdo)	pork, pig	6.1
	ṣérka	(cerca)	near	3.1
	ṣérka—de		near to	3.1
	ṣínko, —∅	(cinco)	five	2.1
	ṣyénto, —∅	(ciento)	hundred	7.1
	ṣyéntos, —as		hundreds	7.1

/t/   /ten/

el	táksı	(taxi)	taxi	3.1
	tál, —∅	(tal)	such	1.1
	ké—tál		how goes it	1.1
			how	4.1
	tambyén	(también)	also, too	5.1
	tánto, —a	(tanto)	so much	4.1
	tánto—gústo—de—konoşérlo		I'm very glad to know (meet) you	4.1
	tárde	(tarde)	late	10.1
la	tárde	(tarde)	afternoon	1.1
	bwénas—tárdes		good afternoon	1.1
	por—la—tárde		during the afternoon	11.1
	te	(te)	you, (to) you (fam)	6.1
			to you	9.1
			yourself	9.1
	tenér	(tener)	to have	2.1
	ténga		have	15.1
	téngo		(I) have	2.1
	tyéne		(you) have	2.1
	tyénes		(you) have (fam)	6.1
	akí—tyéne		here you are	3.1
			here is (are)	7.1
	tenér—ámbre		to be hungry	5.1
	tenér—ke		to have to	8.1
	tenér—la—bondád—de		to be so kind as to, please	15.1

	tenér—rrasón		to be right	6.1
	ténga (see tenér)			
	téngo (see tenér)			
	tí	(ti)	you (fam)	8.1
	kontígo		with you	12.2
la	tıntorería	(tintorería)	cleaner's shop	10.1
	todabía	(todavía)	yet, still	9.1
	tódo, —a	(todo)	all	9.1
			every	10.1
	sóbre—tódo		above all, especially	14.1
	tomár	(tomar)	to take	3.1
el	tomáte	(tomate)	tomato	6.1
	trabahár	(trabajar)	to work	4.1
	tradusír	(traducir)	to translate	2.1
	tradúşka		translate	2.1
	traér	(traer)	to bring	6.1
	tráyga		bring	6.1
el	trágo	(trago)	swallow, drink	10.1
el	tráhe	(traje)	suit	10.1
	trankílo, —a	(tranquilo)	quiet	13.1
	tratár	(tratar)	to treat	6.1
	tratárse—de		to address as	6.1
	tráyga (see traér)			
	trés, —∅	(tres)	three	2.1
	tréşe, —∅	(trece)	thirteen	2.1

	tu, —∅	(tu)	your (fam)	9.1
	tú	(tú)	you (fam)	4.2
	túyo, —a	(tuyo)	your(s) (fam)	9.1
	tu, —∅		your (fam)	9.1
el	tyémpo	(tiempo)	time	11.1
	kon—tyémpo		in time	11.1
	tyéne (see tenér)			
	tyénes (see tenér)			

/u/

	unído, —a	(unido)	united	4.1
	unír	(unir)	to unite	4.1
	úno, —a	(uno)	one	2.1
			a, an	2.3
	un		a, an	2.1
	únos, —as		some, a few	3.1
	ustéd	(usted)	you	1.1

/w/

el	wískı	(whiskey)	whiskey	9.1

/y/

	yá	(ya)	already	5.1
			yet	14.1
			now	15.1
	yó	(yo)	I	4.2

673

AI.2   Index